# A strained partnership?

Manchester University Press

# A strained partnership?

## US–UK relations in the era of détente, 1969–77

Thomas Robb

Manchester University Press
Manchester and New York
distributed in the United States exclusively
by Palgrave Macmillan

Published by Manchester University Press
Oxford Road, Manchester M13 9NR, UK
and Room 400, 175 Fifth Avenue, New York, NY 10010, USA
www.manchesteruniversitypress.co.uk

Distributed in the United States exclusively by
Palgrave Macmillan, 175 Fifth Avenue, New York,
NY 10010, USA

Distributed in Canada exclusively by
UBC Press, University of British Columbia, 2029 West Mall,
Vancouver, BC, Canada V6T 1Z2

British Library Cataloguing-in-Publication Data
A catalogue record for this book is available from the British Library

Library of Congress Cataloging-in-Publication Data applied for

ISBN 978 0 7190 9175 9 hardback

First published 2013



Typeset
by 4word Ltd, Bristol
Printed in Great Britain
by CPI Group (UK) Ltd, Croydon, CR0 4YY

# Contents

# Acknowledgements

I would like to acknowledge the financial support from the University of Wales, Aberystwyth, which largely funded the writing of this book. I would also like to thank Dr R. Gerald Hughes and Professor Len Scott for reading numerous drafts during the writing process. I also send my appreciation to Professor Matthew Jones and Professor Campbell Craig for reading through the entire manuscript and providing detailed and compelling commentary on it. I would also like to acknowledge the insightful commentary provided by the three anonymous reviewers of the manuscript.

Those that have assisted in the finding of materials at the various archives I have visited in the writing of this work deserve my thanks. Special mention goes to the staff at the Gerald R. Ford presidential library in Ann Arbor, Michigan who went beyond the call of duty in locating material. Their dedication and professionalism serves as a fine model for all to follow.

Dr David Gill, Dr Christopher Curran, Mrs Alison Curran and Dr Michael Seibold all deserve a mention for reading through various drafts. Special mention should be given to Dr Gill for reading through the entire manuscript, various drafts, and for discussing the project at length. As an emerging scholar himself, I know that he greatly benefitted from our discussions on all things to do with Richard Nixon and Henry Kissinger, but I would like to thank him for his time nonetheless. I would like to thank my parents, Gail and Keith, for their financial and logistical support in writing this book. Without the use of their motor vehicles, I could not have travelled to and from the multiple train stations that have become such a highlight of my life. Likewise, without the storage facilities provided at Rutland I could not have stored all of my various books and documents that were needed in the writing of this book. As it is apparently standard practice, I should also acknowledge my two siblings, Hilary and Alec, for annoying me immensely throughout the writing of this book.

Mr Kitty, the neighbour's cat, deserves a mention for keeping me entertained during the final drafting of the book. Finally, I would like to thank Donna who has supported me throughout my entire academic career (and, for her sins, continues to do so). Without her insisting I actually attend lectures or visit the library, then I would simply have never started, let alone finished, the writing of this book. It is to her that I dedicate this book.

# Abbreviations

| | |
|---|---|
| ABM | Anti-Ballistic Missile |
| BAOR | British Army of the Rhine |
| CBMs | Confidence Building Measures |
| CDS | Chief of the Defence Staff, UK |
| CSCE | Conference on Security and Cooperation in Europe |
| DBPO | Documents on British Policy Overseas |
| DEFCON | Defense readiness condition (US) |
| DEFE | Defence Files, UK National Archive |
| EEC | European Economic Community |
| FCO | Foreign and Commonwealth Office, UK |
| FO | Foreign Office, UK |
| FRG | Federal Republic of Germany |
| FRUS | Foreign Relations of the United States |
| FY | Financial Year |
| G10 | Group of Ten |
| GCHQ | Government Communications Headquarters, UK |
| GDP | Gross Domestic Product |
| GFL | Gerald Ford Library |
| HAK | Henry Alfred Kissinger |
| HAKTELCONS | Henry A. Kissinger Transcripts of Telephone conversations |
| HWP | Harold Wilson Papers |
| IDF | Israeli Defense Force |
| IMF | International Monetary Fund |
| JCP | James Callaghan Papers |
| JCS | Joint Chiefs of Staff, US |
| JIC | Joint Intelligence Committee, UK |
| MBFR | Mutual and Balanced Force Reductions |

| | |
|---|---|
| MDA | Mutual Defence Agreement |
| MOD | Ministry of Defence, UK |
| NAII | National Archives II, College Park, Maryland, US |
| NATO | North Atlantic Treaty Organization |
| NPMP | Nixon Presidential Materials Project, US |
| NSA | National Security Agency |
| NSAMC | National Security Adviser Memorandum of Conversations |
| NSC | National Security Council, US |
| NSCDM | National Security Council Decision Memorandum |
| NSCIHF | National Security Council Institutional (H) Files |
| NSDM | National Security Decision Memorandum |
| NSSM | National Security Study Memorandum |
| PRC | People's Republic of China |
| PREM | Prime Minister Files, UK National Archives |
| PSBR | Public Sector Borrowing Requirement (UK) |
| RAF | Royal Air Force |
| SALT | Strategic Arms Limitation Talks |
| Telcon | Telephone Conversation Transcript |
| TNA | The National Archives, Kew, UK |
| UNSC | United Nations Security Council |
| USAF | United States Air Force |
| USSR | The Union of Soviet Socialist Republics |
| *WHY* | *White House Years* (Henry Kissinger's memoir) |
| WSAG | Washington Special Actions Group |
| *YOR* | *Years of Renewal* (Henry Kissinger's memoir) |
| *YOU* | *Years of Upheaval* (Henry Kissinger's memoir) |

# 1

# Introduction

*American leaders saw it [to be] in their self-interest to obtain British advice before taking major decisions. It was an extraordinary relationship because it rested on no legal claim; it was formalized by no document; it was carried forward by succeeding British governments as if no alternatives were conceivable. Britain's influence was great precisely because it never insisted on it; the 'special relationship' demonstrated the value of intangibles.*

Henry Kissinger's assessment of the US–UK 'special relationship'[1]

## Introduction

The above quote from Henry Kissinger, who served as US national security adviser (1969–75) and US secretary of state (1973–77) under presidents Richard M. Nixon (1969–74) and Gerald R. Ford (1974–77), gives the impression that the US–UK special relationship functioned in a cooperative manner during his years in office. Moreover it suggests that British policy-makers could also exercise a decisive influence upon the course of US foreign policy. Readers will find that a quite different picture emerges in the following chapters. During the period under examination, the US–UK special relationship would come under severe strain. Demonstrative of this was the fact that on a number of separate occasions the most 'special' areas of US–UK cooperation, which related to the intelligence and nuclear aspects of the relationship, were suspended at the behest of Washington because of wider US–UK political disagreements. Indeed, by the end of 1973, it appeared as if the special relationship was at an end with both Richard Nixon and Henry Kissinger declaring it to be 'over'.[2]

Yet, in spite of such rhetoric, the US–UK relationship remained extremely resolute. The decision by Edward Heath in late 1973 to upgrade Britain's strategic nuclear deterrent ensured US–UK nuclear cooperation would continue for at least another generation. Intimate cooperation between the two countries with regard to international diplomacy was also evident throughout the period. Similarly, the intelligence relationship between the two countries continued throughout the era and beyond. Thus, cooperation, as well competition, was a continual feature of the US–UK relationship during the years under examination here.

Whilst cooperation and competition are the two main features of the relationship, there is, however, another key element that is largely overlooked by scholars analysing the relationship, that being coercive diplomacy. Traditionally, scholars believe that the coercive elements of US foreign policy were a tactic applied by the United States towards its foes, such as the Soviet Union (USSR), the People's Republic of China (PRC) and North Vietnam. It is shown, in contrast to existing accounts, that this aspect of US diplomacy was also applied to its relationship with the United Kingdom. By utilising new documentary evidence unearthed in both US and British archives, it is demonstrated that the United States sought to convince British policy-makers to pursue alternative policy choices on a number of different occasions by utilising its security relationship with the United Kingdom as a means of political leverage. For instance, during what Henry Kissinger would term the 'Year of Europe', the United States would suspend its intelligence and nuclear cooperation with the United Kingdom to persuade British policy-makers to pursue a more amenable foreign policy line. As shown later in the book, this was a rather successful policy and unsurprisingly we see the United States pursuing a similar course when US–UK disagreement emerged in subsequent years.

Existing accounts of the Nixon–Heath years (1970–74) have tended to emphasise the points of difference and antagonism between the two countries. The relationship is depicted as being fraught with difficulty either because of Heath's European ambitions, which necessitated a loosening of the ties with Washington, or because of Washington's pursuit of détente on a bilateral basis which resulted in the US–UK relationship being largely ignored. Regardless of how you attribute the cause of the difficulties in the relationship, all accounts agree that the Nixon–Heath years were largely antagonistic for US–UK relations.[3]

In opposition to this, it is suggested below that the Nixon–Heath years are better understood as having consisted of two distinct phases. The years between 1970 and 1972 saw a failure to address fundamental points of difference between London and Washington. Consequently, US–UK differences about the course of détente, EEC entry, NATO restructuring, potential strategic arms limitations between the US and USSR and progress towards an Arab–Israeli settlement came to a head in 1973–74, when the United States sought to bring some definitive conclusions to these subjects. The period 1970–72 should also be seen as a transitional one for US–UK relations. Détente meant that a less antagonistic Cold War was evolving and the imperative for close US–UK cooperation therefore diminished. Added to this, the Heath government's confirmation of the British withdrawal East of Suez meant that the opportunity for potential US–UK interaction declined. Along with this, a number of policy decisions concerning the breakdown of the Bretton Woods system; the war between India and Pakistan in 1971; the evolution of triangular diplomacy between the US, USSR and PRC, and Britain's bid for membership of the EEC caused difficulties for US–UK relations. In spite of this, there was also a remarkable amount of cooperation between the two sides which is often overlooked or downplayed in existing accounts of the Nixon–Heath years. Thus, we see nuclear diplomacy being actively re-energised as Heath's government sought to find an upgrade to its strategic nuclear deterrent. Likewise, British intelligence worked closely with its American counterparts. Finally, British diplomats and officials had considerable contact with the leading figures within the Nixon White House. The early years of the Nixon–Heath epoch were hardly ones of unmitigated antagonism that they are so often presented as being.

The years 1973–74 were undoubtedly a more troubling time for US–UK relations, when differences surrounding the 'Year of Europe', the fourth Arab–Israeli War and the subsequent oil crisis led to serious discord. Nevertheless, scholars should not overlook that intelligence, nuclear and diplomatic cooperation did continue throughout this period. Indeed, in 1974 Edward Heath confirmed that US–UK nuclear cooperation would continue for at least another generation when he approved the updating of Britain's strategic nuclear deterrent. Thus, the Heath years should not be viewed as ones of constant disagreement. Rather, the archival record which is now open to scholars provides us with a more nuanced assessment of the relationship where considerable cooperation and profound disagreement as well as coercive diplomacy were the hallmarks of the relationship.

US–UK relations between 1974 and 1977 witnessed rather less bellicosity than seen in the Nixon–Heath years. However, a number of important points have been omitted in existing historical accounts. US threats relating to the continuation of US–UK nuclear and intelligence collaboration were made periodically as a means of influencing British defence policy. This coercive diplomacy is an element of the relationship that is much underappreciated within the literature of the US–UK special relationship. Further to this, it is demonstrated that this coercive diplomacy was only partially successful. By 1976

Harold Wilson had concluded that US threats to reappraise its security cooperation with London if the Wilson government enacted further defence cutbacks were mere bluster and he subsequently largely ignored them. Wilson was right to conclude that the United States had little intention of permanently severing the defence relationship it had with London. However, he miscalculated just how seriously the defence cutbacks affected how US policy-makers viewed the United Kingdom as an ally. As his successor, James Callaghan, would find out, this would have serious consequences for British interests during the 1976–77 IMF crisis.

## Book organisation

The book is divided into four core chapters which are, broadly speaking, chronologically organised and focus upon the political–diplomatic dynamics of the US–UK relationship during 1969–77. They all begin with a brief overview of the existing literature, and this is followed by an analytical narrative of key US–UK interaction within the designated timeframe. Chapters 2 and 3 focus upon the Nixon years (i.e. 1969–74), whilst Chapters 4 and 5 are concerned with the administration of President Ford (1974–77). The book addresses several interconnected topics and questions. It analyses how the US reacted to British membership of the European Economic Community (EEC), as well as providing an examination of how US–UK relations were conducted within the context of international superpower détente. Broader themes of economic decline; intelligence and nuclear collaboration; and US and UK conceptions of multilateral diplomacy are also studied.

Chapter 2 illustrates that the Nixon administration re-assessed whether the US should continue to support British membership of the EEC. Throughout the Eisenhower, Kennedy and Johnson administrations, the US had encouraged its British counterparts to join the EEC for largely economic and wider political reasons. However, in the 1960s a number of US policy-makers had begun to make arguments about the detrimental impact that EEC expansion would have upon US economic interests.[4] Nixon's economic advisers repeated this advice, with John Connally – the US Treasury Secretary – being especially vocal in making such arguments. Economics, though important for Nixon, were never the determining factor behind US policy towards British membership of the EEC. For the president, longer-term strategic and political considerations would determine policy, and these were the areas that were seriously analysed by Nixon and his chief foreign policy adviser, Henry Kissinger. While both raised doubts as to whether British membership of the EEC benefitted long-term US interests, they reluctantly concluded that US support for this should be given. As Nixon was aware, the United States was largely powerless in determining whether Britain would become a member of the EEC. More important yet was the concern that without EEC membership the US would be 'saddled with the UK and the pound in a permanent client status'.[5] Along with this, Nixon also believed that British membership of the EEC could encourage Europe to accept the burden-sharing concept he was keen to foster. In the next two years, such aspirations failed to materialise and, as Kissinger noted, Nixon would come to regret supporting British membership of the EEC.[6]

Chapter 2 also explores several areas of US–UK interaction vis-à-vis détente. Particular attention is given to the ongoing Strategic Arms Limitation Talks (SALT), the Conference on Security and Cooperation in Europe (CSCE) and the Mutual and Balanced Force Reduction (MBFR) negotiations. Nixon's triangular diplomacy with the USSR and the PRC, and the subsequent impact this would have upon US foreign policy actions – notably during the India–Pakistan war – are also examined. All of these areas witnessed US–UK disagreement. Heath's government feared that superpower cooperation in SALT could prevent future US–UK nuclear cooperation. It was the view of the Heath administration that MBFR could seriously impinge on British security interests, and that the onset of triangular diplomacy was needlessly distorting US policy.

However, as Chapter 2 argues, one should not forget that, despite the many difficulties for US–UK relations, there existed many points of agreement and examples of cooperation. Moreover, it should not be overlooked that Nixon and Heath actually re-established closer US–UK interaction in the nuclear realm with US–UK working groups convening to discuss the upgrading of Britain's Polaris nuclear deterrent. Equally, the intelligence relationship between the two countries continued throughout this period. Nor should it be forgotten that Heath publicly supported Nixon's Vietnam policies even in the face of severe criticism from his European allies. Coupled with this, British officials managed to establish remarkably close contact with Henry Kissinger which enabled them to learn of US policy intentions (if not actually influence them a great deal). SALT, MBFR and the CSCE were also matters which were to be resolved via diplomatic consultation between the two countries, and the existence of disagreement should not be taken as a demonstration of an antagonistic US–UK relationship. This chapter therefore provides a rather more mixed assessment of US–UK relations than is currently available.

Chapter 3 marks the rapid decline of the Nixon–Heath relationship into one of open disagreement between the two countries. Such was the deterioration in relations that both Nixon and Kissinger would declare that the special relationship was over, and both intelligence and nuclear collaboration between the two sides were suspended on a number of occasions at Washington's urging. This chapter highlights that US–UK relations had assumed a virtually antagonistic agenda because of differences surrounding what Henry Kissinger termed the 'Year of Europe'. Kissinger envisaged that a 'Declaration of Principles' would be made by the US, the newly enlarged EEC and NATO. This declaration would encapsulate all areas of US–European interaction, and in practical terms this meant that monetary and trade discussions would no longer be conducted in isolation from military–security negotiations.[7] In essence then, the Nixon–Kissinger worldview of 'linkage' was to be formally applied to US–European relations.[8]

It was the interpretation of how this policy agenda would be implemented that separated US and British policy-makers. Of course, Kissinger's insistence that the Europeans be assigned a year was seen in British circles as deeply patronising. However, matters of substance were what really divided US and British opinion. Central to British concerns was the fact that Kissinger's motive for the project was believed to be less than altruistic. At best, the implementation of 'linkage' to US–European relations would allow the US to extract preferential economic terms in trade and monetary discussions by utilising their security commitments to Europe. This, in the British assessment, would be unfavourable to their interests and therefore they sought to avoid the level of 'linkage' to US–European relations that Kissinger wanted. Darker assessments of US intentions also loomed large in British thinking. In particular, it was thought that Kissinger was seeking to 'divide and rule' the newly enlarged EEC for his own purposes, and was using this 'Year of Europe' scheme to create tension and discord amongst the EEC member states. It was for these reasons, then, that the British rejected Kissinger's proposal to work bilaterally in creating a Declaration of Principles and were generally uncooperative towards the idea.

As for the US, it came to the conclusion that British intransigence signalled that the valuable bilateral relationship with Britain was being substituted for a US–EEC relationship built on a rather more competitive agenda. The seriousness of such political disputes resulted in the more practical aspects of US–UK cooperation being affected, and on two occasions US–UK intelligence and nuclear cooperation were temporarily suspended by the US. This occurred as a form of political punishment, but the US – especially Henry Kissinger – also saw this as a policy tool. Kissinger believed that, by utilising aspects of the US–UK relationship, he could achieve policy results in other areas. This feature of Kissinger's foreign policy is another demonstration of his worldview that international relations were an interconnected web which the statesman had to manipulate and master in order to achieve policy goals. On this occasion, Kissinger's policy was successful and by placing pressure on other areas of US–UK interaction, particularly that of nuclear and intelligence cooperation, Kissinger was able to gain political movement in regard to the Declaration of Principles.

The chapter then moves on to highlight the severe US–UK discord that resulted from the fourth Arab–Israeli war of October 1973 and the subsequent oil crisis. During the war, Heath decided to pursue what he dubbed a neutralist policy. Accordingly, when American requests for British airbases to launch flyovers of the warzone were made, they were rebuffed. Equally, Heath refused to support US diplomacy in the United Nations Security Council (UNSC) as it was perceived to have been openly pro-Israeli. The most serious moment for US–UK relations followed the decision by the US to move their nuclear forces to Defense Condition III (DEFCON III).[9] The open British hostility to this move led, once again, to US–UK intelligence collaboration being temporarily halted at the behest of the US.

While this chapter highlights the problems within the US–UK relationship, it also points out that the alliance was extremely resilient and that cooperation in many sensitive areas of national security continued. For instance, Kissinger tasked Thomas Brimelow – the deputy permanent under-secretary at the Foreign and Commonwealth Office (FCO) – with drafting the US–USSR's Prevention of Nuclear War Agreement. By November 1973, Heath had decided to upgrade Britain's Polaris strategic nuclear deterrent, which required additional US assistance. Nixon duly approved this request in January 1974.[10] Finally, throughout the Washington Energy Conference of February 1974, the Heath government worked closely with the Nixon administration in finding a collaborative response to the oil embargo. This chapter therefore highlights that much of the existing literature on the Nixon–Heath years has been too focused on the moments of discord and disagreement. By assessing other facets of the relationship, a more nuanced picture of the relationship emerges.

Chapter 4 charts the conduct of US–UK relations following the return to office of Harold Wilson in March 1974. Wilson sought to re-establish closer US–UK relations and hoped it would provide him with a greater level of influence upon US policy that would allow the British a more decisive and influential world role. Wilson, however, was ultimately unsuccessful because his continual defence cutbacks to the UK military weakened the utility of Britain as an ally in the perception of policy-makers in Washington. Also, as the Cyprus crisis of 1974 demonstrated, British policy-makers had limited influence over US policy even when direct British interests were at stake. Such arguments must be carefully qualified and, although a number of scholars have seen the US–UK relationship as almost irrelevant for this period, it has to be remembered that US–UK cooperation continued in numerous areas of extreme importance. US–UK interaction on the updating of Polaris and intelligence sharing serve as the most obvious examples but considerable interaction over the CSCE and MBFR also occurred.[11]

It is also within this chapter that Britain's continued economic problems really come into focus. Indeed, no study of the US–UK relationship would be complete, or even convincing, without taking into account the profound impact that economics had upon US–UK relations. In particular, British economic troubles created the impression throughout the Nixon–Ford administrations that Britain was a declining ally. At its worst, it presented an image that Britain was on the verge of economic and political collapse. Consequently, senior policy-makers in Washington – including President Ford and Kissinger – believed Wilson's government was unable to restore order to Britain's economy. This belief was to be influential in dictating the course of US policy throughout the IMF crisis when a largely uncooperative attitude (at least as perceived by British policy-makers) was adopted by Washington.

The resulting IMF crisis is therefore the predominant focus of Chapter 5. It is demonstrated throughout this chapter that US financial assistance, in the guise that the new Prime Minister James Callaghan wanted, never materialised. Callaghan believed that Britain's position within the Western alliance would ensure that the US would use its influence to ensure that the IMF would provide preferential loan conditions. The Ford administration, however, did not believe Britain warranted such treatment. It is tempting to see the Callaghan–Ford epoch as one where the US–UK relationship was largely irrelevant for serving their respective interests. However, as noted elsewhere, many of the institutionalised aspects of US–UK cooperation, notably in the security/defence realms, continued. In other areas, US–UK cooperation was also in evidence; for instance, the US and UK worked together efficiently in Lebanon and Rhodesia.[12] Nevertheless, the fact that Callaghan over-estimated the degree of importance which the US attached to the UK cannot be ignored. The IMF negotiations were viewed as critically important by Callaghan; the prime minister believed he would be able to obtain preferential financial treatment because of Britain's ability to promote US interests in Europe. Evidently, the Ford White House did not ascribe the same level of importance to its relationship with Britain as those in London did to their relationship with Washington.

The US–UK relationship during 1974–77 should not, however, be seen as a period of unmitigated crisis. Rather, as Britain declined in significance on the world stage, so did the number of occasions in which US and UK policies interacted. Essentially, US–UK diplomacy had to adjust to the reality that Britain was no longer a world power.[13] Further, the more institutionalised aspects of US–UK relations, such as nuclear and intelligence cooperation, continued. Wilson's more hostile attitude towards the EEC was appreciated in Washington and he also lent his support to wider aspects of the US's Cold War policy. This was particularly evident during the final approaches to the CSCE's Final Act in Helsinki. As such, all of this would suggest that the US–UK relationship, in the period under consideration, is one that is rather more multifaceted and complex than existing accounts would suggest.[14]

## Sources

The UK's 'Thirty Year Rule' has resulted in the recent declassification of large amounts of government documentation (1970–1979). The US has also steadily released archival material from this era. This work has drawn heavily upon such material in constructing its argument and analysis. Indeed, the archival historian is particularly blessed when studying the Nixon–Ford administrations. The taping system which Richard Nixon installed within the White House, which have come to be termed the 'White House Tapes', give an insight into the creation of US foreign policy, and contain hours of conversation between the president and his senior advisers. In a similar fashion to his boss, Henry Kissinger also had a penchant for recording his conversations, and scholars have access to thousands of Kissinger's verbatim records of telephone conversations and meetings with US and foreign officials, such as Richard Nixon, Gerald Ford, Brent Scowcroft, James Schlesinger, Alexander Haig, Alec Douglas-Home, Sir Burke Trend, Lord Cromer and James Callaghan.

Historians, however, must use these materials with the utmost caution. Nixon's recording device within the White House was automatically activated on hearing a voice, and, therefore, captured all of the conversations held within the various rooms bugged by the president. On listening to the tapes, the historian finds that the discussions are often disjointed, range over a number of issues, and on a number of occasions can be considered as examples of when the president is seeking to 'let off steam'.[15] As Edward Keefer, the general editor of the *Foreign Relations of the United States* documentary series, wisely points out:

> The Nixon tapes are often raw, incoherent, rambling, and repetitive ... They must be used with caution, because Nixon had a tendency to exaggerate, vent, and posture. For example, he would announce that he wanted officials fired on the spot and rant about his intentions or his toughness as a leader. What Nixon says on one day in the heat of the moment is not in itself absolute proof of his intentions, just evidence of his state of mind at that particular time. Obviously, upon reflection a president can change his mind or moderate his attitudes. Multiple examples from the tapes, backed up by other documents, are the best way to discern Nixon's real motivations and reasoning.[16]

Even though the tapes do need to be used with caution, they offer a valuable and unique insight into how foreign policy was conceived and debated in the Nixon White House and are used throughout this work. Along with this, the policy-making papers from the White House, the State Department, the Pentagon and the National Security Council have been utilised in the construction of this work. This material has been sourced from the various presidential libraries, the United States National Archive II, and the various volumes of the collected documentary editions of the *Foreign Relations of the United States* (*FRUS*) series. By utilising this material, a more nuanced and fuller understanding of US foreign policy-making can be advanced. The telephone transcripts of Henry Kissinger serve as one such example. From these it is possible to learn Kissinger's private intentions about a particular subject, learn his often candid assessments of his colleagues and international counterparts, or discern the tactical nuances that went into his approach to diplomacy. By using this material the historian has a unique insight into the creation and formulation of US foreign policy during this period.

On the British side, the predominant material has been drawn from government documentation available at the National Archives (formerly the Public Records Office) in Kew, Surrey. This includes material from the Foreign and Commonwealth Office (FCO), Ministry of Defence (MOD), Treasury and the Cabinet. The private papers of former policy-makers and officials, including the likes of Harold Wilson and James Callaghan, have also been utilised. All of this archival material has been triangulated with secondary works, oral history interviews with former officials, and the voluminous memoirs that have been written by many of the protagonists featured in this work.

It would, however, be remiss not to point out that there are several important omissions in the source material. In particular, the private papers of Henry Kissinger and Edward Heath were not available to consult during the writing of this work. Kissinger's private papers, which supposedly consist of over 33 tonnes of material, are stored in the Library of Congress, and cannot be consulted publicly until five years after his death.[17] The papers of Edward Heath, who died in 2005, are also unavailable as they are waiting to be catalogued.[18] While such source material always has the potential to aid our understanding of the period, the contemporary historian has to accept that only partial access to the documentary record can be obtained. Moreover, the amount of material that is available for consultation is extremely detailed and, indeed, far outweighs that available to scholars who study many earlier eras.

By utilising this source material, this work provides a more thorough understanding of the US–UK relationship. Importantly, it allows many of the arguments made within the memoirs of the former policy-making protagonists to be cross-referenced with the government records and accordingly challenged and corrected. This new material also allows scholars to have a better insight into how policy is created and executed. As such, the arguments advanced throughout this work are substantially supported by the documentary record and need not be curtailed due to a lack of documentary evidence. Indeed, as John Lewis Gaddis correctly asserts, the writing of any history is conducted and produced within its own moment in history. In view of that, a history of the Cold War written in 2013 should, and probably will, be very different from one that is produced one hundred years later.[19]

## Special relationship?

Since the end of the Second World War, for policy-makers and academics alike, both the practice and study of US–UK relations has been dominated by the idea that a special relationship exists between the two countries. While close US–UK political and military cooperation had been apparent during earlier periods, the special relationship is largely believed to have been born during the unique conditions which the realities of total war fostered.[20] Winston Churchill – British prime minister, 1940–45 and 1951–55 – is usually credited with bringing the phrase special relationship into the popular imagination.[21] Churchill, who himself was half-American, had spoken of the special relationship throughout the Second World War, but it was not until after the war, during his 1946 'Iron Curtain' speech at Fulton, Missouri, that the phrase special relationship would enter the 'lexicon of international politics'.[22] During this speech Churchill explained that a special relationship between English-speaking peoples was required to avert another global war. As Churchill eloquently espoused:

> Neither the sure prevention of war, nor the continuous rise of world organization will be gained without what I have called the fraternal association of the English-speaking peoples. This means a special relationship between the British Commonwealth and Empire and the United States.[23]

Defining what this special relationship is has been a matter of some debate amongst scholars. Alex Danchev has divided the various arguments surrounding the special relationship into three broad schools of thought: what he terms the 'Evangelical', 'Functionalist' and the 'Terminalist'.[24] The Evangelical school has largely bought into the idea championed by Churchill that the US–UK special relationship is based upon a shared cultural and political philosophy on how international politics should operate. In a typically evangelical fashion, H. C. Allen explained the special relationship thus: 'Happily, the intimacy of Anglo-American relations is by no means solely dependent upon the powerful but sometimes fickle bond of emotion; it has manifold links embedded deep in the lives of both peoples.'[25]

Others have treated such interpretations with scepticism. As David Reynolds has noted about the origins of the special relationship, it 'grew out of a sense of shared threat and mutual need'.[26] Such assessments provide a 'Functionalist' interpretation of the US–UK relationship. Drawing upon a 'realist' understanding of international affairs, the US–UK special relationship is driven by national interests, rather than shared cultural or social values. Intelligence, nuclear and wider defence cooperation are at the core of the special relationship, and are undertaken and sustained because they suit the interests of each power. This is perhaps best highlighted by the words of James Callaghan when he explained to those who could not understand how a Republican president could work with a Labour prime minister, 'We both accepted that the interests of our two countries and of the Alliance transcended political differences'.[27] More bluntly, Peter Carrington – British secretary of state for defence, 1970–74, and foreign and commonwealth secretary, 1979–82 – noted that: 'It's always been national interests. People like to bang on about the special relationship but it's always interests.'[28]

Terminalist arguments draw on similar ideas for explaining the special relationship. For these commentators, the special relationship was sustained by mutual security concerns, but gradually eroded in its significance as the Cold War progressed because of Britain's dwindling military and economic significance. As Sir Michael Howard noted in 1986, if the special relationship existed for the US, then it was only because of the memory of Winston Churchill, which persisted throughout the American psyche.[29] Similarly, the likes of John Dickie predicted the demise of the special relationship once the rationale of Cold War security had been removed.[30] Dickie was perhaps too hasty in announcing the end of the special relationship. The resurrection of the special relationship was clearly evidenced throughout the Bush–Blair years (2001–2007). As two scholars of US–UK relations have noted, the special relationship remains the 'Lazarus' within international affairs.[31]

This work prefers to avoid adjudicating as to whether or not it can be said that a special relationship existed during the era under consideration. At first glance this approach may appear curious, but the reason for pursuing such a course is based upon several key factors. The first of these is that utilising the actual term special relationship brings an array of problems. The biggest of these is actually defining what is meant by the term 'special' and what exactly the phrase is referring to. Does it, for instance, refer to intelligence sharing, nuclear cooperation, or the overall political relationship? Can there be an economically competitive relationship but concurrently a special relationship in the security realm? Should scholars look for some sort of special cultural ties between the two countries? As there is little clarity on this matter, it is left to individual scholars to decide for themselves as to what the special relationship refers to. This then results in a rather haphazard approach for analysing the US–UK relationship.

Further to this, the term also inevitably leads to comparative analysis with other eras, and with other relationships enjoyed by both states with third actors.[32] This is clearly highlighted in many existing accounts of US–UK relations. 'No personal rapport developed between the rough spoken Texan President [Lyndon Johnson] and the wily British Prime Minister [Harold Wilson], nothing like the relationship that had been built up by Macmillan with Eisenhower and Kennedy,' claim two authors.[33] Wilson's period of government in the 1960s was 'less special' than that enjoyed under the governments of the half-American Harold Macmillan (1957–63).[34] The Cold War special relationship was 'not as comprehensive or special' as that experienced during the Second World War, according to another scholar.[35] This comparative approach is problematic for studying US–UK relations during 1969–77 because whether this era is less special in comparison to another is largely immaterial for understanding the relationship during this timeframe. Comparing the 'specialness' in one era with another provides only a superficial assessment of the period under question. Moreover, the idea of something being 'special' is not a fixed concept. Rather it is something that can only ever be relative to something else. Thus, by continually debating whether or not the US–UK relationship is special or, as current jargon would have it, 'essential', very little about the events in question can be understood.

While this work prefers to avoid assessing whether the US–UK relationship was special or not throughout this period, it does situate itself largely within the Functionalist school of interpreting the relationship. The discussion of mutual interests and antagonisms is central to the analysis, as is the military and economic interaction and competition between the two countries. This approach is taken because these areas of US–UK interaction were deemed by the actual policy-making elites to be the most important for promoting their respective interests. For the vast majority of both US and UK policy-makers, material interests were central to their understanding of US–UK interaction.[36] Richard Nixon, for instance, regarded power as the central conduit of international relations. Likewise, for Henry Kissinger, 'international relations cannot be conducted without an awareness of power relationships'.[37] Edward Heath was equally frank in articulating that 'realism' had to be the bedrock of any British foreign policy.[38] The following chapters, therefore, provide an analysis of the key political engagements between the two countries.

## The context for US–UK relations

The Nixon presidency has long fascinated historians, political scientists, journalists and psychologists, with the personality of Nixon himself attracting particular scrutiny.[39] It is the president's often contradictory personality that has come to dominate large swaths of the literature on the Nixon presidency. This, to some degree, is understandable given the amount of attention those who worked with the president have themselves given the subject. Indeed, nearly all those who worked closely with the president have remarked on his contradictory personality.[40] As one former Nixon associate recollected: 'One part of Richard Nixon is exceptionally considerate, exceptionally caring, sentimental, generous of spirit, kind. Another part is coldly calculating, devious, craftily manipulative. A third part is angry, vindictive, ill-tempered, mean-spirited.'[41] For George Schultz – who served as Nixon's Treasury Secretary, 1972–74 – the president demonstrated 'brilliance' in creating foreign policy strategy, but could also exhibit a peculiar amount of insecurity for a man who was the president of the United States.[42] In the opinion of Henry Kissinger a popular myth has developed that Richard Nixon 'was a man given to histrionics, to shouting his prejudices at cowed subordinates, and to dominating his environment by conveying his views with great, and even overpowering insistence – frequently under the influence of alcohol'. Rather, in Kissinger's own assessment, 'The Richard Nixon with whom I worked on a daily basis for five and a half years was generally soft spoken, withdrawn, and quite shy'.[43]

Likewise, the personality and psychology of Henry Kissinger has attracted a lot of attention. For some, Kissinger was akin to a modern-day Metternich, who shrewdly conducted US foreign policy at a time of considerable challenge for the US.[44] Others have viewed Kissinger's record less kindly.[45] Some have gone as far to suggest that Kissinger's actions equate to those of a 'war criminal' and that he should be arrested for his misdemeanours.[46] Regardless of where one stands on this, it is indisputable that Kissinger received remarkable attention both in and out of office. One historian has even estimated that Kissinger has been the subject of the largest number of inquiries of any US secretary of state.[47] What is evident is that 'Kissingerology' continues to be a flourishing industry, with the now nonagenarian Kissinger still commanding the attention of the world's policy-making elite and media.[48]

Whilst there is much to be gained from analysing the personalities of Nixon and Kissinger, their actions, decisions and policies must be placed properly within the context of the international and domestic system in which they operated. Many existing accounts fail to actually do this and, worse yet, several historians have subscribed to a 'personality disorder' theory of the Nixon presidency. For these commentators, Nixon's personality traits – especially the 'darker' elements – largely explain the course of US foreign policy under his tutelage.[49] Such is the power of this train of thought that work undertaken by one usually authoritative author opens with the sentence: 'Richard Nixon was a peculiar person.'[50]

This work prefers to avoid placing so much emphasis upon the supposedly peculiar personalities of Richard Nixon and Henry Kissinger. This is not to downplay the role of individuals in making and executing foreign policy. As one leading commentator on international relations theory notes, 'the international distribution of power can drive countries' behaviour only by influencing the decisions of flesh and blood officials'.[51] Given this, US foreign policy is better understood by contextualising the world situation, as understood by US policy-makers at the time.[52] Thus, structural factors, domestic interests, and identity politics all influenced the decisions undertaken by US policy-makers.[53] It is by taking this approach that one can better appreciate and explain why certain policy choices were undertaken throughout the period.[54]

On taking office in January 1969, Nixon was confronted with a myriad of domestic and foreign policy problems: a worsening economy, strategic nuclear parity with the USSR and, most pressing of all, the ongoing Vietnam War.[55] The domestic discontent the Vietnam War created had undermined Lyndon Johnson's presidency, and Nixon was aware that seeking a solution to Vietnam was as much a domestic as a foreign policy imperative. Vietnam, however, was only part of a more general problem that, in Nixon's assessment, the US faced at the onset of his presidency. For Nixon, the US had overstretched its resources throughout the 1960s in trying to maintain all of its global commitments, and had subsequently fallen into the Vietnam misadventure, seen its leadership of the Western alliance undermined, now faced the reality of nuclear parity with the USSR and had witnessed the weakening of American economic power.[56] When taken together, Nixon concluded that the US no longer held the position of global supremacy that he perceived it to have had during the Eisenhower administration, in which he served as vice-president (1953–61). Indeed, the new president wondered whether the USSR was now the 'number one' world power. Nixon was not alone in reaching such a conclusion, given that the senior advisers surrounding him largely shared his opinion of America's declining international position.[57]

Following his defeat for the presidency in 1960, and his subsequent failure to capture the Californian Governorship in 1962, Nixon had watched America's political situation unfold as somewhat of an outsider. His years outside politics were not misspent and they allowed him to conceive new policies to implement, if he was given the opportunity.[58] Nixon devised a number of strategies for resolving both domestic and foreign policy problems, and these could often be quite radical in their nature. For instance, he seriously contemplated establishing a new political party that would draw in the 'left' of the Republican Party and dissatisfied southern Democrats.[59]

It was in the realm of foreign policy, however, where Nixon's real interest lay, and here too he sought to impart fresh thinking into US policy. Nixon possessed a worldview that held international relations between states to be a single web of interlinked and interconnected actors and institutions (Kissinger, too, was strongly attracted to this model). This, in turn, led to an American approach that is often termed 'linkage'. As the term implies, the globe consisted of a network of states, statespeople and systems that were there to be mastered and manipulated to one's own advantage. This new outlook in foreign policy was to be applied to America's foes and allies alike. As Nixon remarked in private, it was now the time to 'play our allies and hit our foes'.[60]

The other major innovation in US foreign policy expressed itself as the so-called 'Nixon Doctrine'. Ostensibly aimed at avoiding Vietnam-style embroilments in the future, the Nixon Doctrine also articulated a future vision of US foreign policy. For Nixon, there were five centres of world power: the US, the USSR, the PRC, Western Europe and Japan, but within this the US and the USSR were the dominant actors. However, Nixon sought to limit direct US involvement globally, because the economic and domestic burdens of maintaining such commitments could no longer be endured. In particular, the damage Vietnam had caused for the US meant that future assistance to regional allies would have to be limited to American money and material. While not explicitly ruling out direct US military assistance, the Nixon Doctrine illustrated a determination to lessen America's global commitments.[61]

Reducing America's global presence was seen to pose a number of challenges for the US, especially in relation to the possible actions of the USSR. As both Nixon and Kissinger realised, a lessening of American commitments could be misinterpreted by Moscow as a sign that the US would not oppose Soviet aggrandisement. Thus, a dual strategy would be pursued. This would involve improving relations with Moscow through a policy of détente (an easing of strained relations) that would enable Moscow to see that it would benefit more from superpower cooperation, rather than confrontation.[62] Along with this, American power and influence could be maintained by improving regional alliances and distributing the military burdens of the alliances more equitably. NATO, therefore, would be one area receiving this new attention from Washington and its members were now being encouraged to provide a greater material commitment to the alliance. This policy took the label of 'burden-sharing'.[63]

Like the US, the beginning of the 1970s was a point of re-assessment for the UK. Since the end of the Second World War, close US–UK relations had been seen as a means of ensuring Britain's global influence.[64] Robert Cecil – first secretary in the British Embassy in Washington in the first years of the Cold War – explained how the special relationship was:

> a means of making sure that if this little British gunboat was following in the wake of the American battleship ... on the bridge ... the Americans would be receiving messages from the British who had this long experience of international affairs and knew so much more about things than the Americans did, or so we liked to think.[65]

Harold Macmillan perhaps typified this type of thinking when he referred to Britain playing the role of Greece to the American Roman Empire. Macmillan had made this in reference to how Britain would run the Allied Headquarters in Africa during the Second World War. When prime minister he made similar remarks to his foreign secretary, Selwyn Lloyd.[66] Tony Blair – British prime minister, 1997–2007 – less eloquently noted that close US–UK relations gave Britain 'immediate purchase' and a 'huge position' in influencing the course of US foreign policy.[67] From both of these assessments it is implied that Britain would be able to utilise its network of global bases and its well-practised diplomacy, coupled with its military and intelligence capabilities, to exercise a decisive influence over US foreign policy. Whether the British government ever had the level of influence over US policy that it sought is questionable. Regardless, as Henry Kissinger perceptively noted: 'Whatever the "reality" of the "special relationship," Britain has tried hard to give the impression to the outside world that American policy is strongly influenced, if not guided, by London.'[68]

Maintaining such an illusion throughout the course of the Cold War became increasingly difficult for British policy-makers as economic problems and the unwillingness of subsequent governments to maintain Britain's global military commitments clearly challenged the idea of Britain acting as a global lieutenant to the United States. Continued British economic weakness, typified by the devaluation of its currency in 1967 and the transition of the British Empire into a Commonwealth, along with the 1967 decision by the Wilson government to withdraw all British forces 'East of Suez', cemented both the image and the reality that the UK was no longer a global power.[69] Much of the rationale then for close US–UK relations was undermined by this set of events. Accordingly, from the 1960s onwards, membership of the EEC was seen by British policy-makers as a means of achieving the twin objectives of improving Britain's economic performance and its international influence. The French president, Charles de Gaulle, however, scuppered such aspirations when he twice vetoed British membership of the EEC (1963 and 1967). Harold Wilson, however, refused to relent and began the third application. Therefore, when

Heath assumed power in June 1970, he inherited a situation where British foreign policy was on a more European-focused trajectory. This was a course the new prime minister was unlikely to alter because he was deeply committed to gaining British membership of the EEC.[70]

It is within this broader context then that US–UK relations are analysed throughout the subsequent chapters. As shown, the challenges that détente, economic decline, retreat from global obligations and membership of the EEC created were to be ones that would nearly lead to a fundamental break in the US–UK relationship. Nonetheless, and in spite of these challenges, the institutionalised aspects of the relationship, notably intelligence and nuclear collaboration, remained. Indeed, close US–UK cooperation, however one might view it, remained a rather resilient feature of US–UK interaction.

## Notes

1 Henry Kissinger, *The White House Years* (Boston, MA: Little, Brown and Company, 1979) (hereafter: *WHY*), p. 90.

2 The following telephone conversations between Nixon and Kissinger are illuminating on this point. See: Telephone conversation transcript (hereafter: Telcon): The President–HAK [Kissinger], 9 August 1973, Henry A. Kissinger Telephone Conversation Transcripts (hereafter: HAKTELCONS), Nixon Presidential Materials Project, National Archive II, College Park, Maryland, USA (hereafter: NPMP); Telcon: The President–Kissinger, 13 August 1973, *ibid.*; Telcon: The President–Kissinger, 14 August 1973, *ibid.*

3 Christopher Hill and Christopher Lord, 'The Foreign Policy of the Heath Government' in Stuart Ball and Anthony Seldon (eds.), *The Heath Government 1970–1974: A Reappraisal* (London: Longman, 1996), pp. 285–6; Keith Hamilton, 'Britain, France and America's Year of Europe, 1973', *Diplomacy and Statecraft*, 17:4 (2006), 872–5; Catherine Hynes, *The Year That Never Was: Heath, The Nixon Administration and the Year of Europe* (Dublin: University College Dublin Press, 2009); Alex Spelling, 'Edward Heath and Anglo-American Relations 1970–1974: A Reappraisal', *Diplomacy and Statecraft*, 20:4 (2009), 640–58; Niklas Rossbach, *Heath, Nixon and the Rebirth of the Special Relationship: Britain, the US and the EC, 1969–74* (Basingstoke: Palgrave Macmillan, 2009); Daniel Möckli, *European Foreign Policy during the Cold War: Heath, Brandt, Pompidou and the Dream of Political Unity* (London: I.B. Tauris, 2009); Andrew Scott, *Allies Apart: Heath, Nixon and the Anglo-American Relationship* (Basingstoke: Palgrave Macmillan, 2011).

4 Geir Lundestad, *'Empire' by Integration: The United States and European Integration, 1945–1997* (Oxford: Oxford University Press, 1998), pp. 13–28.

5 National Security Study Memorandum (hereafter: NSSM) 79 and 91: Enlargement of the European Community: Implications for the US and Policy Options, attached to Martin J. Hillenbrand to Henry Kissinger, 23 April 1970, National Security Council Institutional (H) Files (hereafter: NSCIHF), Study Memorandums, National Security Study Memorandums, Box H-164, NPMP.

6 Kissinger, *WHY*, pp. 937–8.
7 Hynes, *The Year*, pp. 109–10.
8 The concept of 'linkage' is explained in greater detail within note 60.
9 This refers to the readiness of the US military. It ranges from DEFCON I, when forces are at their highest state of readiness just short of war, to DEFCON V, which is the 'normal readiness posture'. For a full explanation see: Scott Sagan, *The Limits of Safety: Organizations, Accidents, and Nuclear Weapons* (Princeton: Princeton University Press, 1993), pp. 64–5.
10 The National Archives, Kew, Surrey (hereafter: TNA): PREM 15/2038 The President to the Prime Minister, undated, January 1974.
11 John Baylis, 'British Nuclear Doctrine: The "Moscow Criterion" and the Polaris Improvement Programme', *Contemporary British History*, 19:1 (2005), 53–65.
12 Henry Kissinger, *Years of Renewal* (New York: Simon & Schuster, 1999) (hereafter: *YOR*), pp. 1006–10.
13 Klaus Larres, 'International and Security Relations Within Europe', in Mary Fulbrook (ed.), *Europe Since 1945* (Oxford: Oxford University Press, 2001), pp. 212–13.
14 See Note 3 for examples of existing works.
15 The Nixon tapes have all been put online by Luke Nichter. See: http://nixontapes.org. For edited transcripts of the tapes see: Stanley Kutler, *The Wars of Watergate: The Last Crisis of Richard Nixon* (New York: Norton, 1990).
16 Edward C. Keefer, 'Key Sources for Nixon's Foreign Policy', p. 3. Available from: www.shafr.org/passport/2007/august/keefer.pdf (Accessed 11 July 2010).
17 Bruce P. Montgomery, 'Source Material: Sequestered from the Court of History: The Kissinger Transcripts', *Presidential Studies Quarterly*, 34:4 (2004), 867–90; Asaf Siniver, 'Source Material: The Truth is Out There: The Recently Released NSC Institutional Files of the Nixon Presidency', *Presidential Studies Quarterly*, 34:2 (2004), 449–54; Keith Nelson, 'Détente Over Thirty Years' in Robert D. Schulzinger (ed.), *A Companion to American Foreign Relations* (Oxford: Blackwell, 2003), p. 436.
18 Philip Ziegler, *Edward Heath: The Authorised Biography* (London: HarperPress, 2010), p. 627.
19 John Lewis Gaddis, *We Now Know: Rethinking Cold War History* (Oxford: Oxford University Press, 1997), pp. vii–viii. On the problems confronting historians of the recent past see: Marc Trachtenberg, *The Craft of International History: A Guide to Method* (Princeton: Princeton University Press, 2006), pp. 146–162.
20 Some believe it to have much earlier origins. Iestyn Adams, *Brothers Across the Ocean: British Foreign Policy and the Origins of the Anglo-American 'Special Relationship' 1900–1905* (London: I.B. Tauris, 2005).
21 John Charmley, *Churchill's Grand Alliance: The Anglo-American Special Relationship 1940–57* (London: Hodder & Stoughton, 1995), p. 3.
22 The 'Iron Curtain' speech, as it is often dubbed, is in fact titled 'The Sinews of Peace' and was delivered on 5 March 1946 in Fulton, Missouri, USA. See: David Reynolds, *In Command of History: Churchill Fighting and Writing the Second World War* (London: Allen Lane, 2004), pp. 43–4.
23 'The Sinews of Peace', 5 March 1946, in Robert Rhodes James (ed.), *Winston S. Churchill: His Complete Speeches 1897–1963* (London: Chelsea House Publishers, 1974), Vol. VII, p. 7289.

24 Alex Danchev, 'The Cold War "Special Relationship" Revisited', *Diplomacy and Statecraft*, 17:3 (2006), 579–95.

25 Harry Cranbrook Allen, *Great Britain and the United States: A History of Anglo-American Relations 1783–1952* (London: Odhams, 1954), pp. 17–18.

26 David Reynolds, 'Roosevelt, Churchill, and the Wartime Anglo-American Alliance, 1939–1945: Towards a New Synthesis', in W. M. Roger Louis and Hedley Bull (eds.), *The Special Relationship: Anglo-American Relations Since 1945* (Oxford: Clarendon Press, 1986), p. 39.

27 James Callaghan, *Time & Chance* (London: Collins, 1987), p. 430.

28 David Gill, 'Peter Carrington', in Jennifer Mackby and Paul Cornish, *US–UK Nuclear Cooperation after Fifty Years* (Washington DC: CSIS Press, 2008), p. 267.

29 Sir Michael Howard, 'Afterword: The "Special Relationship"', in Louis and Bull, *Anglo-American Relations*, p. 387.

30 John Dickie, *'Special' No More. Anglo-American Relations: Rhetoric and Reality* (London: Weidenfeld & Nicolson, 1994), pp. 1–10.

31 Steve Marsh, 'September 11 and Anglo-American relations: Reaffirming the Special Relationship', *Journal of Transatlantic Studies*, 1:1, Supplement (2003), 56–75; Steve Marsh and John Baylis, 'The Anglo-American "Special Relationship": The Lazarus of International Relations', *Diplomacy and Statecraft*, 17:1 (2006), 173–211.

32 For instance: John Dumbrell and Axel Schäfer (eds.), *America's Special Relationships* (London: Routledge, 2009).

33 David Dimbleby and David Reynolds, *An Ocean Apart: The Relationship Between Britain and America in the Twentieth Century* (New York: Random House, 1988), p. 264.

34 Ritchie Ovendale, *Anglo-American Relations in the Twentieth Century* (Basingstoke: Macmillan, 1998), pp. 120–31; D. Richard Thorpe, *Alec Douglas-Home* (London: Sinclair-Stevenson, 1996), p. 431.

35 Alan Dobson, 'Anglo-American Relations and Diverging Economic Defence Policies in the 1950s and 1960s', in Jonathan Hollowell (ed.), *Twentieth Century Anglo-American Relations* (Basingstoke: Macmillan, 2001), p. 143.

36 Bruce Kuklick, *Blind Oracles: Intellectuals and War from Kennan to Kissinger* (Princeton: Princeton University Press, 2006), pp. 182–92.

37 Henry A. Kissinger, 'Reflections on American Diplomacy', *Foreign Affairs*, 35:1 (1956), 42.

38 Edward Heath, 'Realism in British Foreign Policy', *Foreign Affairs*, 48:1 (1969), 39–50.

39 For the most recent and comprehensive accounts see: Conrad Black, *Richard Milhous Nixon: The Invincible Quest* (London: Quercus, 2007); Robert Dallek, *Nixon and Kissinger: Partners in Power* (London: Allen Lane, 2007). For an overview of the scholarship concerning Nixon see Melvin Small (ed.), *A Companion to Richard M. Nixon* (Malden: Wiley-Blackwell, 2011).

40 John Dean, *Blind Ambition* (New York: Simon & Schuster, 1976); Harry Robbins Haldeman, *The Ends of Power* (New York: Times Books, 1978); John Ehrlichman, *Witness to Power: The Nixon Years* (New York: Simon & Schuster, 1982); Alexander Haig, *Inner Circles: How America Changed the World* (New York: Warner Books, 1992); John Connally and Mickey Herskowitz, *In History's Shadow: An American Odyssey* (New York: Hyperion Books, 1993), pp. 254–7; Robert H. Ferrell (ed.), *Inside the Nixon*

*Administration: The Secret Diary of Arthur Burns, 1969–1974* (Lawrence: University of Kansas, 2010).

41 Raymond Price, *With Nixon* (New York: The Viking Press, 1977), p. 29.

42 George P. Shultz, *Turmoil and Triumph: My Years as Secretary of State* (Oxford: Maxwell Macmillan International, 1993), p. 9.

43 Kissinger, *YOR*, pp. 54–5.

44 Stephen Graubard, *Kissinger: Portrait of a Mind* (New York: Norton, 1973); Marvin Kalb and Bernard Kalb, *Kissinger* (London: Hutchinson, 1974); David Landau, *Kissinger: The Uses of Power* (London: Robson, 1974); Coral Bell, *The Diplomacy of Détente: The Kissinger Era* (London: Martin Robertson, 1977).

45 Seymour Hersh, *The Price of Power: Kissinger in the Nixon White House* (New York: Summit Books, 1983).

46 Christopher Hitchens, *The Trial of Henry Kissinger* (London: Verso, 2001).

47 Robert D. Schulzinger, *Henry Kissinger: Doctor of Diplomacy* (New York: Columbia University Press, 1989), pp. x–xi.

48 This is a term taken from the Kissinger biographer, Jussi Hanhimäki. See: Jussi Hanhimäki, '"Dr Kissinger" or "Mr Henry"? Kissingerology, Thirty Years and Counting', *Diplomatic History*, 27:5 (2003), 637–76; 'Henry Kissinger talks to Simon Schama', *FT Weekend Magazine*, 21–22 May 2011, 14–19.

49 Peter Rodman, *Presidential Command: Power, Leadership and the Making of Foreign Policy from Richard Nixon to George W. Bush* (New York: Alfred Knopf, 2009), p. 56.

50 Tore T. Peterson, *Richard Nixon, Great Britain and the Anglo-American Alignment in the Persian Gulf and Arabian Peninsula: Making Allies out of Clients* (Brighton: Sussex Academic Press, 2009), p. 1.

51 Gideon Rose, 'Review Article: Neoclassical Realism Theories of Foreign Policy', *World Politics*, 51 (1998), 144–72. Quote at p. 158.

52 Some of the best works on the 1970s that provide this contextual information are as follows: Beth Bailey and David Farber (eds.), *America in the 70s* (Lawrence: University of Kansas, 2004); Jeremi Suri, *Power and Protest: Global Revolution and the Rise of Détente* (Cambridge, MA: Harvard University Press, 2005), pp. 164–259; Rick Perlstein, *Nixonland: The Rise of a President and the Fracturing of America* (New York: Scribner, 2010).

53 For some general works which note the influence of domestic factors upon the foreign policy of the Nixon administration, see: Jussi Hanhimäki, 'Global Visions and Parochial Politics: The Persistent Dilemma of the American Century', *Diplomatic History*, 27:4 (2003), 423–47; Dominic Sandbrook, 'Salesmanship and Substance: The Influence of Domestic Policy and Watergate', in Fredrik Logevall and Andrew Preston (eds.), *Nixon in the World: American Foreign Relations, 1969–1977* (Oxford: Oxford University Press, 2008), pp. 85–106; Campbell Craig and Fredrick Logevall, *America's Cold War: The Politics of Insecurity* (Cambridge, MA: Harvard University Press, 2009), pp. 252–88; Thomas Alan Schwartz, '"Henry, ... Winning an Election is Terribly Important": Partisan Politics in the History of U.S. Foreign Relations', *Diplomatic History*, 33:2 (2009), 173–90.

54 Odd Arne Westad, 'The Cold War and the International History of the Twentieth Century', in Melvyn P. Leffler and Odd Arne Westad (eds.), *The Cambridge History of the Cold War: Origins* (Cambridge: Cambridge University Press, 2010), pp. 1–3.

55 Memorandum from the President's Assistant for National Security Affairs-Designate [Kissinger] to President-elect Nixon, 27 December 1968, in *Foreign Relations of the United States: Organization and Management of U.S. Foreign Policy, 1969–1972* (Washington DC: United States Government Printing Office, 2006), Vol. II, Doc.1, p. 8.

56 Mark A. Pollack and Gregory C. Shaffer, 'Transatlantic Governance in Historical and Theoretical Perspective', in Mark A. Pollack and Gregory C. Shaffer (eds.), *Transatlantic Governance in the Global Economy* (Oxford: Rowman & Littlefield, 2001), pp. 9–12; Allen J. Matusow, 'Richard Nixon and the Failed War Against the Trading World', *Diplomatic History*, 27:5 (2003), 767–72; Frank Costigliola, 'US Foreign Policy From Kennedy to Johnson', in Melvyn Leffler and Odd Arne Westad (eds.), *The Cambridge History of the Cold War, Volume 2, Crises and Détente* (Cambridge: Cambridge University Press, 2010), pp. 131–2.

57 Harry Robbins Haldeman, *Haldeman Diaries: Inside the Nixon White House* (London: Putnam, 1994), p. 215; Monica Crowley, *Nixon in Winter: The Final Revelations* (New York: Random House, 1998), p. 11; Telcon: Henry Kissinger–James Retson, 1 May 1969, HAKTELCONS; Memorandum of Conversation, Henry Kissinger, James Schlesinger, National Security Adviser Files, Memoranda of Conversations (hereafter NSAMC), Box 9, Gerald Ford Library, Ann Arbor, Michigan, USA (hereafter: GFL).

58 Richard Nixon, 'Asia after Viet Nam', *Foreign Affairs*, 46:1 (1967), 111–25.

59 Robert Mason, "'I was Going to Build a New Republican Party and Majority": Richard Nixon as Party Leader, 1969–73', *Journal of American Studies*, 39:3 (2005), 463–83.

60 Nixon Tapes, 8 March 1971, Nixon–Rumsfeld Tapes, conversation 463–6, available at http://nixontapes.org (Accessed 11 September 2011). On Kissinger's worldview see: Jeremi Suri, *Henry Kissinger and the American Century* (Cambridge, MA: Harvard University Press, 2007), pp. 138–96. On the intellectual origins of 'linkage' and its ramifications for US foreign policy see: Robert D. Schulzinger, 'Détente in the Nixon-Ford Years 1969–1976' in Leffler and Westad (eds.), *Crises and Détente*, pp. 377–8; Raymond Garthoff, *Détente and Confrontation: American-Soviet Relations from Nixon to Reagan* (Washington DC: The Brookings Institution, 1994), pp. 28–39. On linkage see: Henry Kissinger, *Diplomacy* (New York: Simon & Schuster, 1994), pp. 715–19, 733, 740–1, 754–5, 758–9; Thomas Otte, 'Kissinger', in Geoffrey Berridge, Thomas Otte and Maurice Keens-Soper (eds.), *Diplomatic Theory From Machiavelli to Kissinger* (Basingstoke: Palgrave, 2001), pp. 196–7; David C. Geyer, 'The Missing Link: Henry Kissinger and the Back-channel Negotiations over Berlin' in David C. Geyer and Bernd Schaefer (eds.), *American Détente and German Ostpolitik, 1969–1972* (Washington DC: German Historical Institute, 2004), p. 80.

61 Address to the Nation on the War in Vietnam, 3 November 1969, *Public Papers of the Presidents of the United States, Richard Nixon, 1969* (Washington DC: United States Government Printing Office, 1971), pp. 901–9; Jeffrey Kimball, 'The Nixon Doctrine: A Saga of Misunderstanding', *Presidential Studies Quarterly*, 36:1 (2006), 59–74.

62 Dieter Dekke, 'The Scholar Statesman: Henry Kissinger', *Journal of Transatlantic Studies*, 6:3 (2008), 252–6; John Lewis Gaddis, 'Grand Strategies in the Cold War', in Leffler and Westad (eds.), *Crises and Détente*, pp. 14–16; Marc Trachtenberg, 'The structure of great power politics, 1963–1975', in Leffler and Westad (eds.), *Crises and Détente*, pp. 492–9; Jeremi Suri, 'Henry Kissinger and American Grand Strategy', in Logevall and Preston (eds.), *Nixon in the World*, pp. 67–84.

63 Argyris G. Andrianopoulos, *Western Europe in Kissinger's Global Strategy* (Basingstoke: Macmillan, 1988), pp. 90–100.
64 David Reynolds, *The Creation of the Anglo-American Alliance 1937–41: A Study in Competitive Co-operation* (London: Europa Publishing, 1981), pp. 284–5. Good overviews on Britain in the 1970s are provided by: Alwyn W. Turner, *Crisis? What Crisis?: Britain in the 1970s* (London: Aurum, 2008); Dominic Sandbrook, *State of Emergency: The Way We Were: Britain, 1970–1974* (London: Penguin, 2011). For a broader overview see: Gerard DeGroot, *The Seventies Unplugged: A Kaleidoscopic Look at a Violent Decade* (Basingstoke: Macmillan, 2010).
65 Peter Hennessy, *Never Again: Britain 1945–1951* (London: Vintage, 1993), p. 365.
66 Christopher Hitchens, *Blood, Class and Nostalgia: Anglo-American Ironies* (London: Farrar, Straus & Giroux, 1990), p. 23; Harold Macmillan Papers, MS Macmillan, dep. c. 347, M279/57, Macmillan to Lloyd, 16 June 1957, Bodleian Library, Oxford University, United Kingdom.
67 Tony Blair, *A Journey* (London: Hutchinson, 2010), p. 410.
68 Henry A. Kissinger, *The Troubled Partnership: A Reappraisal of the Atlantic Alliance* (New York: McGraw-Hill for the Council on Foreign Relations, 1965), p. 78.
69 Paul Kennedy, *The Realities Behind Diplomacy: Background Influences on British External Policy, 1865–1980* (London: Fontana, 1981), pp. 315–44; Kathleen Burk, *Old World, New World: Great Britain and America from the Beginning* (Boston, MA: Little, Brown and Company, 2009), p. 579.
70 Hugo Young, *The Blessed Plot* (London: Macmillan, 1998), p. 218–19; Nigel Ashton, 'Harold Macmillan and the "Golden Days" of Anglo-American Relations', *Diplomatic History*, 29:4 (2005), 691–723; R. Gerald Hughes, *Britain, Germany and the Cold War: The Search for a European Détente, 1949–1967* (London: Routledge, 2007), pp. 150–9; Hynes, *The Year*, pp. 11–17.

# 2

# Re-assessing foreign policy 1969–72

*There could be no special partnership between Britain and the United States, even if Britain wanted it.*

Prime Minister Heath to President Pompidou, May 1971[1]

## The jilted lover

According to Henry Kissinger, Edward Heath rejected a close working partnership with Richard Nixon, which left him feeling akin to that of a 'jilted lover'.[2] Kissinger's analysis has had an incredible impact upon the subsequent scholarly assessments of the US–UK relationship. As Heath's official biographer Philip Ziegler has claimed, 'Certainly it was no fault of President Nixon's if the special relationship languished'.[3] As the argument runs, Heath was determined to attain membership of the EEC because this would bolster a stagnant British economy, and promote Britain's international influence. France, having vetoed British membership on two previous occasions in 1963 and 1967, had to be convinced that Britain could be a 'European country'. Accordingly, Heath disassociated from the US–UK special relationship in order to prove his European credentials, and thus undermine the perennial French fear that Britain would act as an American Trojan Horse within the EEC.[4]

This interpretation has been challenged by other scholars. Rather than it being London's enthusiasm for a weakening of the special relationship, the cause of this lay with Washington. The Nixon administration's secretive foreign policy resulted in Britain being ignored and British policy-makers therefore sought to re-galvanise their influence internationally by entrenching a European foreign policy.[5] Other commentators have attempted to synthesise such arguments. The Nixon administration's indifference towards the special relationship coupled with a British foreign policy pursuing a more European path resulted in the special relationship becoming near redundant. It was only once the consequences of the global economic and energy crisis of 1973–74 became apparent that the special relationship became prevalent again.[6]

Central in many of these accounts is the role played by certain individual policy-makers. Henry Kissinger, in particular, is seen to have had a malevolent effect upon US–UK relations.[7] As one leading scholar of US–UK relations declares, US–UK difficulties 'certainly owed something to Kissinger's ego'.[8] This line of argument appears especially popular amongst former British officials.[9] Certainly, as recent scholarship has demonstrated, Kissinger's penchant for presenting himself as the archetypal proponent of *realpolitik* should be challenged, given that his actions could be dictated by anger, jealously and suspicion of his bureaucratic rivals.[10] Personalities, and especially that of Kissinger, did have an impact, often a detrimental one, upon the course of US–UK relations.[11] Nonetheless, such arguments should not be taken too far. US–UK relations are far greater than simply the behaviour of a few men. Indeed, if one is to accept the arguments of some scholars, one would be left with the impression that the entire US–UK relationship was virtually single-handedly controlled by Henry Kissinger. While personal relations in the conduct of international affairs are important, they are not overriding in determining the course of relations between states. Economic, security, political and domestic factors all play an important role in determining the development of events. Accordingly, these areas feature prominently below.[12]

Existing accounts have also tended to focus too heavily upon moments of crisis and acrimony between the two states. US–UK differences concerning the ceasing of the post-World War II Bretton Woods economic consensus, the India–Pakistan War, the 'Year of Europe' and the fourth Arab–Israeli War have all been emphasised. This is not unreasonable given the sometimes serious ramifications which emanated from such disagreements. Yet, as other analysts have highlighted, focusing solely on such events presents a distorted image of this era, and continued military, nuclear and intelligence cooperation between the two countries was hardly symbolic of a relationship that was supposedly 'All at sea'.[13]

Accordingly, it is argued below that certain aspects of the US–UK relationship functioned smoothly throughout this period (1969–72). In contradiction to the typical portrayal of Edward Heath actively shunning close US–UK cooperation, it is shown that in some areas it was actively re-energised.[14] This was most obvious related to the updating of Britain's strategic nuclear weapons system, Polaris. Where US–UK difficulties did arise, these stemmed from differences towards détente, EEC entry and the re-ordering of the world's financial system.

For US–UK relations, 1969–72 should be seen as a period of transition, rather than one of crisis. Nevertheless, it must be remembered that many areas of difficulty for US–UK relations were largely ignored by policy-makers during this time. As shown throughout subsequent chapters, these unresolved differences were to create a number of problems for US–UK relations in the following years.

## Dramatis personae

Nixon, as with all presidents, brought his own style of conducting foreign affairs to the White House.[15] He was determined to centralise the creation of foreign policy in the White House because he was distrustful of the traditional centres of power in Washington. In Nixon's assessment, his years as vice-president (1953–61) had demonstrated how the Washington bureaucracy was able to manipulate the president into pursuing choices which 'they' wanted. In Nixon's estimation, the CIA was full of 'Ivy League Liberals' who disdained him. Worse yet, Nixon distrusted the work of the CIA and believed that many of its analysts had a tendency to utilise intelligence as a means to support pre-existing conclusions.[16]

As one former director of the CIA (DCI) recalls, Nixon 'despised' the agency, not least because he was convinced that it had worked with John F. Kennedy in the 1960 presidential election to undermine his candidacy.[17] As such, the role of the DCI (Richard Helms) was severely curtailed, and all intelligence assessments were instructed to run through the office of Henry Kissinger.[18] Kissinger also made sure that Helms would never meet with the president alone, and that all intelligence estimates that were to reach the president had to be in Kissinger's possession 'at least 48 hours' beforehand.[19] This meant that all of the intelligence assessments that were to reach the president could be vetted by Kissinger and duly influenced according to his design. As national security adviser, therefore, Kissinger effectively functioned as Nixon's 'principal' intelligence officer. It is with authority then that Richard H. Immerman notes, 'Richard Nixon had no use for sources of intelligence other than his own – which meant Henry Kissinger's'.[20]

The new president's opinion of the State Department was little better. As one prominent journalist recollected, Nixon 'distrusted the state department which he considered both fuzzy minded and a nest of holdover liberal Democrats'.[21] Nixon's disdain for the State Department is captured well by his comment that it was staffed by 'striped pant faggots'.[22] Worse still, the president believed that the existing Washington bureaucracy was actively seeking to undermine his policies. In order to overcome this, Nixon wanted to replace all of the existing bureaucrats with his own appointees.[23] On matters related to foreign policy,

Nixon was determined to centralise its creation and execution from within the White House. Nixon believed that a sort of inertia had enveloped US foreign policy, and it was only through the White House that foreign policy could be properly debated and re-conceptualised. In the subsequent years, the opinions of the CIA, Pentagon and State Department were to be largely ignored. As Arthur Schlesinger noted, Nixon's conduct really did mark the zenith of the 'Imperial Presidency'.[24]

Nixon was aided in this ambition by employing a very small circle of advisers in which policy choices would be debated and decided. This circle included Chief of Staff H. R. Haldeman, Deputy Chief of Staff John Ehrlichman, Treasury Secretary John Connally and National Security Adviser Henry Kissinger. Haldeman's position within the administration was particularly important given that Nixon wanted all matters of substance to be channelled through him. Such was Haldeman's importance that he was referred to by Nixon as his 'lord high executioner'. In fact, the president made clear in one Cabinet meeting: 'When [Haldeman] talks, it's me talking.' According to a number of White House insiders, nobody, not even Kissinger, could ignore Haldeman.[25]

Whilst not immune to Haldeman's presence, at least in advising the president on foreign policy matters, Kissinger reigned supreme.[26] Kissinger managed to achieve this in a number of ways. First, he had been quick to centralise as much power in his office as possible. Thus, Kissinger – under the direction of Nixon – sought to change the Washington bureaucracy, in order to strip the traditional centres of influence of their power. The State Department was Kissinger's first target and, in spite of meeting resistance, he was successful in diminishing its influence by forcing through a number of changes.[27] Kissinger did this by first warning against following Lyndon Johnson's 'Tuesday Lunch' decision-making approach. As Kissinger suggested, this approach meant that the 'discussants are frequently inadequately briefed and often unfamiliar with the nuances of the issues before them'.[28] To avoid this in the new administration, Kissinger advised that the National Security Council should return as the principal forum for discussing and deciding US policy. Here, the national security adviser (Kissinger), working under the 'direction of the President', would determine the agenda and lead the discussion.[29] This won Nixon's approval and the first National Security Decision Memorandum (NSDM) issued under him stated that the National Security Council would be the 'principal forum for issues requiring inter-agency decisions and setting basic national objectives'. NSDM Number 2 re-affirmed this.[30] Nixon was even more explicit within private communications with Kissinger.[31] The State Department also lost a number of its advisory roles within the administration. For instance, the collective group meetings between various bodies were taken away from the State Department and placed in the hands of Kissinger.[32]

Kissinger's position within the administration as the number one foreign policy adviser was therefore endorsed at the onset of the Nixon administration. Nixon's decision to re-establish the National Security Council as the primary body for debating and deciding US foreign policy enabled Kissinger to enact a tremendous amount of influence upon the course of US policy. However, it should be remembered that Kissinger's position within the bureaucracy was far from supreme. His biggest challenge was that he did not have an institutional base from which to operate in the same fashion that a secretary of state or defense would have. Instead, Kissinger relied solely upon the continued good will of the president himself. Thus, although Nixon gave greater prominence to his national security adviser, it was the president who assumed the dominant role in the Nixon–Kissinger relationship and it was Nixon who established the general outlines of foreign policy. It was Kissinger's job to then turn these general ambitions of the president into reality.[33] One former Nixon White House insider eloquently summarises the relationship thus: 'Many of America's moves in this period originated with Kissinger, but Kissinger was operating within the Nixon framework.'[34]

On the face of it, it is perhaps curious that a book which deals with US foreign policy has yet to mention the role played by the US secretary of state. William Rogers was appointed as secretary of state in 1969, and had worked with Nixon as a partner within the same New York law firm, had advised him as a senator on the Alger Hiss case and had served as the Attorney General during the Eisenhower administration with him. Given this, one would naturally presume that Rogers would have had a major role to play in US foreign policy-making but in reality he had limited influence upon significant aspects of US foreign policy. The institutional changes to the Washington bureaucracy ensured that the State Department's influence was curtailed, and Nixon's disdain for the department meant he had little time for it anyhow. As such, Rogers' main area of concern was with trying to resolve the Arab–Israeli conflict. Even this had only been given to Rogers largely because of Nixon's belief that Kissinger's Jewish background would leave him incapable of pursuing a path which was not profoundly pro-Israeli.[35] Thus, Rogers' influence upon US–UK relations was limited and occurred only sporadically.

Melvin Laird, as Nixon's defense secretary, had a much more influential role in US foreign policy which can largely be attributed to his superb bureaucratic in-fighting skills.[36] However, on the major issues, Kissinger usually managed to triumph. More importantly, Kissinger had a far more consistent record of supporting Nixon on the most crucial issues. On all of the critical events during the early days of Nixon's first term, be it Cuba, the potential Syria–Jordan war and the escalation of hostilities in Vietnam, Kissinger steadfastly supported the president which, in turn, gave Kissinger more influence with Nixon.[37] Laird, however, was still important for US–UK relations and obvious areas where his influence would be felt included the MBFR negotiations and debates about wider NATO restructuring. Laird's position on the upgrading of Britain's Polaris fleet was also of crucial significance for British interests. Nevertheless, UK policy-makers would predominantly gain access to Nixon via Kissinger.[38] Given this, it is the person of Henry Kissinger that features heavily in subsequent chapters.

In comparison to Nixon's distrust of the bureaucracy, Heath worked well with his civil service. Heath leaned heavily on Robert Armstrong – his principal private secretary – especially on matters related to European and domestic policy. Douglas Hurd, who would go on to become foreign and commonwealth secretary during the Thatcher and Major governments (1989–95), and Donald Maitland, who acted as Heath's press secretary, also enjoyed a close professional relationship with the prime minister. Heath also actively sought the advice of Lord Carrington, secretary of state for defence (1970–74), on defence and security issues.[39]

Burke Trend, the Cabinet secretary, enjoyed a somewhat mixed relationship with Heath. Apparently, his Socratic method in proffering advice irritated Heath and he was also judged to have been too close with the former prime minister, Harold Wilson. However, for US–UK relations, and in matters regarding defence and wider foreign policy, Heath realised that Trend was indispensable, because Trend was, as one author put it, 'Heath's link-man with Nixon'.[40] Trend achieved this position largely as a result of Nixon's insistence that the usual channels for international communication, i.e. via the State Department, be bypassed. Instead, foreign governments deemed of importance were encouraged to communicate all sensitive and important matters via Henry Kissinger. This backchannel method is usually associated with Kissinger and Anatoly Dobrynin, the Soviet Union's ambassador to Washington (1962–86). However, the British also engaged in backchannel diplomacy with Rowley Cromer (UK ambassador to Washington, 1971–74) first acting as the main liaison, and Trend gradually assuming the role from 1971/2 onwards.[41]

Other key individuals for the management of US–UK relations included Rowley Cromer, Denis Greenhill, Thomas Brimelow, Richard Sykes and Charles Powell.[42] Cromer was the former governor of the Bank of England, and had acted as an unofficial adviser to the Conservative Party during the Labour governments of Harold Wilson (1964–70). Cromer's reward for this was to be appointed as the ambassador to Washington.[43] Greenhill and Brimelow were the two officials from the Foreign and Commonwealth Office who had the most contact with the Nixon administration. Sykes and Powell were both important as they attended many of the meetings between Cromer and key US officials. Once the Kissinger–Trend backchannel was established, they attended these meetings too.[44]

Little has been said so far about foreign and commonwealth secretary Alec Douglas-Home. While he was certainly not marginalised in foreign policy-making, Heath was keen to dominate the areas of foreign policy that he felt were most important. Such aspects included Britain's application to the EEC and the conduct of US–UK relations. Furthermore, whilst Douglas-Home established a cordial relationship with his opposite number William Rogers, and was held in high regard by both Nixon and Kissinger, the reality was that points of importance were communicated and discussed via backchannels. Consequently, communication about matters of substance largely took place through Rowley Cromer and, later, Burke Trend.[45]

## Maintaining a presence East of Suez

On assuming office, Heath was faced with a number of associated difficulties regarding the economy. Heath had inherited an economy with an unexpected budget deficit and his economic problems were compounded by the fact that his chancellor of the exchequer, Iain Macleod, passed away soon after taking office. Macleod, who had spent his years in opposition crafting an alternative economic agenda for the country, was replaced by Anthony Barber who, by own admission, was ill-prepared for the job.[46] In foreign affairs, two immediate points were prevalent: whether to endorse the 1967 decision to withdraw British military forces East of Suez, and how to attain membership of the EEC. Both of these topics had obvious consequences for US–UK relations.[47]

Throughout the 1960s, the US had made several efforts to convince the British to maintain their East of Suez commitments.[48] This presence included the two sovereign bases in Aden and Singapore, agreements to uphold security in a number of states, and a number of smaller bases located east of the Suez Canal. In total the British committed close to 90,000 troops to upholding this role. Such efforts proved superfluous when Wilson announced in 1967 that Britain would begin a phased withdrawal of its forces East of Suez. By January 1968, Wilson had decided that this process would be accelerated and British forces would be withdrawn by the end of 1971.[49] Such announcements deeply irritated Washington with Lyndon Johnson giving the impression that a British withdrawal signalled that the US would have to stand alone in the defence of the entire Western bloc.[50]

Once Nixon took office in January 1969, he too attempted to convince Wilson that he should reverse the East of Suez decision. Nixon believed that Britain had a role to play globally and he lamented the decision not to support Britain during the Suez crisis (1956–57) because it resulted in Britain hastening its global retreat, which had only damaged the long-term interests of the

US.[51] Added to this, Nixon wanted a more self-reliant Europe. In practical terms this meant Europe would contribute more fully to its own defence needs. This took the moniker 'burden-sharing'. A whole host of domestic, strategic and economic factors were behind Nixon's desire for burden-sharing. For one, the way in which Lyndon Johnson had financed the Vietnam War had created serious problems for the US economy. Thus, there was an economic imperative for the United States to lessen its spending commitments. The American misadventure in Vietnam had also encouraged calls that the United States could not offer open-ended commitments to foreign powers which would involve huge manpower and monetary resources. Therefore, on the domestic front Nixon was facing Congressional and public opinion pressures to reduce America's global commitments. In such a context, it is not a surprise that Heath's allusion within the 1970 Conservative Party manifesto to reverse the decision to withdraw East of Suez was met with approval in Washington.[52]

Running alongside this potential change in British defence policies were the efforts of the Nixon administration to share the burden of NATO's conventional forces more equally throughout the alliance. This was driven not only by the aforementioned factors but by the increasingly apparent reality of nuclear parity. NATO had adopted the doctrine of 'flexible response' in 1967 which superseded the previous policy of 'Massive Retaliation', that being that any Soviet military aggression against US allies would be met with a full strategic nuclear response. Flexible response was designed to place a heavier reliance upon conventional forces in a world where rough nuclear parity meant Massive Retaliation was deemed no longer credible. This, so the theory ran, would offer decision-makers greater flexibility during a confrontation with the USSR and prevent a scenario where a president of the United States would be forced to surrender or precipitate a nuclear Armageddon in response to any Soviet military aggression in Europe.[53] However, NATO's force levels fell well short of being able to realistically pursue this flexible response strategy. As Nixon's team had been informed prior to taking office, and soon concluded once in office, the Warsaw Pact held an advantage in conventional forces and had also reached parity with the United States in the nuclear realm.[54] Given this, we can see why Nixon questioned whether NATO's heavy reliance on nuclear weapons was credible under such circumstances. As Nixon bluntly stated, '[the] nuclear umbrella in NATO [was] a lot of crap'.[55] Less crudely, he informed Heath that the era of 'nuclear standoff' had dawned.[56] As a result, Nixon concluded that a far greater emphasis had to be given to conventional forces. Only by improving these would a credible deterrence posture be posed towards the USSR.[57]

Kissinger agreed largely with Nixon's assessments on the dangers that nuclear parity posed for Western security. During his time at Harvard, Kissinger had made similar arguments to those now being pushed by Nixon and in 1970 he repeated such thinking to the president.[58] As Kissinger noted:

> We no longer can count on our nuclear weapons to deter Soviet aggressiveness or threat of using force. With near parity in strategic weapons the Soviets probably assume that we could not credibly threaten their use except when faced with a direct attack on the US itself.[59]

Kissinger was not alone in offering such gloomy advice. The president's other advisers, including Laird and Rogers, were equally pessimistic about the evolving strategic situation.[60]

The Nixon administration therefore assumed a dual strategy towards the British. They first sought to convince both the Wilson and Heath governments to contribute further resources to the NATO alliance. They tried also to persuade the British to reverse their decision to withdraw their forces East of Suez and therefore encouraged Heath to retain as large a commitment as possible.[61] Such an approach proved, ultimately, to be a wasted effort. With respect to NATO, the British government refused to bow to American pressure. With regard to the East of Suez decision, Wilson remained unperturbed and stuck with his original decision. Heath, while wanting to implement a full reversal of Wilson's policy, found that it was not easily reversible. The new prime minister therefore largely endorsed Wilson's East of Suez plans.[62]

The only discernible difference was that Britain signed a Five Power Pact Treaty with Australia, New Zealand, Malaysia and Singapore. It was not, however, a major defence treaty. As Lord Carrington put it, 'There was no question of completely putting the clock back; we accepted much of the situation as we found it'.[63] However, it should be remembered that the agreement did ensure that the British retained a symbolic global military role which Wilson's plans would have eliminated. For Nixon, this did provide a small token victory. In relation to Britain's NATO commitments, American efforts were equally pointless. The Heath government made it clear that Britain would not be contributing greater resources to NATO. All that the Heath administration offered was their auspices in trying to convince fellow NATO members to increase their own contributions.[64]

## Doing as much as they can

The manner in which the Nixon administration should react to Heath's defence review was vigorously debated in Washington. Melvin Laird, who was ever conscious of Congressional opinion, wanted to send a message to London that defence cuts were intolerable. In his assessment, Congressional demands for US troop withdrawals globally, and in particular throughout Europe, would become more vehement because of British defence cuts. The US, therefore, should threaten to withdraw its troops from NATO unilaterally. This, Laird hoped, would force the British into retracting their own defence cuts. However, Laird's advice did not attract much support within the administration. His deputy, David Packard, suggested that a public rebuke of Heath's decision should be issued; the approach was endorsed by William Rogers.[65]

Aside from Laird, there appeared little appetite at this stage for a major confrontation with the UK over their defence spending. As other US officials advised, to pursue Laird's course, or even the less bellicose options put forward by Packard and Rogers, would do little to serve US interests. As George Springsteen reasoned, the UK still contributed, as a proportion of Gross Domestic Product (GDP), the most of any European state to NATO.[66] Therefore, to publicly admonish the Heath administration would be an unproductive course. More important yet, Laird's approach was unlikely to actually change the British decision, meaning a confrontation would actually not serve any meaningful objective.[67] This line of argument gained the support of Kissinger's advisers. Helmut Sonnenfeldt, Kissinger's key aide for European affairs, argued that whilst Britain's defence commitment had not increased, Heath had not agreed to the scale of cutbacks envisaged under Wilson.[68] This clearly resonated with Kissinger. 'The fact is that the British have probably done about as much as they can,' Kissinger informed the president.[69] Such advice won the president's backing. Consequently, no public rebuke was issued; nor were any threats of US troop withdrawals from Europe made. Instead, when US officials met with their British counterparts, a sympathetic tone, along the terms outlined by Kissinger, was employed.[70]

The White House took Heath's decision rather philosophically given that it ran contrary to Nixon's policy of burden-sharing. For US–UK relations, Heath's confirmation of Wilson's East of Suez policy had reduced Britain's utility as an ally to the US. This, however, was not an event deemed to be terminal in the eyes of the Nixon White House. Kissinger had argued against the notion of a public rebuke because of the president's desire to establish solid relations with the new Conservative government.[71] Moreover, the five power defence agreement did provide the US with a symbolic partner on the world stage, in that the US could plausibly argue that it was not alone in trying to maintain global stability. Thus, as one author has recently noted, the East of Suez decision did not mean the end of Britain's ability to actually project global power.[72] Yet, Heath's decision did signify the increasingly Euro-centric nature of British defence and foreign policy. As Lord Carrington wrote, 'Defence had come full circle. It was not only to start but almost to end at home.'[73] Furthermore, the British had been perceived by the Nixon administration to have undermined US interests. As shown in subsequent chapters, when US–UK opinion collided, the Nixon administration would not always react in such a subdued manner.

## EEC expansion: A future competitor?

As Denis Greenhill argued, for Edward Heath, 'Europe came first'.[74] Heath had demonstrated this desire during a series of lectures at Harvard University in 1967 where he noted that Britain should reconfigure its foreign policy priorities away from the 'Atlantic Community' and the Commonwealth. Instead, Britain would shape a new Europe, which would act as a genuine third power centre in a world dominated by the superpowers. Thus, as one early biographer of Heath noted, the EEC was a vehicle in which Britain could ensure a world role 'commensurate with the role that she enjoyed in the past'.[75]

Traditionally, historical accounts have tended to present Heath's EEC policy as a zero sum affair. For these authors, Heath rejected a close relationship with the US in order to gain EEC membership.[76] When Heath read a biography of himself in which it was claimed he wanted to abandon the special relationship, he scribbled in the margin 'No'.[77] Heath was correct to reject this line of argument. Certainly, Heath brought his own particular brand of realism to the US–UK relationship; he refused to accept that US–UK cooperation was always beneficial to British interests. For instance, soon after assuming office, Heath ordered an assessment of US usage of British bases globally and wanted to know whether it was in the British interest to grant US access to these bases. Both Douglas-Home and Carrington responded that it was in Britain's interest, arguing that it allowed Britain to continue exploiting US expertise in the nuclear and intelligence realms.[78]

Nevertheless, Heath querying US rights to British bases does not automatically imply that he wished to terminate such cooperation. Rather, Heath wanted to ensure that the US–UK relationship, as it had traditionally been conceived by British policy-making elites, actually continued to promote British interests. Relevant aspects of the relationship, such as nuclear and intelligence sharing would be allowed to continue whereas other elements, such as international summitry, would be allowed to slip.[79] Europe then was seen by Heath as a way of maintaining Britain's international position and would, much in Ernest Bevin's vein of 'pillars', act as one pillar for British interests. The other pillar, the US–UK relationship, would be retained and utilised as and when needed.[80] None of this was seen as particularly controversial (at this stage anyhow) from Washington's perspective. The Nixon administration wished to pursue its détente agenda in a largely bilateral fashion. British international decline in recent years also undermined notions that it could act as America's global lieutenant. However, as Kissinger explained, the US was not blessed with many close allies and the US 'should not discourage those who feel they have a special friendship for us'.[81]

Close US–UK relations had been sought by British policy-makers as a means of upholding British global interests since the end of the Second World War.[82] Similarly, Harold Macmillan looked towards British membership of the EEC as a mechanism for managing Britain's changing international circumstances. Wilson's government also sought a similar objective. Macmillan and Wilson, however, were both reluctant converts to the European project. They came to the conclusion that British membership of the EEC was essential for maintaining British relevance in a world dominated by the superpowers. They also believed that EEC membership could help to improve Britain's economic fortunes. Heath's Euro-centric policy should not, therefore, be viewed as revolutionary in the field of British foreign policy.[83]

Heath differed from his predecessors, however, in that he was more passionately committed to the European ideal. For Heath, British membership of the EEC was imperative, not only for ensuring Britain could continue a relevant world role, but also for maintaining European peace and stability. As one commentator noted soon after Heath's accession to office, 'Mr Heath will use all his power' to prove that Britain could win admission into the EEC.[84] First, Heath's background made him a suitable candidate for trying to obtain membership to a club that had eluded both Macmillan and Wilson as he had been the chief negotiator for UK membership to the EEC under the Macmillan government (1960–63).[85] Witnessing Charles de Gaulle veto British membership, and his citing of the US–UK special relationship as the reason for his action, provided Heath with first-hand experience of France's suspicion of the US–UK relationship.[86] As Donald Maitland opined, Heath 'drew the clear lesson from the events of 1962/63 that the French held the key' to EEC membership.[87] Given this, once in office, Heath would court France and sought to convince French president Georges Pompidou that Britain should be admitted into the EEC.

Why then was Heath determined to enter the EEC? Some have suggested that he was passionately committed to the ideal of European integration as a means of ensuring the continent's future peace, stability and prosperity. Whilst this view is not without merit, Heath's policy was also driven by pragmatism and a desire to ensure that the UK could retain an influential role in world affairs. Heath, however, also wanted to move further and faster towards an integrated political Europe, which would have common foreign and defence policies. Indeed, it was Heath's intention to utilise the expansion of the EEC as a vehicle for promoting this ambition in 1973. It was this feature of Heath's European policy that marked his fundamentally different approach to that of his predecessors.[88]

Regardless of the actual route taken, the fact remained that British membership of the EEC would have a profound impact upon US–UK relations. Obviously, if the British followed the protectionist trade and monetary policies as practised by the EEC, this would have ramifications for US economic interests. Politically, given the notion that the EEC would create some type of 'common' foreign and political policies, this would at the very least change the nature of US–UK diplomacy.[89]

What then of US policy? Since the creation of the EEC, successive US administrations had encouraged British membership as it was commonly believed this would revitalise the British economy and ensure Europe was driven by a friendly power.[90] The Nixon administration did not automatically subscribe to such thinking. Certainly, the president reassured both Wilson and Heath on multiple occasions that the US supported British membership.[91] Furthermore, Nixon even offered clandestine US support for Britain's application.[92] Given that this was the flagship policy of the Heath government, it is perhaps not surprising that the president would make such utterances in a bilateral conversation. If, however, one studies the documentary record of the internal debates in Washington, it becomes clear that considerable anxiety about British membership of the EEC existed.

Soon after coming to power, the Nixon administration undertook a serious review of US policy towards EEC enlargement. Nixon's economic advisers were pushing the president to reconsider US support for EEC expansion and, reiterating the types of argument put forward since the mid-1960s, they suggested that EEC expansion would have a detrimental impact upon US economic interests. Nixon came under further pressure from domestic constituents with the Republican leadership advising that he should be more robust in challenging the protectionist trading practices of the EEC.[93] As Sonnenfeldt recalled, some US policy-makers were concerned about the possible development of an economic 'fortress Europe'.[94]

John Connally, the confidant of Nixon and US Treasury Secretary, was especially vocal in emphasising such thinking. In Connally's opinion, EEC enlargement would only have negative consequences for US economic interests because it would increase the number of countries that would adopt protectionist policies.[95] Connally appears to have been somewhat of a *bête noire* for British policy-making elites. Greenhill noted that Connally 'roughly handled' the British chancellor of the exchequer, Anthony Barber, during meetings. Heath was equally frustrated with Connally and he remarked that they had 'killed the wrong man at Dallas'. Officials tasked with Britain's EEC negotiations even speculated as to whether Connally was advising Nixon against supporting British membership.[96]

Economic arguments, though important in the opinion of Nixon, were not critical in determining US policy towards British membership of the EEC. Nixon accepted that Heath was determined to obtain British membership of the EEC and, as a result, US economic interests were likely to suffer. This, though, would be counterbalanced by the political benefits derived from British membership.[97] As the president candidly explained, the 'economic guys' should be 'screwing' one another, and 'there ought to be a lot of screwing going on' but fundamentally 'the political aspects of our relations should be overriding for both sides'.[98] In a less robust fashion, Nixon issued a memorandum in January 1971 that explained US economic policy had to 'maintain close coordination with basic foreign policy objectives'.[99] In the final assessment, Nixon was not prepared to sacrifice the political–military relationship with Europe for short-term economic gains.[100]

As the president made clear, the political aspects of EEC enlargement were what fundamentally mattered. On this topic, Nixon's political advisers presented conflicting advice. Walter Annenberg, the US ambassador to the UK, argued that British membership would advance US interests as it increased the likelihood that Europe would have a more 'outward' looking mentality, implying that Europe would assume a greater role in the global containment of the USSR. It also created the potential that the EEC would assume a greater proportion of the European defence burden.[101] Similar advice was provided by the State Department which supported their position by bringing in wider European questions, notably concerns about West Germany. They suggested that British membership was required because it would act as a natural counterweight to West German dominance of the EEC. Perhaps these arguments held particular resonance with the president given his ongoing concerns vis-à-vis West Germany's policy of *Ostpolitik*.[102]

The State Department's advice was largely a regurgitation of what it had recommended throughout the Kennedy–Johnson years.[103] Unsurprisingly, given the growing bureaucratic squabbling between the State Department and Kissinger, such advice was met with little sympathy from him or his aides.[104] In October 1969, after prompting from his subordinates, Kissinger ordered a review of US policy towards EEC enlargement.[105] Kissinger himself was reticent about EEC enlargement, given that his tendency to see international relations through a realist perspective provoked apprehension towards the emergence of another bloc of powers.[106] As Kissinger had written in 1965, 'European unity is not a major cure-all for Atlantic disagreements. In many respects it may magnify rather than reduce differences.'[107] Kissinger articulated similar arguments when in government, arguing that an 'independent Europe could prove to be a competitive power center with the US'.[108]

Such evidence should not be taken as indicative of Kissinger's European policy. It has to be remembered that Kissinger balanced such judgements by arguing, 'Our security and our prosperity are both insolubly linked with the security and prosperity of Western Europe'.[109] For Kissinger, American security could not be divorced from that of Western Europe. Moreover, economics, which was being pushed so heavily as a reason against supporting EEC expansion, was actually of marginal concern to Kissinger. He was notorious for demonstrating a lack of knowledge of, or interest in, economics during his early years in office. As Arthur Burns, the chairman of the Federal Reserve, noted, Kissinger was, self-admittedly, 'ignorant' about economics.[110]

The report ordered by Kissinger about EEC enlargement was largely supportive of the concept and it noted that it was, in the main, in the interests of the US. As the report reasoned, if Britain failed to gain entry into the EEC, it 'might well leave us saddled with the UK and the pound in a permanent client status'. This would have obvious negative economic consequences, but any hopes of increased military burden-sharing would also be negated.[111] A month later, another paper on EEC expansion was produced that largely repeated this argument.[112] These internal working papers were finally established as a National Security Decision Memorandum which concluded that the US would 'support ... expansion of the membership of the Community'.[113]

Nixon thus re-affirmed the earlier policy of the Kennedy–Johnson administrations of supporting British membership of the EEC. This did not, however, cement US policy. Rather, highly influential US officials continued to question the wisdom of pursuing this course. Nixon's economic advisers continued with their onslaught of advice, suggesting a more proactive approach should be taken to defend US economic interests.[114] It was clear during the breakdown of the Bretton Woods system in 1971 that Nixon was following some of this advice. Whilst his economic advisers were far from unanimous in their support for taking a tougher line in trade disputes, the advice from the likes of John Connally won through.[115] Accordingly, as Donald Rumsfeld noted, Nixon decided to 'grab the old shotgun and pull the trigger'.[116] This took the form of halting dollar–gold convertibility and placing a 10 per cent surcharge on all imports. These decisions were reached in the utmost secrecy and took scant regard for America's allies. By the beginning of 1972, it is right to conclude that, at least in the economic realm, US–European relations had turned into a 'competitive relationship'.[117]

Kissinger and his staff also remained less than convinced that US interests were best served by encouraging British membership of the EEC. Sonnenfeldt took his concerns to the president, where he complained about the EEC's lack of leadership and the unwillingness of the European states to contribute more fully to the NATO alliance. Nixon agreed with this assessment, noting that there was a 'vacuum of leadership in Europe which we must fill'. Even Annenberg had tempered his earlier advice, warning: 'Heath is thinking "Britain first" and wants Britain to command respect in the world. As we noted in our last examination of British foreign policy last December this assertive attitude is bound to result in differences between us.' US policy-makers, whilst officially supporting British membership of the EEC, were privately far more reticent.[118]

Regardless of US policy, it became increasingly obvious that Britain would attain membership of the EEC. Following a long meeting between Heath and Pompidou in May 1971, a fundamental agreement had been struck to allow British entry into the EEC. Following further negotiations, it was confirmed that Britain would enter the EEC on 1 January 1973.[119] This clearly signified that the British had, at some level at least, accepted that their future interests would largely be bound to those of the European region. No longer would the UK seek a global role on the scale that it had done previously and it also signalled that the Heath government was determined to operate within the framework of the EEC. This would mean that the UK would be looking to establish not only common economic policies with their EEC partners but *political* ones also.[120] All of this created the potential for US–UK disagreements in the near future.

## Détente and its consequence

Since taking office, Nixon had sought to reconfigure US foreign policy in order to confront the myriad problems facing the US. Amongst the most pressing included the American extrication from Vietnam, along with the worsening economic situation. For Nixon, the US was facing a gradual decline in its global power and this needed to be tackled. Détente was the policy through which these circumstances were managed.[121] The establishment of détente with the USSR, the opening to the PRC, and the subsequent impact this would have upon US foreign policy actions – notably during the India–Pakistan War – had profound ramifications for US–UK relations. Negotiations encouraged by the détente process, notably the CSCE and MBFR, also produced US–UK difference but also considerable diplomatic consultation.

During Nixon and Heath's first meeting, the president insisted he wanted close US–UK consultation which would not only occur during moments of crisis but would rather become a routine activity.[122] Throughout the ensuing years, this declaration would prove rather hollow. For example, Nixon's opening to the PRC was conducted without any prior consultation with the

British. Likewise, Nixon's major Vietnam policies, including the incursion into Cambodia, the Easter bombings, and the Christmas bombings of 1972, were taken without even a modicum of discussion with their British ally taking place.[123] The deepening of US–USSR bilateral diplomacy also largely excluded the British. Ironically, since the governments of Macmillan and Wilson, British policy had sought to achieve superpower détente. Once achieved, it was now viewed as being just as irksome as superpower confrontation![124] As Kissinger astutely noted in his memoirs, détente had created a predicament where the Europeans 'dreaded a US–Soviet condominium'.[125] Or, as he suggested in private conversation, the real reason the Europeans were distrustful of détente was that they 'didn't do it themselves'.[126] As another commentator stated in 1970, 'for Europeans, contemporary America is doubtless a less certain protector, a less committed partner'.[127] Certainly, such descriptions applied to many parts of the British policy-making establishment.

Before assuming office, both Nixon and Kissinger had argued that the US had to engineer a rapprochement with the PRC.[128] Once in the White House, the president set out to accomplish this and by November 1971, following many months of intricate and secretive diplomacy, US efforts paid off. Nixon was invited to the PRC; his visit was set for February 1972.[129] There should have been very little in Nixon's rapprochement with the PRC to have caused US–UK disagreement. British policy had traditionally been more amenable to Mao's China than that of the US and Britain had officially recognised the PRC in January 1950 (leading to disagreement between London and Washington).[130] Moreover, when Heath had taken power, he too was seeking to improve relations with the PRC.[131] US–UK problems largely existed due to the manner in which the president established his opening to the PRC, because Nixon demanded that the US–PRC rapprochement be conducted with the utmost of secrecy – only four days prior notification was given to British officials regarding the president's forthcoming visit to the PRC.[132] This was hardly a sufficient amount of time for Britain to proffer advice on Nixon's endeavours. The limited pre-warning, coupled with the total lack of consultation, contradicted Nixon's earlier espousal of a desire for 'close and continual' US–UK consultation. Heath was also personally piqued by Nixon's actions, because he had kept the US fully informed of his own efforts to improve relations with the PRC. Nixon's conduct stood in stark contrast to this.[133]

Aside from upsetting Heath personally, the opening to the PRC had other discernible effects upon US–UK relations. The most obvious ramification was the policy pursued by the US during the India–Pakistan War (December 1971), which was governed by wider geopolitical considerations to the neglect of the realities driving the conflict on the ground.[134] Border disputes between China and India had led to war in 1962 and China had subsequently supported

Pakistan as a counterweight to Indian power (which was in turn supported by the USSR). Indian–Pakistani tensions were running high over the future of East Pakistan (modern-day Bangladesh), and the possibility of an Indian–Chinese confrontation mounted. From the perspective of the Nixon White House, the signing of the Indian–Soviet treaty of August 1971 confirmed their long-held suspicions about Indian 'neutralism' in the Cold War and heightened the possibility of an Indian–Soviet conflagration with China–Pakistan.[135]

This context, together with the importance Nixon attached to the PRC opening, resulted in the US 'tilting' towards Pakistan during the India–Pakistan war.[136] With the war barely three days old, Pakistan was faring badly, and the naval losses of two destroyers and a submarine gave naval superiority to Indian forces. Further, the Indian army – if not supreme – was forcing its Pakistan counterpart to retreat from East Pakistan.[137] The Nixon White House watched the unfolding events with increasing alarm, and therefore sought a ceasefire agreement in the United Nations Security Council (UNSC) which was designed to halt the fighting and leave the Pakistani forces in East Pakistan.

US policy was designed primarily with a view to supporting Pakistan's president Yahya Khan, as Pakistan under his rule provided a useful bulwark against what the US perceived was Soviet-backed Indian expansion in the region. Thus, the US ambassador at the United Nations, George H. Bush, labelled the Indians as the aggressor in the war, and called for a ceasefire which would return East Pakistan to Pakistani control.[138] This turn of events, however, brought US and UK policy into direct conflict. British officials believed that the war had erupted as a result of Pakistani provocation. Moreover, the British did not view the conflict through the Cold War lens that Washington did and concluded that Indian actions were in response to local factors and were not designed as a smokescreen for possible Soviet aggrandisement in the region. For these reasons, Heath rejected the US ceasefire terms.[139]

Following further fighting, East Pakistan was annexed and declared independent by India. US moves to influence the outcome had been largely ineffective. For instance, the despatching of a US naval task force to act as a 'signal' to the USSR against interfering was unable to prevent the Pakistani army suffering a military defeat at the hands of Indian forces.[140] In Washington, recrimination was the order of the day. Both Nixon and Kissinger believed that if the British had supported their UNSC Resolution then the war could have been stopped before Pakistan's defeat.[141] Not all shared this assessment, and other US officials had little sympathy with Kissinger's 'tantrums'. Nixon's chief of staff, H. R. Haldeman, believed the US response to the war had been ill-conceived and that Kissinger's actions had created a diplomatic 'loss' for the US. In his assessment, blaming the British was solely designed by Kissinger to deflect attention away from this fact.[142]

Whether the British supporting a UN resolution would have made much difference is largely a moot point. What mattered for US–UK relations was the fact that both Nixon and Kissinger believed the British had undermined their policies. Therefore, a president–prime minister summit scheduled to take place in Bermuda in December 1971 was perhaps an impromptu moment for such an event to be held. Nonetheless, as Sonnenfeldt noted, it gave the opportunity for Britain and America to 'mend fences'.[143] British diplomats welcomed this American attitude. The FCO was especially keen to exploit the summit; they saw it as an opportunity to repair some of the fallout over both the Bretton Woods collapse and the India–Pakistan war.[144]

At the summit, Nixon and Kissinger elaborated on their recent policy initiatives. They explained why they had not been able to communicate their decision over the China opening but promised that, 'We'd like to keep you informed on a personal basis' about US policy in the upcoming months. They also explained their policy regarding the India–Pakistan war. Again, Nixon promised to establish firmer US–UK consultations to avoid future misunderstandings of one another's policies. Nixon also explained why he had adopted his economic policies during the year.[145]

In addition, US–UK nuclear cooperation was discussed with the ongoing Polaris Improvement Project, initiated soon after Heath had won office, being of greatest importance, given that it required additional US assistance. The president gave his personal assurance that this cooperation would continue.[146] The discussions appeared to have met the FCO's ambition of ensuring recent US–UK difficulty did not impinge upon the wider relationship. Moreover, Nixon had announced at the beginning of the conference that the US would abolish the 10 per cent surcharge upon all imports that it had enacted earlier in the year.[147] While not undertaken because of Heath's diplomacy, the fact remained that the timing of the announcement coincided with the start of the Bermuda talks, thus affording the prime minister the allure of international influence upon US policy decisions.

## Theory and reality

The Bermuda Conference gave an impression that recent difficulties in US–UK relations were in the past. As one newspaper reported, the US–UK relationship was embarking upon a 'new era', but one in which the Atlantic alliance remained as the 'cornerstone of the free world's defence'.[148] Publicly, the president's press secretary, Ron Ziegler, also gave the impression that Nixon had enjoyed his talks with Heath.[149] When Heath arrived back in London, he conveyed a similar impression that recent US–UK difficulties were now settled.

He informed his colleagues that he had managed to get US agreement for increased diplomatic consultation and that the US would keep his government fully informed about the developing superpower relationship.[150] US officialdom did little to disabuse their British counterparts of such an opinion.[151]

This new era in US–UK openness was quickly shown to be illusory. Nixon's visit to the PRC (21–28 February 1972) illustrated that the assurances he had given to Heath were little more than words.[152] British officialdom received no more information regarding the US visit than any other European power. Thus, the FCO had to rely upon television coverage to gauge how the visit was progressing. Moreover, such a predicament heightened British suspicions of US motives and about what the US was actually discussing with the PRC.[153]

Lord Cromer was subsequently ordered to 'smoke out' Kissinger to ascertain the US's motives.[154] Cromer, for his part, was clearly more relaxed about the American silence than his colleagues. Whilst Nixon had declared his visit to the PRC as 'the week that changed the world', Cromer believed that the lack of communication could be attributed to American embarrassment at not having reached any substantive agreements with the PRC. This view was also shared by the UK Joint Intelligence Committee (JIC).[155] A survey of the memorandums of the conversations which took place between Chairman Mao, Prime Minister Chou En Lai, President Nixon, and Henry Kissinger appear to somewhat undermine such an assessment.[156] The subject of Taiwan, though originally dismissed by Kissinger in his memoirs as having been a peripheral issue and thus mentioned only briefly, was discussed in detail.[157] Obviously, a potential change in America's military and legal commitments to Taiwan would have practical implications for Asia. Moreover, the Shanghai communiqué – coupled with the geopolitical implications of the visit – demonstrated the rising significance of the US–PRC relationship on the global stage.[158]

Despite Cromer's personal assessment, he followed his instructions and sought to learn more from Kissinger. The British ambassador was to have little success. Unable to gain an audience with Kissinger, he had to make do with a debriefing from William Rogers. Cromer was under no illusions as to what Rogers would be able to divulge and complained to London: 'I doubt whether we shall learn a great deal from this source.'[159] President Nixon's personal correspondence with Heath also produced little more information. British officials had little unique US information with which to determine the outcome of Nixon's China visit. Instead, their assessments were drawn from the Shanghai communiqué, Secretary Rogers' briefing to NATO, and discussions with minor US officials.[160]

Nixon's personal promise to keep Heath informed regarding his thinking on world affairs was not apparent during his visit to the PRC. It should not be forgotten, however, that Heath did actually support Nixon's rapprochement with the

PRC. Indeed, British support of Nixon's PRC policies won him approval. The British had been 'damn good' about the PRC opening, Nixon declared during a private meeting. 'We couldn't have a better ally' was the opinion of William Rogers.[161] Evidently the British government had presented an outward impression of warmth to their American colleagues, but the lack of consultation over the PRC opening generated resentment in London. The prime minister wanted to be better informed than he was. Washington, however, was not forthcoming on this occasion.

The reason for this was manifold. As outlined above, the Nixon administration had conducted their diplomacy with the PRC in an extremely secretive fashion. The possibility of US–PRC interaction being leaked prior to Nixon officially opening relations was something the president was not prepared to risk. There was, however, a wider structural issue at play, and that was simply that the UK was no longer important or powerful enough to warrant close consultation on all facets of US foreign policy.[162] UK policy-makers certainly would have preferred deep consultative discussions with their US counterparts. Given the importance attached to Hong Kong by the British, perhaps there was a legitimate basis of complaint. Regardless, the Nixon administration appeared none too interested in British sensibilities. As the president summed up in conversation:

> Heath – comes here, he loves to talk about, 'Oh, how was your trip to China?' He likes to talk about the Russian arms, what we're going to do about [unclear] of course he does. And what's going to happen in the Mideast, and what can we do. But he knows, as he talks to me, that what the British do doesn't make a damn bit of a difference in the world anymore. It's too bad, but it's true.[163]

## SALT and Moscow

Following Nixon's visit to the PRC, he once again shocked onlookers by announcing a visit to the USSR. As with the PRC opening, the strictest secrecy was employed in engineering this summit. Again, the British were only given brief notice about the visit.[164] British officials were deeply concerned about Nixon's latest gambit and the FCO commissioned a paper that would pre-empt any 'fait accomplis' that Britain would have to face as a result of the Moscow summit. A US–USSR summit was seen to hold much greater potential for damaging British interests than the US–PRC rapprochement not least because of the nuclear negotiations that these talks entailed. Of particular concern was the subject of SALT because the Moscow summit would potentially conclude some agreement which British policy-makers feared would undermine existing US–UK nuclear arrangements.[165]

The SALT process had begun during the Johnson administration and, even though US involvement in Vietnam had strained US–USSR relations, by 1968 Lyndon Johnson had decided to visit the USSR where nuclear arms limitation was to be a topic open for serious discussion. Events, however, interceded in such plans and the USSR's invasion of Czechoslovakia in August 1968 made it politically impractical for the US president to visit the USSR, and thus the proposed trip was cancelled. With the visit cancelled, progress on SALT stalled and it was not until the Nixon administration took power in January 1969 that SALT would begin again.[166]

For the Nixon administration, SALT was to be taken as one point in the overarching policy of linkage. SALT, therefore, would be linked to advances in other areas of US–USSR interaction. In particular, the US government was determined not to move on SALT until a satisfactory Berlin agreement had been reached with Moscow.[167] SALT was also conducted on a bilateral basis between the two superpowers. As Nixon candidly put it in discussion with the Soviet ambassador to the United States, Anatoly Dobrynin:

> Let's be realistic. The key to this sort of thing [SALT] is what the two major nuclear powers will do. It is a question of leadership at the top – I don't mean at the top of governments, but at the top of this group of five.[168]

Such an attitude was worrying from the British perspective as any SALT agreement could have consequences for British interests. A general concern was that SALT would gradually erode the US nuclear guarantee to NATO. This, of course, was hardly a new phenomenon. Since the origins of NATO, a perennial British concern had been that the US would loosen its nuclear commitments. More specifically was the worry that the US would agree a SALT treaty that would prevent future US–UK nuclear cooperation.[169]

It should not be forgotten that Heath's government supported the general concept of SALT because it was deemed to promote long-term British interests as it would halt a needless arms race and encourage a more stable international order.[170] Nonetheless, there were specific points of interest where SALT concerned the British government. These included the possibility of an Anti-ballistic Missile (ABM) Treaty, a 'No Transfer' agreement and a reduction in Forward Base Systems. Perhaps the most worrisome aspect was the possibility that SALT would curtail existing and future US–UK nuclear weapons cooperation. The 'No Transfer' possibility was, therefore, viewed with particular concern. Officials within the MOD had ascertained that the US had agreed with the Soviets to not circumvent a SALT agreement by providing 'significant' nuclear weapons to a third party. It also suggested that nuclear assistance, i.e. providing other states with nuclear technology, would be limited or entirely outlawed.[171]

This had obvious ramifications for Britain's Polaris deterrent yet the US had made no mention of this directly to them.[172] Instead, the British government learned this information from Raymond Garthoff, a member of the US SALT negotiating team. However, Garthoff did not represent White House policy because Nixon preferred to negotiate the substance of SALT through Kissinger's backchannel with Anatoly Dobrynin.[173] This was obviously problematic from the British perspective as they were unaware of the content of these meetings. While the British received briefings on the general thrust of US policy (something Nixon had insisted on, much to the chagrin of his defense secretary, Melvin Laird), the fact remained that British policy-makers felt they were not adequately briefed about US intentions.[174] As such, we can see from British documentation that a general trend can be discerned: as US–USSR détente established itself, British fears of US–UK nuclear cooperation being curtailed increased.[175]

Once Nixon's visit to Moscow was under way (May 1972), Heath sought to gather as much information as possible about the trip. Establishing the finer details of the SALT agreement was viewed as fundamentally important. Compared to China, British officials were much more successful. To be sure, the British ambassador in Moscow, John Killick, reported that he had nothing of substance to inform London. 'We seem to be out in the cold' was Solly Zuckerman's appraisal.[176] Heath, however, was not as much 'out in the cold' as such reports would suggest. Unbeknownst to Killick and Zuckerman, Kissinger had agreed to keep Trend privately informed of American negotiations at the summit.[177] Regardless of this channel, British officials continued to suspect that the Americans were not supplying them with the full picture. To compensate for this, Douglas-Home ordered the British Embassy in Washington to try to elicit further information from Kissinger. While gaining more knowledge, the British remained sceptical about US policy.[178]

Though British officials may have been nervous about the likely contents of a US–USSR nuclear arms agreement, the ones reached, in particular the interim SALT I agreement and the ABM treaty, were on balance viewed optimistically.[179] The ABM treaty was generally interpreted as being in the British interest because it had prevented the widespread deployment of ABMs. Those tasked with analysing such matters believed that widespread ABM deployment would have led to serious questions about the credibility of Britain's nuclear deterrent. Therefore, the final US–USSR agreement to limit their ABM deployment to only two sites, and for the ABMs to total only 100 interceptors apiece, was seen to have prevented their widespread deployment.[180]

The US was not ignorant of potential British and NATO concerns about what SALT meant for future security cooperation. Nixon had sought to reassure Heath that the US government would never enter into an agreement with the Soviet Union that would undermine Britain's nuclear ability.[181] The president also publicly sought to reassure his allies and in a joint session of Congress Nixon stated that:

> By the same token, we must stand steadfastly with our NATO partners if negotiations leading us to a new détente and a mutual reduction of forces in Europe are to be productive. Maintaining the strength, integrity, and steadfastness of our free world alliances is the foundation on which all of our other initiatives for peace and security in the world must rest. As we seek better relations with those who have been our adversaries, we will not let down our friends and allies around the world.[182]

None of these reassurances did much to alleviate suspicions within the FCO or MOD in London. Thus, both departments continued to advise the prime minister that he should seek to bilaterally utilise his relationship with Nixon to gain more information about US policy.[183]

These continued British feelings of marginalisation were reported to Washington, which presented an interesting conundrum for US policy-makers. Since the outset of détente, key US officials had feared this could create the 'atmospherics of peace', which in turn could be exploited by the USSR.[184] Superpower détente could also easily be perceived as superpower duplicity and British officials made this known to Kissinger and Rogers on numerous occasions.[185] Given Nixon's exploits in China, along with the signing of the SALT and ABM agreements, US policy-makers were especially conscious of such accusations.[186] Consequently, the president attempted to sooth British concerns about a potential superpower condominium. Nixon assured Trend that the US would not 'go off' with the USSR and establish agreements that would negatively infringe upon the allies of the US. Nixon offered 'very private President to Prime Minister talks through the White House Channel' to further explain the content of US–USSR diplomacy.[187]

Nixon's offer of bilateral contact did little to quell British suspicions. Reports continued to arrive in Washington about British concerns towards détente, superpower summitry and SALT. Kissinger's visit to Moscow in September 1972 was reported by David Kennedy, the US permanent representative to NATO, to have raised particular concern.[188] Such reporting was, however, contradicted by Secretary Rogers. He informed the president that the British were satisfied with the consultation they were receiving over US–USSR bilateral diplomacy with Kissinger's personal briefings being particularly appreciated.[189]

In private, British assessments were much more in keeping with the analysis offered by Kennedy. British officialdom remained highly sceptical about the entire direction of the détente process. As the highly influential JIC argued, whilst superpower summits were unlikely to fundamentally alter the foreign policy of either superpower, the increased communication between the two superpowers underscored the 'special nature' of their relationship. This would set in motion the opportunity for further exclusive superpower summits which increased the likelihood of a superpower settlement that would undermine British security interests.[190]

The US engaging more heavily in bilateral diplomacy with the USSR thus served to increase British concerns about détente. Indeed, at the Moscow summit in May 1972 the two superpowers had gone some way to institutionalising their relationship when they signed an agreement of 'basic principles' which would underpin US–USSR conduct of foreign affairs.[191] Interestingly, this increased superpower bilateralism appears to have had a direct impact on Britain's European policy as the extension of superpower bilateral diplomacy supported Heath's argument that EEC membership was essential for safeguarding Britain's interests in a world dominated by two superpowers.[192] As one Cabinet briefing paper stated: 'The spectacle of the two superpowers locked in private talks for over a week, with most of the US Government machinery excluded, reinforces the need for progress towards a common European foreign policy.'[193] The Nixon administration's level of briefings on the PRC and Moscow openings irritated officials in Whitehall. The president did not feel he needed to consult with Britain in order to achieve what he wanted. On the actual substance of the talks, this was clearly the case. The US could consult the British if they desired, but ultimately British opinion was of little weight. US policy, however, was hardly conducive to alliance solidarity.

On the one hand we can appreciate why British officials continued to be sceptical about American policy. The Nixon administration was never really forthcoming in providing the level of detail about their discussions with the USSR which could have perhaps alleviated British fears. Added to this was the fact that the British government was at this stage in the process of analysing whether or not their own strategic nuclear deterrent, Polaris, required upgrading and, if it did, then deciding what the preferred method for achieving this was. Obviously, reaching a decision would be dictated in large measure by the American attitude, and the likely American response to any British request for further nuclear assistance would be influenced by the US's own strategic arms programmes and any legal obligations to which they had committed. Even in such a context, British fears that the US would permanently undermine the US–UK nuclear relationship in order to secure a US–USSR nuclear arms agreement were slightly exaggerated. The Nixon administration did not believe it had to reach any agreement on 'third party' nuclear weapons in order to achieve a SALT agreement. As Nixon and Kissinger had made clear during private conversations with Soviet officials, the US would not enter into negotiations with the USSR about the British nuclear deterrent.[194] Nevertheless, British concerns about the reliability of the United States continued.

## CSCE and MBFR

As the US and USSR continued their détente agenda, other areas of international diplomacy continued to be a source of US–UK disagreement. The first of these related to the possibility of a CSCE. The USSR had sought a CSCE since the 1950s, because it saw this as a potential opportunity for ratifying the post-World War II borders of Europe.[195] Regardless of actual Soviet intentions, this was how the Nixon administration viewed Soviet motives.[196] Until the beginning of the 1970s there had been limited progress on the CSCE. Previously, the USSR had insisted that the CSCE should be conducted exclusively between the USSR and European states. This insistence to exclude the US realistically prevented any further development on the CSCE. By 1970, however, the USSR accepted that the US should be present in the CSCE negotiations. The CSCE was now a subject that could no longer be ignored. As Kissinger explained to Nixon, a refusal to engage in the CSCE would give the USSR an easy propaganda victory. More worryingly, US obduracy could result in Western Europe negotiating bilaterally with the USSR, and reaching an agreement which could undermine US interests.[197]

For the Nixon administration, such changes were unwelcome. The CSCE was seen by the president and Kissinger as an irritant. One of Kissinger's aides claimed that Kissinger viewed the CSCE with 'disdain'.[198] Certainly, if you go through the US documentation pertaining to the CSCE, you will find numerous examples of both Nixon and Kissinger casting scorn upon the entire CSCE process.[199] This lack of interest in the CSCE has been noted by several writers.[200] Nevertheless, all of this misses a broader point. While the Nixon White House had little enthusiasm for the CSCE, it was viewed as another tool in which the US could exert leverage upon the USSR. This meant progress on the CSCE would be linked directly to matters deemed more important, such as Vietnam, SALT and a Berlin settlement. Washington believed that the Soviets were enthusiastic about the CSCE; delaying movement on the CSCE then was seen as having the potential to soften Soviet policy in other areas. Accordingly, US policy directly linked progress on a Berlin settlement with movement on the CSCE.[201]

Senior members of Heath's government were equally disdainful about the idea of a CSCE. Douglas-Home, for instance, told American officials that he would prefer the CSCE to never take place. The CSCE was a 'horrifying prospect', he later told William Rogers.[202] Lord Carrington made similar views known. For Carrington, the CSCE would create the impression that the USSR no longer posed a threat to Western security, and would critically undermine efforts to improve NATO's defence commitments.[203] In spite of this, the British understood that given that East–West relations were improving within the broader climate of détente, resisting the CSCE would become increasingly difficult. Other states, notably West Germany and France, were looking to the CSCE as a means of significantly improving East–West relations and were actively pursuing a policy that would see one come into being. In a sense, Douglas-Home was correct when he claimed that the CSCE was 'unavoidable'.[204]

While the Nixon administration was seeking to extrapolate concessions in other areas of US–USSR diplomacy for participating in the CSCE, the Heath administration sought a quick conclusion to the project. For the British, this would ensure that nothing of substance would be dealt with. Furthermore, it would also prevent any type of superpower deal that would trade the CSCE for some larger prize. The British, therefore, sought to be actively engaged in the negotiations in order to craft the CSCE according to their interests. This position was reported to Washington and one telegram noted, the British government believed: 'The West does not stand to gain from a CSCE so the Allies should try to get the Conference over with quickly rather than dawdle unduly over probably fruitless efforts to secure substantive results'. Internal studies in Washington only confirmed that this was actual British policy.[205]

Clearly, US and UK policy towards the CSCE contradicted one another. The US sought a long, drawn-out negotiation as a means of convincing the USSR to take a softer line in other areas of its foreign policy. The British, meanwhile, wanted a speedy resolution to the project and a CSCE which dealt with little in the form of substance. Nonetheless, it was not until 1972 that these differences began to have a practical effect upon US–UK relations. With the signing of the first protocol on a Berlin settlement in September 1971, Western European enthusiasm for a CSCE grew. This only encouraged the British to find a common Western negotiating position regarding the CSCE. The US, meanwhile, was encouraging its Western allies to delay progress. Nixon, having achieved Soviet movement with regards to Berlin, decided now to delay progress on the CSCE until the Soviets had made substantive moves on MBFR and arms control.[206]

This policy shift in Washington did not sit well with those in London. As Denis Greenhill complained to his deputy, Thomas Brimelow:

> I find the American attitude ... rather disturbing. If they are going to lie low at the Conference it will greatly weaken our defences against a Russian attempt to steam roller an undesirable Declaration of Principles. The Americans may not like the idea of the conference any more than we do and may rightly blame the Europeans for permitting it to come about. But it would be very serious if they abandoned us at this point and let the Russians have a major propaganda victory.[207]

That there was a tactical conflict in US and UK policy should not have come as a surprise to Washington. Douglas-Home had informed Rogers that trying to stall the CSCE would only provide a propaganda coup for the USSR and as such the West should seek its swift conclusion. Both Nixon and Kissinger were aware of British thinking: 'The British believe that a Conference is an unavoidable evil, should be given short shrift, and closed out as quickly as possible with minimum damage'.[208]

Being aware of British policy did not mean that the Nixon administration was happy with it and they continued to seek to delay the CSCE. Indeed, it was their stated ambition to avoid any CSCE agreement in 1972.[209] However, British negotiators at the CSCE were pushing for a resolution to the project. From the perspective of the US, British policy was clearly undermining their wider foreign policy objectives. Simply put, if the British managed to force through a CSCE agreement then the US would have less leverage in persuading the USSR to adopt a less hostile stance on matters deemed to be of greater importance by Washington, i.e. arms control and MBFR. The president, therefore, took the opportunity during a meeting with Burke Trend to repeat US policy and admonish British behaviour at the CSCE negotiations. As Trend reported to London, Nixon claimed that Britain's CSCE policy had harmed Western interests. The US wanted the negotiations to be dragged out for as long as possible as this would allow the West to enact a degree of influence on other areas of Soviet policy. The line which British policy was pursuing had squandered this political leverage.[210]

While aware of US dissatisfaction, it did little to affect the course of British policy. More broadly, British efforts were all rather moot given the evolution of events. A swift resolution to the CSCE appeared unlikely given that the Multilateral Preparatory Talks, which convened in November 1972, had representatives from over 35 countries. Aside from the simple mass of countries present was the more important problem that little common agreement existed between them. Thus, it was always likely that finding a common agreement would be an arduous process. Events would later prove this to be the case, given that the CSCE would not be concluded until August 1975.

In spite of US–UK disagreements over the CSCE, it should not be seen as indicative of a relationship fraught with difficulties.[211] Certainly differences of opinion existed regarding the substance of what a CSCE should contain and the tactical approach each side should take towards it. However, there were no major ramifications for US–UK relations. Differences on the CSCE were not seriously impairing good relations, as both countries were kept informed of one another's policy intentions. Such differences are better viewed as a natural policy schism between two countries. Furthermore, the CSCE was simply not important enough at this stage to have serious consequences for bilateral relations.

## MBFR

The spectre of MBFR was an area of deeper concern for US and UK policy-makers. As Kissinger expressed, if the MBFR was not handled correctly, it had the potential to 'screw' the entire NATO alliance.[212] Likewise, the British government believed MBFR could potentially damage its security interests. British concerns centred on a large reduction in NATO's conventional forces on a symmetrical basis. This meant that both sides would reduce their forces equally. Internal studies produced by the British Ministry of Defence revealed that NATO's conventional force position would relatively worsen vis-à-vis the Warsaw Pact if such a policy was enacted. Accordingly, NATO would have to rely more heavily on nuclear weapons for occasions when their use would have been deemed inappropriate. As such, a ceiling approach to the negotiations was preferable which meant that an agreement on a set number of forces which each side could possess would be sought.[213]

Regardless of the actual specifics, Heath's government wanted the MBFR to be vigorously analysed within NATO. Substantive policy was to be agreed in this forum and only then would serious negotiations with the Warsaw Pact begin. Heath's government clearly attached great significance to this given that, during the first high-level meeting with the Nixon administration, both Carrington and Douglas-Home made their reservations known about MBFR. Both argued that NATO required force modernisation, and that an MBFR agreement would only undermine efforts to convince NATO members to improve their defence efforts.[214]

When he assumed the presidency, Nixon gave little attention to MBFR and it was only by the middle of 1971 that this position began to alter due to a number of interlocking factors. Economics was clearly one reason behind this change given that the balance of payments difficulties facing the US had become particularly acute by 1971. MBFR was, thus, viewed as an opportunity to reduce America's military burden and help ease such economic problems.[215] MBFR was also seen as an attractive way of hedging against unilateral reductions in military forces by NATO members. The thinking ran that NATO members would enact force reductions regardless of any MBFR settlement being reached. Therefore, an MBFR agreement could allow NATO to reduce its forces without having to suffer the strategic consequences of this being done unilaterally.[216]

Domestic politics were also prevalent in altering US policy. Confronting a hostile Congress which demanded troop reductions globally (in 1971 the Democrat Senator George McGovern, who would contest the 1972 presidential election, called for the halving of American forces in Europe), the MBFR offered a way for Nixon to reduce America's commitments while maintaining a rough equivalence with the USSR.[217] Melvin Laird was especially conscious of the domestic pressures being placed upon the administration. Although initially against NATO troop reductions, Laird advised Nixon that NATO troop reductions were needed to mitigate Congressional demands. In particular, Senator Mike Mansfield was leading a sustained attack against the administration's unwillingness to reduce its global military presence, and its failure to convince its allies to increase their own military efforts. As such, Laird wanted the US to inform NATO that it would have to accept an increased reliance on tactical nuclear weapons for its defence, unless greater burden-sharing was enacted.[218]

Kissinger was also feeling the effect of Congressional opinion and the rejection of the Nixon administration's foreign aid budget gave added emphasis to the growing reluctance of the US Congress to continue to fund the US's global defence efforts.[219] Following further pressure from Mansfield to reduce America's European force levels, Kissinger suggested to Nixon that a 'visible effort to get MBFR underway' was needed to placate Congress.[220] This then serves as a reminder to scholars that domestic political factors can have a profound impact upon the course of foreign policy decisions.[221]

As a consequence of these factors, US MBFR policy was built upon twin pillars. It would seek to convince NATO to contribute more to the alliance. If this was achieved, then the US could reduce its own commitments without affecting the overall make-up of NATO's conventional forces. If this was unsuccessful, then the US would seriously negotiate with the USSR on an MBFR settlement. Nixon's position, however, was to avoid reaching any hasty settlement. Rather, US policy was designed to give an impression to Congress that the administration was seriously seeking to reduce America's military burdens in Europe.[222] The president had no intention of being forced into finding a quick agreement by US Senators.

Heath's government found this shift in US policy all rather disconcerting. Douglas-Home and Carrington still believed NATO would likely be disadvantaged by *any* MBFR agreement. While understanding Nixon's need to placate Congressional critics, they remained concerned that even beginning MBFR negotiations could seriously damage British security interests.[223] British officials communicated these concerns clearly to their American counterparts and Annenberg reported that 'the more the British look at MBFR, the more they dislike it. They see only a very small margin of safety for NATO in such negotiations.'[224] At the highest level, Heath expressed British worries to Nixon and Douglas-Home repeated similar concerns to Rogers.[225]

Such complaints were met with little sympathy within the Nixon administration. As one aide informed Kissinger, 'As you know, NATO generally takes a more pessimistic view of the conventional balance in Europe than our own inter-agency analysis has shown'.[226] However, the US was keen to placate their British ally and so Nixon informed Heath that MBFR was only being countenanced as it was a necessary 'holding action' against his domestic critics and offered further 'consultation and discussion'. Despite Nixon's efforts, reports continued to arrive in Washington outlining British concerns towards MBFR.[227]

Like the CSCE negotiations, the long drawn out process of establishing an MBFR settlement was to be a continual source of disagreement between British and American officials. This, however, must be viewed in its proper context. The differences over MBFR were not seen as a point of major difficulty at this stage. Rather, it was a subject which both US and UK officials discussed at considerable length amongst themselves. Indeed, such a state of affairs should be deemed a natural part of diplomacy between states. Disagreement on matters as intricate and detailed as MBFR are always likely to occur between two countries which varied so much in what each would deem to be their vital national interests. The fact that such disagreements were discussed often and at length between US and UK officials is perhaps indicative of a close, though not harmonious, relationship between the two countries' policy-makers.

## Conclusion

In opposition to existing accounts that tend to paint an overly dark assessment of US–UK relations during 1969–72, many aspects of US–UK cooperation functioned remarkably smoothly.[228] Public and private support for Nixon's policies in Vietnam was provided by the prime minister. Likewise, Heath would articulate public support for Nixon's détente project more generally.[229] In a similar fashion, Heath received the public backing from the president with regard to British membership of the EEC. Moreover, US–UK interaction was maintained and reinvigorated in this period. This was clearly demonstrated in the intelligence realm where the 'JIC Net' continued. In keeping with other eras, the station chief of the CIA was also invited to attend the meetings of the JIC. The National Security Agency (NSA), and its British counterpart, Government Communications Headquarters (GCHQ), continued their intelligence relationship. On the nuclear side, US–UK working groups, which had been put on hiatus in the Wilson era, were once again resurrected to discuss potential avenues for upgrading Polaris.[230]

Nevertheless, one should not paint an overly optimistic picture of US–UK relations at this time. Many of the key foreign policy objectives of each state were causing deep concern in their respective capitals. British policy towards the EEC was met with deep scepticism in Washington. The policies emanating from détente created resentment and distrust in London. As one British newspaper had correctly predicted following Nixon's inauguration, the spectre of superpower negotiation would create 'anxieties' in London.[231] These anxieties were predicated upon the belief that superpower discussion would lead to superpower condominium, and, in turn, see vital Western security interests being sacrificed. Few predicated, however, that superpower détente would have larger ramifications for US–UK relations. This was seen throughout Nixon's efforts to court the PRC and the impact this had upon US policy throughout the India–Pakistan war. Nixon's international economic policies, most obviously in halting dollar to gold convertibility, again resulted in problems between the two countries. It also led to calls in London for closer US–EEC interaction. Most importantly, several unresolved points of difference (namely, Britain's role within the EEC) would have severe ramifications for US–UK bilateral relations throughout 1973–74. It is to this that we now turn.

## Notes

1 Edward Heath, *The Course of My Life: The Autobiography of Edward Heath* (London: Hodder & Stoughton, 1998), p. 370.

2 Kissinger, *WHY*, pp. 932–3.

3 Ziegler, *Heath*, p. 374.

4 For an overview of Kissinger's influence in the subsequent writing of Cold War history see: Robert Kagan, 'The Revisionist: How Henry Kissinger Won the Cold War, or So He Thinks', *The New Republic*, 220:25 (1999), 38–48. Also see: Andrew Roth, *Heath and the Heathmen* (London: Routledge, 1972), pp. 227–8; Fredrick Samuel Northedge, *Descent From Power: British Foreign Policy 1945–1973* (London: George Allen & Unwin, 1974), p. 354; Robert M. Hathaway, *Great Britain and the United States: Special Relations Since World War II* (Boston: Twayne, 1990), pp. 97–8; Robin Renwick, *Fighting With Allies: America and Britain in Peace and War* (Basingstoke: Macmillan, 1996), pp. 206–11; John Baylis, *Anglo-American Relations Since 1939:*

*The Enduring Alliance* (Manchester: Manchester University Press, 1997), p. 168; Sean Greenwood, *Britain and the Cold War 1945–91* (Basingstoke: Macmillan, 2000), pp. 177–8.

5 Hill and Lord, 'The Foreign Policy of the Heath Government', pp. 285–6; Hamilton, 'Britain, France and America's Year of Europe'; Scott, *Allies Apart*.

6 Hynes, *The Year*; Rossbach, *Rebirth*.

7 Spelling, 'Edward Heath and Anglo-American Relations', 640–58.

8 Burk, *Old World*, p. 625.

9 John Killick, British Diplomatic Oral History Project, Churchill College, Cambridge University (hereafter: BDOHP), p. 30.

10 Barbara Keys, 'Henry Kissinger: The Emotional Statesman', *Diplomatic History*, 35:4 (2011), 587–609.

11 One only has to survey the despatches sent from the UK Ambassador in Washington, Lord Cromer, to realise that Kissinger's operational methods, and often prickly personality, were not that well received in British circles. See for example TNA: FCO 82/177 Lord Cromer to Denis Greenhill, 27 April 1972; TNA: FCO 82/183 Lord Cromer to Denis Greenhill, 27 November 1972; TNA: FCO 82/178 Lord Cromer to Denis Greenhill, 15 December 1972.

12 The impression is given within Hynes, *The Year*; Rossbach, *Rebirth*. On the point in the text see: Philip Pomper, 'Historians and Individual Agency', *History and Theory*, 35:3 (1996), 281–308; John Young, *Twentieth Century Diplomacy: A Case Study of British Practice, 1963–1976* (Cambridge: Cambridge University Press, 2008), pp. 4–6.

13 David Dimbleby and David Reynolds termed the period 1973–1980 'All at sea'. Dimbleby and Reynolds, *An Ocean Apart*, pp. 307–22. Also: John Baylis, *Anglo-American Defence Relations 1939–1984: The Special Relationship* (Basingstoke: Macmillan, 1984), pp. 99–115; Michael Chichester and John Wilkinson, *The Uncertain Ally: British Defence Policy 1960–1980* (Aldershot: Gower, 1982), pp. 43–56.

14 For accounts that downplay cooperation see: Hynes, *The Year*; Rossbach, *Rebirth*; Scott, *Allies Apart*.

15 For a good overview on how the political system operates in Washington see: John P. Burke, *The Institutional Presidency: Organizing and Managing the White House from FDR to Clinton* (Baltimore: The Johns Hopkins University Press, 2000); Paul R. Viotti, *American Foreign Policy and National Security: A Documentary Record* (New Jersey: Pearson, 2005), pp. 320–45.

16 Roger Morris, *Uncertain Greatness: Henry Kissinger and American Foreign Policy* (New York: Quartet Books, 1978), p. 63; Christopher Andrew, *For the President's Eyes Only: Secret Intelligence and the American Presidency from Washington to Bush* (London: HarperCollins, 1996), pp. 350–96. For an example of Nixon's complaints about the CIA see: Memorandum from [Name not declassified] of the Central Intelligence Agency to Director of Central Intelligence Helms, 18 June 1969, in *FRUS 1969–1976: Organization and Management*, Vol. II, Doc. 191, pp. 388–9.

17 Stansfield Turner, *Burn Before Reading: Presidents, CIA Directors and Secret Intelligence* (New York: Hyperion, 2005), pp. 122–37; Andrew, *For the President's Eyes Only*, pp. 350–1.

18 Richard Helms and William Hood, *A Look Over My Shoulder: A Life in the Central Intelligence Agency* (New York: Random House, 2003), pp. 382–3.

19 Tim Weiner, *Legacy of Ashes: The History of the CIA* (London: Penguin, 2007), pp. 342–3; Memorandum from Frank Chaplin of the National Security Council Staff to the Director of Central Intelligence Helms, 23 January 1969, in *FRUS 1969–1976: Organization and Management*, Vol. II, Doc. 182, p. 370.

20 Richard H. Immerman, 'Intelligence and Strategy: Historicizing Psychology, Politics, and Policy', *Diplomatic History*, 32:1 (2008), 16; David Robarge, 'Leadership in an Intelligence Organization: The Directors of Central Intelligence and the CIA', in Loch Johnson (ed.), *The Oxford Handbook of National Security Intelligence* (New York: Oxford University Press, 2010), p. 495.

21 C. L. Sulzberger, *The World and Richard Nixon* (New York: Prentice Hall Press, 1987), p. 168.

22 Iwan Morgan, *Nixon* (London: Arnold, 2002), p. 132; Memorandum of Conversation, 6 June 1974, File: June 6, 1974, Nixon, Schlesinger, NSAMC, Box 4, GFL.

23 Haldeman, *Haldeman Diaries*, p. 309; Jurek Martin, 'Nixon Still Has 200 Senior Posts to Fill', *Financial Times*, 24 January 1974, p. 5.

24 Rodman, *Presidential Command*, pp. 36–56; Immerman, 'Intelligence and Strategy', p. 16; Arthur Schlesinger, *The Imperial Presidency* (Boston: Houghton Mifflin, 1973).

25 Haldeman, *The Ends of Power*, pp. 51–3; Haldeman, *Haldeman Diaries*, pp. 51–3; 309, 311; Dean, *Blind Ambition*, p. 65; Ehrlichman, *Witness to Power*, pp. 78–80.

26 On the role of the National Security Adviser see: John Prados, *Keepers of the Keys: A History of the National Security Council from Truman to Bush* (New York: Random House, 1994).

27 U. Alexis Johnson, *The Right Hand of Power* (New York: Prentice-Hall, 1984), pp. 513–14; Memorandum from the President's Assistant for National Security Affairs-Designate [Kissinger] to President-Elect Nixon, 7 January 1969 in *FRUS 1969–1976: Organization and Management*, Vol. II, Doc. 3, pp. 11–14.

28 Johnson had held a weekly lunch where his principal advisers met to discuss and create policy. See Kissinger's critique of this here: Memorandum from the President's Assistant for National Security Affairs-Designate [Kissinger] to President-Elect Nixon, 27 December 1968, in *FRUS 1969–1976: Organization and Management*, Vol. II, Doc. 2, pp. 2–3. Quote at p. 3.

29 *Ibid.*, p. 4.

30 For the quote see: National Security Decision Memorandum 1, 20 January 1969, NSCIHF, Policy Papers, National Security Council Decision Memorandum (hereafter: NSCDM), Box H-209, NPMP. Also see: National Security Decision Memorandum 2, 20 January 1969, NSCIHF, Policy Papers, NSCDM, Box H-209, NPMP. For a good overview of Kissinger's NSC see: Gerry Argyris Andrianopoulos, *Kissinger and Brzezinski: The NSC and the Struggle for Control of US National Security Policy* (Basingstoke: Macmillan, 1991).

31 Memorandum for the President-Elect from Henry A. Kissinger, 7 January 1969, NSCIHF, Policy Papers, NSCDM, Box H-209, NPMP; Memorandum for Henry Kissinger from RN [Nixon], 13 January 1969, NSCIHF, Policy Papers, NSCDM, Box H-209, NPMP.

32 Editorial Note, in *FRUS 1969–1976: Organization and Management*, Vol. II, Doc. 2, pp. 10–11.

33 Jussi Hanhimäki, *The Flawed Architect: Henry Kissinger and American Foreign Policy* (Oxford: Oxford Univeristy Press, 2004), pp. 23–8.

34 Price, *With Nixon*, p. 305.

35 Hanhimäki, *Flawed*, p. 28.

36 Kissinger, *WHY*, pp. 32–33. Laird's skill as a bureaucratic fighter was acknowledged by Nixon when he commented that 'he was the most devious man in Washington'. Given Nixon's own political skills, this was quite the compliment. For the quote see Cynthia Helms, *An Intriguing Life: A Memoir of War, Washington and Marriage to an American Spymaster* (Oxford: Rowman & Littlefield, 2012), pp. 110–11.

37 Hanhimäki, *Flawed*, pp. 92–3.

38 Rodman, *Presidential Command*, pp. 36–56.

39 Peter Hennessy, *The Prime Minister: The Office and its Holders Since 1945* (London: Penguin, 2000), pp. 337–45; Dennis Kavanagh and Anthony Seldon, *The Powers Behind the Prime Minister: The Hidden Influence of Number Ten* (London: HarperCollins, 1999), pp. 77–8.

40 Peter Hennessy, *Whitehall* (London: Pimlico, 2001, revised edition), p. 215.

41 *Ibid.*

42 Cromer served as the British Ambassador to Washington, 1971–74. Greenhill was the Permanent Under-Secretary (PUS) at the Foreign and Commonwealth Office (FCO), 1969–73. Brimelow was the Deputy PUS at the FCO, 1969–73, before assuming the position as PUS, 1973–75. Sykes was the Minister at the Washington Embassy, 1970–74. Powell was Cromer's Private Secretary, 1971–74.

43 An award that Cromer would soon come to regret being granted! See Thorpe, *Alec Douglas-Home*, pp. 411–12; Alexander Spelling, 'Lord Cromer, 1971–74', in Michael Hopkins, Saul Kelly and John Young (eds.), *The Washington Embassy: British Ambassadors to the United States, 1939–77* (Basingstoke: Palgrave Macmillan, 2009), pp. 189–208.

44 Denis Greenhill, *More by Accident* (York: Wilton, 1992), pp. 130–50; Denis Greenhill, BDOHP, pp. 1–10; Charles Powell, BDOHP, p. 8.

45 Ziegler, *Heath*, pp. 388–9; Spelling, 'Lord Cromer', in Hopkins et al., *The Washington Embassy*, pp. 189–208.

46 Heath, *The Course*, pp. 325–53; Robert Shepherd, *Iain Macleod: A Biography* (London: Hutchinson, 1994), pp. 529–36.

47 Ongoing commercial disputes were causing US–UK difficulties. See Raj Roy, 'The Politics of Planes and Engines: Anglo-American Relations During the Rolls-Royce–Lockheed Crisis, 1970–1971' in Matthias Schulz and Thomas A. Schwartz (eds.), *The Strained Alliance: U.S.–European Relations from Nixon to Carter* (Cambridge: Cambridge University Press, 2009), pp. 172–5.

48 John Dumbrell, 'The Johnson Administration and the British Labour Government: Vietnam, the Pound and East of Suez', *Journal of American Studies*, 30:2 (1996), 211–31; Saki Dockrill, *Britain's Retreat from East of Suez: The Choice Between Europe and the World?* (Basingstoke: Palgrave Macmillan, 2002).

49 David M. McCourt, 'What was Britain's "East of Suez" Role? Reassessing the Withdrawal, 1964–1968', *Diplomacy and Statecraft*, 20:3 (2009), 454–5; Philip Ziegler, *Wilson: The Authorised Life* (London: Weidenfeld & Nicolson, 1993), pp. 329–31.

50 Lyndon Johnson to Harold Wilson, 11 January 1968, National Security File, Special Head of State Correspondence, United Kingdom, Lyndon Baines Johnson Library, Austin, Texas, USA (hereafter: LBJ Library). Thanks to Dr David Gill for bringing this document to my attention.

51 Richard Nixon, *The Memoirs of Richard Nixon,* (London: Grosset & Dunlap, 1978), p. 179.

52 On the domestic pressures facing the Nixon administration see: Dominic Sandbrook, 'Salesmanship and Substance: The Influence of Domestic Policy and Watergate', in Logevall and Preston, *Nixon in the World*, pp. 85–106; Jussi Hanhimäki, 'Global Visions and Parochial Politics'; Thomas Alan Schwartz, '"Winning an Election is Terribly Important"; Thomas Alan Schwartz, 'Henry Kissinger: Realism, Domestic Politics, and the Struggle against Exceptionalism in American Foreign Policy', *Diplomacy and Statecraft*, 22:1 (2011), 121–41. For the other points mentioned see: Nixon, *Memoirs*, pp. 370–5; Kissinger, *WHY*, pp. 73–81. For the Conservative Party 1970 manifesto see: 'A Better Tomorrow', 1970 Conservative Party Election Manifesto, available at: www.conservative-party.net/manifestos/1970/1970-conservative-manifesto.shtml (Accessed 12 January 2012).

53 Francis Gavin, 'The Myth of Flexible Response: US Strategy in Europe During the 1960s', *International History Review*, 23:4 (2001), 847–75.

54 V. A. Walters to Dr Kissinger, 31 December 1968, National Security Council Files, Henry A. Kissinger Office Files, HAK Administrative & Staff Files – Transition, Box 1, NPMP; Memorandum for the President's File from Henry A. Kissinger, 20 December 1971, President's Office Files, Memoranda for the President, Box 87, NPMP.

55 Marc Trachtenberg, 'The Structure of Great Power Politics, 1963–1975', in Leffler and Westad (eds.), *Crises and Détente*, p. 491.

56 William Burr (ed.), *The Kissinger Transcripts: The Top Secret Talks With Beijing and Moscow* (New York: The New Press, 1998), p. 10.

57 William Burr, 'The Nixon Administration, the "Horror Strategy," and the Search for Limited Nuclear Options, 1969–1972', *Journal of Cold War Studies*, 7:3 (2005), 34–78.

58 Henry Kissinger, 'Introduction', in Henry Kissinger (ed.), *Problems of National Strategy: A Book of Readings* (London: Praeger, 1965), p. 5.

59 Memorandum for the President from Henry A. Kissinger, undated (circa October 1970), NSCIHF, Meeting Files: National Security Council Meetings, Box H-029, NPMP.

60 Memorandum for the President's Office Files from Henry Kissinger, 18 August 1970, President Office Files, Memoranda for the President, Box 82, NPMP; Memorandum for the President from William P. Rogers, 22 September 1970, NSCIHF, National Security Decision Memorandums (hereafter: NSDM), Box H-221, NPMP.

61 Memorandum for the President from Henry A. Kissinger, undated (circa October 1970), NSCIHF, Meeting Files: National Security Council Meetings, Box H-029, NPMP; Memorandum for the President from Henry Kissinger, 14 October 1970, President Office Files, Memoranda for the President, Box 82, NPMP; Memorandum of Conversation, 23 September 1970, RG 59 General Records of the Department of State, Subject Numeric Files, 1970–73, Political & Defense, Box 2650, National Archives II, College Park, Maryland, USA (hereafter: NAII); Memorandum of Conversation, 3 October 1970, *ibid.*

62 Lord Peter Carrington, *Reflect on Things Past* (London: HarperCollins, 1988), pp. 218–20.

63 *Ibid.*, p. 218.

64 Memorandum of Conversation, 23 September 1970, RG 59 General Records of the Department of State, Subject Numeric Files, 1970–73, Political & Defense, Box 2650, NAII.

65 This can all be followed within: Dale Van Atta, *With Honor: Melvin Laird in War, Peace and Politics* (Madison: The University of Wisconsin Press, 2008), pp. 285–90; Memorandum for the President from Melvin Laird, 14 October 1970, NSCIHF, Study Memorandums, National Security Study Memorandums, Box H-167, NPMP; Memorandum for Assistant to the President for National Security Affairs [Kissinger] from David Packard, 12 November 1970, NSCIHF, NSDM, Box H-219, NPMP; Memorandum for Mr Kissinger from Helmut Sonnenfeldt, 30 October 1970, *ibid.*

66 George Springsteen was a career diplomat within the State Department. In 1973, he was appointed as special assistant to Kissinger.

67 George S. Springsteen to the Under-Secretary of State [Irwin], 20 November 1970, RG 59 General Records of the Department of State, Subject Numeric Files 1970–73, Political & Defense, Box 2848, NAII.

68 Memorandum for Mr Kissinger from Helmut Sonnenfeldt, 30 October 1970, NSCIHF, NSDM, Box H-219, NPMP.

69 Memorandum for the President from Henry A. Kissinger, 3 November 1970, *ibid.* Interestingly, Edward Heath was arguing much the same point to Cyrus Sulzberger, the lead foreign correspondent for the *New York Times*. See: C. L. Sulzberger, *An Age of Mediocrity, Memoirs and Diaries: 1963–1972* (New York: Macmillan, 1973), pp. 693–4.

70 Johnson to Ambassador in London Embassy, Tel. 193761, 24 November 1970, RG 59 General Records of the Department of State, Subject Numeric Files 1970–73, Political & Defense, Box 2848, NAII.

71 Memorandum for Mr Kissinger from Helmut Sonnenfeldt, 30 October 1970, NSCIHF, NSDM, Box H-219, NPMP; Memorandum for the President from Henry A. Kissinger, 3 November 1970, NSCIHF, NSDM, Box H-219, NPMP.

72 McCourt, 'Britain's "East of Suez" Role', pp. 468–9.

73 Carrington, *Reflect*, p. 219.

74 Greenhill, *More by Accident*, pp. 147, 167. On Heath's diplomacy to gain British membership of the EEC see: Sir Con O'Neill, *Britain's Entry into the European Community: Report on the Negotiations of 1970–72* (London: Routledge, 2000).

75 These points were delivered in the Godkin Lecture of 1967 at Harvard University. They were re-printed in: Edward Heath, *Old World, New Horizons: Britain, the Common Market and the Atlantic Alliance* (London: Oxford University Press, 1970). For the quote see: George Hutchinson, *Edward Heath: A Personal and Political Biography* (London: Longman, 1970), pp. 101–2. Also see: Margaret Laing, *Edward Heath: Prime Minister* (London: Sidgwick & Jackson, 1972), pp. 124–47; John Campbell, *Edward Heath: A Biography* (London: Jonathan Cape, 1993), pp. 108–38.

76 Gottfried Niedhart, 'U.S. Détente and West German Ostpolitik: Parallels and Frictions', in Schultz and Schwartz (eds.), *Strained Alliance*, p. 35; C. J. Bartlett, *The 'Special*

*Relationship': A Political History of Anglo-American Relations since 1945* (London: Longman, 1992), p. 130.

77 Ziegler, *Heath*, p. 374.

78 TNA: PREM 15/2077 Heath to Douglas-Home, 8 September 1970; TNA: PREM 15/2077 Douglas-Home to the Prime Minister, 18 September 1970.

79 John Young, *The Labour Governments 1964–70: International Policy* (Manchester: Manchester University Press, 2003), pp. 142–65.

80 Bevin served as British Foreign Secretary, 1945–51. On his espousal of the 'pillars' strategy see Marc Trachtenberg, *A Constructed Peace: The Making of the European Settlement, 1945–1963* (New Jersey: Princeton University Press, 1999), pp. 115–16. For a different interpretation see: Niklas Rossbach, 'Edward Heath's Vision and the Year of Europe', in Morten Rasmussen and Ann-Christina Lauring Knudsen (eds.), *The Road to a United Europe: Interpretations of the Process of European Integration* (Brussels: Peter Lang, 2009), pp. 69–84.

81 Kissinger, *WHY*, p. 91.

82 Reynolds, *The Creation of the Anglo-American Alliance*, pp. 284–5; Klaus Larres, *Churchill's Cold War: The Politics of Personal Diplomacy* (New Haven: Yale University Press, 2002), pp. xiv–xv.

83 Michael Stewart, 'Britain, Europe and the Alliance', *Foreign Affairs*, 48:4 (1970), 655; Ashton, 'Harold Macmillan and the "Golden Days" of Anglo-American Relations', pp. 691–724; James Ellison, *The United States, Britain and the Transatlantic Crisis: Rising to the Gaullist Challenge, 1963–68* (Basingstoke: Palgrave Macmillan, 2007), pp. 139–63.

84 M. H. Fisher, 'A Marked Continuity', *Financial Times*, 20 June 1970, p. 13.

85 Denis MacShane, *Heath* (London: Haus Publishing, 2006), pp. 46–7.

86 Robert Gibson, *Best of Enemies: Anglo-French Relations Since the Norman Conquest* (London: Sinclair Stevenson, 1995), pp. 303–13; Erin Mahan, *Kennedy, de Gaulle and Western Europe* (Basingstoke: Palgrave, 2002), pp. 136–42; Heath, *Course*, pp. 201–40.

87 Donald Maitland, BDOHP, p. 20.

88 Ilaria Poggiolini, 'How the Heath Government Revised the European Lesson: British Transition to EC Membership, 1972', in Antonio Varsori (ed.), *Inside the European Community: Actors and Policies in European Integration From the Rome Treaty to the Creation of the Snake* (Brussels: Bruylant, 2006), pp. 313–46.

89 Stephen George, *Britain and European Integration Since 1945* (Oxford: Basil Blackwell, 1991), pp. 49–51; Rossbach, *Rebirth*, p. 3; David Sanders, *Losing an Empire, Finding a Role: British Foreign Policy since 1945* (Basingstoke: Macmillan, 1990), pp. 146–7.

90 Lundestad, *'Empire' by Integration*, pp. 13–28; Trachtenberg, *A Constructed Peace*, pp. 114–25.

91 Memorandum of Conversation, 1 May 1969, *Foreign Relations of the United States 1969–1974: Foreign Economic Policy; International Monetary Policy, 1969–1972* (Washington: United States Government Printing Office, 2001), Vol. III, Doc. 122, p. 319; TNA: FCO 46/591 Note of a Meeting held in the Oval Office, 27 January 1970; Memorandum of Conversation, 27 January 1970, NSCIHF, Presidential/HAK Memcons, Box 1023, NPMP; Memorandum of Conversation, 17 December 1970, NSCIHF, Presidential-HAK Memcons, Box 1024, NPMP; Memorandum for the

President's File from Henry A. Kissinger, 20 December 1971, President's Office Files, Memoranda for the President, Box 87, NPMP.

92 Kissinger, *WHY*, pp. 937–8.

93 Memorandum for the President's Office Files from Patrick J. Buchanan, 17 November 1970, President's Office Files, Memoranda for the President, Box 83, NPMP; Paper prepared by Consultants, undated, *FRUS 1969–1976; Foreign Economic Policy*, Vol. III, Doc. 26, p. 69; Klaus Larres, 'Assertive Supremacy and Enlightened Self-Interest: The United States and the "Unity of Europe"', *AICGS Transatlantic Perspectives*, December 2009, pp. 3–6, from: www.aicgs.org/publication/assertive-supremacy-and-enlightened-self-interest-the-united-states-and-the-%E2%80%9Cunity-of-europe%E2%80%9D/ (Accessed 27 March 2011).

94 Helmut Sonnenfeldt interview, *The Foreign affairs Oral History Collection of the Association for Diplomatic Studies and Training*, from: http://memory.loc.gov/cgi-bin/query/D?mfdip:6:./temp/~ammem_XnbX (Accessed 11 July 2009).

95 Connally, *In History's Shadow*, pp. 244–5; Rossbach, *Rebirth*, pp. 56–68.

96 Connally had been riding in the same car as President John F. Kennedy when he was assassinated. For the alleged comment see: Roth, *Heath and the Heathmen*, p. 224. For the other quote see: Greenhill, *More by Accident*, p. 166. Interestingly, Barber only refers to Connally in a positive fashion throughout his memoirs. See: Anthony Barber, *Taking the Tide* (London: Michael Russell, 1996), pp. 113–14. The archival record undermines this positive portrayal however. For instance: TNA: PREM 15/361 Tickell to Con O'Neill, 15 October 1971; TNA: PREM 15/361 Tickell to Moon, 18 October 1971.

97 Memorandum for Henry Kissinger from C. Fred Bergsten, 6 May 1970, NSCIHF, Senior Review Group Meetings, Box H-042, NPMP; Memorandum for the President's Office Files from Patrick J. Buchanan, 17 November 1970, President's Office Files, Memoranda for the President, Box 83, NPMP; Memorandum of Conversation, 17 December 1970, NSCIHF, Presidential-HAK Memcons, Box 1024, NPMP.

98 Memorandum for the President's File from Peter Flanigan, 11 September 1972, President's Office Files, Memoranda for the President, Box 89, NPMP.

99 Memorandum by President Nixon, 18 January 1971, *FRUS 1969–1976, Organization and Management*, Vol. II, Doc. 374, pp. 811–12.

100 Memorandum from the President's Assistant for National Security Affairs [Kissinger] to President Nixon, 28 January 1969, *FRUS 1969–1976; Foreign Economic Policy*, Vol. III, Doc. 4, pp. 6–7; Action Memorandum from the President's Assistant for National Security Affairs [Kissinger] to President Nixon, 25 June 1969, *ibid.*, Doc. 131, p. 345–7; Memorandum from C. Fred Bergsten of the National Security Council Staff to the President's Special Assistant for National Security Affairs [Kissinger] 21 April 1971, *ibid.*, Doc. 64, p. 156; Memorandum of Conversation, 25 July 1972, *ibid.*, Doc. 236, pp. 642–3.

101 Walter Annenberg to William P. Rogers, 12 February 1971, RG 59 General Records of the Department of State, Entry 1613, Box, 961, NAII.

102 All of this policy advice can be followed throughout: Memorandum for the President from Henry Kissinger, 17 June 1970, NSCIHF, Senior Review Group Meetings, Box H-042, NPMP; Information Memorandum from Ernest Johnston of the National Security Council Staff to the President's Assistant for National Security Affairs

[Kissinger], 10 May 1971, *FRUS 1969–1976; Foreign Economic Policy*, Vol. III, Doc. 154, pp. 431–2; State Department Summary: Enlargement of the European Community: Implications for the US and Policy Options, undated (circa June 1970), NSCIHF, Senior Review Group Meetings, Box H-042, NPMP. On Nixon's concerns about *Ostpolitik* see: Gottfried Niedhart, 'U.S. Détente and West German Ostpolitik: Parallels and Frictions', in Schulz and Schwartz (eds.), *The Strained Alliance*, pp. 23–44; Bernd Schaefer, 'The Nixon Administration and West German Ostpolitik', in *ibid.*, pp. 45–64.

103 Lundestad, *'Empire' by Integration*, pp. 13–28; Oliver Bange, *The EEC Crisis of 1963: Kennedy, Macmillan, de Gaulle and Adenauer in Conflict* (Basingstoke: Macmillan, 2000), pp. 37–49.

104 Memorandum for Dr Kissinger from C. Fred Bergsten and Helmut Sonnenfeldt, 7 November, 1969, NSCIHF, Study Memorandums, National Security Study Memorandums, Box H-164, NPMP.

105 Memorandum for Dr Kissinger from C. Fred Bergsten and Helmut Sonnenfeldt, 7 October 1969, *ibid.*, Henry Kissinger to the Secretary of State et al., 13 October 1969, *ibid.*

106 As noted by one former US official. See J. Robert Schaetzel, *The Unhinged Alliance: America and the European Community* (London: Harper & Row, 1975), pp. 51–2.

107 Kissinger, *Troubled Partnership*, p. 232.

108 Discussion of United States Policy Toward Europe: NSC Meeting, 28 January 1970, NSCIHF, Meeting Files, National Security Council Meetings, Box H-026; NPMP; Memorandum from the Deputy under-Secretary of State for Economic Affairs [Samuels] to the President's Assistant for National Security Affairs [Kissinger] 20 August 1970, *FRUS 1969–1976; Foreign Economic Policy*, Vol. III, Doc. 43, p. 110.

109 Discussion of United States Policy toward Europe: Part 1 – Alternative Structure, attached to Memorandum for the Vice President et al. from Henry A. Kissinger, 26 January 1970, NSCIHF, Meeting Files, National Security Council Meetings, Box H-026, NPMP.

110 Ferrell (ed.), *The Secret Diary of Arthur Burns*, p. 66. One example that demonstrates Kissinger's thinking about global economic matters is contained within: Action Memorandum from the President's Assistant for National Security Affairs [Kissinger] to President Nixon, 25 June 1969, *FRUS 1969–1976; Foreign Economic Policy*, Vol. III, Doc. 131, p. 345. As global monetary issues became a keener part of international diplomacy, Kissinger's knowledge of economics would improve. See: Rodman, *Presidential Command*, pp. 106–7.

111 All quotes within: NSSM 79 and 91: Enlargement of the European Community: Implications for the US and Policy Options, attached to Martin J. Hillenbrand to Henry Kissinger, 23 April 1970, NSCIHF, Study Memorandums, National Security Study Memorandums, Box H-164, NPMP.

112 National Security Decision Memorandum: US Policy toward the European Community, 30 May 1970, attached to Henry Kissinger to Deputy under-Secretary of State Samuels et al., 30 May 1970, NSCIHF, Senior Review Group Meetings, Box H-042, NPMP.

113 National Security Decision Memorandum 68, 3 July 1970, NSCIHF, Policy Papers, National Security Decision Memorandums, Box H-217, NPMP.

114 Report by the President's Assistant for International Economic Affairs [Flanigan] 20 June 1972, *FRUS 1969–1976; Foreign Economic Policy*, Vol. III, Doc. 91, p. 223; Memorandum from Acting Secretary of State Irwin to President Nixon, 20 October 1972, *ibid.*, Doc. 105, pp. 275–9; Paper prepared in the State Department, Undated, *ibid.*, Doc. 108, p. 287; Report by the President's Assistant for International Economic Affairs [Flanigan] 20 June 1972, *ibid.*, Doc. 91, p. 227.

115 Connally managed to override the objections of Arthur Burns. In his opinion, closing the 'gold window' was 'a tragedy for mankind'. See: Ferrell (ed.), *The Secret Diary of Arthur Burns*, pp. 49–50; Connally, *In History's Shadow*, pp. 240–5.

116 At this stage of his career, Rumsfeld served in the Nixon White House as Counsellor to the President, a role that was predominantly focused upon domestic and economic matters. He would go on to serve in the Ford White House, as Chief of Staff (1974–75) and then as Secretary of Defense (1975–77). Rumsfeld would then return to the White House as Secretary of Defense under President George W. Bush (2001–06). For the quote see: Donald Rumsfeld, *Known and Unknown: A Memoir* (London: Sentinel, 2011), p. 139.

117 William C. Cromwell, *The United States and the European Pillar: The Strained Alliance* (Basingstoke: Macmillan, 1992), pp. 72–3; Matusow, 'Richard Nixon and the Failed War against the Trading World', 767–72; Hubert Zimmermann, 'Western Europe and the American Challenge: Conflict and Cooperation in Technology and Monetary Policy, 1965–1973', in Marc Trachtenberg (ed.), *Between Empire and Alliance: America and Europe During the Cold War* (New York: Rowman & Littlefield, 2003), pp. 127–55; Francis J. Gavin, *Gold, Dollars, and Power: The Politics of International Monetary Relations, 1958–1971* (Chapel Hill: The University of North Carolina Press, 2004); William Glenn Gray, 'Floating the System: Germany, the United States, and the Breakdown of Bretton Woods, 1969–1973', *Diplomatic History*, 31:2 (2007), 295–323. For the quote see: Allen Matusow, *Nixon's Economy: Boom, Busts, Dollars and Votes* (Lawrence: University Press of Kansas, 1998), pp. 130–3.

118 For Kissinger's apprehension see: Memorandum for the Record: Conversation with Dr Kissinger and Mr Lucet, 8 November 1971, National Security Council Files, Box 678, NPMP. For the Nixon quote see: Memorandum for Helmut Sonnenfeldt from Al Haig, 3 September 1970, NSCIHF, Meeting Files, Senior Review Group Meetings, Box H-047, NPMP. For Annenberg's quote see: Walter Annenberg to William P. Rogers, 12 February 1971, RG 59 General Records of the Department of State, Entry 1613, Box, 961, NAII.

119 The British record of these discussions can be followed within TNA: PREM 15/2241. See: Pompidou's statement to the press following his talks in: Jussi Hanhimäki and Odd Arne Westad (eds.), *The Cold War: A History in Documents and Eyewitness Accounts* (Oxford: Oxford University Press, 2003), p. 339. Also see: Philip Bell, *France and Britain 1940–1994: The Long Separation* (London: Longman, 1997), pp. 218–26.

120 Ziegler, *Heath*, pp. 292–7.

121 John Lewis Gaddis, 'Grand Strategies in the Cold War', in Leffler and Westad (eds.), *Crises and Détente*, pp. 14–16; Marc Trachtenberg, 'The Structure of Great Power Politics, 1963–1975', in *ibid.*, pp. 492–9; Jeremi Suri, 'Henry Kissinger and American Grand Strategy', in Logevall and Preston (eds.), *Nixon in the World*, pp. 67–84.

122 TNA: FCO 7/1815 Record of a Meeting between the Prime Minister and President Nixon at Chequers, 3 October 1970.

123 For the rather candid assessment that the British knew very little about the president's Vietnam intentions see: TNA: FCO 82/178 Lord Cromer to Denis Greenhill, 15 December 1972. Providing solace was the fact that the British government was just as poorly informed as the US State Department and CIA. In Cromer's estimation, only Kissinger and his deputy, Alexander Haig, were abreast of Nixon's thinking.
124 Geraint Hughes, *Harold Wilson's Cold War: The Labour Government and East-West Politics, 1964–1970* (Rochester: The Boydell Press, 2009), pp. 112–38.
125 Kissinger, *WHY*, p. 94.
126 Kenneth Weisbrode, *The Atlantic Century: Four Generations of Extraordinary Diplomats Who Forged America's Vital Alliance With Europe* (Cambridge, MA: Da Capo Press, 2009), p. 213.
127 Zbiginiew Brzezinski, 'America and Europe', *Foreign Affairs*, 49:1 (1970), 11–30.
128 Richard Nixon, 'Asia After Viet Nam', pp. 111–25; Jeremi Suri, 'Henry Kissinger and the Geopolitics of Globalisation', in Niall Ferguson, Charles Maier, Erez Manela, Daniel Sargent (eds.), *The Shock the Global: The 1970s in Perspective* (Cambridge, MA: Harvard University Press, 2010), p. 183.
129 Amongst the highlights of the US–PRC rapprochement was Kissinger's secret visit to China in July 1971. This involved Kissinger feigning illness during a visit to Pakistan thus allowing him to secretly fly to China. See: Nixon, *Memoirs*, pp. 544–59; Kissinger, *WHY*, pp. 163–94, 684–787. For an entire monograph devoted to the US–PRC rapprochement see: Margaret Macmillan, *Seize the Hour: When Nixon Met Mao* (London: John Murray, 2006). On the diplomacy leading to the opening of relations with the PRC see: Morris, *Uncertain Greatness*, pp. 203–8; Margaret Macmillan, 'Nixon, Kissinger, and the Opening to China', in Logevall and Preston (eds.), *Nixon in the World*, p. 108.
130 Lanxin Xiang, 'The Recognition Controversy: Anglo-American Relations in China, 1949', *Journal of Contemporary History*, 27:2 (1992), 319–43.
131 Keith Hamilton, 'A "Week that Changed the World": Britain and Nixon's China Visit of 21-28 Feb 1972', *Diplomacy and Statecraft*, 15:1 (2004), 117–35.
132 TNA: PREM 15/1988 Lord Cromer to FCO, 25 November 1971.
133 For the quote see: TNA: FCO 7/1815 Record of a Meeting between the Prime Minister and President Nixon at Chequers, 3 October 1970. On the points raised see: Macmillan, *When Nixon Met Mao*, p. 199; Roth, *Heath and the Heathmen*, p. 224; Hamilton, 'A "Week that Changed the World"', 118–21.
134 J. R. Saigal, *Pakistan Splits: The Birth of Bangladesh* (Washington: Manas, 2000); Robert J. McMahon, 'The Danger of Geopolitical Fantasies: Nixon, Kissinger and the South Asia Crisis of 1971', in Logevall and Preston (eds.), *Nixon in the World*, pp. 249–68; Luke A. Nichter and Richard A. Moss, 'Superpower Relations, Backchannels and the Subcontinent', *Pakistaniaat: A Journal of Pakistan Studies*, 2:3 (2010), 47–75.
135 Kissinger, *WHY*, pp. 866–9; Odd Arne Westad, *The Global Cold War: Third World Interventions and the Making of our Times* (Cambridge: Cambridge University Press, 2006), pp. 160–70.
136 Richard Thornton, *The Nixon–Kissinger Years: The Reshaping of American Foreign Policy* (St. Paul, MN: Paragon House, 2001 2nd edition), pp. 113–22; Nichter and Moss, 'Superpower Relations', 46–9.
137 'Naval Victory Claim by India', *Daily Telegraph*, 6 December, 1971, p. 1.

138 Bush would go on to become president of the United States (1989–93). Tom Wicker, *One of Us: Richard Nixon and the American Dream* (New York: Random House, 1991), pp. 665–7.

139 Haldeman, *The Haldeman Diaries*, pp. 380–2; TNA: PREM 15/715 Edward Heath to President Nixon, 13 December 1971.

140 Elmo R. Zumwalt, *On Watch: A Memoir* (Arlington: Zumwalt & Associates, 1976), p. 367.

141 Telcon: Kissinger–The President, 17 December 1971, HAKTELCONS.

142 Haldeman, *The Haldeman Diaries*, p. 381.

143 TNA: FCO 82/63 Burke Trend to Lord Cromer, 29 November, 1971.

144 TNA: FCO 82/63 H. T. A. Overton to Mr Hankey and Thomas Brimelow, 24 November 1971; TNA: FCO 82/67 Steering Brief, Fourth draft, Undated.

145 Memorandum for the President's File by the President's Assistant for National Security Affairs [Kissinger], 20 December 1971, *Foreign Relations of the United States 1969–1976: Foundations of Foreign Policy, 1969–1972* (Washington: United States Government Printing Office, 2003), Vol. I, , Doc. 102, p. 353.

146 Memorandum for the President's File from Henry A. Kissinger, 20 December 1971, President's Office Files, Memoranda for the President, Box 87, NPMP.

147 John Graham, 'Nixon: Surcharge is Ended', *Financial Times*, 21 December 1971, p. 1.

148 'Heath and Nixon Hail New Era', *Daily Telegraph*, 22 December 1971, p. 1.

149 'Nixon Very Pleased', *Daily Telegraph*, 21 December, 1971, p. 20.

150 TNA: FCO 82/183 H. T. A. Overton to Mr Hankey, 7 January 1972.

151 Memorandum of Conversation, 23 December 1971, RG 59 General Records of the Department of State, Subject Numeric Files, 1970–73, Box 2649, NAII.

152 A good overview on the significance of this summit is contained within David Reynolds, *Summits: Six Meetings that Shaped the Twentieth Century* (London: Allen Lane, 2007), pp. 207–61.

153 TNA: FCO 21/982 H. T. A. Overton to T. A. K. Elliott, 22 February 1972; TNA: FCO 21/983 Denis Greenhill to Lord Cromer, 23 March 1972.

154 TNA: FCO 21/983 H. T. A. Overton to T. A. K. Elliot, 24 March 1972.

155 TNA: FCO 21/983 Lord Cromer to Denis Greenhill, 16 March 1972; TNA: PREM 15/1988 JIC(A)(72)(SA) 41, 28 February 1972.

156 Memorandum of Conversation, 21 February 1972, President's Office Files, Memoranda for the President, Box 87, NPMP; Memorandum of Conversation, 22 February 1972, *ibid.*

157 Kissinger, *WHY*, p. 1062. This was a point Kissinger rectified within: Henry Kissinger, *On China* (London: Allen Lane, 2011), pp. 236–74.

158 Nancy Bernkopf Tucker, 'Taiwan Expendable? Nixon and Kissinger Go to China', *The Journal of American History*, 92:1 (2005), 109–35; Jung Chang and Jon Halliday, *Mao: The Unknown Story* (London: Vintage, 2007), pp. 706–8; Macmillan, *Seize the Hour*, pp. 225–65.

159 TNA: PREM 15/1988 Lord Cromer to FCO, 2 March 1972.

160 TNA: PREM 15/1988 Richard Nixon to Edward Heath, 6 July 1972; TNA: FCO 21/983 R. M. Evans to Mr Wilford, 16 May 1972.

161 Conversation Among President Nixon, his Assistant for National Security Affairs [Kissinger], White House Chief of Staff [Haldeman], and Secretary of State Rogers,

11 May 1972, *Foreign Relations of the United States 1969–1976, Soviet Union October 1971–May 1972* (Washington: United States Government Printing Office, 2006), Vol. XIV, Doc. 217, p. 813.

162 As noted within Sonnenfeldt Note, October 1970, National Security Council Files, President's Trip Files, Box 466, NPMP.

163 Conversation Among President Nixon, the Chairman of the Federal Reserve System Board of Governors [Burns], the Director of the Office of Management and Budget [Ash], the Chairman of the Council of Economic Advisers [Stein], Secretary of the Treasury Shultz, and the under-Secretary of the Treasury for Monetary Affairs [Volcker], 3 March 1973, *Foreign Relations of the United States 1969–1976: Foreign Economic Policy, 1973–1976* (Washington: United States Government Printing Office, 2009), Vol. XXXI, Doc. 16, p. 68.

164 Robert D. Schulzinger, 'Détente in the Nixon-Ford years, 1969–1976', in Leffler and Westad (eds.), *Crises and* Détente, pp. 378–82.

165 Or, at least, this was the opinion of some British officials. See: TNA: FCO 28/2027 H. T. A. Overton to Mr Rose, 24 February 1972.

166 Lyndon Baines Johnson, *The Vantage Point: Perspectives of the Presidency 1963–1969* (London: Weidenfeld & Nicolson, 1972), pp. 489–99; Gerard Smith, *DoubleTalk: The Story of SALT I* (New York: Doubleday, 1980), pp. 15–21.

167 Memorandum for Mr Kissinger from Helmut Sonnenfeldt, 22 June 1970, National Security Council Files: SALT, Box 878, NPMP.

168 Memorandum for the President's Files, 15 June 1971, White House Special Files, President's Office Files, Memoranda for the President, Box 85, NPMP.

169 TNA: CAB 164/936 Mac [Victor Macklen] to P. J. Hudson, 30 July 1970; TNA: FCO 45/595 SALT: The Defence Department, attached to Denis Greenhill to the Private Secretary, 1970; Trachtenberg, *Constructed Peace*, pp. 283–351.

170 Edoardo Sorvillo, 'Caught in the Middle of the Transatlantic Security Dilemma. Great Britain, the United States and Western European Security, 1970–1973', *Journal of Transatlantic Studies*, 8:1 (2010), 70.

171 Lawrence Freedman, *Britain and Nuclear Weapons* (London: Macmillan, 1980), pp. 40–5.

172 TNA: CAB 164/936 P. J. Hudson to Burke Trend, 1 March 1971; TNA: CAB 164/937 C. M. Rose to Edward Peck, 21 June 1971; TNA: CAB 133/408 Brief by the Foreign and Commonwealth Office, 22 June 1971; TNA: PREM 15/1272 Brief No. 4, attached to Burke Trend to the Prime Minister, 23 June 1971; TNA: CAB 164/937 MD Butler to C. M. Rose, 28 June 1971.

173 This dual approach to negotiating SALT did not sit well with the US lead negotiator, Gerard Smith. The title of his memoir reveals the bitterness he still felt about this approach. See: Smith, *DoubleTalk*, pp. 200–79. Also see Paul Nitze, *From Hiroshima to Glasnost: At the Centre of Decision* (London: Weidenfeld & Nicolson, 1989), pp. 308–10; Raymond Garthoff, *A Journey Through the Cold War: A Memoir of Containment and Coexistence* (Washington: The Brookings Institute, 2001), pp. 243–76.

174 Laird feared that NATO members would leak US policy to the USSR and therefore undermine their diplomacy. See: Memorandum for Mr Kissinger from Helmut Sonnenfeldt, 27 April 1970, National Security Council Files, SALT, Box 877, NPMP; Memorandum for the Secretary of Defense from Henry A. Kissinger, 4 May 1970,

*ibid.*; Memorandum for the Assistant to the President for National Security Affairs from Melvin Laird, 27 April 1970, *ibid.* On British concerns see: TNA: CAB 164/936 Douglas-Home to Washington, Tel. 2476, 2 November 1970; TNA: CAB 164/937 M. D. Butler to R. M. Tesh, 10 June 1971; TNA: CAB 164/937 M. D. Butler to R. M. Tesh, 16 June 1971.

175 TNA: PREM 15/1359 Solly Zuckerman to the Prime Minister, 17 July 1970; TNA: FCO 146/4649 Meeting between the Defence Secretary and H.M. Ambassador, Paris, 2 March 1971; TNA: PREM 15/299 Burke Trend to the Prime Minister, 4 March 1971; TNA: CAB 133/408 Brief by the Foreign and Commonwealth Office, 22 June 1971; TNA: PREM 15/1272 Brief No. 4, Burke Trend to Prime Minister, 23 June 1971; TNA: PREM 15/1359 Annex A, attached to Robert Armstrong to Robert Andrew, 15 April 1972; TNA: FCO 41/987 Prime Minister's Meeting with President Nixon, Brief No. 3, T. L. A. Daunt to B. M. Norbury, 1 December, 1972.

176 TNA: FCO 28/2027 Killick to FCO, 16 May 1972; TNA: FCO 28/2027 Killick to FCO, 24 May 1972; TNA: PREM 15/775 S. Zuckerman to the Prime Minister, 17 May 1972.

177 TNA: FCO 28/2027 Denis Greenhill to Thomas Brimelow, 8 March 1972.

178 TNA: FCO 28/2028 Douglas-Home to Washington, 13 June 1972; TNA: FCO 28/2028 H. T. A. Overton to T. A. K. Elliott, 9 June 1972.

179 On the details of both agreements see: Lawrence Freedman, *The Evolution of Nuclear Strategy* (Basingstoke: Palgrave Macmillan, 2003 3rd edition), pp. 391–7.

180 Memorandum of Conversation, 15 February 1972, *FRUS 1969–1976, Soviet Union*, Vol. XIV, Doc. 51, pp. 179–80; Memorandum from Helmut Sonnenfeldt of the National Security Council Staff to the President's Assistant for National Security Affairs [Kissinger], 5 April 1972, *ibid.*, Doc. 83, pp. 260–1, notes 2, 3, 4.

181 TNA: FCO 82/205 President [Nixon] to the Prime Minister, 8 June 1972.

182 Address to a Joint Session of the Congress on Return from Austria, the Soviet Union, Iran, and Poland, 1 June 1972, *Public Papers of the Presidents of the United States: Richard Nixon, 1972* (Washington: United States Government Printing Office, 1974), Doc. 188, p. 664.

183 TNA: FCO 41/987 Prime Minister's Meeting with President Nixon, Brief No. 3, attached to T. L. A. Daunt to B. M. Norbury, 1 December, 1972.

184 Rodman, *Presidential Command*, pp. 106–7.

185 TNA: CAB 133/408 Note of a Meeting held in Sir Denis Greenhill's Office, 25 June 1971. Also see: Douglas-Home's comments in: Sir A. Douglas-Home to Sir D. Wilson, 1 December 1970, G. Bennett and K. A. Hamilton, *Documents on British Policy Overseas: Britain and the Soviet Union 1968–1972* (London: The Stationery Office, 1997), Vol. I, Doc. 57, pp. 287–9; Ambassador in London to Secretary of State, Tel. London 402, 16 January 1970, RG 59 General Records of the Department of State, Subject Numeric Files 1970–73, Political & Defense, Box 2848, NAII.

186 US Mission NATO [Kennedy] to the Secretary of State [Rogers], June 1972, RG 59 General Records of the Department of State, Entry 1613, Box 2703, NAII.

187 Memorandum from the President's File from Henry A. Kissinger, 28 July 1972, President's Office Files, Memoranda for the President, Box 89, NPMP.

188 For the Secretary [Rogers] from Ambassador Kennedy, Tel. USNATO 3570, September 1972, National Security Council Files, Henry A. Kissinger Office Files, HAK Trip Files, Box 24, NPMP.

189 Memorandum for the President from the Secretary of State, 23 September 1972, RG 59 General Records of the Department of State, Subject Numeric Files, 1970–73, Box 2649, NAII.
190 TNA: FCO 28/2029 JIC(A)(72)(CIG)191, 5 June 1972.
191 For British concerns see: TNA: FCO 82/197 P. Craddock to Burke Trend, 18 September 1972.
192 Scott, *Allies Apart*, pp. 15–16.
193 TNA: FCO 28/2028 President Nixon's visit to Moscow: Brief for Cabinet, 6 June 1972.
194 Memorandum from the President's Assistant for National Security Affairs [Kissinger] to President Nixon, 24 December, 1969, *Foreign Relations of the United States 1969–1976: Soviet Union, January 1969–October 1970* (Washington: United States Government Printing Office, 2006), Vol. XII, Doc. 110, p. 338; Memorandum of Conversation, 22 April 1972, *FRUS 1969–1976, Soviet Union*, Vol. XIV, Doc. 139, p. 532. This memorandum in *FRUS* differs from the one available in the US archive. See: Memorandum of Conversation 22 April 1972, National Security Council Files, Henry A. Kissinger Office Files, Country Files-Europe–USSR, Box 72, NPMP.
195 Svetlana Savranskaya, 'Unintended Consequences: Soviet Interests, Expectations and Reactions to the Helsinki Final Act', in Oliver Bange and Gottfried Niedhart (eds.), *Helsinki 1975 and the Transformation of Europe* (Oxford: Berghahn Books, 2008), pp. 175–8.
196 Memorandum for the President from Henry Kissinger: NSC Consideration of NATO Issues, Mutual Force Reductions, European Security Conference, undated (circa October 1971), NSCIHF, National Security Council Meetings, Box H-032, NPMP.
197 NSC Consideration of NATO Issues, Mutual Force Reductions, European Security Conference, Memorandum for the President from Henry Kissinger, undated (circa October 1971), NSCIHF, National Security Council Meetings, Box H-032, NPMP. There is a burgeoning literature about the CSCE. For a good overview see: Angela Romano, *From Détente in Europe to European Détente: How the West Shaped the Helsinki CSCE* (London: Peter Lang, 2009).
198 William G. Hyland, *Mortal Rivals: Superpower Relations from Nixon to Reagan* (New York: Random House, 1987), p. 114.
199 Editorial Note, *Foreign Relations of the United States 1969–1976, European Security* (Washington: United States Government Printing Office, 2008), Vol. XXXIX, Doc. 108, p. 327; Memorandum of Conversation, 22 March 1974, *ibid.*, Doc. 192, p. 573; Memorandum of Conversation, 28 August 1974, *ibid.*, Doc. 245, p. 717; Minutes of Secretary of State Kissinger's Staff Meeting, 5 December, 1974, *ibid.*, Doc. 262, pp. 763–7; Memorandum of Conversation, 30 January 1975, *ibid.*, Doc. 269, p. 786; Memorandum of Conversation, 16 February 1975, *ibid.*, Doc. 270, p. 792; Memorandum of Conversation, 15 August 1974, *ibid.*, Doc. 243, p. 713.
200 Garthoff, *Détente and Confrontation*, p. 532; Angela Romano, 'Détente, Entente, or Linkage? The Helsinki Conference on Security and Cooperation in Europe in U.S. Relations with the Soviet Union', *Diplomatic History*, 33:4 (2009), 703–22.
201 Jussi Hanhimäki, '"They Can Write it in Swahili": Kissinger, the Soviets, and the Helsinki Accords, 1973–1975', *The Journal of Transatlantic Studies*, 1:1 (2003), 37–58; Michael Cotey Morgan, 'The United States and the Making of the Helsinki Final Act' in Logevall and Preston (eds.), *Nixon in the World*, p. 178. On Kissinger's espousal of such

thinking see: European Security Issues, Background Paper, Part 1, President's Trip Files, National Security Council Files, Box 667, NPMP; NSC Consideration of NATO Issues, Mutual Force Reductions, European Security Conference, Memorandum for the President from Henry Kissinger, undated (circa October 1971), NSCIHF, National Security Council Meetings, Box H-032, NPMP.

202 Memorandum of Conversation, 3 October 1970, RG 59 General Records of the Department of State, Subject Numeric Files, 1970–73, Political and Defense, Box 2650, NAII; TNA: FCO 30/1744 Record of Conversation between the Foreign and Commonwealth Secretary and the United States Secretary of State, 1 February 1973.

203 TNA: FCO 7/1814 Record of a Meeting held at Chequers, 3 October 1970.

204 TNA: FCO 82/197 Record of Conversation, 14 September 1972; TNA: PREM 15/1273 Record of Conversation between the Foreign and Commonwealth Secretary and Dr Henry Kissinger, 14 September 1972. On broader European developments towards the CSCE see: Bange and Niedhart (eds.), *Helsinki 1975*; Romano, *From Détente in Europe*; Richard Davy, 'Helsinki Myths: Setting the Record Straight on the Final Act of the CSCE, 1975', *Cold War History*, 9:1 (2009), 1–22; Romano, 'Détente, Entente, or Linkage?'; Douglas E. Selvage, 'Transforming the Soviet Sphere of Influence? U.S.-Soviet Détente and Eastern Europe, 1969–1976', *Diplomatic History*, 33:4 (2009), 671–88.

205 For British thinking see: Record of the Seventh Meeting of the Conference of HM representatives in Eastern Europe, 8 May 1970, in G. Bennett and K. A. Hamilton, *Documents on British Policy Overseas: Détente in Europe, 1972–1976* (London: The Stationery Office, 2001), Vol. III, Doc. 46, p. 19; Minute from Mr Tickell to Mr Wiggin, 6 March 1972, *ibid.*, Doc. 2, pp. 16–18; Record of the Seventh Meeting of the Conference of HM representatives in Eastern Europe, 8 May 1970, in G. Bennett and K. A. Hamilton, *Documents on British Policy Overseas: Britain and the Soviet Union 1968–1972* (London: The Stationery Office, 1997), Vol. I, Doc. 46, p. 235. For the quote see: Ambassador in Bonn Embassy to Secretary of State, Tel. Bonn 1299, January 1972, NSCIHF, Study Memorandums, NSCSM, Box H-171, NPMP. Also see: Ambassador in London Embassy to Secretary of State, Tel. London 9567, October 1971, NSCIHF, Study Memorandums, National Security Study Memorandums, Box H-187, NPMP; CSCE Interagency Task Force: Interim Report, 3 March 1972, NSCIHF, Meeting Files, Senior Review Group Meetings, Box H-061, NPMP.

206 Romano, *From Détente in Europe*, pp. 85–9.

207 TNA: FCO 82/193 Denis Greenhill to Thomas Brimelow, 2 October 1972.

208 For quote see: Analytical Summary: MBFR and CSCE, attached to Memorandum for Dr Kissinger from Helmut Sonnenfeldt and Phil Odeen, 24 March 1972, NSCIHF, Meeting Files, Senior Review Group Meetings, Box H-061, NPMP. Also see: CSCE Interagency Task Force: Interim Report, 3 March 1972, NSCIHF, Meeting Files, Senior Review Group Meetings, Box H-061, NPMP; TNA: FCO 44/533 Record of a Conversation between the Foreign and Commonwealth Secretary and Mr William Rogers, 20 December 1971.

209 NSDM 162: Presidential Guidance on Mutual and Balanced Force Reduction and a European Conference, 2 December 1971, NSCIHF, National Security Council Files, Box H-032, NPMP.

210 TNA: PREM 15/1272 Record of Discussion with Dr Kissinger, 28 July 1972.

211 In opposition to the assessments of: Hynes, *The Year*; Rossbach, *Rebirth*.
212 Discussion between John McCloy and Henry Kissinger, 11 November 1971, White House Tapes, Tape 014–062a, from: http://nixontapes.org (Accessed 11 September 2009).
213 TNA: DEFE 48/513 DOAE Project 147: Analysis of US MBFR Proposals, Dr D. P. Dare et al., September 1971, Table V.
214 TNA: FCO 7/1814 Record of a Meeting held at Chequers, 3 October 1970; TNA: PREM 15/1272 Burke Trend to Prime Minister, 23 June 1971, Brief No. 1.
215 Memorandum for the President from Henry A. Kissinger, undated, NSCIHF, Meeting Files, Senior Review Group Meetings, Box H-061, NPMP.
216 Memorandum for the President from Henry A. Kissinger, undated, NSCIHF, Meeting Files, Senior Review Group Meetings, Box H-061, NPMP.
217 Lawrence S. Kaplan, *NATO Divided, NATO United: The Evolution of an Alliance* (Westport: Praeger, 2004), pp. 51–4; Hubert Zimmermann, 'The Improbable Permanence of a Commitment: America's Troop Presence in Europe During the Cold War', *Journal of Cold War Studies*, 11:1 (2009), 19–26.
218 Van Atta, *Melvin Laird*, pp. 288–9.
219 Memorandum for the President from Henry A. Kissinger, undated, NSCIHF, Meeting Files, Senior Review Group Meetings, Box H-061, NPMP; Guy de Jonquières, 'Urgent Moves in the U.S. to Save Some of Aid Programme', *Financial Times*, 1 November 1971, p. 1.
220 Memorandum for the President from Henry A. Kissinger, undated, NSCIHF, Meeting Files, Senior Review Group Meetings, Box H-061, NPMP.
221 A number of works have focused more keenly upon the interplay between domestic politics and their influence on the course of US foreign policy. For the best overviews see: Melvin Small, *Democracy and Diplomacy: The Impact of Domestic Politics on U.S. Foreign Policy, 1789–1994* (Baltimore: Johns Hopkins University Press, 1996); Julian E. Zelizer, *Arsenals of Democracy: The Politics of National Security – From World War II to the War on Terrorism* (New York: Basic Books, 2010).
222 Zimmermann, 'The Improbable Permanence', 23.
223 TNA: DEFE 13/880 C [Lord Carrington] to CDS [Admiral Peter Hill-Norton], 17 May 1971; TNA: DEFE 13/880 C [Lord Carrington] to CDS [Admiral Peter Hill-Norton], 16 August 1971.
224 From Ambassador in London Embassy to the Secretary of State, Tel. London 6728, July 1971, RG 59 General Records of the Department of State, Subject Numeric Files, 1970–73, Political & Defense, Box 2658, NAII. Also see: Memorandum for Henry Kissinger from John Irwin, 17 September 1971, NSCIHF, Study Memorandums, National Security Study Memorandums, Box H-171, NPMP.
225 TNA: PREM 15/1272 Brief No. 1, Burke Trend to Prime Minister, 23 June 1971; TNA: FCO 82/71 Record of a Conversation between the Foreign and Commonwealth Secretary and Mr William Rogers, 20 December, 1971.
226 Memorandum for Dr Kissinger from K. Wayne Smith, 16 February 1971, NSCIHF, Study Memorandums, NSCSM, Box H-167, NPMP.
227 For the quote see: TNA: FCO 82/71 Record of Plenary Session between the UK and US Delegation, 21 December 1971. Further British complaints are within: Annual Assessment for the United Kingdom, From the Ambassador in London to the Secretary

of State, 14 February 1972, RG 59 General Records of the Department of State, Subject Numeric Files, 1970–73, Political & Defense, Box 2658, NAII; Memorandum for Dr Kissinger from Helmut Sonnenfeldt and Phil Odeen, 24 March 1972, NSCIHF, Meeting Files, Senior Review Group Meetings, Box H-061, NPMP.

228 Such examples include: Hynes, *The Year*; Rossbach, *Rebirth*.

229 See Heath's public speech to this effect contained within TNA: FCO 7/1837 Freeman to Foreign and Commonwealth Office, 23 December, 1970. For Heath articulating his support for Nixon's Vietnam policies see TNA: FCO 7/1815 Record of a Meeting between the Prime Minister and President Nixon at Chequers, 3 October 1970.

230 TNA: FCO 82/1884 P. R. H. Wright to D. F. Murray, 14 July 1972; John Dickie, *How British Foreign Policy Works* (London: I.B. Tauris, 2004), pp. 105–7; Richard J. Aldrich, *GCHQ: The Uncensored Story of Britain's Most Secret Intelligence Agency* (London: HarperPress, 2010), pp. 277–366; Baylis, 'Moscow Criterion'.

231 'Nixon's Appeal', *Daily Telegraph*, 21 January 1969, p. 16.

# 3

# A year of discord
## 1973–74

*No special relations. Correct. They'll [Britain] have the relation with the French.*

President Nixon to Henry Kissinger, 9 August 1973[1]

## A year of discord

At the onset of 1973, the US–UK relationship was entering a new epoch. The East of Suez withdrawal had lessened Britain's global commitments and Britain officially entered the EEC on 1 January 1973. Heath was determined to chart a more Euro-centric British foreign policy, which would involve the creation of common political, foreign, monetary and energy policies within the EEC. The US had also undergone a re-assessment of its global position and the Nixon administration had reconfigured US foreign policy with its détente agenda. The Paris Peace Accords (January 1973) officially ended the US's involvement in Vietnam, and superpower détente had resulted in the opening to the PRC and the establishment of US–Soviet bilateral diplomacy. 1973, therefore, presented new circumstances in which US–UK relations would be conducted, and it was the adaptation to this that created a number of problems for US–UK relations.[2]

First, Britain's membership of the EEC created procedural difficulties for bilateral interaction, given that the EEC was seeking to produce common policies on a plethora of topics, including monetary, trade and energy cooperation. It also envisaged the establishment of common political and foreign policies. How the US would interact with the expanded EEC was a source of continued difficulty for American and British policy-makers. Aside from procedural problems, Heath was determined to operate as a fully-fledged member of the EEC. This meant that US–UK diplomacy could not be an avenue for solving US–EEC matters. This was another area which caused much angst in Washington and led to profound consequences for US–UK relations, including the short-term postponement of nuclear and intelligence cooperation.

All of these US–UK difficulties were surrounded by the gradual erosion of President Nixon's authority because of the Watergate scandal.[3] Even though Kissinger would dismiss Watergate as a 'school boy prank' and equated it to 'a bunch of dogs snapping at the heels' of the president, the issue would soon dominate Nixon's agenda.[4] It was, as Kissinger noted, obvious that foreign policy issues were no longer Nixon's top priority, and testament to this is that the annotations and comments the president had always provided on briefing papers were now no longer made. Nixon – who was seriously considering firing Kissinger at the beginning of 1973, and who had promoted James Schlesinger to defense secretary in part to temper Kissinger's dominance of foreign policy – reluctantly accepted that US foreign policy would largely be directed by Henry Kissinger.[5]

Watergate and the impact it had upon the foreign policy decisions taken by the Nixon administration would also have a malign impact upon US–UK relations. For instance, UK policy in a number of areas was informed by the president's domestic problems. One of the most important was the bearing it had upon Heath's decision to upgrade Polaris. Likewise, US foreign policy decisions could hardly be immune from Watergate. US policy-makers believed that Nixon's domestic troubles explained, in part, why Britain refused to embrace the 'Year of Europe'. Such beliefs contributed to the more antagonistic policies undertaken by the US throughout 1973–74.[6]

This chapter is broken into three parts with the 'Year of Europe' comprising the opening third. Following this is an assessment of US–UK relations during the fourth Arab–Israeli war. Finally, the oil crisis which followed, along with the Washington Energy Conference of February 1974, which was convened to solve this, are analysed within the context of US–UK relations. For US–UK relations, the common theme throughout 1973–74 is largely one of acrimony. British policy-makers, including the prime minister, believed Kissinger's 'Year of Europe' was a ploy designed to dominate the nascent common foreign policy of the EEC. For their part, US policy-makers believed that a valuable bilateral relationship with the UK was being replaced by one built upon distrust and competition. The seriousness of such political disputes resulted in the more practical aspects of US–UK cooperation being affected. On two occasions, the US temporarily halted intelligence and nuclear cooperation because of broader political disagreements. This occurred as a form of political punishment, but it was also seen as a policy tool by Kissinger. In sum, Kissinger utilised US–UK bilateral cooperation as a means of encouraging the British to take a less hostile approach to American political initiatives. This was witnessed during the 'Year of Europe' as a means of altering the perceived antagonistic policies of the British government; in the immediate aftermath of the fourth Arab–Israeli war, in order to prevent the British pursuing a policy which would undermine Kissinger's 'shuttle diplomacy'; and throughout the Washington Energy Conference, as a means of ensuring that the British government supported Washington's energy proposals. This coercive element in Kissinger's foreign policy is something traditionally associated with his approach in relation to America's adversaries, but, as shown below, it was applied to America's British ally as well.[7]

In spite of these political differences, and serious bilateral disputes, US–UK cooperation continued in a number of highly sensitive realms. For instance, Kissinger tasked Thomas Brimelow with drafting the US–USSR Prevention of Nuclear War Agreement.[8] By November 1973, Heath had decided to upgrade Polaris. This required additional US assistance which Nixon approved in January 1974.[9] Finally, throughout the Washington Energy Conference of February 1974, the Heath government worked closely with the Nixon administration even at the cost of sacrificing EEC cohesiveness. This was largely done in order to protect Britain's oil interests. Presented below then is a picture which highlights an antagonistic relationship between the two countries, but one which, although strained to near breaking point, survived intact and, indeed, by the time Edward Heath left office in February 1974, had been reinvigorated by the nuclear agreements between the two sides.

## 'Year of Europe': Origins and motives

The 'Year of Europe' had its genesis in the autumn of 1972. The creation of superpower détente and finding a solution to the Vietnam War had dominated the agenda of the president's first term, and throughout the administration there was a belief that the US had somewhat neglected their relationship with Europe. As Donald Rumsfeld recollected, the fact that he was appointed as Nixon's third representative to NATO in February 1973 – following David Kennedy's resignation some eight months earlier – suggested that the Nixon 'administration's interest in [NATO] was at best modest'.[10] More important still was that Nixon believed that relations with Europe were taking on a new competitive form. Certainly, throughout 1969–72, the US–EEC economic relationship had manifested in fierce competition, and political changes that were evolving would present new challenges for US–EEC relations. The most pressing was that the EEC was seeking to formulate an independent voice in international affairs. Clearly, regardless of what form this actually took, it would have some bearing on the future course of US–EEC relations.

With EEC expansion confirmed at the beginning of 1973, Nixon sensed this was an opportune moment to address the situation.[11] What then did the recently re-elected president envisage? Simply, Nixon had the ambitious agenda to re-conceptualise US–EEC relations. In practical terms, this meant that all aspects of US–EEC relations would be dealt with as a whole; discussions pertaining to monetary or trade matters would no longer be conducted in total isolation from those in the military/security realm. This, in British circles, took the moniker of the 'one ball of wax thesis'.[12] It appeared, more appropriately, as an extension of Nixon's linkage approach to foreign policy. Linkage, as seen in US foreign policy towards the USSR, would now be more explicitly applied to Europe.

US motives behind the 'Year of Europe' created considerable debate, with Henry Kissinger providing his own weighty analysis. Kissinger suggested the initiative was required to revitalise relations with both Europe and NATO. NATO's conventional force position vis-à-vis the Warsaw Pact was steadily worsening and, in an age of nuclear parity, NATO's nuclear deterrent was deemed to have become less credible. US–EEC economic disputes were also jeopardising the political–military relationship. As such, a Declaration of Principles would be created. This would outline the future basis of US–EEC practices and overhaul NATO's conventional forces. Finally, it would prevent economic disputes having a detrimental impact on US–European political–military affairs.[13]

A number of authors have largely accepted Kissinger's argument.[14] Without doubt, one of the motivating factors behind the 'Year of Europe' was genuinely to improve NATO's force posture, given that both Nixon and Kissinger had raised serious concerns about NATO's capabilities ever since assuming office. Nixon had even opined that NATO was 'finished' unless a modernisation programme was undertaken and in February 1973 repeated such concerns.[15] Kissinger largely agreed with Nixon's view of NATO and had a long history, dating back to his time at Harvard, of suggesting that NATO needed to overhaul both its conventional and nuclear forces. Likewise, as a part-time adviser to the Kennedy administration, he had made similar arguments.[16]

Assessments drawn up for Kissinger in the 1970s only endorsed these pessimistic views. Two of Kissinger's aides, for instance, described NATO as 'decaying' and, during one conversation between Kissinger and secretary of defense James Schlesinger, both men agreed that a conventional arms attack by the Warsaw Pact would lead to the collapse of NATO![17] Attention upon NATO in 1973 was also consistent with earlier policy espousals, given that Kissinger had suggested in 1971 that once SALT and British membership to the EEC had been settled, the issues surrounding NATO would be tackled.[18] Therefore, at one level, the 'Year of Europe' can be viewed as an attempt to improve NATO.

Other commentators have interpreted Kissinger's motives differently, with Robert Dallek suggesting that the 'Year of Europe' was designed as a means to focus attention away from Watergate. Others have been more cynical in their interpretation of US motives with the argument being put forth that the

'Year of Europe' was devised to re-establish US 'hegemony' over Europe and to prevent the EEC challenging US leadership of the Atlantic alliance. For Mario Del Pero, Kissinger's policy was even darker. Kissinger employed 'classical realist' traits in seeking to 'divide and rule' the EEC, which would ensure that the EEC's attempts to establish a common foreign policy would not be formed on an independent basis. Rather, it would accord, generally, to the contours of US wishes and, even more importantly, would not be able to challenge US primacy within the Atlantic alliance.[19]

Watergate as an explanation for Kissinger's 'Year of Europe' is only part of the story. While domestic factors can have a strong influence upon the course of US foreign policy, and were certainly important during the Nixon administration, the reality is that the 'Year of Europe' had its origins in September 1972, some five months *before* Watergate became a political problem for the president.[20] This chapter also rejects the argument that the 'Year of Europe' was a means of ensuring US hegemony over the EEC's emerging common foreign policy. No archival evidence is used to support these claims and there is also little wider evidence provided that convincingly illustrates that the 'Year of Europe' was designed to ensure the US could dominate the EEC.

As Kissinger suggested in his memoirs, the 'Year of Europe' was calculated to re-invigorate NATO and to provide a symbolic gesture of Atlantic solidarity.[21] This was not, however, the sole intention behind the project. Rather, the president and Kissinger decided that a 'Year of Europe' was necessary in order to encapsulate all aspects of US–EEC relations. This meant that the continuing imbalance between the military contributions of the US and the European powers to the defence of Europe could no longer persist. The expansion of the EEC meant trade and monetary practices which were disadvantageous to the United States could not be negotiated in complete isolation from military-security matters. US policy, therefore, sought to ensure that the EEC could not continue to operate bilaterally in the economic realm, whilst still expecting the US to contribute so considerably to Europe's defence needs. In sum, the Nixon–Kissinger theory of linkage was to be applied to US–EEC relations.[22] Kissinger himself best summarised the US objectives in conversation with Nixon:

> Eventually we can force them [EEC] into a position where they have to talk to us on these matters [economics], or we will talk separately on our matters. And they can't insist that MBFR, nuclear treaty, and so forth, we cannot operate without consultation ... I would use this, at least – at a minimum, you'll get out of it a better tone in the other discussion.[23]

This does not mean, however, that the 'Year of Europe' was designed to enforce US hegemony over Europe. Certainly, Nixon and Kissinger wanted to ensure that the US remained the dominant partner within NATO. This, however, would not be achieved by dividing and ruling the EEC. Rather, in their assessment, this would occur naturally because of simple power realities. It should be pointed out that documentary evidence does exist that illustrates that the US was seeking to 'divide and rule' the EEC. Nevertheless, this was not the original intention of the 'Year of Europe' project. Rather, it was simply a tactic that was employed once US policy-makers realised that the EEC was not going to cooperate in producing their much-wanted Declaration of Principles. The ultimate objective was not to divide the EEC; it was to reconfigure US–EEC relations that accepted the new economic, military and political realities of the alliance.

Gaining economic advantage from Europe's reliance upon US military guarantees was also a peripheral objective of the 'Year of Europe'. Nixon was not prepared to forfeit the political relationship with Europe solely to achieve economic advantages.[24] This was a position Kissinger agreed with. As one of Kissinger's closest advisers reminded him, it was not in the interests of the US to sacrifice the US–European security relationship for 'citrus fruits'.[25] For Kissinger, political considerations would predominantly outweigh economic factors. US policy sought to mitigate the economic consequences of EEC expansion, but this would not be achieved at the cost of permanently alienating America's European allies.

## Theory and practice

In September 1972, Nixon discussed his intention to refocus upon US–European relations once his re-election had been guaranteed.[26] Such thinking was rapidly transmitted to British officials, and was positively met, with Burke Trend informing Kissinger that such an initiative would be welcome.[27] With Nixon securing his re-election in November 1972, this re-appraisal began. However, the atmosphere for such an initiative was less than ideal given that the US Christmas bombing campaign of North Vietnam had been roundly condemned by Europe's leaders. This soured Nixon's opinion towards such critics and, indeed, made him re-assess the nature of the entire NATO alliance.[28] As Nixon articulated in conversation, NATO 'had been an alliance of interest and friendship'; now it was 'just an alliance of interest'.[29] Clearly the president's personal feelings towards European leaders were less than ideal for re-affirming the solidarity of transatlantic relations, but the exception to this was Nixon's attitude towards Edward Heath. Heath's personal relationship with Nixon may have ended in 'mutual contempt' but at the beginning of 1973 Heath was held in high regard by the president. Heath, alone amongst European leaders, had given his public support for US actions in Vietnam, and such support had not gone unnoticed in the White House.[30] British officials observed that Nixon's attitude towards Heath had warmed. Indeed, Lord Cromer suggested Nixon viewed Britain as the 'blue eyed boy'.[31]

Heath's visit to Washington and Camp David in February 1973 presented an opportunity to exploit this favourability. Kissinger termed the visit 'interesting but inconclusive'.[32] The minutes of the meetings largely corroborate Kissinger's assessment as decisions pertaining to nuclear cooperation, trade, monetary reform and re-configuring NATO's force posture were all deferred for a future date.[33] It was only on the issue of the CSCE and MBFR that real policy differences were discussed. With SALT achieved, a peace treaty signed in Vietnam and the establishment of triangular diplomacy, Nixon was now determined to settle other matters. In particular, the president wanted progress on SALT II and on MBFR. To support such ambitions, Nixon and Kissinger envisaged some type of linkage between the MBFR and CSCE negotiations.[34] They argued that the CSCE should be quickly settled, on the proviso that MBFR negotiations would begin soon after. In anticipation of this, Nixon wanted NATO to agree upon their MBFR objectives, with September 1973 being given as a final date by which this should all be settled by.[35]

The Nixon–Heath meeting also indicated that the US would no longer tolerate the criticism it had received for trying to settle a number of East–West issues. Kissinger argued that SALT and MBFR were necessary, both for domestic and strategic reasons, and that he would not accept open hostility to them from America's allies. Kissinger warned Heath:

> Europe really must stop being so suspicious about the risk of a bilateral deal between the Soviet and United States Governments in this matter. If the Europeans went on pestering Washington on this issue, the United States Government might be driven to the point where they had no alternative but actually to conclude a deal of this kind.[36]

In April, Kissinger repeated a similar message to Trend.[37] This was in general accordance with Kissinger's private complaints about Britain's attitude towards SALT and MBFR. According to Kissinger, the British had a 'desire to be a spokesman in NATO against the US'.[38]

This shift in emphasis towards the CSCE and MBFR left Heath's government uneasy. Certainly, Heath had sought a swift resolution to the CSCE since 1970, but since then two years had passed and the negotiations had become broader in scope and more complicated in design. For the British, trying to find a common Western negotiating platform in Kissinger's timeframe would be difficult, and even more concerning for British policy-makers was the possibility that a hasty settlement could result in the West agreeing to terms not properly considered.[39] This is a point which Trend and Sykes conveyed to Kissinger in June 1973, but they were unable to convince him of the merits of their argument.[40] As the year progressed, the CSCE and MBFR discussions became ensnared in wider US–UK difficulties pertaining to the 'Year of Europe'. What were once seen as 'natural' policy differences had now assumed vital significance.

During the Camp David talks, Nixon took the opportunity to explain how the following year would be used to refocus upon the US–European alliance. Nixon revealed his preferred method for implementing such changes: 'We must try to recreate the wartime habit of getting together for really intimate and deep discussions in a relaxed atmosphere – discussions which range over the whole field of the problems, political, military and economic, which we faced together.'[41] Heath's response is not recorded in the British memorandum of the conversation, but his subsequent actions indicated his disinclination to react positively to such a proposition because the prime minister told his Cabinet colleagues that Britain should cooperate with the US only after full consultation with Britain's EEC partners.[42] Given his determination for Britain to act as a fully-fledged member of the EEC, it would have been contradictory for Heath to have agreed to solve US–EEC matters on a US–UK basis. Nevertheless, it should not be overlooked that Heath had not ruled out negotiations. Heath simply differed with Nixon on how these would be conducted. Given this, the *Daily Telegraph* newspaper was quite correct to predict that 'hard bargaining' between the US and the EEC lay ahead.[43]

Heath may have been averse to operating bilaterally with the US, but the opposite impression was transmitted to Washington. On 5 March 1973, British officials met with Kissinger and Nixon's plans for US–EEC relations were discussed. Kissinger suggested private US–UK talks be held to discuss the subject and the British delegation gave their approval. The British record of this meeting does not explicitly state that agreement was given to Kissinger's proposal but from the memorandum of the meeting this obviously occurred because Trend enquired when this meeting should convene. Secondly, the FCO's internal history on the 'Year of Europe' noted that British agreement to Kissinger's offer was given during this meeting.[44]

Within the British policy-making bureaucracy there was an element of disagreement (or misunderstanding) over the direction of British policy. Heath was opposed to US–UK bilateralism for solving matters concerning the EEC. Heath's officials, however, had given the reverse impression to Kissinger, and this is a point which existing scholarship has crucially overlooked. British policy, as articulated to Kissinger, ran contrary to Heath's wishes, and it was this contradiction in British policy that would contribute to the US–UK diplomatic furore throughout the summer of 1973.

Kissinger launched the 'Year of Europe' publicly on 23 April 1973 in a speech that had not even been seen by the State Department prior to its announcement.[45] Perhaps if it had, the speech writers would have worded his statements a little more delicately as the announcement for a 'Year of Europe' caused enormous offence in European capitals. Kissinger proposed that the US and the EEC would issue a Declaration of Principles which would institutionalise US–EEC relations. This would be achieved by interconnecting all aspects of US–EEC interaction in some type of formal document, which would then be signed by the respective leaders later in the year. Kissinger also envisaged that the 'Year of Europe' would encompass an overhaul of NATO's military structure. It is interesting to note that Kissinger's proposals had distinct similarities with earlier arguments he had made prior to obtaining office. Also, a National Security Council study memorandum, composed in July 1970, had many similarities. Kissinger's initiative appears, therefore, to have been the manifestation of his earlier thinking.[46]

Kissinger's speech, however, contained a less than flattering analysis about the role Europe could play on the global stage. In private, Kissinger had described Europe as 'basically irrelevant' in shaping global events. The president and other senior US officials were also expressing similar sentiments.[47] Kissinger's analysis of Europe in his speech, while not as blunt as those espoused privately, did make it clear that Europe's interests were strictly regional whereas, in contrast, the US had global interests and responsibilities. Such insights, even if accurate, hardly created the ideal atmosphere for re-confirming Atlantic solidarity, or, more importantly, winning support for his proposals. As Kissinger retrospectively acknowledged, 'It may not have been wise to make reality explicit'.[48] Indeed, it appeared so and, as Raymond Garthoff has pointed out, 'The Europeans were not amused to be assigned a "year" by the Americans'.[49] This certainly applied to Heath, who was furious with Kissinger. 'For Henry Kissinger to announce a Year of Europe without consulting any of us was rather like my standing between the lions in Trafalgar Square and announcing that we were embarking on a year to save America,' Heath lambasted.[50] Another unnamed European official equated Kissinger's proposal as akin to an unfaithful husband's declaration of a 'year of the wife'.[51]

In spite of Heath's personal intransigence, Kissinger's proposal was given serious attention in British circles. Cromer sent his opinion to London, explaining that Kissinger wanted the declaration to produce substantive conclusions, rather than woolly phraseology. Britain would, thus, have to respond in this spirit and do so in a timely fashion, given that the US was eagerly awaiting the European response. Trend produced a similar analysis for the prime minister. As Trend advised Heath, despite its vague content and other shortcomings, 'it would not be in our interest to rebuff' Kissinger's proposals. As he further warned the prime minister, the Nixon administration was attaching significant importance to this project, and the British would thus be wise to react accordingly.[52] Indeed, few could be in any doubt as to the degree of importance Nixon was personally attaching to the 'Year of Europe' as he made it known to the media that he desired the Europeans to respond in the same spirit as that which greeted the Marshall Plan in 1947.[53]

The president was soon to be disappointed by the European response. 'The speech is clearly an important one with a constructive intent' was the FCO's public reaction.[54] Privately within the FCO, a rather more cautious attitude was adopted. For the MOD, the proposals were welcome as long as the initiative brought real improvements to NATO. The majority of British scepticism emanated from the Treasury, which feared that an all-encompassing declaration would result in Kissinger exploiting Europe's reliance on US security guarantees to the economic advantage of the US. The Treasury was also nonplussed at the American initiative because it trampled over European efforts to coordinate EEC monetary policy. In April 1973, a European reserve fund had been established that was designed to streamline EEC monetary policy, yet Kissinger's ambition to seek US–EEC monetary reform would clearly challenge this.[55]

The concern that the US would use its military contributions to Europe for economic gain was not unique to the Treasury. Senior policy-makers and officials across various departments, including the prime minister, were sceptical of establishing a single framework in which US–EEC relations should be conducted.[56] As Paul Lewis, the US editor for the *Financial Times*, perceptively noted:

> Dr Kissinger clearly implies a connection between the economic concessions the US wants from the Common Market and its readiness to remain committed to Europe's defence – although this 'linkage' has always been opposed by the Europeans.[57]

Though British officials differed with Kissinger on the substance of a Declaration of Principles, they had not rejected its creation. Instead, they wanted further negotiations on the subject. How this would be done created a problem for the prime minister. Heath wanted to fully consult his EEC partners about wider US–EEC negotiations. The obvious problem of pursuing such a course was that the EEC had no foreign minister who could undertake this task. Kissinger therefore proposed that the declaration could be negotiated bilaterally with individual EEC members, yet when Nixon had suggested such a course earlier in the year Heath had been against it. The prime minister's position appears not to have concerned Burke Trend all that much given that in May 1973 he again expressed British interest in bilateral discussions. Trend did add some caveats to his support, warning that it would be difficult to persuade France to support Kissinger's ideas. As such, it was preferable for Kissinger alone to convince the French of his plans. Regardless, the fact remained that British officials had again indicated their support for Kissinger's bilateral approach in creating some sort of declaration.[58]

What is curious about all of this is that Heath was being supplied with full briefings of the Trend–Kissinger meetings. Why then did the prime minister never instruct Trend to inform Kissinger of his true thinking regarding the creation of the declaration? Perhaps Heath simply never read the relevant papers. Alternatively, the prime minister could have felt it was a matter that was easily reconcilable. Maybe, however, Heath was happy for Trend to mislead Kissinger in order to avoid any recriminations. Whatever the reason behind this confusion, the point remained that Kissinger believed the UK was willing to operate bilaterally in establishing a declaration. Such evidence undermines arguments that it was the 'obsessive secrecy' of the Nixon administration that created US–UK misunderstandings throughout the 'Year of Europe'.[59] These arguments have largely accepted the accusations levelled at the Nixon administration by British officials at the time. Not surprisingly, these officials blamed their US counterparts for US–UK antagonism and failed to highlight how their own actions may have contributed to difficulties. On closer inspection of the documentary record, it becomes apparent that the British government's own bureaucratic inertia was just as instrumental in creating the US–UK misunderstanding.

## British reversal

This Trend–Kissinger agreement collapsed in the following months and US–UK bilateral discussion on the declaration also came to a halt. Kissinger has suggested that British membership of the EEC explains this. According to Kissinger, the need to appear as a 'good European' resulted in Britain following the French, who had taken an extremely negative attitude towards the idea. US–UK bilateralism was therefore stopped to appease French wishes.[60] This argument is not without merit as the prime minister was certainly concerned with causing an Anglo–French dispute because of the 'Year of Europe' concept.[61] The French factor was, however, just one determinant behind the British reversal in operating bilaterally with the US. Two fundamentally important reasons were also behind this reversal. First, Heath had never supported the bilateral approach and, secondly, British officials who gave their agreement to operate bilaterally in creating the declaration began to question Kissinger's motives and decided bilateralism was a dangerous path to pursue. As the year progressed, Kissinger's declaration was no longer seen as an opportunity to reconfigure US–EEC relations, but rather as a device in which Kissinger could, at best, ensure American primacy within the alliance. At worse, it was seen as a US attempt to establish a new framework for US–EEC relations that would allow the US to dominate the nascent common foreign policy of the EEC and extract preferential economic treatment from the EEC.

In May 1973, Heath departed for Paris where he discussed the declaration with the French president, Georges Pompidou. French scepticism towards the project was evident and Pompidou even alleged it was a Kissinger ploy to 'divide and rule' the EEC. Less cynically, Pompidou suggested that it was designed to flatter the ego of President Nixon. Interestingly, Heath rejected this assessment and made a robust defence of the US-inspired 'Year of Europe' and then urged Pompidou to undertake the necessary preparatory measures so the project could seriously progress. Such appeals, however, made little impression upon the French president.[62]

Subsequently, when Heath returned to London he convened a meeting of the European Unit. Here, the 'Year of Europe', France's attitude, and the likely consequences for British interests were discussed at length. After much deliberation, the prime minister concluded that the British tactic would be to 'lie low'. Only once Pompidou's meeting with Nixon (scheduled for 30 May to 1 June 1973 in Reykjavik) was finished could a firm British response to the 'Year of Europe' proposals be put forward.[63] This, then, was the beginning of the British decision to reverse bilateral cooperation with the US over the 'Year of Europe'.

Following the US–Franco summit in Reykjavik, the French foreign minister Michel Jobert publicly rejected Kissinger's desired procedural process for creating a declaration.[64] For Heath this was troublesome, as he realised that any sort of US–French confrontation over the 'Year of Europe' was likely to force the British to 'takes sides' and harm British interests. Heath, therefore, came to the conclusion that the best way to safeguard the British position was to react with a non-reaction. Consequently, London informed Washington that it would take no further action until this US–Franco disagreement had been resolved.[65] Jobert's public announcement also scuppered the ambitions of Trend and Brimelow. They had accepted the idea that US–UK working groups should be established to work on draft versions of the declaration but following Jobert's démarche, this idea was scrapped. Clearly, British policy was being influenced by France and, as Alistair Noble has rightly suggested, the 'British were anxious to demonstrate their European credentials'.[66]

In London, deliberation about the next course of action was the order of the day. Advice provided by Trend and the FCO still suggested that the British should react positively to Kissinger's 'Year of Europe' proposals, and that they needed to go some way to producing a draft version of the Declaration of Principles. As such, the British should ask Kissinger to provide them with a draft version of the declaration, from which they would then consult with West Germany and produce a response. Once UK–West German consultation had been completed, the two would then present their response to France, and from here tripartite discussions could commence and produce a unified European response to the 'Year of Europe'.[67]

The prime minister partially accepted this advice and instructed his officials to obtain a draft of the declaration from the US, which would then be discussed with the West Germans. However, Heath added the caveat that Britain should try to create two separate declarations which would specifically separate economic and security matters.[68] Unfortunately for the British, this plan quickly came unstuck, because the discussion of the draft declaration with the US and West Germans was to remain secret – yet, unbeknownst to the prime minister, the French had learned of these discussions. Thus, a rather embarrassing situation for Heath developed when he met with Jobert on 2 July 1973, and the French foreign minister made it clear that he knew of the UK–US–West German efforts to create a declaration, and that he was unhappy with the situation. Indeed, it appears as if a rather acrimonious discussion took place between Heath and Jobert, leaving the British in no doubt that the French were not prepared to establish a declaration in this fashion, and, moreover, the French even suggested that the creation of any declaration was unnecessary.[69] In spite of Jobert's reaction, the British decided that they would seek to win his support for the declaration later that month but they were simply wasting their time as Jobert again rebuffed any talk of creating a declaration. Added to this, the French remained angry with the British for trying to move forward with the 'Year of Europe' in a manner that would emphasise US–UK bilateralism. In their assessment, all of the members of the EEC had to act in unison, and would all have to be properly consulted before any progress towards creating a Declaration of Principles could be made.[70]

Heath's policy was now broken. He had sought to produce two declarations that would explicitly separate economic and security issues but, by attempting to push the process forward by engaging in US–UK and UK–West German bilateralism, he had attracted the scorn of France. With Heath's policy ruined, he altered course and decided that bilateralism could no longer continue and that the EEC would have to act as a collective. Consequently, Heath outlined to Nixon that US–UK bilateral discussions pertaining to the declaration would be transmitted to all EEC member states. Furthermore, UK–EEC discussion on the declaration would remain private, i.e. out of the purview of the US.[71] Heath had therefore effectively closed down the US–UK path for establishing the declaration.

In part, Heath was driven to this because he wanted to lessen French antagonism towards Britain. Heath also realised it would have been superfluous to have presented a US–UK agreement to France if it was likely to be rejected out of hand. The prime minister was, therefore, attempting to convince the French of the merits of the declaration, and from here a common EEC response to the US initiative could be given.[72] This does not, however, explain the entire situation. Heath, along with other senior policy-makers and officials, suspected from the outset of 1973 that the US could be tempted to extract preferential economic terms from the EEC by exploiting its continuing security commitments to Europe.[73] These deep-rooted anxieties began to come into the open as the year continued.

British policy-makers pointed to a number of actions in Kissinger's behaviour that suggested his policy towards the EEC was less than altruistic, and that his diplomacy was designed to exploit the differences between the EEC member states for the gain of the US. For instance, Kissinger had informed the British that a draft version of the declaration had been made exclusively available to them. Heath was concerned that Kissinger was being less than frank with him and he was right to be suspicious as Kissinger had established backchannel communications with French and West German officials, and in this realm he was also providing them with 'exclusive' draft versions of the declaration.[74]

Kissinger's rivalry with Secretary Rogers further contributed to British suspicions. Rogers contradicted Kissinger's claim that the Americans had not drafted different versions of the declaration, and had informed Douglas-Home that at least four competing versions existed. In contrast, Kissinger was claiming that he had only created one version of the declaration. Given this, it is easy to appreciate why the British reached the opinion that Kissinger was providing competing versions of the declaration to different countries in order to maximise his negotiating position.[75]

This, then, was the background in which Burke Trend was to liaise with Kissinger at the end of July 1973. Trend should have expected that this meeting was likely to be uncomfortable, because four days prior to his arrival Nixon had despatched a scathing letter to Heath. In it Nixon had lamented Heath's decision to cancel US–UK bilateralism for creating the declaration and outlined a number of other areas where US–UK relations were becoming difficult.[76] In his memoirs, Kissinger described his meeting with Trend as a 'painful session'.[77] This was somewhat of an understatement because the meeting descended into near acrimony. Nixon had instructed Kissinger to give Trend 'my worst' if he 'was being difficult'.[78] As the record of the meeting suggests, Trend, in Kissinger's analysis, was presumably 'being difficult'.

In the actual meeting, Trend refused to provide Kissinger with FCO memorandums of UK–EEC discussions about the declaration. 'If old friends treated the US Government like that, the US would deal with them as they did with Luxembourg,' Kissinger blasted. Kissinger continued with his warnings and explained that there would be 'major consequences' for the US–UK relationship if Heath insisted on making their bilateral conversations known to other EEC members.[79] This obviously had the desired effect because Trend, on a 'one time basis', handed the requested records to Kissinger.[80] That evening, Trend contacted Kissinger via telephone, and whilst the conversation was conciliatory in its tone, Kissinger's fundamental point, that US–UK bilateralism should be restored in order to create the declaration, remained. It was obvious now that whatever the intentions behind the 'Year of Europe', it had clearly turned 'into an adversary procedure'.[81]

Kissinger's behaviour in this meeting provoked a serious examination in British circles. Richard Sykes, who was present at the Kissinger–Trend encounter, sent his analysis to Thomas Brimelow and suggested that the pressure emanating from the Watergate scandal was forcing President Nixon to seek quick foreign policy successes. The slow British reaction towards the 'Year of Europe' had therefore angered the president and resulted in Kissinger's reaction.[82] Given the domestic problems engulfing Nixon, this was not an unreasonable conclusion. Nevertheless, this analysis fundamentally missed the point that from Kissinger's perspective the British had agreed to bilaterally discuss and draft the declaration. The British had reneged on this, and this, therefore, was the real source of the US's irritation toward Britain.

One day after the Kissinger–Trend meeting, Kissinger noted the 'Year of Europe' could go into 'low gear'.[83] The sincerity of this is betrayed by Kissinger's actions and he was still determined to establish some sort of substantive agreements. Kissinger now altered his tactics and, instead of bemoaning the lack of US–UK cooperation, he enacted a series of measures to ensure a more amenable policy from the British. What should be remembered is that Kissinger's policy of producing a declaration which accepted linkage had not changed. What had altered was Kissinger's tactics in achieving this objective. In conversation with his staff, Kissinger made it clear that 'They [UK] can't milk us for everything in the name of special channel'.[84] Kissinger explained how he would now attempt to influence British policy. 'We are going to try to bust the Europeans. The French can be useful in this. We hit the British, ignore the French and deal with the Germans and Italians.' As Kissinger concluded, 'We must break up the Europeans'.[85]

## Hitting the British

As Nixon wrote in 1980, 'diplomacy can be used either as a sword or as a needle – as a weapon or an instrument of union'.[86] To influence British policy, the president took the 'sword' approach on this occasion. Similarly, America's other principal European allies were also to face the wrath of the Nixon administration. Kissinger apparently intimated that he would use his influence on Wall Street to 'wreck' the French economy, and threats of withdrawing US troops and curtailing military assistance to West Germany were also made.[87]

How the British would be dealt with became clearer in the following weeks. The area in which the Americans decided to apply pressure concerned the closest area of the US–UK relationship, namely intelligence and nuclear weapons cooperation. The US thus suspended its existing intelligence and nuclear cooperation with the UK. 'I am cutting [Britain] off from intelligence special information they are getting here,' Kissinger informed the president. 'No more special relations,' Nixon agreed.[88]

US–UK nuclear cooperation was the next area to be used by Kissinger as a means of influencing British foreign policy. Suspending nuclear cooperation was perhaps the most powerful tool in the US arsenal, because Britain depended significantly on US assistance with its Polaris force. For example, one report supplied to Heath (November 1970) suggested that, 'The British strategic deterrent is at present entirely dependent upon our continued access to US information and material'.[89] UK reliance was further exacerbated by the programme to update Polaris, as only the US would be able to provide the necessary technical cooperation for the timely and safe update to Polaris.[90]

Given this obvious area of vulnerability, nuclear cooperation was the next area of US–UK cooperation that American policy-makers sought to utilise to bring about a change in British policy. First, James Schlesinger postponed a meeting with British officials regarding the upgrading of Polaris. Schlesinger cited his inability to review the necessary briefing material as he had only recently been appointed as secretary of defense, but in reality it was a plan concocted with Kissinger to pressure the British into engaging bilaterally over the declaration. At the end of the month, Schlesinger was still refusing to meet with the British about Polaris, and in spite of British officials being 'desperate' to ascertain the American position on whether Poseidon (the latest US Submarine Launch Ballistic Missile nuclear weapons system) would be sold to the UK, he refused to yield.[91]

Further to this, Kissinger also instructed US Treasury Secretary George Shultz to stop any special information being given to the British pertaining to ongoing monetary discussions. As he reasoned: 'I want to get your area synchronized with ours so that they [Britain] can't claim a special relationship in one field and really put it to us in other fields'.[92] In sum, under Kissinger's direction, US policy had created a coherent and coordinated response towards the UK's unwillingness to cooperate in regard to the 'Year of Europe' proposals. Kissinger had targeted the most sensitive areas of US–UK bilateralism to invoke a policy change in London, and in the following weeks this would come about.

Kissinger's actions got the desired effect from London and caused a considerable stir throughout British policy-making circles. Four meetings of the JIC were convened throughout August and September to discuss the American action. Other British officials hypothesised about American behaviour.[93] More importantly, the combined actions of Kissinger and Schlesinger had a significant impact on British policy as the British now took the 'lead' in trying to formulate the declaration with the EEC.[94] This saw the British engaging in active diplomacy with their EEC colleagues, especially France. Indeed, it was mooted as to what concessions Britain could offer to France in return for a more constructive attitude. Such efforts failed to shift French policy and Jobert made it clear that France would not be rushed into producing a draft declaration.[95]

It has to be pointed out that since the outset of the 'Year of Europe' Heath had sought agreement with the US over the declaration and had made multiple attempts to convince the French to go along with the idea. Whilst US action hastened the British into trying to produce the declaration, it had not fundamentally altered what the British wanted to achieve. Most obviously, the British would still not agree that the declaration had to interlink all aspects of US–EEC interaction, and they still sought a declaration that explicitly separated economic and security aspects of the relationship.

Where US pressure on US–UK bilateral cooperation had its greatest success was in reversing Heath's decision to refuse to discuss the declaration bilaterally. Heath's other policy, to provide full records of US–UK discussions on the declaration to the EEC, was also dropped. Indeed, a total reversal of British policy was enacted; but it also went further. The British now briefed the US on their discussions with EEC members about the declaration. This was undertaken by Richard Sykes who met with Helmut Sonnenfeldt and informed him about British intentions towards the upcoming EEC conference in Copenhagen. Sykes articulated that this was being done as Heath wanted to 'maintain a firm bilateral relationship'. Heath had written to Nixon declaring his intention to maintain 'close' bilateral contact, and this was evidently the manifestation of this desire.[96]

By the beginning of September 1973, the EEC was reaching some limited decisions on the contents of the declaration. For example, it was decided to establish a spokesperson for the EEC who would then act as the main representative for US–EEC interaction. However, even this ran afoul of Washington given that, earlier in the year, Kissinger had shown his opposition towards such an idea, and this latest announcement only soured his opinion further.[97]

Nevertheless, some positive progress did also appear to be developing as the EEC announced how the declaration would be completed procedurally and what it would (provisionally) contain. Such was the speed of this that a draft version of the declaration was delivered to the US on 19 September 1973.[98]

Though the EEC had produced this draft in a relatively short space of time, Kissinger was far from pleased with it and, during his meeting with Douglas-Home on 24 September 1973, he made his displeasure known.[99] During this meeting Kissinger was extremely forthright in bemoaning the conduct of both the EEC and the British throughout the previous months, and complained that 'It was worse than dealing with the Soviets'. Douglas-Home refused to engage in reprisals and instead claimed that the US and UK fundamentally agreed that a declaration needed to be created. Where the two countries differed was in how this would be achieved procedurally.[100] Douglas-Home was being disingenuous, given that a fundamental difference with Kissinger did exist. The UK did not want US–EEC relations to be institutionalised according to the American concept of linkage. Moreover, their enthusiasm for the project had only been reignited following the coercive diplomacy enacted by the US against key British interests.

At the end of Douglas-Home's visit, US officials began to evaluate the contents of the EEC's draft declaration. Sonnenfeldt informed Kissinger that it was 'sound' in places, but in others it was 'ludicrous'.[101] The EEC draft explicitly separated economic, political and security issues, which clearly contradicted Kissinger's intention to interconnect such areas. Moreover, it indicated that US bilateral pressure upon the UK and wider EEC had failed to convince them that this should be applied to US–EEC relations.[102] Whilst differences in substance still persisted over the declaration, the EEC had shown itself willing to negotiate and further progress in creating the declaration took place in the latter half of September 1973. Events in the Middle East, however, would come to intercede in the creation of the declaration. The differences which emanated from this would threaten to cause lasting damage to the US–UK relationship.

## The nadir for US–UK relations

On 6 October 1973, war broke out between Israel and the axis of Egypt–Syria. US intelligence was largely caught unawares by the outbreak of war. As Ray S. Cline, the director of the Bureau of Intelligence and Research, opined, US intelligence assessments had been 'brainwashed by the Israelis', who in turn had 'brainwashed themselves' into believing that the Arab states would not launch a pre-emptive strike.[103] British intelligence was equally poor. One day prior to the war, Sir Philip Adams, UK ambassador to Cairo, reported that Egyptian military moves were not indicative of preparations for war. As he informed London, 'There has been no, repeat, no, evidence of panic here or offensive intentions.'[104] As subsequent events showed, this assessment was somewhat inaccurate.

On a number of distinct issues US and UK interpretations on how to respond to the conflict clashed. The first area of US–UK debate revolved around the use of British airbases in Cyprus for reconnaissance overflights of the warzone. The second concerned how a ceasefire should be negotiated within the UNSC. The US airlift to Israel was to be the third area of US–UK antagonism. The final point related to the US DEFCON III decision of 25 October 1973.

That US and UK policy differed was perhaps to be expected given that their respective policies towards the Middle East had often clashed since the beginning of the Cold War. With Heath coming to office this only continued, and his ambition of resolving the Arab–Israeli conflict caused further US–UK disagreement. Heath had signalled his intention to find a resolution to the Arab–Israeli conflict soon after assuming office and this solution, as Douglas-Home publicly declared in October 1970 during a speech at Harrogate, would be based on the general contours of UN Resolution 242. Briefly summarised, this meant that Israel would have to surrender the land it had occupied following its victory in the 1967 Six Day War.[105] Given Nixon's 'even-handed' policy towards the Arab–Israeli dispute, there should have been little problem in supporting Heath's approach. Indeed, William Rogers's peace proposals, dubbed the 'Rogers Plan', were largely in line with Heath's own thinking. However, it was soon apparent that Nixon was undermining his secretary of state's ambitions, and in 1971 Nixon authorised a large-scale military shipment for Israel and little pressure was placed upon Israel to reach an agreement with its Arab neighbours. By 1972–73, Nixon had, in real terms, dropped the Rogers Plan and was pursuing a more traditional pro-Israeli policy.[106]

When conflict erupted in October 1973, longer-term political differences, coupled with recent US–UK antagonism, were likely to see relations strained.[107] This said, shorter-term problems were, from Kissinger's perspective at least, immaterial and the seriousness of the conflict meant US–UK differences had to be put to one side.[108] Events would show this not to be the case, and US–UK discord was obvious from the outset. This stemmed from longer-term differences towards implementing a lasting political settlement in the region, and shorter-term difficulties contributed to a suspicious atmosphere towards each other's policy objectives. Fundamentally, however, US and UK policies were seeking competing objectives. Heath wished to remain 'neutral' throughout the conflict as this would safeguard British oil supplies, and he wanted to find a lasting political solution that would largely endorse UN Resolution 242. The US, under Kissinger's direction, saw things differently. According to

Kissinger's thinking, the war presented an opportunity for a lasting political settlement that would predominantly exclude the USSR from the region. It was this competing idea then, on how a lasting Arab–Israeli settlement would be created, which really led to severe US–UK animosity.[109]

## The ceasefire

When fighting broke out in the Middle East, policy-makers in Washington and London expected a swift Israeli victory. Indicative of this is the fact that during a meeting of the Washington Special Actions Group (WSAG), convened on 6 October 1973, all of the advice proffered suggested that Israel would achieve a rapid military victory.[110] Thus, for Nixon and Kissinger, the biggest concern was that the USSR would intervene to prevent a military humiliation of its Arab allies. Events soon showed that believing an easy Israeli victory would come about was misplaced. Rather than Israel turning the Syrian front into a 'turkey shoot', it was the Israelis who found they were retreating across the Golan Heights.[111]

The information coming out of the region was unclear and, to better determine the balance of the conflict, the United States Air Force (USAF) wanted to undertake reconnaissance overflights of the warzone. British airbases in Cyprus were ideally situated geographically to launch such overflights, and a request was put to the Heath government to utilise these facilities. The British deliberated this request at length and various ideas were put forward. It was suggested that if the flights could remain secret, or at least plausible deniability could be ensured, then approval should be given. Heath remained reluctant because he suspected that the US would provide the Israelis with the intelligence gathered from these reconnaissance overflights. Of course, this would have undermined his efforts to remain neutral during the conflict and he therefore refused to grant approval for the American request.[112]

In spite of this early warning sign that British policy would not be amenable to US requests, Kissinger refused to take heed. Now the US secretary of state sought assistance from the British in the UNSC. Kissinger proposed that the British table a ceasefire resolution in the UNSC, which would call for a ceasefire and a return to the status quo ante bellum.[113] London was less than enthusiastic with Kissinger's idea and, when he had initially suggested this course to Lord Cromer, British reluctance was evident. Indeed, the British ambassador rejected Kissinger's offer because British information indicated that the Egyptian president, Anwar Sadat, would reject such ceasefire proposals. Kissinger was unwilling to demur, and again he contacted Cromer and attempted to convince him of his ceasefire plan. Kissinger guaranteed that

Egypt would accept a ceasefire resolution if it was tabled by Britain. Cromer relented and suggested that it was 'well worth the effort' if Egypt would agree to such terms.[114]

Cromer reported his conversations with Kissinger to London.[115] Kissinger's argument that Egypt would agree to a ceasefire that insisted on a return to the status quo ante bellum ran in contradiction to the information received from the British ambassador to Cairo, Philip Adams. Accordingly, Douglas-Home ordered Adams to meet with Sadat, in order to learn his real position about ceasefire terms. Adams duly reported on his discussions and confirmed that Sadat would not accept a ceasefire which insisted on a return to the status quo ante bellum.[116]

On 13 October 1973, Heath convened a meeting at Chequers where the war was discussed in detail. Maintaining Britain's oil supply was clearly at the top of his agenda, and he reasoned that the current tactic of neutrality assured that the British government could not be accused of being pro-Israeli and would hopefully prevent any possible oil embargo by the Arab states being enacted against the British. Coupled with this, it was also apparent that Kissinger's ceasefire proposal was viewed as either some sort of 'trick' or as a means of preserving superpower détente. Again, British anxiety towards Kissinger's real foreign policy intentions surfaced and it was concluded that Britain would not table any ceasefire resolution proposing a return to the status quo ante bellum. In the UNSC, Kissinger's ceasefire proposal had effectively collapsed.[117]

The airlift to Israel proved to be the third area which witnessed US–UK disagreement. At the onset of hostilities, the Israelis had lobbied the Americans for military aid, but this had been met coolly in Washington. As Schlesinger had warned during the WSAG of 6 October 1973, 'Our shipping any stuff into Israel blows any image we may have as an honest broker.'[118] Consequently, Israeli demands for F-4 Phantom II fighter jets and M60 tanks were rebuffed.[119] Agreement was given, however, to re-supply Israel with ammunition, but even this was conditioned on the fact that Israel had to provide its own airliners to pick it up. Three days into the fighting, Israel had endured serious military losses, with a total of over 250 tanks and 49 fighter jets being lost. The Israeli ambassador in Washington, Simcha Dinitz, consequently stepped up his lobbying for American assistance and this was partially successful because Nixon agreed to supply five F-4 Phantom IIs. Crucially, the stipulation that Israel had to provide its own transportation remained, thus allowing the Americans to retain the impression that they were not directly re-supplying Israel.[120]

This created a dilemma for Kissinger. His entire response to the conflict was driven by his overarching ambition of excluding the USSR from the region, and designed so that all of the belligerents realised that only the US could establish a lasting political settlement. As such, the ceasefire proposal was built upon the proviso that Israel would, at the very least, be militarily dominant on the Syrian front, because this would ensure the Arab states would be willing to negotiate. As Kissinger put it: 'Our interests are not identical with Israel's. We want Israel to win so the Arabs will turn to us.'[121] As such, American involvement in re-supplying Israel had to be kept to a minimum so as to present an image to Egypt and Syria that the US was not seeking to advance Israel's position at their expense. This would enable the US to appear as an 'honest broker' and assume the position of kingmaker in any political settlement. Unfortunately for the US secretary of state, military events on the ground would intercede and made such an approach impossible to pursue.[122]

Events in the war soon led to further Israeli calls for US assistance. An Israeli counter-attack on the Syrian front had ground to a halt because of a lack of equipment, and now they demanded that the US re-supply them directly via airlift. With Israeli calls becoming more vehement for a re-supply, Washington was forced into making a decision.[123] Whilst Kissinger remained reluctant, Schlesinger advised Nixon that the US undertake the re-supply with its own transport planes. The US secretary of defense suspected that if the US refused to provide Israel with the needed material it could well be militarily defeated. In turn, this could lead Israel into being tempted to utilise its nuclear arsenal to ensure its security.[124] Making an Israeli military defeat more likely was the fact that the USSR was re-supplying both Egypt and Syria.[125] Nixon understood that supplying Israel with any sort of material would attract criticism, so he concluded that the US may as well supply Israel with what it actually required to win the war. As Nixon simply put it: 'You'll get as much blame for three [aircraft] as for twenty-five ... Do what will do the job.'[126] Thus, the president ordered a full re-supply via airlift for Israel.

The airlift was to act as the catalyst for the third schism in US–UK relations. With the president ordering an open airlift to Israel, the question of how this would be conducted had to be determined. The USAF wanted to use its transport planes from European airfields, because this would both shorten the flight time to the warzone and increase flight safety. This request was to prove problematic for the British as agreeing to it would clearly undermine Heath's policy of neutrality. The likelihood that Britain would agree that US aircraft could re-supply Israel from its airbases, given the earlier refusal to even allow reconnaissance overflights from British bases in Cyprus, was therefore slim. Heath had demonstrated his desire to remain neutral when he had refused to support Kissinger's ceasefire proposal in the UNSC, and had also refused to supply ammunition and spare parts for British-made Israeli Centurion tanks. Walter Annenberg was surely correct then to inform Washington that a US request to use the US airbase at Mildenhall would be rejected. As Kissinger wrote, 'There was never a formal refusal on the airlift because it had been made plain that we should not ask.'[127]

## Nuclear alert

The collapsed ceasefire proposal and the refusal of the British to acquiesce in the airlift deeply irritated key policy-makers in Washington.[128] However irksome this was, it was a matter that need not have resulted in a great US–UK quarrel. Testament to this was the fact that Kissinger dismissed using US–UK nuclear cooperation as a form of leverage in obtaining a more amenable British policy.[129] At this juncture, Kissinger did not feel that US–UK political disagreement warranted such a stern US reaction. In the following days this was to change because of US–UK differences over the US response to a letter received by the Soviet premier, Leonid Brezhnev. The US decision to move their military, including their nuclear arsenal, to a heightened state of alert, DEFCON III, was to prove deleterious for US–UK relations.

With both superpowers now openly airlifting material to their respective allies, a further round of diplomatic activity was undertaken which saw Kissinger flying to Moscow, Tel Aviv and London for various talks.[130] A ceasefire agreement was the result of these efforts but, once back in Washington, Kissinger found his brokered ceasefire had already begun to crumble. After a further round of diplomacy, UN Resolution 339 was passed, which insisted a ceasefire be enacted along an unspecified line and for a UN observer force to be despatched to the region.[131]

Whilst the diplomacy was being acted out, the Israeli Defense Force (IDF) had surrounded the Egyptian Third Army. Sadat realised that his army was on the verge of destruction, and even more worrying was that, if the Third Army collapsed, the road to Cairo was open for the IDF.[132] Consequently, Sadat despatched a letter to Nixon which called for direct US intervention to implement the ceasefire. Sadat went as far as to suggest: 'I am formally asking you to intervene effectively, even if that necessitates the use of forces, in order to guarantee the full implementation of the ceasefire resolution in accordance with the joint US–USSR agreement.'[133] The Egyptian leader was to be disappointed because Nixon's reply made it clear that the US would not despatch military forces to establish the ceasefire.[134]

Kissinger, meanwhile, was concerned that Sadat would reach out to the USSR and offer the same terms as those suggested to the US. As Kissinger lamented to the Israeli ambassador, Simcha Dinitz, 'if the Soviets put some divisions in there then you will have outsmarted yourselves'.[135] As Kissinger feared, Sadat did just this and asked the USSR to deploy forces into the region to prevent the further destruction of his military. This now led to a series of telegrams between the US and USSR which gradually became more confrontational in their tone.[136] On 24 October 1973, Brezhnev delivered a letter which requested that a joint US–Soviet force be despatched to the region. As Brezhnev wrote: 'Let us together, the Soviet Union and the United States, urgently dispatch to Egypt Soviet and American contingents, with their mission the implementation of the decision of the Security Council of August 22 and 23...'[137] More vital yet, Brezhnev outlined that: 'I will say it straight that if you find it impossible to act jointly with us in this matter, we should be faced with the necessity urgently to consider the question of taking appropriate steps unilaterally.'[138]

Historians have debated whether or not this letter should have been interpreted as a Soviet threat to deploy forces into the region and much ambiguity still clouds what motivated Brezhnev to send this letter to Nixon.[139] Regardless, in Washington at least, Brezhnev's letter was viewed as a Soviet notice to invade the Middle East, with Kissinger explaining to Alexander Haig, now the president's chief of staff, that he had 'just had a letter from Brezhnev asking us to send forces in together or he would send them in alone'.[140] At the time, other US policy-makers had reached a similarly dark conclusion, with Admiral Thomas Moorer, the chairman of the Joint Chiefs of Staff, describing Brezhnev's letter a 'real piss-swisher'.[141]

A meeting of the WSAG was thus convened to decide the US response. Kissinger chaired the meeting and it was here that it was decided that US forces should be placed onto a heightened state of military alert: DEFCON III.[142] Along with this, the US moved two of its aircraft carriers closer to the conflict zone, placed on alert its troops in Europe, alerted the 82nd Airborne Division, and recalled a number of its strategic bombers from the Pacific region.[143] 'Words were not making our point – we needed action, even the shock of a military alert,' Nixon retrospectively argued.[144]

Given Nixon's domestic problems, the decision to move to DEFCON III can, perhaps, be viewed as an offshoot of this. Kissinger would note in conversation with Alexander Haig that US domestic troubles were having a bearing on the course of US foreign policy. More importantly, Kissinger believed that the actions of the USSR were being driven by Nixon's weakening domestic position. As he remarked, 'You cannot be sure how much of this is due to our domestic crises'.[145] Aside from this, there was an overarching concern that the USSR would commit troops to the Middle East, and from the outset of the conflict it had been US policy to marginalise the USSR from the Middle East. Agreeing to a joint US–Soviet task force would have contradicted this objective. As Odd Arne Westad has correctly pointed out, détente had its limitations vis-à-vis US–Soviet cooperation.[146] Or, as Anatoly Dobrynin more bluntly noted: 'The rivalry would remain. Détente had its limits.'[147]

America's European allies were not informed, much less consulted, on the decision to move US nuclear forces to DEFCON III. As one newspaper exclaimed, the NATO alliance had been 'kept in the dark'.[148] This has long been believed to have applied to the UK as well.[149] Whilst the WSAG may not have consulted with the British on moving to DEFCON III, Kissinger did inform Cromer about the decision. Kissinger made a point in showing how privileged Britain was to receive this information, as Cromer was the only European ambassador informed about the contents of the Brezhnev letter that had sparked the DEFCON III alert.[150] Cromer failed, however, to convey this message to London prior to the DEFCON III move having become public knowledge. Quite why this happened is unclear, and the seriousness of this led Heath to order an inquiry into why this had occurred. Whatever the cause, Heath was never informed prior to the US move becoming public knowledge, but this was the result of London's bureaucratic failings.[151]

Kissinger had, therefore, informed the British of the DEFCON III move, and in doing so he also requested Britain's 'very strong support'.[152] The fact remained, however, that the prime minister believed the American military moves had been undertaken without prior warning, and he therefore publicly rebuked the American action.[153] This hardly accorded with the 'very strong support' Kissinger had sought. The move was also viewed with trepidation in London, and MPs in the House of Commons went as far as to cast aspersions about the mental stability of President Nixon.[154] While the foreign secretary dismissed these claims, his own ambassador to Washington was filing reports that expressed the very same thing![155]

Events would fortunately see superpower confrontation averted. Moscow picked up the American military moves, and Nixon had also sent a conciliatory note to Brezhnev on 25 October 1973. Together these convinced the Soviet leader that he should retract his statement to despatch Soviet forces to the conflict zone. The UNSC thus agreed that a 'police force' could be sent to the region, but it would not be allowed to consist of any troops from the United States, USSR, UK or France, and with this agreement in place the spectre of an immediate US–Soviet confrontation abated.[156]

For US–UK relations, events in the Middle East had led to a number of acrimonious altercations. However, the fact that the British attempted to distance themselves from US policy should hardly have come as a surprise. On the first day of the conflict, Kissinger had been warned that Britain (and other Western European states) would 'dissociate themselves from the US in order to insure access to Arab oil'.[157] Likewise, during the WSAG of 6 October 1973, William Simon, William Colby and James Schlesinger had all suggested that the European states would be hit hardest by an oil embargo and would 'begin to scream' if one were to be enacted.[158] Nonetheless, Kissinger thought that the UK would support US actions, but events proved that this was not to be the case. The UK had not acted in the fashion Kissinger expected and, moreover, he believed he had been personally let down by the course of British policy. In his estimation, the British were 'jackals' who had ruined his UN ceasefire proposals at the beginning of the conflict.[159]

The information Kissinger obtained later on only confirmed his negative view of British policy, because he learned that the British ambassador in Cairo, Phillip Adams, had actively scuppered his efforts at introducing a ceasefire over the course of 12–13 October 1973.[160] British opposition to the airlift and nuclear alert had also demonstrated a frustrating degree of opposition to American policy. As a result of this, Kissinger – after prompting from Schlesinger – wanted to 'reconsider our European policy'.[161] For US–UK relations this even touched the 'most special' area of the relationship, that of intelligence cooperation. As William Colby stated in the WSAG convened to discuss American Middle East policy, 'they [UK] can't have a special relationship with us and do what they are doing'.[162] Kissinger evidently concurred, as he again temporarily ordered a suspension of US–UK intelligence cooperation.[163]

In London, Heath believed that Nixon's domestic problems had driven the US decision to move to DEFCON III, which, in turn, was seen as a grossly disproportionate reaction to the situation.[164] Perhaps the prime minister was correct to think that domestic politics had played a part in the decision. However, he failed to grasp that US policy was determined to exclude the USSR from the region, and US actions were conditioned in pursuit of this ambition. Regardless, Heath was nonplussed by American actions and was determined to ascertain why the US had employed the tactics they had. He therefore ordered the JIC assessment staff and the FCO to analyse US conduct throughout the war. When both of these reported, they only endorsed the prime minister's earlier thinking that the American response had been overblown, and was driven by the domestic problems engulfing the president.[165]

## The allure of oil

As a means of influencing international support against Israel, several of the Arab oil-producing states enacted an oil embargo following the outbreak of the fourth Arab–Israeli war. As one author has noted, the oil embargo 'threatened the unity and prosperity of the West'.[166] Likewise, the repercussions of the oil embargo threatened to deal a permanent blow to the US–UK relationship. The Washington Energy Conference, convened in February 1974 to solve this oil crisis, was also seen by Washington as an opportunity to confront French leadership of the nascent common foreign policy of the EEC. The UK was seen as useful in achieving such ambitions, and by applying pressure upon British policy-makers – in the guise of threatening a permanent severance in US security commitments to Europe unless support for US-inspired oil plans were made, and threatening to outbid all competitors for spare oil, thus forcing its price higher – Kissinger believed the British would break with competing French ideas towards the oil conference. As events would demonstrate, this was an astute assessment.

For the Heath government, the severity of the oil embargo and the decisions taken to solve it served as a seminal moment in the foreign policy of his government. As the energy conference illustrated, Heath was able to work intimately with Washington in order to safeguard British security and economic interests. This approach, however, critically undermined his wider foreign policy of operating collectively within the framework of the EEC. Ultimately, therefore, Heath sacrificed his wider European ambitions to secure British interests, thus demonstrating the pragmatism inherent within his approach to foreign policy.

Such an argument, however, must be carefully qualified. US foreign policy at the Washington Energy Conference was not seeking to dominate EEC foreign policy, and such allegations are over-exaggerated and are not actually grounded in documentary evidence.[167] Certainly, Kissinger was in a combative mood towards the European states and was not prepared – as he put it – to 'keep financing them' because they continued 'screwing us in the Middle East'.[168] Nonetheless, this only explains a part of Kissinger's overarching approach towards the ongoing energy crisis. Rather, US policy was built around the premise that EEC foreign policy could no longer be dominated by French Gaullist ideas, which the Americans believed would take an anti-American agenda. It would also guarantee that Kissinger's evolving Middle East diplomacy would not be undercut by any Euro–Arab dialogue that had emerged following the outbreak of the October War.[169]

Likewise, British policy at the Washington Energy Conference must be carefully explained. Only reluctantly did the Heath government accept US demands for collective consumer action in response to the oil embargo. The break with France at the energy conference was something that Heath only endorsed once it became apparent that they would not agree to collective consumer action, which would, in his estimation, result in the price of oil rising steeply and do untold damage to both the British economy and his political position. Once Heath had decided upon this course (by mid-January 1974), he showed once again that he was quickly able to engage in close US–UK contact in order to secure his objectives.

Heath had long been concerned about the West's increasing dependency upon Middle East oil, and he rightly suspected that the Arab states would, in the fullness of time, seek to gain control over their oil reserves. Moreover, he believed a future Arab–Israeli war would cause severe disruption to Western oil supplies.[170] Such fears were soon realised once the fourth Arab–Israeli war broke out as, on 16 October 1973, Arab oil-producing states increased the per barrel price of oil from $3.01 to $5.12. At the Kuwait City summit on 17 October 1973, the Arab oil producers announced a reduction in oil production of 5 per cent per month. This would continue until an Arab–Israeli settlement predicated upon UN Resolution 242 was achieved. The Arab oil producers further announced that only 'friendly' countries could purchase oil. This status would only be afforded to states that demonstrated their commitment to finding an Arab–Israeli settlement according to UN Resolution 242.[171]

This created a myriad of problems for Heath as, in comparison to the US, Britain relied much more upon the continued supply of Arab oil. For instance, over 60 per cent of Britain's petroleum usage was sourced from the Arab states.[172] Escalating oil prices also harmed Britain's balance of payments position, and not only was this economically deleterious for Britain, but for the prime minister it was also becoming a political liability.[173] Because of the potential for an oil shortage, Heath asked the British public to curb their energy use. This even involved a plea that British households limit their heating use to one room! Petrol rationing was seriously debated within the Cabinet, and it was eventually decided to implement speed restrictions on British roads as a means to conserve British petroleum reserves. For Heath, then, the oil embargo was as much a domestic as an international issue.[174]

On 6 November 1973, the EEC declared that it would seek to find a resolution to the Arab–Israeli conflict according to UN Resolution 242, which Heath fully endorsed. As he argued, it was essential to support this so as to prevent the oil embargo being applied to Britain. On one level, Heath's decision was a success given that Britain was categorised as a 'friendly' nation and thus ensured the right to continue purchasing Arab oil. Further, on 18 November 1973, the Arab oil-producing states met in Vienna where it was announced that, in 'appreciation' of the EEC's position, the 5 per cent cutback in oil production that was supposed to begin at the end of that month would be postponed. Heath's tactics had ensured Britain retained access to Arab oil, both safeguarding oil access and preventing further damage to the British economy.[175]

The prime minister's actions were not without wider consequences, and for US–UK relations his decisions had a deeply negative impact. British support for the EEC declaration irritated Washington and, retrospectively, Kissinger would describe Heath's decision as 'horrible'.[176] Cromer was next to face Kissinger's wrath, and throughout November Kissinger levelled his dissatisfaction with British policy on at least three occasions.[177] Schlesinger also lent his weight to Kissinger's complaints and during a meeting of NATO representatives he accused Britain of 'decayed Gaullism'.[178] Privately, American assessments were even more scathing. In Schlesinger's estimation, the British had demonstrated throughout the entire Middle East crisis that they were simply 'incompetent'. For Kissinger, the British had acted like 'shits'.[179]

By the end of November, Kissinger was declaring that the 'special relationship' was collapsing. With a touch of flamboyance, Kissinger warned Cromer that if British policy was to be antagonistic towards the US then, 'This was the worst decision since the Greek city states confronted Alexander'.[180] Kissinger also had a policy paper drawn up that analysed various avenues for punishing the British. The paper concluded that long-term punishment was inadvisable because it would only damage US interests. While accepting this, Kissinger decided that a short-term punishment was necessary, and thus decided to once again halt US–UK intelligence cooperation.[181]

Kissinger's ferocious response can be explained by the fact that British actions appeared to undermine his efforts to find a long-term Arab–Israeli settlement. At this point, the US secretary of state was engaged in his Middle East 'shuttle diplomacy' and was attempting to find an agreement on which Israel would withdraw from the lands it had occupied during the latter stages of the recent war. While this was ongoing, the British – along with their EEC partners – had publicly articulated that UN Resolution 242 should be the basis of any final Arab–Israeli settlement (thus Israel would have to withdraw from the land it had occupied in the Six Day War in 1967). Given this, it was hardly unreasonable for Kissinger to conclude that this public diplomacy was going to undermine his own efforts. Moreover, Kissinger had no intention of finding an agreement according to UN Resolution 242, because in his assessment it was simply impractical to expect Israel to accept such conditions; he privately referred to such demands as a 'joke'.[182] More importantly, Sadat was also making it known to the US secretary of state that this was an unnecessary precondition for Egypt to agree to a lasting political settlement. Given this, in Kissinger's opinion, European efforts – via their 'Euro–Arab' dialogue – to implement UN Resolution 242 only complicated his efforts to establish a ceasefire agreement and find a permanent political solution.[183]

While Kissinger continued to broker an Arab–Israeli agreement, the Arab oil ministers met in Kuwait. Here, they decreed that the 5 per cent cuts which they had cancelled for December 1973 would be re-imposed upon those states which 'don't provide concrete evidence of friendliness such as by showing they are putting pressure on the United States or Israel'.[184] This was a clear signal to the European powers that continued access to oil was conditioned upon their efforts to convince the US secretary of state to seek an Arab–Israeli settlement according to UN Resolution 242. The dilemma facing Heath was therefore clear: if access to Arab oil was to continue, the separate policy initiative towards an Arab–Israeli settlement would have to continue. This, however, would run the risk of infuriating the US further.[185]

Even though Britain enjoyed the right to purchase Arab oil, it still had to absorb the price increase – which was particularly unpalatable given the worsening state of Britain's economy. For Heath, the oil embargo could not have struck at a more inopportune moment, given that the ongoing miners' strike was restricting the amount of coal (still Britain's largest source of energy) available at the very moment that Britain's second largest source of energy, oil, was undergoing extreme price increases. This was having a ruinous effect upon Britain's industrial and social well-being, not to mention the negative effect it was having upon Heath's political popularity. These domestic reasons alone meant that from Heath's viewpoint it was imperative to find some sort of solution to the oil embargo.[186]

From the perspective of the US, the status quo was also undesirable given that it was faced with a full Arab oil embargo, and that bilateral oil deals were forcing the price of oil that it could purchase even higher. For instance, oil from Nigeria was commanding around $17 per barrel, and Japan was purchasing oil from Egypt at just over $10 per barrel. To place this in context, at the outset of October 1973 oil was trading at just over $3 per barrel. The price of oil had, therefore, at least trebled in less than three months.[187]

Given these circumstances, it was no exaggeration when Nixon declared that the US faced an energy crisis in November 1973. To overcome this, Nixon launched 'Project Independence' which would seek to make the US energy self-sufficient by 1980.[188] Such was the seriousness of the situation that US policy-makers even discussed a possible invasion of the Middle East in order to secure the oil fields. Kissinger, for instance, told a group of journalists that the Arab states had better find a way of cooperating with the consumer nations 'if they don't want to go the way of the Greek city states'.[189] James Schlesinger was making similar comments.[190] Yet, in spite of such rhetoric, it appears as if Kissinger and Schlesinger had little intention of actually militarily seizing the oil fields. Indeed, the fact that Kissinger had made his point to a group of journalists indicates that such statements were designed to be made public in order to exert political pressure against the Arab oil states.[191]

Therefore, both the US and UK had a strong interest in seeking some sort of a solution to the oil embargo. The form it would take, however, was to be a point which would again result in disagreement between the two countries. This stated, the process illustrated several important things regarding Heath's approach to foreign policy. During the lead-up to the conference, Heath engaged in secret bilateral diplomacy with the US. Heath also broke with his ambition to establish common EEC policies, and followed the US's lead for a collective consumer response to the oil embargo. By doing this, Heath revealed his ability to work closely with Washington when he believed that it better promoted British interests.

Prior to a meeting of NATO representatives, Cromer suggested that some type of gesture to affirm US–UK solidarity should be made to placate US anger.[192] The prime minister was in no mood to be offering such gestures. From the record available, Heath's thinking on this matter appears to be most peculiar. In an official 'Note for the Record', it is recorded that Heath did not believe US–UK relations were confronted with any particular problems.[193] Perhaps this can be explained as a secretarial error? However, if this was Heath's thinking then he may have been suffering from a short-term memory lapse given that recent political differences had seen the suspension of US–UK intelligence and nuclear cooperation. Nor does it equate with how Heath was acting in other fields relating to US–UK relations. For example, the British decision to opt for the Super Antelope upgrade to Polaris was not relayed to the US at this moment. The reason for the delay was because of wider US–UK political differences. Heath was also deeply angered by the behaviour of senior US policy-makers and complained to the Italian prime minister about Henry Kissinger's 'schizophrenic' approach towards Europe.[194]

It was thus left to Douglas-Home to mollify the US. Privately, Douglas-Home agreed with the prime minister that Kissinger's approach during the 'Year of Europe' was the reason for all of the US–UK acrimony, but he followed Cromer's advice and despatched a conciliatory letter to the US secretary of state.[195] In it, Douglas-Home explained that Britain viewed the US as the 'lynchpin' of its foreign and defence policies, and wanted to reassure Kissinger that it was not the intention of the British government to deliberately take contrary policies to those pursued by the US.[196] Such efforts failed to calm Kissinger and the British found that he was in a pugnacious mood at the NATO conference. Complaints, akin to those he had been making to Cromer in Washington, were repeated in this arena.[197] Interestingly, other US officials were less rambunctious than Kissinger, and Schlesinger, who had been scathing about recent British actions, had reportedly been attempting to 'mend fences'. Even Kissinger's anger appeared to be directed more at the European powers than Britain.[198]

## Kissinger in London

As the oil embargo continued, Western states sought bilateral agreements with producer states to maintain their oil supplies. Heath's government was no exception to this and quickly secured an agreement with Iran in November 1973. Kissinger watched this with increasing dissatisfaction and reasoned that such action would only push the price of oil upwards and be self-defeating in the long term. For the US secretary of state, the continuation of such policies was simply 'suicidal'.[199] Kissinger, therefore, proposed that a collaborative consumer response to the oil embargo be found, and during his trip to London (12 December 1973) he took the opportunity to publicly articulate such thinking. Here it was suggested that a small group of senior officials should convene to formulate a collective energy policy which would prevent 'beggar thy neighbour' bilateral oil deals; i.e. the decrease in supply would be mitigated by lowering demand through the implementation of oil-sharing programmes and making collective bids to other oil producers.[200]

Publicly, Heath gave his strong support to Kissinger's proposals, which naturally won his approval, and a rather sycophantic letter was subsequently delivered to the prime minister. Under the surface, US–UK differences were more apparent, and Heath scrawled 'Pompous ass' on the top of Kissinger's letter.[201] Others, meanwhile, were rather more suspicious of Kissinger's motives, and Julian Amery, a Conservative MP and adviser to Douglas-Home, suggested Kissinger's goal was to ensure US dominance of the oil industry.[202] While British officials scrutinised Kissinger's proposals, the US secretary of state began to gauge support for an energy conference, and, following further oil price increases, Kissinger announced his intention to form an Energy Action Group which would assemble in the near future, find common agreement, and seek to break the oil embargo.[203]

At this stage, Heath wanted some form of collective consumer approach and Kissinger had, at the very least, provided one alternative with his Energy Action Group, but this also presented a number of interlinked difficulties. The first of these surrounded what Kissinger's intentions actually were. Throughout the entire 'Year of Europe' process, Heath had been concerned with allowing the US too much influence over the formulation of EEC policies. Kissinger's proposed Energy Action Group, regardless of the actual form it took, would have some consequences for ongoing EEC discussions on energy cooperation, and potentially it could limit EEC cooperation in this area. Heath, therefore, did not want to accept Kissinger's idea if it destroyed his wider EEC ambitions of collective political/economic cooperation. Some of Kissinger's other ideas on what the Energy Action Group would seek, especially the notion of actively driving down the price of oil, were simply deemed to be unrealisable objectives. This stated, Heath thought Kissinger's idea was not without merit and he agreed with the basic premise that a collective consumer approach had to be found. Where Heath differed was with the substance, rather than with the fundamental idea, of an Energy Action Group.[204]

Nevertheless, Heath was still confronted with a problem in relation to the EEC as the French had made their opposition to Kissinger's latest plans abundantly clear. Instead, France suggested that bilateral oil deals should continue until a collective EEC energy policy was formulated, and only once this had been achieved could EEC members engage with other powers about energy matters. For Heath this appealed little, for he well knew that creating a collective energy policy within the EEC would take some time. Moreover, continuing with bilateral oil deals would only drive the price of oil higher, damaging the British economy further by increasing the cost of consumer goods and thus importing inflation into the economy. Such a set of circumstances was hardly designed to help a prime minister who was already struggling to maintain his political popularity.[205]

As the British debated what the preferred course of action was, the US took the initiative in trying to alleviate the damage caused by the oil embargo. Nixon had agreed to Kissinger's idea to hold an energy conference amongst the principal consumer states, and thus invited Britain to attend this energy conference in Washington. The following day this invitation was reiterated publicly during a press conference held jointly by Kissinger and the US 'Energy Czar' William Simon, where the world's principal consumer nations of oil were invited to meet in Washington in February 1974. Following this, Nixon delivered a formal letter of invitation.[206]

As Kissinger realised, a public invitation would force the British to make a decision: they would either support his proposals or they would continue to engage in bilateral oil deals.[207] Either way, the US would have confirmation of British intentions and could react accordingly. Heath had to decide whether Britain would attend the conference and then how Britain would actually be represented (either as an individual state or as a member of the EEC). It also forced the British to decide on their course of action, and in essence they had two real choices. They could follow the US lead and agree to collective action, but this would mean forsaking bilateral oil deals and risking a confrontation with France. Alternatively, Heath could support the French line: find an EEC common energy policy, and continue with bilateral oil deals in the interim. Heath soon showed that he would back Kissinger's plan and did so because, in the final assessment, it was far preferable to the one being proposed by the French.

In Brussels, little common agreement existed on how best to react to the US invitation but French hostility to the entire Kissinger-inspired scheme was evident. Nevertheless, on 15 January, Nixon's invitation was discussed at the EEC Council of Ministers and an agreement was reached that the EEC would be represented at the conference by the president of the Council of Ministers. As this was a rotating position, individual member states were free to send their own representatives, and Heath therefore accepted Nixon's invitation.[208]

Interestingly, Heath had decided to attend the energy conference regardless of the position of the EEC.[209] Heath was not going to jeopardise Britain's oil supplies because the EEC could not formulate an agreed position and he was fully aware that Britain had to ensure it had access to affordable oil. The most obvious concern was that Heath's political authority in the UK was being undermined by continuing industrial relations problems, which, in turn, were being exacerbated by the oil crisis. The rising price of oil was also having severe inflationary effects upon Britain's economy, resulting in a sharp increase in the price of food and energy. The economic and social problems which were magnified by the oil embargo were encouraging Heath's opponents within the Conservative Party to seek his removal. It is not too much of an overstatement to claim that the oil embargo was threatening the political life of the prime minister.[210] Attending the energy conference would thus afford Heath the opportunity to tackle these problems. If the conference could formulate some collective consumer response to the oil embargo then it would have the benefit of stabilising the price of oil because it would rule out competitive bidding and prevent price escalation. Heath, therefore, was set on attending the conference, regardless of what the EEC's Council of Ministers decided.[211]

In relation to foreign policy, Heath had demonstrated his ability to work closely with the Nixon administration when he decided it suited his and British interests to do so. The prime minister resorted to US–UK bilateralism to ensure the energy conference would be successful, and was quite prepared to undermine EEC unity in order to achieve this. First, Heath sent Sir John Hunt, the British Cabinet secretary, to the US to speak confidentially with Kissinger.[212] This visit was designed to be kept secret from Britain's EEC partners. Kissinger, however, was rather less circumspect in keeping this meeting confidential, as he informed Dan Rather, the CBS journalist, of the clandestine British visit. Heath also sent Jack Rampton, the permanent under-secretary at the Department of Energy, to liaise with the Nixon administration, and knowledge of this meeting was also to be withheld from the wider EEC. For Heath, the seriousness of the oil crisis, coupled with the EEC's inability to reach a workable solution to combat it, meant that he was prepared to seek solutions with the US.[213]

Following US–UK discussions, the US delivered an aide memoire which outlined the finer details of the upcoming energy conference. This suggested that the energy conference would seek to reverse the price increase in oil, create a new institution that would complete follow-up work from the conference, and would also look to intensify 'economic and monetary policy cooperation to deal with the consequences of the present situation'.[214] Such suggestions caused concern within the British policy-making elite, because throughout the 'Year of Europe' initiative Heath had wanted to avoid interlinking US–EEC economic cooperation. Now it appeared as if Kissinger was once again proposing such a course.

On 5 February 1974, another European Council Meeting convened and it was here that a mandate which laid down a series of 'ground rules' for the upcoming energy conference was created.[215] The French were of the opinion that this mandate meant that all members of the EEC agreed that pre-existing institutions, such as the Organisation for Economic Cooperation and Development (OECD), the International Monetary Fund (IMF) and the World Bank, would undertake the follow-up work resulting from the conference. The French thought that the EEC had agreed that it would not accept the American proposal to create a new institution to deal with any follow-up work. As Jobert bluntly told one British official, 'no follow up – full stop'.[216]

Heath's government deliberately interpreted the mandate differently, and certain officials went as far as to suggest that the mandate did not forbid agreement to follow-up machinery being created. Hugh Overton, of the North American Department, suggested Britain should sign up to Kissinger's Energy Action Group. Other officials were less direct but articulated much the same opinion. Indeed, Douglas-Home concluded that the EEC mandate would not prohibit a positive outcome from the conference. As Douglas-Home was fully aware, the US regarded a positive outcome as one where the conference agreed to create a new institution to deal with the follow-up work. It appears then as if the Heath government was countenancing the possibility that the British should break with the EEC and support the American plans, in order to secure Britain's oil interests.[217]

For Kissinger, this played directly into his wider objectives in relation to Europe. In particular, Kissinger was trying to prevent French domination of the EEC's policy agenda, which he believed would result in a common foreign policy premised on an anti-American agenda. As Kissinger candidly put it in one conversation, 'We must break up the Europeans.'[218] Kissinger, therefore, was actively seeking to exploit the differences between EEC members, so as to cause friction and discord between the various states, and in turn prevent the other states of the EEC from simply acquiescing in French decisions. As such, the EEC would less likely follow the more independent and, as perceived in Washington, belligerent policies that France pursued in its bilateral dealings with the United States.

Nevertheless, the prime minister remained ambivalent towards many aspects of Kissinger's energy plans, and US statements to attempt to roll back oil prices were met with particular incredulity. US ideas of coordinating US–EEC monetary and trade practices were met with equal disdain. Heath, however, accepted the need for an energy conference and was also prepared to countenance the creation of a new institution to solve the oil crisis. British support existed behind the fundamental idea of international energy cooperation and it was only the details of this which now divided US and UK policy-makers.[219]

## Bandaid on a cancer

In Washington, France remained the *bête noire* for US policy-makers and, when Jobert again made it clear to Kissinger that France would not be supporting any common consumer solutions to the oil crisis, it only annoyed opinion further.[220] As James Schlesinger would recollect, at this point relations with France were experiencing a 'rather irritating period'.[221] At the time, he was rather more candid. The 'worst bastards' was Schlesinger's appraisal of French policy. 'Unadulterated bastards' was Kissinger's even more abrasive assessment.[222] Such comments were evidently not restricted to private audiences, as one British newspaper reported that Kissinger had described the EEC as 'jackals'.[223]

In spite of this, Kissinger was determined that his plans for the energy conference would not be scuppered by France. To ensure success, Kissinger explained that it was his intention to isolate France within the EEC and he would achieve this by winning British and West German support for his energy proposals by being as 'brutal' as necessary.[224] In practical terms this involved a twofold approach. First, this required Kissinger articulating that if a collective consumer response to the oil embargo could not be agreed then the US would outbid all of the competition in order to secure oil. Given the economic power of the US, this was a threat which the US could see through. The second phase involved linking the continuation of US military-security guarantees to Europe directly to support for his energy plans. Nixon queried whether this was a sensible stratagem, and Kissinger himself accepted that his tactics were akin to that of putting a 'bandaid on a cancer'. Nevertheless, the US secretary of state's argument won through.[225]

Interestingly, Kissinger never suggested that US–UK nuclear or intelligence cooperation would be revoked if support for his energy conference was not forthcoming. In fact, Kissinger recommended to Nixon that additional support for Britain's Polaris fleet should be given in January 1974, which Nixon accepted.[226] Such actions may at first appear contradictory to Kissinger's broader policy agenda. However, Kissinger decided that linking US–UK nuclear and intelligence cooperation to finding an energy agreement was not required at this point. Rather, he emphasised in conversation with British officials that if a common consumer response could not be found then the US would respond by simply outbidding all other consumer states.[227] Clearly such utterances demonstrated just how much importance the US attached to finding an agreement at the upcoming energy conference. Further to this, Kissinger and other US officials were making it known publicly that they viewed the energy conference as a 'crucial – perhaps even a final – test of Western political cooperation'.[228] This dual tactic had the desired effect upon British policy-making elites. As such, Lord Carrington – now serving as the British secretary of state for energy – informed Walter Annenberg that Britain would support the US '100 per cent' at the upcoming energy conference.[229]

The conference opened on 11 February 1974. Kissinger tabled his plans for overcoming the oil embargo, and outlined that the Western consumer nations should establish a coordinating group. This would establish a coordinated consumer response to the oil embargo and, once an agreed upon position had been established, a foreign ministers' conference between the consumer and producer states would convene to find a settlement to the oil embargo.[230] As Kissinger had expected, Jobert opposed his proposals.[231] This, however, was not really all that problematic from Kissinger's perspective, because US policy-makers had understood prior to the conference that there was little possibility of obtaining an agreement between all of the parties present. Rather, the US objective was to obtain approval for Kissinger's plans from as many of the other delegates as possible. As events unfolded, the US came to see that this approach would be successful. In Douglas-Home's plenary speech he accepted Kissinger's proposal that some sort of follow-up machinery should be established and representatives from other EEC nations, notably the West Germans and Dutch, made statements along similar lines. Jobert was therefore alone in opposing the follow-up machinery. With Douglas-Home then confirming that Britain would support the creation of a new institution to deal with global energy matters, the image of a united EEC was completely erased.[232]

As the first day of the energy conference drew to a close, Kissinger assessed the situation for Alexander Haig. 'So far so good,' the US secretary of state reported.[233] For Kissinger, things were indeed looking favourable given that Douglas-Home had given British agreement for establishing follow-up machinery and the West German and Japanese delegations had also lent their support.[234] In sum then, the world's largest consumers of oil had agreed to work collectively with the United States. More significant still was the fact that all the EEC members, except France, had agreed that they would approve Kissinger's proposals as national governments if common EEC agreement could not be found.[235] 'It's not us against Europe, it's France against us,' Kissinger explained to Nixon.[236] Indeed, Jobert's refusal to agree to follow-up machinery had left him isolated, and Kissinger's adroit diplomacy at this stage had gone some way to engineering this situation.

The decision by the other EEC members to operate as single representatives had isolated France, and importantly it averted a confrontation between the US and the EEC. Instead, the situation resulted in France being outside of the consensus opinion of the conference, and French officials could only publicly bemoan the behaviour of the other EEC states and accuse the US of 'seeking to impose a Pax Americana on her would-be satellites in the West'.[237] This outcome delighted Kissinger, who boasted to his deputy Brent Scowcroft that: 'We have broken the Community, just as I always thought I wanted to ... I think its [sic] going to be a good lesson to the French not to monkey around with us.'[238]

The British position was rather less jubilant than this, given it had been Douglas-Home's intention at the beginning of the conference to obtain collective agreement. This now appeared unlikely and his last-minute efforts to obtain French agreement were futile.[239] Regardless of French opposition, a communiqué was issued in which it was agreed that an emergency oil-sharing programme would be established for dealing with the 'next crisis'. An International Energy Agency was also created which would oversee this emergency oil-sharing programme, and which would also create a means of 'harmonizing and making parallel the energy policies of the Western countries'.[240] The communiqué also explicitly made the linkage between energy, trade and monetary matters, as it stated:

> General Conclusion. They [the states who signed the communiqué] affirmed, that, in the pursuit of national policies, whether in the trade, monetary or energy fields, effort should be made to harmonize the interests of each country on the one hand and the maintenance of the world economic system on the other.[241]

This is an important point often overlooked by commentators when assessing the 'Year of Europe'. Throughout the year, Heath had fought against American efforts to apply linkage to US–EEC relations; yet at the Washington Energy Conference, Heath, to some degree, accepted this. Kissinger had also demonstrated at the conference that US leadership of the Atlantic alliance had been assured and, as viewed in Washington, the French challenge to American primacy in the Western alliance had been overcome.

## Lessons for the future

Publicly, the Nixon White House gave an impression of satisfaction with the results of the Washington Energy Conference. Privately, however, Nixon's thinking was rather more mixed. The conference had failed to achieve the spectacular results which the president believed could have dissipated some of his domestic critics.[242] In spite of this, Nixon and Kissinger believed the Washington Energy Conference had achieved important political aims vis-à-vis the EEC. As Nixon articulated, 'The point is the European Community instead of having that silly unanimity rule, learned they can't gang up against us and we can use it now, we can use it on trade, security, with everything else'.[243] Kissinger was equally elated by the results and in conversation with the president explained: 'Last week, Mr President, the Community took a decision and today they split apart on it eight to one. It is a lesson to everybody.'[244] As Kissinger noted to Brent Scowcroft, 'It taught us an important lesson, if we really throw our weight around we can have our own way'.[245]

The Washington Energy Conference was, then, an important event from the standpoint of the Nixon White House, because it provided a valuable lesson in how to operate towards the EEC. It would not be unfair to suggest it was somewhat of a watershed for the Nixon administration's foreign policy towards the EEC. Nixon and Kissinger had questioned the wisdom of supporting EEC expansion and British membership of the EEC, and by 1973 both had concluded that this was no longer always in the American interest. As Nixon told one former US ambassador to West Germany, 'I share your concerns with European unity. It is no longer necessarily desirable'.[246] As Nixon had feared, the EEC would act in unison in opposition to American interests, and this fear had become a reality throughout the 'Year of Europe'. The British had shown that they were quite prepared to stand in opposition to American policy throughout the year, and it was membership of the EEC that was believed to have caused this new, uncooperative attitude in London. As such, for Schlesinger, 'It was a mistake getting Great Britain into the Common Market'. In Kissinger's opinion, 'It was a tragic mistake'.[247]

US policy-makers may have lamented this changed international dynamic, but it also provided them with an opportunity to alter the trajectory of events. Or, as one scholar has neatly noted, it afforded US policy-makers the chance to rescue 'choice from circumstance'. In essence, although the likes of Kissinger were restrained by the structure in which they operated, they still had to make decisions which could affect the course of events positively or negatively for US interests.[248] The decisions which were undertaken in the lead-up to the Washington Energy Conference, and the effects these had upon the policies pursued by London, demonstrated that Washington could garner the necessary support for its policies if it was willing to be forceful enough. As Kissinger had promised Nixon earlier in the year, 'the Europeans will be on their knees by the end of this year'.[249] By the end of the Washington Energy Conference, the US secretary of state had certainly delivered on this promise.

British officials fully understood that the energy conference would have profound political ramifications for the future course of British foreign policy. Denis Greenhill has suggested that it demonstrated the primacy of the US in the transatlantic relationship and, accordingly, those in Whitehall who had argued for a more Euro-centric British foreign policy were severely undermined.[250] The Paris correspondent of the *Financial*

*Times* perhaps best captured the wider ramification for Britain's European policy, when he wrote:

> The Washington Oil conference has at least one salutary result which has nothing to do with energy policies. It has shown up the absurdity of the so-called joint European positions based on texts which accommodate the conflicting positions of all the nine partners and has demonstrated to France that it cannot hope to impose its views on the other Common Market member countries indefinitely.[251]

Other British officials were rather more concerned that the EEC's inability to formulate a common position would actively encourage the US to 'divide and rule' the Community. Or, as another put it, the results of the energy conference would only encourage Kissinger to 'impose his will' upon Europe.[252] For the prime minister, however, this was something which he was willing to risk. As he was well aware, obtaining agreement with the US was imperative if bilateral oil deals were not to spiral out of control.[253] The fear that bilateralism would result in a 'beggar thy neighbour' approach – which would devastate Britain's economy, and perhaps end Heath's political career – convinced him that the UK had to lend its support to US energy proposals, even at the cost of sacrificing EEC unity.

## Conclusion

When assessing this difficult period for US–UK relations, scholars should not forget that close cooperation between the two states continued. The intelligence and nuclear cooperation between the two countries continued throughout the year and, moreover, in January 1974, the US–UK nuclear relationship was re-energised when the British requested additional US assistance for their update of Polaris. Likewise, US–UK diplomatic cooperation was quite unique in that Thomas Brimelow was given the responsibility by Henry Kissinger to help draft a US–USSR agreement on the prevention of nuclear war.[254]

Even recognising this, the level of diplomatic and political acrimony between the two countries had led to the temporary suspension of this cooperation on more than one occasion. More important yet was that the events of the year clearly highlighted the disparity in power within the US–UK relationship. The US had re-asserted its authority and demonstrated that if the UK was to pursue a policy path which Washington deemed would damage its vital interests, then this would not go unanswered. The practical demonstration of what this meant had been given when the US had halted intelligence and nuclear cooperation in response to political decisions taken by the Heath government throughout the year. This coercive diplomacy had the desired impact upon the course of British foreign policy. Whilst Heath's decision-making at the Washington oil conference was not solely dictated by American pressure, the US government believed that it could ensure its interests were better protected if it decided to 'throw its weight around'. Given this, it should not be a surprise that in the following chapters we will see that this was exactly the approach that the Nixon and Ford administrations would take when dealing with their British ally.

## Notes

1 Telcon: The President–HAK, 9 August 1973, HAKTELCONS.
2 Kennedy, *The Realities Behind Diplomacy*, pp. 381–4.
3 For a good overview see: Fred Emery, *Watergate: The Corruption and Fall of Richard Nixon* (London: Jonathan Cape, 1994).
4 Stanley Kutler, *Abuse of Power: The New Nixon Tapes* (New York: The Free Press, 1997), p. 458; Haig, *Inner Circles*, pp. 321–408.
5 On Nixon considering firing Kissinger see: Anthony Summers, *The Arrogance of Power: The Secret World of Richard Nixon* (London: Victor Gollancz, 2000), pp. 451–2; Chuck Colson, *Born Again* (New York: Crossings Classics, 1976), pp. 73–5. During this conversation with Schlesinger, Nixon reveals that he intended for Schlesinger to balance Kissinger's domination of US foreign policy. See: Memorandum of Conversation, 6 June 1974, File: June 6, 1974, Nixon, Schlesinger, NSAMC, 1973–1977, Box 4, GFL.
6 Thomas Robb, 'Antelope, Poseidon or a Hybrid: The Upgrading of the British Strategic Nuclear Deterrent, 1970–1974', *Journal of Strategic Studies*, 33:6 (2010), 811–13; Telcon: President-HAK, 23 September 1973, HAKTELCONS.
7 A point completely overlooked in existing accounts of the US–UK relationship. See for example: Hynes, *The Year*; Rossbach, *Rebirth*; Scott, *Allies Apart*.
8 This was termed Operation Hullabaloo. See: Stephen R. Twigge, 'Operation Hullabaloo: Henry Kissinger, British Diplomacy, and the Agreement on the Prevention of Nuclear War', in *Diplomatic History*, 33:4 (2009), 689–701.
9 TNA: PREM 15/2038 The President to the Prime Minister, undated, January 1974.
10 Rumsfeld, *Known and Unknown*, p. 149.
11 Memorandum of Conversation, 10 September 1972, National Security Council Files: Henry A. Kissinger Office Files, HAK Trip Files, Box 24, NPMP.
12 Alistair Noble, 'Kissinger's Year of Europe, Britain's Year of Choice', in Schulz and Schwartz (eds.), *The Strained Alliance*, p. 223.
13 Henry Kissinger, *Years of Upheaval* (Boston, MA, Little, Brown and Company, 1982) (hereafter: *YOU*), pp. 128–38.
14 Sulzberger, *The World and Richard Nixon*, pp. 208–9; Alaistair Horne, *Kissinger: 1973, The Crucial Year* (New York: Simon & Schuster, 2009), p. 110; Hanhimäki, *Flawed*, p. 275; Möckli, *European Foreign Policy*, pp. 143–5; Daniel Möckli, 'Asserting Europe's

Distinct Identity: The EC Nine and Kissinger's Year of Europe', in Schulz and Schwartz (eds.), *The Strained Alliance*, pp. 195–6; Silvia Pietrantonio, 'The Year That Never Was: 1973 and the Crisis Between the United States and the European Community', *Journal of Transatlantic Studies*, 8:2 (2010), 158–77.

15 Conversation between President Nixon and his Assistant for National Security Affairs [Kissinger], 19 April 1972, *FRUS 1969–1976, Soviet Union*, Vol. XIV, Doc. 126, p. 445; Memorandum for the President's File from Ronald L. Ziegler, 15 February 1973, President Office Files, Memoranda for the President, Box 91, NPMP.

16 Henry A. Kissinger, *Nuclear Weapons and Foreign Policy* (New York: Harper and Brothers, 1957); Henry A. Kissinger, *The Troubled Partnership*; Memorandum for Mr Bundy from Henry A. Kissinger, 3 October 1961, File: Kissinger Series, 36 Confidential, Papers of President Kennedy, National Security Files, Kissinger Series, Box 463A, John F. Kennedy Library, Boston, Massachusetts, USA.

17 Memorandum for Dr Kissinger from Phil Odeen and Helmut Sonnenfeldt, 28 June 1972, NSCIHF, Senior Review Group Meetings, Box H-064, NPMP; Memorandum of Conversation, 2 July 1973: File: July 2, 1973, Kissinger-Schlesinger-Moorer, NSAMC, Box 2, GFL.

18 NSSM-123: US–UK Nuclear Relations, Analytical Summary, attached to Memorandum for under-Secretary John Irwin et al. from Jeanne W. Davies, 2 July 1971, NSCIHF, Study Memorandums, Box H-182, NPMP.

19 Dallek, *Partners in Power*, pp. 473–6; Rossbach, *Rebirth*, pp. 155–60; Youri Devuyst, 'American Attitudes on European Political Integration – The Nixon–Kissinger Legacy', *IES Working Paper*, 2:1 (2007), 19; Mario Del Pero, *The Eccentric Realist: Henry Kissinger and the Shaping of American Foreign Policy* (Ithaca: Cornell University Press, 2010), pp. 93–9.

20 Fredrik Logevall, 'A Critique of Containment,' *Diplomatic History*, 28:4 (2004), 473–99; Robert McMahon, 'Diplomatic History and Policy History: Finding Common Ground', *Journal of Policy History*, 17:1 (2005), 94; Schwartz, 'Partisan Politics in the History of U.S. Foreign Relations', 173–90; Sandbrook, 'The Influence of Domestic Policy and Watergate', in Logevall and Preston (eds.), *Nixon in the World*, pp. 85–103; Julian F. Zelizer, 'Détente and Domestic Politics', *Diplomatic History*, 33:4 (2009), 653–70.

21 Kissinger, *YOU*, pp. 128–38.

22 Marc Trachtenberg, 'The French Factor in US Foreign Policy during the Nixon-Pompidou period, 1969–74', *Journal of Cold War Studies*, 13:1 (2011), 4–59. For evidence of this as the cornerstone of US objectives see: Memorandum for the President's Office File from David N. Parker, 25 May 1973, President Office Files, Memoranda for the President, Box 91, NPMP; Conversation Among President Nixon, the President's Assistant for National Security Affairs [Kissinger], and Secretary of the Treasury, Shultz, 3 March 1973, *FRUS: Foreign Economic Policy*, Vol. XXXI, Doc. 17, pp. 72–91.

23 Conversation Among President Nixon, the President's Assistant for National Security Affairs [Kissinger], and Secretary of the Treasury, Shultz, 3 March 1973, *FRUS: Foreign Economic Policy*, Vol. XXXI, Doc. 17, pp. 84–5.

24 Memorandum for the President's File from Peter Flanigan, 11 September 1972, President's Office Files, Memoranda for the President, Box 89, NPMP.

25 Memorandum for Mr Kissinger from Helmut Sonnenfeldt, 30 January 1973, NSCIHF, Senior Review Group Meetings, Box H-066, NPMP.

26 Memorandum of Conversation, 10 September 1972, National Security Council Files: Henry A. Kissinger Office Files, HAK Trip Files, Box 24, NPMP.

27 TNA: PREM 15/1273 Record of a Discussion with Dr Kissinger, 14 September 1972; TNA: FCO 82/177 Charles Powell Minute, J. A. N. Graham to A. A. Acland, 24 November 1972; TNA: FCO 82/193 Secretary of the Cabinet's Meeting with Dr Kissinger, 20 October 1972.

28 On the bombing see Stephen E. Ambrose, 'The Christmas Bombing', in Robert Cowley, *The Cold War: A Military History* (New York: Random House, 2006), pp. 397–418. On the wider points made see Memorandum for the President's Office Files from B/Gen Brent Scowcroft, 15 February 1973, President Office Files, Memoranda for the President, Box 91, NPMP; Memorandum for the President's Files from Henry A. Kissinger, 10 April 1973, President Office Files, Memoranda for the President, Box 91, NPMP; Conversation Among President Nixon, the Chairman of the Federal Reserve System Board of Governors [Burns], the Director of the Office of Management and Budget [Ash], the Chairman of the Council of Economic Advisers [Stein], Secretary of the Treasury Shultz, and the under-Secretary of the Treasury for Monetary Affairs [Volcker], 3 March 1973, *FRUS 1969–1976, Foreign Economic Policy*, Vol. XXXI, Doc. 16, p. 68.

29 Memorandum for the President's Office Files from B/Gen Brent Scowcroft, 15 February 1973, President's Office Files, Memoranda for the President, Box 91, NPMP.

30 Raymond Seitz, *Over Here* (London: Weidenfeld & Nicolson, 1998), pp. 316–17; Memorandum for the President's Office Files from B/Gen Brent Scowcroft, 15 February 1973, President's Office Files, Memoranda for the President, Box 91, NPMP; Memorandum for the President's Files from Henry A. Kissinger, 10 April 1973, President's Office Files, Memoranda for the President, Box 91, NPMP.

31 TNA: FCO 59/931 Prime Minister's Meeting with President Nixon, 1–2 February H. T. A. Overton Minute, 12 February 1973; TNA: FCO 82/294 Lord Cromer to Denis Greenhill, 17 January 1973.

32 Kissinger, *YOU*, p. 142.

33 TNA: FCO 82/303 Record of a Discussion at Camp David, 2 February 1973.

34 This direct linkage only materialised in 1974. This was something that Kissinger would later regret. See: Memorandum of Conversation, 26 May 1975, File: May 26, 1975 Ford–Kissinger, NSAMC, Box 12, GFL.

35 TNA: FCO 82/303 Record of Discussion at Camp David, 2 February 1973.

36 *Ibid.*

37 TNA: FCO 82/311 Record of a Discussion at the British Embassy, Washington DC, 19 April 1973.

38 Memorandum of Conversation, 5 March 1973, *FRUS 1969–1976, European Security*, Vol. XXXIX, Doc. 131, p. 402, Note 3.

39 The British were concerned with the pace of American decision making. For instance, they were critical of the Basic Principles agreement signed during the Moscow Summit in May 1972. In the British assessment, the US had signed this agreement without fully understanding all of the consequences. A repetition of this was something the British were keen to avoid. See Reynolds, *Summits*, p. 251.

40 TNA: CAB 164/1233 Record of a Meeting held in the British Embassy, Washington DC, 4 June 1973.

41 TNA: FCO 82/303 Record of Discussion at Camp David, 2 February 1973.

42 TNA: CAB 130/671 GEN 161 (73) 21 March 1973; TNA: CAB 130/671 GEN 161 (73) 1, 30 March 1973.

43 'Atlantic Cross-Currents', *Daily Telegraph*, 25 April 1973, p. 18.

44 TNA: FCO 73/135 Record of a Conversation at the British Embassy, Washington DC, 5 March 1973; TNA: PREM 15/2089 The Year of Europe: The Impact on Transatlantic and Anglo-American Relations: An Analytical Account, February–July 1973.

45 Stephen E. Ambrose, *Nixon: Ruin and Recovery 1973–1990* (New York: Simon & Schuster, 1991), p. 168.

46 James Mayall and Cornelia Navari (eds.), *The End of the Post-War Era: Documents on Great-Power Relations, 1968–1975* (Cambridge: Cambridge University Press, 1980), pp. 360–7; Suri, 'Geopolitics of Globalisation' in Logevall and Preston (eds.), *Nixon in the World*, p. 178; National Security Decision Memorandum 68, 3 July 1970, NSCIHF, NSDM, Box H-217, NPMP.

47 For the quote see Dallek, *Partners in Power*, p. 466. Other examples include: Conversation Among President Nixon, the Chairman of the Federal Reserve System Board of Governors [Burns], the Director of the Office of Management and Budget [Ash], the Chairman of the Council of Economic Advisers [Stein], Secretary of the Treasury Shultz, and the under-Secretary of the Treasury for Monetary Affairs [Volcker], 3 March 1973, *FRUS: 1973–1976, Foreign Economic Policy*, Vol. XXXI, Doc. 16, p. 68.

48 Kissinger, *YOU*, p. 161.

49 Garthoff, *A Journey Through the Cold War*, p. 288.

50 Heath, *The Course*, p. 493.

51 John Stoessinger, *Henry Kissinger: The Anguish of Power* (New York: W.W. Norton, 1976), p. 219.

52 TNA: PREM 15/1362 Rowley Cromer to the Prime Minister, 23 April 1973; TNA: PREM 15/1362 Burke Trend to the Prime Minister, 24 April 1973; Trend to Heath, 2 May 1973, in *Documents on British Policy Overseas* (hereafter: *DBPO*), series III, vol. IV, Doc. 81, A04075 (CD-ROM).

53 Peter Jenkins, 'US Eagerly Awaits Europe's Response to New Atlantic Charter', *Manchester Guardian*, 25 April 1973, p. 2.

54 John Bourne, 'Whitehall Welcomes Kissinger's "Charter" Call', *Financial Times*, 25 April 1973, p. 15.

55 TNA: T 355/80 F. R. Barratt to Mr I. P. Wilson, 19 June 1973; TNA: T355/80, I. P. Wilson to Mr Bailey, 20 June 1973. Also see: Lord Carrington's Meeting with acting secretary Johnson to ambassador in London Embassy [Annenberg], Tel. 193761, 24 November 1970, RG 59 General Records of the Department of State, Subject Numeric Files 1970–73, Political & Defense, Box 2848, NAII. Also see: Lord Carrington, *Reflect*, pp. 228–33; Hynes, *The Year*, pp. 106–8.

56 Hynes, *The Year*, pp. 138–42; Noble, 'Kissinger's Year of Europe', p. 223.

57 Paul Lewis, 'Importance of Atlantic Charter Call Stressed', *Financial Times*, 25 April 1973, p. 5.

58 TNA: PREM 15/1984 Burke Trend to Lord Bridges, 11 May 1973.

59 Spelling, 'Edward Heath', pp. 650–1; Hynes, *The Year*, pp. 196–222; Burk, *Old World*, p. 625.

60 Kissinger, *YOU*, pp. 162–3. On French policy during the 'Year of Europe' see: Aurélie Gfeller, *Building a European Identity: France, the United States, and the Oil Shock, 1973–1974* (New York: Berghahn Books, 2012).

61 TNA: CAB 164/1232 Burke Trend to the Prime Minister, 19 March 1973.

62 TNA: PREM 15/1541 Record of a Conversation between the Prime Minister and the President of the French Republic, 21 May 1973.

63 TNA: CAB 134/3625 European Unit: Minutes of a Meeting Held in Conference Room E, Cabinet Office, 23 May 1973.

64 Kissinger wanted a meeting of deputy foreign ministers to convene where the details of the Declaration of Principles would be negotiated and agreed. This would be followed by a foreign ministers' conference where the final Declaration of Principles would be signed. Jobert flatly rejected this publicly and he refused to put forward a competing modus operandi. See: Möckli, *European Foreign Policy*, pp. 156–8; Claudia Hiepel, 'Kissinger's Year of Europe: A Challenge for the EC and the Franco-German Relationship', in Jan van der Harst, *Beyond the Customs Union: The European Community's Quest for Deepening, Widening and Completion, 1969–75* (Brussels: Bruylant, 2007), p. 284. On the US–French discussions see: Memoranda for the President's File, 27 May 1973, White House Special Files, President's Office Files, Box 91, NPMP.

65 TNA: CAB 164/1233 Burke Trend to Lord Cromer, 8 June 1973.

66 TNA: CAB 164/1233 Record of a Meeting Held in the British Embassy, Washington DC, 4 June 1973. For the quote see Noble, 'Kissinger's Year of Europe', p. 221.

67 TNA: CAB 164/1234 Foreign and Commonwealth Office to the Prime Minister, 18 June 1973; TNA: CAB 164/1234 Burke Trend to Prime Minister, 19 June 1973.

68 TNA: CAB 130/671 GEN 161 (73) 20 June 1973.

69 Hynes, *The Year*, pp. 160–1.

70 TNA: CAB 164/1234 Denis Greenhill to Burke Trend, 6 July 1973; TNA: CAB 164/1235 Michael Palliser to J. O. Wright, 24 July 1973; TNA: CAB 134/3625 European Unit: Minutes of a Meeting Held in Conference Room E, Cabinet Office, 27 June 1973.

71 Kissinger, *YOU*, p. 189.

72 Hynes, *The Year*, pp. 158–61.

73 TNA: FCO 59/931 Rowley Cromer to Denis Greenhill, 19 January 1973; TNA: FCO 59/930 Draft Brief, attached to Private Secretary to Lord Bridges, undated (circa January 1973); Greenhill, *More by Accident*, p. 147.

74 Möckli, *European Foreign Policy*, pp. 146–7.

75 TNA: CAB 164/1234 Foreign and Commonwealth Office to the Prime Minister, 18 June 1973.

76 TNA: PREM 15/1981 Richard Nixon to Edward Heath, 26 July 1973.

77 Kissinger, *YOU*, pp. 191–2.

78 Telcon: President–Kissinger, 30 July 1973, HAKTELCONS.

79 TNA: FCO 82/311 Record of a Meeting, 30 July 1973.

80 Telcon: The President–HAK, 9 August 1973, HAKTELCONS; TNA: FCO 82/311 Record of a Meeting, 30 July 1973.

81 Telcon: Mr Kissinger–Sir Burke Trend, 30 July 1973, HAKTELCONS. Quote in: Sulzberger, *The World and Richard Nixon*, p. 218.
82 TNA: FCO 82/311 R. A. Sykes to Thomas Brimelow, 13 August 1973.
83 Telcon: Secretary Rush–Kissinger, 31 July 1973, HAKTELCONS.
84 Memorandum of Conversation, 7 August 1973, *FRUS 1969–1976, European Security*, Vol. XXXIX, Doc. 342, p. 999. Similar comments were made to the US Treasury Secretary George Shultz. See: Telcon: Kissinger–Shultz, 15 August 1973, HAKTELCONS.
85 Memorandum of Conversation, 17 August 1973: File: August 17, 1973, Kissinger–Schlesinger–John S. Foster, NSAMC, Box 2, GFL.
86 Richard Nixon, *The Real War* (New York: Warner Books, 1980), p. 269.
87 Horne, *Kissinger*, p. 120; Fabian Hilfrich, 'West Germany's Long Year of Europe: Bonn between Europe and the United States', in Schulz and Schwartz (eds.), *The Strained Alliance*, pp. 242–7.
88 Telcon: The President–HAK, 9 August 1973, HAKTELCONS. Quite what areas were shut down is not clear from the existing source material. However, UK documentation does suggest that some aspect of the intelligence relationship was shut down at this point. See: TNA: FCO 82/311 Richard Sykes to Thomas Brimelow, 13 August 1973. The 1973 intelligence cancellation is also referred to by James Callaghan, then foreign and commonwealth secretary, in 1975. See: TNA: PREM 16/733 James Callaghan to the Prime Minister, 22 July 1975.
89 TNA: PREM 15/299 Anglo-French Nuclear Cooperation in the Defence Field: Paper prepared by the Foreign and Commonwealth Office, attached to Solly Zuckerman to the Prime Minister, 5 November 1970. In 1971, both Lord Cromer and Lord Carrington repeated such arguments. See: TNA: PREM 15/787 Cromer to the FCO, 17 April 1971; TNA: CAB 130/506 GEN 25 (71) 1st, 5 March 1971.
90 TNA: PREM 15/1359 Appendix 1 to Annex B, attached to Robert Armstrong to Robert Andrew, 15 April 1972; TNA: CAB 164/1232 United States–United Kingdom Discussions on European Security: Analysis of Objectives, attached to Howard Smith to Burke Trend, 2 March 1973.
91 Schlesinger was appointed US secretary of defense in July 1973. For Schlesinger's discussion with Kissinger about this see: Memorandum of Conversation, 9 August 1973: File: August 9, 1973 Kissinger–Schlesinger, NSAMC, Box 2, GFL. On the other points made see Telcon: James Schlesinger–Henry A. Kissinger, 28 August 1973, HAKTELCONS. British officials were under orders from the Prime Minister to establish the American position in relation to selling Poseidon to the UK. See: TNA: PREM 15/1360 Tel 1277, Douglas-Home to Washington, 15 June 1973; TNA: PREM 15/1360 Tel 1276, Douglas-Home to Washington, 15 June 1973; TNA: PREM 15/1360 Burke Trend to the Prime Minister, 31 August 1973.
92 Telcon: Kissinger–Shultz, 15 August 1973, HAKTELCONS.
93 Aldrich, *GCHQ*, p. 289; TNA: 82/311 R. A. Sykes to Thomas Brimelow, 13 August 1973.
94 Möckli, *European Foreign Policy*, pp. 170–6.
95 Hamilton, 'Year of Europe', 882; TNA: CAB 164/1235 Record of Conversation between Sir Thomas Brimelow and the French Foreign Minister, 29 August 1973; TNA: CAB 164/1235 AW to Burke Trend, 22 August 1973.

96 Memorandum of Conversation, 7 September 1973, RG 59 General Records of the Department of State, Subject Numeric Files, 1970–73, Box 2649, NAII; TNA: FCO 82/321 Message from the Prime Minister to the President, Tom Bridges to M. Alexander, 4 September 1973.

97 Memorandum for Mr Kissinger from Helmut Sonnenfeldt, 11 September 1973, RG 59 General Records of the Department of State, Subject Numeric Files, 1970–73, Box 2649, NAII.

98 Hamilton, 'Year of Europe', 882.

99 On 22 September 1973, Kissinger had been sworn in as the 56th US secretary of state. Kissinger retained his role as National Security Adviser.

100 TNA: FCO 82/310 Record of Conversation, 24 September 1973.

101 Memorandum for Secretary Kissinger from Helmut Sonnenfeldt, 3 October 1973, National Security Council Files, Country Files–Europe, Box 679, NPMP.

102 Geir Lundestad, *The United States and Western Europe since 1945: From 'Empire' by Integration to Transatlantic Drift* (Oxford: Oxford University Press, 2003), pp. 182–3.

103 Minutes of the Secretary of State's Staff Meeting, 23 October 1973, in *Foreign Relations of the United States 1969–1976: Arab–Israeli Crisis and War, 1973* (Washington: United States Government Printing Office, 2011), Vol. XXV, Doc. 250, p. 699. On the failure of US intelligence see: U. Joseph-Bar, *The Watchmen Fell Asleep: The Surprise of Yom Kippur and its Sources* (New York: State University of New York Press, 2005); Robert Litwak, *Détente and the Nixon Doctrine: American Foreign Policy and the Pursuit of Stability, 1969–1976* (Cambridge: Cambridge University Press, 1986), p. 158.

104 TNA: FCO 93/254 Adams to FCO, Tel. 742, 6 October 1973. On British intelligence failures see Geraint Hughes, 'Britain, The Transatlantic Alliance, and the Arab-Israeli War of 1973', *Journal of Cold War Studies*, 10:2 (2008), 17–18.

105 Alec Douglas-Home, *The Way the Wind Blows* (London: Collins, 1978), Appendix B, pp. 296–301.

106 Salim Yaqub, 'The Politics of Stalemate: The Nixon Administration and the Arab-Israeli Conflict, 1969–73', in Nigel Ashton (ed.), *The Cold War in the Middle East: Regional Conflict and the Superpowers, 1969–73* (London: Routledge, 2007), pp. 35–7. For the best recent overview of the origins of the fourth Arab–Israeli war see: Craig Daigle, *Limits of Détente: The United States, the Soviet Union, and the Arab-Israeli conflict, 1969–1973* (New Haven: Yale University Press, 2012).

107 Since Heath had taken office the British had continued to press Washington that the basis of an Arab–Israeli settlement would involve Israel returning to its pre-1967 borders. See for example: Memorandum of Conversation, 3 July 1973, in *FRUS 1969–1976: Arab–Israeli Crisis and War*, Vol. XXV, Doc. 78, pp. 241–2; Memorandum from the Executive Secretary of the Department of State [Eliot] to the President's Assistant for National Security Affairs [Kissinger], 24 July 1973, in *FRUS 1969–1976: Arab-Israeli Crisis and War*, Vol. XXV, Doc. 80, p. 246.

108 Henry Kissinger, *Crisis: The Anatomy of Two Major Foreign Policy Crises* (New York: Simon & Schuster, 2003), p. 58.

109 Matthew Ferraro, *Tough Going: Anglo-American Relations and the Yom Kippur War* (London: iUniverse, 2007), pp. 1–16; Suri, *Kissinger*, pp. 256–67.

110 On the Washington Special Actions Group (WSAG) see: Asaf Siniver, *Nixon, Kissinger, and U.S. Foreign Policy Making* (Cambridge: Cambridge University Press, 2008).

111 Minutes of Washington Special Actions Group Meeting, 6 October 1973, in *FRUS: Arab–Israeli Crisis and War*, Vol. XXV, Doc. 112, pp. 324–37; William Quandt, *Peace Process: American Diplomacy and the Arab–Israeli Conflict Since 1967* (Washington: The Brookings Institute, 2001 revised edition), pp. 106–9; Telcon: Nixon–Kissinger, 7.08 pm, 8 October 1973, HAKTELCONS.

112 Hughes, 'Britain, The Transatlantic Alliance', pp. 21–2.

113 TNA: FCO 93/254 Cromer to FCO, Tel. 3117, 6 October 1973. On Kissinger's motivations see: Telcon: Nixon–Kissinger, 7.08 pm, 8 October 1973; HAKTELCONS; Telcon: Nixon–Kissinger, 8.38 am, 12 October 1973, *ibid.*

114 Kissinger, *Crisis*, pp. 204–5. Cromer had evidently received word from London about Egyptian reluctance given that the prime minister had on 12 October 1973 been told that Egypt would not agree to a ceasefire. See: TNA: PREM 15/1765 Lord Bridges to Prime Minister, Message 6 No. 10 to Blackpool, 12 October 1973. Kissinger's source appears to have been the Soviet Ambassador, Anatoly Dobrynin. Kissinger, *Crisis*, pp. 192–3, 204–5.

115 TNA: PREM 15/1765 Cromer to FCO, Tel. 0340, 13 October 1973.

116 TNA: PREM 15/1765 Douglas-Home to Cairo, Tel. 2305, 12 October 1973; TNA: PREM 15/1765 Adams to FCO, Tel. 0432, 13 October 1973. Douglas-Home rang Kissinger and informed him of this latest information. See: Telcon: Kissinger–Douglas-Home, 2.38 pm, 13 October 1973, HAKTELCONS.

117 TNA: PREM 15/1765 Record of a Meeting at Chequers, 13 October 1973; Donald Maitland, *Diverse Times, Sundry Places* (London: Alpha Press, 1996), pp. 197–8.

118 Minutes of Washington Special Actions Group Meeting, 6 October 1973, in *FRUS 1969–1976: Arab–Israeli Crisis and War*, Vol. XXV, Doc. 112, p. 333.

119 *Ibid.*, pp. 324–37; Memorandum from William B. Quandt and Donald Stukel of the National Security Council Staff to Secretary of State Kissinger, in *ibid.*, Doc. 129, pp. 377–9.

120 Nixon, *Memoirs*, p. 922.

121 Memorandum of Conversation, 13 October 1973, in *FRUS 1969–1976: Arab–Israeli Crisis and War*, Vol. XXV, Doc. 173, p. 485; Transcript of Telephone Conversation Between President Nixon and Secretary of State Kissinger, 12 October 1976, in *ibid.*, Vol. XXV, Doc. 159, p. 446.

122 Richard Ned Lebow and Janice Gross Stein, *We All Lost the Cold War* (Princeton: Princeton University Press, 1994), p. 222.

123 Kissinger, *Crisis*, pp. 211–12.

124 Seymour Hersh, *The Sampson Option: Israel's Nuclear Arsenal and American Foreign Policy* (New York: Random House, 1991), p. 230.

125 Victor Israelyan, *Inside the Kremlin During the Yom Kippur War* (Pennsylvania: Pennsylvania State University Press, 1995), pp. 58–60.

126 Sulzberger, *The World and Richard Nixon*, p. 185.

127 Ziegler, *Heath*, p. 386; Annenberg to SecState, 16 October 1973, Tel. 1755, National Security Council Files, Box 1174, NPMP. For the quote see: Kissinger, *YOU*, p. 709.

128 Telcon: Schlesinger–Kissinger, 4.15 pm, 13 October 1973, HAKTELCONS; Telcon: Kissinger–Cromer, 4.35 pm, 13 October 1973, *ibid.*; Telcon: Nixon–Kissinger, 9.04 am, 14 October 1973, *ibid.*

129 Telcon: Schlesinger–Kissinger, 4.15 pm, 13 October 1973, *ibid.*

130 Memorandum of Conversation, 21 October 1973, in *FRUS 1969–1976: Arab–Israeli Crisis and War*, Vol. XXV, Doc. 221, pp. 633–40; Memorandum of Conversation, 22 October 1973, *ibid.*, Doc. 229, pp. 650–4; Memorandum of Conversation, 22 October 1973, *ibid.*, Doc. 230, pp. 654–60; Memorandum of Conversation, 22 October 1973, *ibid.*, Doc. 232, pp. 662–6.

131 John Mearsheimer and Stephen Walt, *The Israel Lobby and U.S. Foreign Policy* (London: Allen Lane, 2007), pp. 43–4; Horne, *Kissinger*, p. 294.

132 Chaim Herzog, *The War of Atonement: The Inside Story of the Yom Kippur War* (London: Greenhill, 2003), pp. 244–9.

133 Backchannel Message from Egyptian President Sadat to President Nixon, 23 October 1973, within: Hotline Message from Soviet General Secretary Brezhnev to President Nixon, 23 October 1973, in *FRUS 1969–1976: Arab–Israeli Crisis and War*, Vol. XXV, Doc. 248, p. 687.

134 Backchannel Message from President Nixon to Egyptian President Sadat, 23 October 1973, in *FRUS 1969–1976: Arab–Israeli Crisis and War*, Vol. XXV, Doc. 252, p. 702.

135 Secretary Kissinger–Ambassador Dinitz, Telcon, 24 October 1973, HAKTELCONS.

136 Hotline Message from Soviet General Secretary Brezhnev to President Nixon, 23 October 1973, in *FRUS 1969–1976: Arab-Israeli Crisis and War*, Vol. XXV, Doc. 246, pp. 684–5; Hotline Message from Soviet General Secretary Brezhnev to President Nixon, 23 October 1973, in *ibid.*, Doc. 247, p. 686; Brezhnev's letter to Nixon was read by Anatoly Dobrynin to Kissinger. See: Transcript of Telephone Conversation between Secretary of State Kissinger and the Soviet Ambassador (Dobrynin), 24 October 1973, in *ibid.*, Doc. 258, pp. 709–10. The actual message arrived later that afternoon in Washington: Message from Soviet General Secretary Brezhnev to President Nixon, 24 October 1973, in *ibid.*, Doc. 262, pp. 727–8.

137 Message from Soviet General Secretary Brezhnev to President Nixon, undated (24 October 1973), in *FRUS 1969–1976: Arab–Israeli Crisis and War*, Vol. XXV, Doc. 267, pp. 734–5.

138 *Ibid.* p. 735.

139 Hanhimäki, *Flawed*, pp. 315–17; Horne, *Kissinger*, pp. 298–308; Israelyan, *Inside the Kremlin*, pp. 154–64.

140 Telcon: Secretary Kissinger–Al Haig, 9.50 pm, 24 October 1973, HAKTELCONS.

141 Telcon: Secretary Kissinger–Al Haig, 10.20 pm, 24 October 1973, HAKTELCONS; Memorandum for the Record, 24/25 October 1973, in *FRUS 1969–1976: Arab-Israeli Crisis and War*, Vol. XXV, Doc. 269, pp. 737–42, quote at p. 737.

142 Siniver, *US Foreign Policy Making*, pp. 210–20. Why Nixon was not present has led to accusations that the president, troubled by domestic concerns, had resorted to heavy drinking and was thus incapacitated throughout the evening. Nixon was certainly asleep when the message from Moscow arrived. When Kissinger asked whether he should 'wake up the president' on learning of Brezhnev's letter, he was given an immediate response of 'No' from Alexander Haig. This conversation began at 9.50 pm. See: Telcon: Secretary Kissinger–Al Haig, 9.50 pm, 24 October 1973, HAKTELCONS. The context to Nixon's trouble surrounds the resignation of Vice President Spiro Agnew, who had resigned from office on 10 October 1973 as a quid pro quo for being allowed to plead a no contest to criminal charges of corruption during his tenure as Governor of Maryland. On 20 October, President Nixon fired the special prosecutor

into Watergate, Archibald Cox. This led to the Attorney General, Elliot Richardson, and his deputy, William Ruckelshaus, resigning in protest. This was dubbed by the media as the 'Saturday Night Massacre'. Such was the seriousness of this that Alexander Haig notified Kissinger prior to his arrival back in Washington that he would be returning to 'an environment of major national crisis'. See: Telegram from the White House Chief of Staff [Haig] to Secretary of State Kissinger in Tel Aviv, 22 October 1973, in *FRUS 1969–1976: Arab-Israeli Crisis and War*, Vol. XXV, Doc. 234, p. 668. Also see: Spiro T. Agnew, *Go Quietly or Else* (London: William Morrow, 1980), pp. 15–17; Nixon, *Memoirs*, pp. 912–44. For a good overview see: Horne, *Kissinger*, pp. 301–3.

143 Memorandum for the Record, 24/25 October 1973, in *FRUS 1969–1976: Arab–Israeli Crisis and War*, Vol. XXV, Doc. 269, p. 741.

144 Nixon, *Memoirs*, p. 938.

145 Telcon: Secretary Kissinger–Al Haig, 10.20 pm, 24 October 1973, HAKTELCONS.

146 Westad, *Global Cold War*, pp. 199–200.

147 Anatoly Dobrynin, *In Confidence: Moscow's Ambassador to Six Cold War Presidents* (New York: Times Books, 1996), p. 306.

148 'NATO Chiefs Kept in Dark', *Daily Telegraph*, 26 October 1973, p. 1.

149 Dobson, *Anglo-American Relations*, pp. 142–3; Dickie, *Special No More*, pp. 148–50.

150 Telcon: Lord Cromer–Secretary Kissinger, 25 October 1973, 1.03 am, HAKTELCONS; TNA: PREM 15/1766 Lord Cromer to FCO, 25 October 1973; TNA: PREM 15/1766 Larry Woodman to Lord Bridges, 25 October 1973.

151 Aldrich, *GCHQ*, pp. 293–4.

152 Telcon: Lord Cromer–Secretary Kissinger, 25 October 1973, 1.03 am, HAKTELCONS.

153 Hynes, *The Year*, p. 194.

154 'Anxious MPs Hit Out at Nixon's Orders', *The Sun*, 26 October 1973, p. 1.

155 TNA: PREM 15/1766 Lord Cromer to Secretary of State [Douglas-Home], 20 October 1973.

156 Message from President Nixon to Soviet General Secretary Brezhnev, 25 October 1973, in *FRUS 1969–1976: Arab–Israeli Crisis and War*, Vol. XXV, Doc. 274, pp. 747–8; Israelyan, *Inside the Kremlin*, pp. 178–84; 'Russia Retreats from the Brink', *Daily Telegraph*, 26 October 1973, p. 1.

157 WSAG Meeting: Middle East, Quandt and Stukel to Secretary Kissinger, 6 October 1973, NSC Files, Box H-094, NPMP.

158 Simon was serving at this juncture as the Deputy Treasury Secretary and would head up the Federal Energy Administration that was created to tackle the oil embargo. Colby was the Director of the CIA. See Minutes of Washington Special Actions Group Meeting, 6 October 1973, in *FRUS 1969–1976: Arab–Israeli Crisis and War*, Vol. XXV, Doc. 112, pp. 334–5.

159 Memorandum of Conversation, 24 October 1973, in *FRUS 1969–1976: Arab–Israeli Crisis and War*, Vol. XXV, Doc. 261, p. 724.

160 Memorandum of Conversation, 29 October 1973, in *FRUS 1969–1976: Arab–Israeli Crisis and War*, Vol. XXV, Doc. 298, pp. 787–8; Memorandum of Conversation, 29 November, 1973, in *ibid.*, Doc. 363, pp. 1002–3.

161 Memorandum of Conversation, 24 October 1973, in *ibid.*, Doc. 261, p. 724.

162 *Ibid.*

163 Hynes, *The Year*, p. 210.

164 TNA: PREM 15/1382 Heath to Lord Bridges, 28 October 1973.

165 TNA: CAB 185/13 JIC(A)(73) 43rd Conclusions, 26 October 1973; TNA: PREM 15/1382 Note by Cabinet Office Assessment Staff: The US Alert of 25th October, 29 October 1973.

166 Daniel J. Sargent, 'The United States and Globalization in the 1970s', in Ferguson et al. (eds.), *The Shock of the Global*, p. 49.

167 Devuyst, 'American Attitudes on European Political Integration', p. 19.

168 Minutes of Washington Special Action Groups Meeting, 19 October 1973, in *FRUS 1969–1976: Arab–Israeli Crisis and War*, Vol. XXV, Doc. 208, p. 607.

169 On the Euro–Arab dialogue see: Möckli, *European Foreign Policy*, pp. 198–208, 280–6; Gfeller, *Building a European Identity*, pp. 142–161.

170 Giuliano Garavini, 'Completing Decolonization: The 1973 "Oil Shock" and the Struggle for Economic Rights', *International History Review*, 33:3 (2011), 473–87; TNA: PREM 15/1981 Edward Heath to Richard Nixon, 15 June 1973; Willy Brandt, *People and Politics: The Years 1960–1975* (Boston, MA: Little, Brown and Company, 1978), pp. 466–7.

171 Daniel Yergin, *The Prize: The Epic Quest for Oil, Money and Power* (New York: Pocket Books, 1991), pp. 606–7; David Reynolds, *One World Divisible: A Global History Since 1945* (London: Penguin, 2000), pp. 383–5.

172 Reynolds, *One World Divisible*, p. 383; Fiona Venn, 'International Co-operation versus National Self-interest: The United States and Europe during the 1973–1974 Oil Crisis', in Kathleen Burk and Melvyn Stoakes (eds.), *The United States and the European Alliance since 1945* (Oxford: Berg, 1999), pp. 74–5.

173 All of this was summarised for Kissinger by the US Ambassador to London, Walter Annenberg. See: From AmEmbassy London to SecState Washington DC, 15 October 1973, Document Number: 1973LONDON11901, from: http://aad.archives.gov/aad/createpdf?rid=85557&dt=1573&dl=823 (Accessed 11 June 2009).

174 David Frum, *How We Got Here* (New York: Basic Books, 2000), p. 319; *Hansard*, Fifth Series, Vol. 866, col. 649. In the Cabinet it was agreed that contingency plans had to be drawn up to deal with the probable oil embargo. See: TNA: CAB 128/53 CM(73) 47th Conclusions, Conclusions of a Meeting of the Cabinet, 16 October 1973; TNA: PREM 15/1765 Lord Bridges to the Prime Minister, 11 October 1973.

175 TNA: CAB 128/53 CM(73) 52nd Conclusions, Conclusions of a Meeting of the Cabinet, 1 November 1973; Yergin, *The Prize*, pp. 606–8; Heath, *The Course*, p. 501.

176 Kenneth O. Morgan, *Callaghan: A Life* (Oxford: Oxford University Press, 1997), p. 403.

177 TNA: FCO 73/135 Rowley Cromer to Denis Greenhill, 1 November 1973; TNA: PREM 15/2089 A. A. Acland to Thomas Brimelow, 7 November 1973; TNA: FCO 82/308 Lord Cromer to FCO, 30 November 1973; TNA: FCO 82/308 Lord Cromer to FCO, 1 December 1973.

178 Noble, 'Kissinger's Year of Europe', 232.

179 Memorandum of Conversation, 29 November 1973, in *FRUS 1969–1976: Arab–Israeli Crisis and War*, Vol. XXV, Doc. 363, pp. 1002–3.

180 TNA: PREM 15/2232 Lord Cromer to Secretary of State [Douglas-Home] 24 November 1973.

181 Possible Pressure Points on the UK–Dissatisfaction with the UK as an Ally, George S. Springsteen to the Secretary [Kissinger], October 1973, Subject Numerical Files, 1970–73, Pol UK–US, NAII; Aldrich, *GCHQ*, pp. 296–8.

182 Patrick Tyler, *A World of Trouble: The White House and the Middle East – From the Cold War to the War on Terror* (New York: Farrar, Straus & Giroux, 2009), p. 164.

183 Suri, *Kissinger*, pp. 266–72.

184 Kissinger, *YOU*, p. 883.

185 Möckli, *European Foreign Policy*, pp. 198–208, 280–6.

186 Douglas Hurd, *An End to Promises: A Sketch of Government 1970–74* (London: Collins, 1979), pp. 114–15; TNA: PREM 15/2178 Douglas-Home to Washington, Tel. 2504, 20 December 1973.

187 'Japan Buying Egyptian Oil', *Financial Times*, 8 February 1974, p. 7; Yergin, *The Prize*, p. 615.

188 Memorandum for the President's File: Energy Meeting with State and Local elected Officials, 7 November 1973, White House Special Files, President's Office Files, Memoranda for the President, Box 93, NPMP.

189 Tyler, *A World of Trouble*, p. 174.

190 TNA: PREM 15/1768 JIC(A)(73)34 Middle East: Possible Use of Force by the United States, undated (circa December 1973).

191 Hughes, 'Britain, the Transatlantic Alliance', 33–4. Such rhetoric did, however, provoke serious analysis in British circles. The Joint Intelligence Committee compiled a lengthy assessment about US intentions. See: TNA PREM 15/1768 JIC(A)(73)34 Middle East: Possible Use of Force by the United States, undated (circa December 1973). Also see Kissinger's conversation with the British Cabinet Secretary Sir John Hunt. TNA: PREM 15/2178 Record of a Conversation between the Secretary of the Cabinet and the American Secretary of State held at the White House, 30 January 1974.

192 TNA: PREM 15/2232 Lord Cromer to Secretary of State [Douglas-Home], 24 November 1973.

193 TNA: FCO 82/308 Note for the Record, 29 November 1973.

194 TNA: PREM 15/2038 John Hunt to the Prime Minister, 6 November 1973; TNA: PREM 15/2038 John Hunt to the Prime Minister, 4 December 1973; TNA: PREM 15/2089 Extract from Record of Conversation between the Prime Minister and the Prime Minister of Italy, 9 December 1973.

195 TNA: FCO 30/1685 Mr Alexander to Mr Butler, 26 October 1973.

196 TNA: PREM 15/2089 Douglas-Home to Washington, 28 November 1973.

197 TNA: PREM 15/2232 Record of Conversation between French, German, UK and US Foreign Ministers, 9 December 1973.

198 TNA: PREM 15/2232 John Hunt to Lord Bridges, 11 December 1973; TNA: PREM 15/2232 Edward Peck to FCO, 11 December 1973.

199 Sargent, 'The United States and Globalization' in Ferguson et al. (eds.), *The Shock of the Global*, p. 50.

200 William P. Bundy, *A Tangled Web: The Making of Foreign Policy in the Nixon Presidency* (London: I.B. Tauris, 1998), p. 458; TNA: PREM 15/2232 Record of a Conversation between the Prime Minister, the Foreign and Commonwealth Secretary and Secretary Henry Kissinger, 12 December 1973.

201 For the letter see TNA: PREM 15/2178 Earl Sohm to Alec Douglas-Home, 14 December 1973. For the quote see Ziegler, *Heath*, p. 384.

202 TNA: FCO 55/1102 Julian Amery to Secretary of State, 18 December 1973.

203 Kissinger, *YOU*, p. 885.

204 Readers should follow the material contained within TNA: PREM 15/2178; TNA: FCO 59/1155 and TNA: FCO 59/1156.

205 Hamilton, 'Year of Europe', 887–9.

206 TNA: PREM 15/2178 Richard Nixon to the Prime Minister, attached to Earl D. Sohm to the Prime Minister, 9 January 1974; William E. Simon, *A Time for Reflection* (London: Regnery, 2003), p. 88; Letter to Heads of Government of Major Oil-Consuming Nations Inviting their Participation in a Meeting on International Energy Problems, 10 January 1974, in *Public Papers of the Presidents of the United States, Richard Nixon, 1974*, pp. 9–10.

207 Telcon: Helmut Sonnenfeldt–Secretary Kissinger, 2 January 1974, HAKTELCONS; Kissinger, *YOU*, p. 891.

208 TNA: PREM 15/2178 Palliser to FCO, Tel. 168, 11 January 1974; TNA: PREM 15/2178 Tomkins to FCO, Tel. 40, 11 January 1974; TNA: PREM 15/2178 Tomkins to FCO, Tel. 44, 12 January 1974; TNA: PREM 15/2178 Douglas-Home to Washington, Tel. 120, 17 January 1974; TNA: PREM 15/2178 Douglas-Home to Washington, Tel. 121, 17 January 1974; Reginald Dale, 'EEC Accepts Invitation to U.S. Oil Conference', *Financial Times*, 16 January 1974.

209 TNA: PREM 15/2178 Douglas-Home to Bonn, Tel. 19, 10 January 1974; TNA: PREM 15/2178 Record of a Conversation between the Prime Minister and the Japanese Minister for International Trade and Industry, 11 January 1974; TNA: PREM 15/2178 Douglas-Home to Bonn, Tel. 19, 10 January 1974; TNA: PREM 15/2178 J. L. Taylor to Mr Egerton, 10 January 1974.

210 Ziegler, *Heath*, pp. 401–27; Alan Clark, *The Tories: Conservatives and the Nation State, 1922–1997* (London: Weidenfeld & Nicolson, 1998), pp. 350–3.

211 TNA: FCO 59/1155 N. M. Fenn to Mr Taylor, 29 January 1974; TNA: FCO 59/1155 Brief 1: Washington Energy Meeting, February 1974; TNA: FCO 59/1155 M. D. Butler to Mr Fenn, 28 January 1974.

212 Hunt had replaced the recently retired Burke Trend as Cabinet Secretary.

213 On the Hunt visit see TNA: PREM 15/2178 Douglas-Home to Washington, Tel. 192, 25 January 1974; TNA: PREM 15/2178 Record of a Conversation between the Secretary of the Cabinet and the American Secretary of State held at the White House, 30 January 1974. On Kissinger's indiscretion see Telcon: Secretary Kissinger–Dan Rather, 28 January 1974, HAKTELCONS. On the Rampton visit see TNA: PREM 15/2178 From the White House to the Cabinet Office, undated (circa 3 February 1974); TNA: PREM 15/2235 Message from the Prime Minister to President Nixon, undated (circa 5 February 1974).

214 TNA: FCO 59/1155 Aide Memoire, attached to S. L. Egerton to G. Campbell, 1 February 1974.

215 Hamilton, 'Year of Europe', 889. The mandate is contained within: TNA: FCO 59/1155 Palliser to FCO, Tel. 691, 5 February 1974.

216 Jobert made this explicit in his speech on 6 February 1974. See: TNA: FCO 59/1155 Ewart-Biggs to FCO, Tel 162, 6 February 1974; TNA: FCO 59/1155 N. M. Fenn to Mr

Taylor, 6 February 1974; TNA: FCO 59/1155 Palliser to FCO, Tel. 692, 5 February 1974.

217 TNA: FCO 59/1155 H. T. A. Overton to Mr Fenn, 7 February 1974; TNA: FCO 9/1155 N. M. Fenn to Mr Taylor, 6 February 1974; TNA: FCO 59/1155 From FCO to Immediate Certain Missions Tel. Guidance 21, 8 February 1974; TNA: PREM 15/2179 Sykes to FCO, Tel. 516, 9 February 1974.

218 For the quote see: Memorandum of Conversation, 17 August 1973: File: August 17, 1973 Kissinger–Schlesinger–John S. Foster, NSAMC, Box 2, GFL. Also see: Memorandum of Conversation, 7 August 1973, *FRUS 1969–1976, European Security*, Vol. XXXIX, Doc. 342, p. 999; Telcon: Kissinger–Shultz, 15 August 1973, HAKTELCONS; Telcon: Secretary Kissinger–Helmut Sonnenfeldt, 10 January 1974, *ibid.*; Telcon: Secretary Kissinger–Dan Rather, 28 January 1974, *ibid.*; Telcon: Secretary Kissinger–Mr McCloy, 8 February 1974, 11.10 am, *ibid.*; Telcon: Secretary Kissinger–Mr McCloy, 8 February 1974, 9.40 pm, *ibid.*

219 TNA: PREM 15/2178 Record of a Conversation between the Prime Minister and the German Minister of Finance, 29 January 1974; TNA: FCO 59/1155 The Kissinger Initiative: Draft Steering Brief for the Meeting in Washington on 11 February 1974, attached to G. G. Campbell to J. Taylor, 21 January 1974; TNA: PREM 15/2178 Douglas-Home to Washington, Tel 269, 3 February 1974; TNA: PREM 15/2178 Personal for Sykes from Sir Jack Rampton, undated (circa 3 February 1974); FCO 59/1155 S. J. G. Cambridge to Mr Marshall, 7 February 1974; TNA: FCO 59/1155 P. H. R. Marshall to Mr Butler, 4 February 1974; TNA: FCO 59/1155 S. J. G. Cambridge to Mr Marshall, 7 February 1974; TNA: FCO 59/1156 Steering Brief: Washington Energy Conference 11 February 1974, provided by Department of Energy, 7 February 1974.

220 Telcon: Secretary Kissinger–Helmut Sonnenfeldt, 10 January 1974, HAKTELCONS; Telcon: Secretary Kissinger–Dan Rather, 28 January 1974, *ibid*; Kissinger, *YOU*, pp. 897–906.

221 James Schlesinger, *America at Century's End* (New York: Columbia University Press, 1989), p. 55.

222 Memorandum of Conversation, 8 January 1974, File: January 8, 1974, Kissinger–Schlesinger, NSAMC, Box 3, GFL.

223 *Sunday Telegraph*, 9 February 1974.

224 Telcon: Secretary Kissinger–Mr McCloy, 8 February 1974, 11.10 am, HAKTELCONS; Telcon: Secretary Kissinger–Mr McCloy, 8 February 1974, 9.40 pm, *ibid*; Telcon: Secretary Kissinger–Helmut Sonnenfeldt, 8 February 1974, *ibid.*

225 Memorandum of Conversation, 9 February 1974, File: February 9, 1974, Nixon, Kissinger, George Schultz, William Simon, NSAMC, Box 3, GFL.

226 Memorandum for the President from Kenneth Rush, 17 December 1973, NSCIHF, Study Memorandums, Box H-182, NPMP; Memorandum of Conversation, 8 January 1974, File: January 8, 1974, Kissinger–Schlesinger, NSAMC Box 3, GFL.

227 TNA: PREM 15/2178 Record of a Conversation between the Secretary of the Cabinet and the American Secretary of State held at the White House, 30 January 1974; TNA: PREM 15/2179 Sykes to FCO, Tel. 516, 9 February 1974.

228 Paul Lewis, 'Nixon Seeks Code for Oil Deals', *Financial Times*, 11 February 1974, p. 1.

229 From AmEmbassy London to SecState Washington DC, 7 February 1974, Document

Number: 1974LONDON01769, from: http://aad.archives.gov/aad/createpdf?rid=15773&dt=1572&dl=823 (Accessed 11 July 2009).

230 Hamilton, 'Year of Europe', 889.

231 Kissinger, *YOU*, pp. 913–14.

232 All of which was reported to Nixon. See: Telcon: Secretary Kissinger–President Nixon, 11 February 1974, HAKTELCONS. A British report on events is within TNA: FCO 59/1155 Sykes to FCO, Tel. 533, 11 February 1974. For quote see: Cromwell, *The United States and the European Pillar*, p. 90.

233 Telcon: Secretary Kissinger–Al Haig, 11 February 1974, HAKTELCONS.

234 Telcon: Secretary Kissinger–President Nixon, 11 February 1974, HAKTELCONS.

235 *Ibid.*

236 Telcon: President Nixon–Secretary Kissinger, 12 February 1974, HAKTELCONS.

237 Rupert Cornwell, 'Pompidou Turns a Knife in the European Wound', *Financial Times*, 15 February 1974, p. 6.

238 Telcon: General Scowcroft–Secretary Kissinger, 12 February 1974, HAKTELCONS.

239 TNA: FCO 59/1155 Sykes to FCO, Tel. 562, 13 February 1974.

240 Yergin, *The Prize*, p. 630; TNA: FCO 59/1156 Text: Communiqué of 13 Nation Energy Conference, 14 February 1974. All of the details of the communiqué and what it meant in practical terms were spelt out by Jack Rampton for the Cabinet Secretary. See: TNA: FCO 96/54 Jack Rampton to John Hunt, 15 February 1974.

241 TNA: FCO 59/1156 Text: Communiqué of 13 Nation Energy Conference, 14 February 1974.

242 Bundy, *Tangled Web*, p. 459; Statement at the Conclusion of the Washington Energy Conference, 13 February 1974, in *Public Papers of the Presidents, Richard Nixon, 1974*, p. 165.

243 Telcon: Secretary Kissinger–The President, 14 February 1974, HAKTELCONS.

244 Telcon: Secretary Kissinger–The President, 13 February 1974, *ibid.*

245 Telcon: General Scowcroft–Secretary Kissinger, 14 February 1974, *ibid.*

246 Memorandum for the President's Files: Meeting with John McCloy, 13 March 1973, NSCIHF, Presidential HAK Memcons, Box 1025, NPMP.

247 Memorandum of Conversation, 11 March 1974, File: March 11, 1974, Kissinger, Schlesinger, Joint Chiefs, NSAMC, Box 3, GFL.

248 John Lewis Gaddis, 'Rescuing Choice from Circumstance: The Statecraft of Henry Kissinger', in Gordon A. Craig and Francis L. Loewenheim (eds.), *The Diplomats, 1939–1979* (Princeton, NJ: Princeton University Press, 1994), pp. 564–92.

249 Telcon: The President–HAK, 9 August 1973, HAKTELCONS, Box 24, NPMP.

250 Greenhill, *More by Accident*, p. 158.

251 Robert Mauthner, 'Almost Like the Good Old Days', *Financial Times*, 26 February 1974, p. 6.

252 TNA: FCO 59/1156 Sykes to FCO, Tel. 612, 16 February 1974; TNA: FCO 73/151 Record of Conversation between Mr Wright, Fenn and Cuviller, 15 February 1974. Quote in TNA: FCO 59/1155 M. D. Butler to Mr Wright, 4 February 1974.

253 TNA: PREM 15/2232 Record of a Conversation between the Prime Minister, the Foreign and Commonwealth Secretary and Secretary Henry Kissinger, 12 December 1973.

254 A point articulated within Twigge, 'Operation Hullabaloo', 689–701.

# 4

# Wilson returns
## 1974–76

*You have to operate on the assumption that Great Britain is through.*

Henry Kissinger to President Ford, October 1974[1]

## Introduction

Heath's final months in office were dominated by economic and social problems. Continuing trouble with the trade union movement had resulted in a three-day working week being enforced, and the ongoing oil embargo had led to the British public having to restrict their energy use. This set of circumstances had led to what one popular British newspaper would term as Heath's 'Long agony in No. 10'.[2] Following continuing struggles with the trade union movement, the prime minister decided to call a snap general election under the mantra of 'Who runs Britain?' The electorate gave Heath their answer and, in spite of winning the majority of the popular vote, Heath's Conservative Party failed to achieve a parliamentary majority. Instead, Harold Wilson's Labour Party had won the largest parliamentary contingent, securing him 301 out of a possible 635 seats. This, however, left him 17 seats short of an overall parliamentary majority, and Heath engaged in talks with the leader of the Liberal Party, Jeremy Thorpe, about the possibility of forming a coalition government. Following the inability of the two sides to reach an agreement, Heath was forced to resign as prime minister, and for the third time in a decade Harold Wilson was in office.[3]

For scholars studying US–UK relations, three distinct interpretations of Wilson's final governments have emerged. One interpretation suggests that the US–UK relationship continued to deteriorate in its relevance largely because of Britain's declining significance as a military and political ally to the United States.[4] Others have contradicted such arguments, insisting that Wilson's efforts to revive the 'special relationship' with Washington were indeed successful. To support this, these scholars point to the ongoing intelligence and nuclear relationship and also argue that the UK provided support and, more important still, exacted a degree of influence over the United States' wider Cold War policies.[5] Other writers are more sceptical of this interpretation. While they accept that personal relations between elite figures improved, they question what discernible benefits this achieved for British interests; however, they do accept that elements of the special relationship were retained. As such, this period for US–UK relations was one where the special relationship waned politically but it retained its more practical elements.[6]

The vast majority of these accounts were written before access to large swaths of government documentation was permitted and by utilising this new material such arguments are in need of re-interpretation. Additionally, most accounts have largely marginalised British defence cuts within the broader context of US–UK relations and even works that have focused upon this require clarification.[7] This chapter also challenges the idea that certain areas of US–UK cooperation, namely nuclear and intelligence cooperation, remained sacrosanct.[8] To be sure, this cooperation did continue but existing accounts fail to illustrate that this was an area constantly used by US policy-makers as a means for exerting political leverage upon the Wilson government. Throughout 1974–76, the US threatened to cancel US–UK intelligence and nuclear cooperation in order to lessen the severity of Britain's defence cuts. As will be shown below, this coercive diplomacy, which had worked successfully against the Heath government, was to be rather less successful when applied against Harold Wilson.

## Wilson's foreign policy

As shown previously, US–UK relations in Heath's final year of office were at a near crisis point, and a change of personnel was always likely to improve relations amongst political elites. Harold Wilson, however, was hardly the ideal candidate, given that during his interaction with Nixon in 1969–70 he had personally irritated the president. His appointment of John Freeman, an ardent critic of Nixon, as UK ambassador to Washington in 1968 was especially unwelcome.[9] Personal characteristics aside, Wilson's insistence that Britain keep its accelerated plans for an East of Suez withdrawal, along with his unwillingness to offer a greater commitment to NATO, only vexed US policy-makers further.[10] For Wilson, the fashion in which Washington ignored his efforts at improving East–West relations and bringing a settlement to the Vietnam War hardly engendered a close relationship with Washington.[11]

Wilson may not have had the greatest track record with Nixon but, given recent experiences with Heath, his election was welcomed by both Nixon and Kissinger.[12] The extent to which the president's relationship with Heath had deteriorated is perhaps best illustrated by Nixon's quip that his experiences with Heath had resulted in the improbable: he and Wilson were now 'good friends'.[13] Wilson's return to office also marked a change in British foreign policy that would place a renewed emphasis upon the US–UK relationship. Heath's seemingly Euro-centric foreign policy was to be reversed and Wilson let it known that he would not be trying to create common political policies within the EEC. In fact, Wilson's renegotiation of the terms of Britain's EEC entry even questioned Britain's membership.[14]

Wilson's appointment of James Callaghan as foreign and commonwealth secretary, coupled with the prime minister's willingness to allow Callaghan a degree of freedom in conducting foreign policy that was not afforded during his earlier premierships, further signalled the Labour government's intention to move away from the European course that Heath had charted. Callaghan had opposed British membership of the EEC and believed Heath's European policies had been ill-conceived. On assuming the role as foreign and commonwealth secretary, he was not shy in putting forward his anti-EEC feelings and stated his intention to re-affirm the US–UK relationship.[15]

Such broad assessment must, however, be carefully defined because, despite the scepticism towards the EEC, Wilson and Callaghan did not wish for Britain to leave the Community. As noted elsewhere, the creation of policy-making institutions within the EEC framework received the backing of Wilson and Callaghan throughout the period.[16] Indeed, the whole decision to renegotiate EEC entry was driven largely by internal Labour Party politics. The question of EEC membership had been a deeply divisive topic within the Labour Party and, following EEC membership in 1973, the issue continued to provoke bitter debate.[17] However, the focus had now shifted to debating the terms of entry that Heath's government had secured which were seen by EEC sceptics, including Wilson and Callaghan, as being economically punitive. Wilson had, for instance, described the terms Heath had secured as 'utterly crippling' for the British economy.[18] Therefore, the Labour Party manifesto of 1974 declared that it would renegotiate the terms of EEC membership and, if this was not achieved to the satisfaction of Wilson, Britain would withdraw from the EEC.[19] The likelihood of this happening, however, was improbable. Firstly, Wilson was very unlikely to be tied to his manifesto pledges given his penchant for flexibly interpreting the meaning of such pledges. The prime minister also had no real intention of withdrawing from the EEC because he had reconciled that membership was necessary for Britain's longer-term economic and political well-being. As one British official remarked correctly, 'The renegotiation was in fact largely a sham'.[20]

Wilson's approach was therefore based upon twin pillars. He wanted to re-establish intimate relations with the US, with the hope that this would provide him with unique access and influence over US foreign policy. Concurrently, Wilson intended for Britain to remain in the EEC, as this would allow Britain to derive the economic benefits of EEC membership. In essence, the role Wilson had sought for Britain in the 1960s was to be largely transferred into the 1970s.[21]

## The end of the 'Year of Europe'

On assuming office, Wilson quickly contacted Nixon and informed him that it was his intention to put US–UK relations on a sounder footing.[22] 'The Labour government apparently wants to revive something closely akin to Britain's erstwhile "special relationship" with the United States,' the US ambassador reported from London.[23] In June 1974, Kissinger corroborated this assessment.[24]

Such an overt attempt to re-affirm the US–UK relationship was appreciated at the highest levels of the US government, and Callaghan's appointment was also seen as a positive for US interests.[25] In a rather typical Machiavellian moment between Nixon and Kissinger, both men talked about how it was 'useful' that Wilson wanted to promote closer US–UK relations. Nixon, however, questioned whether Wilson would actually be able to deliver much of substance and mocked that: 'Harold is going to want to have some foreign policy – some little things for his bonnet and he may just start swinging a little weight around'.[26] Nevertheless, Nixon and Kissinger viewed Wilson's foreign policy as useful in safeguarding against French domination of the EEC and preventing it from pursuing an anti-American agenda. It would also ensure that the continuing Euro–Arab dialogue would not undermine US diplomacy in the Middle East.[27]

Although Wilson had signalled an intention to re-emphasise the Atlantic relationship, this did little to alter the Nixon administration's attitude towards Western Europe or have a calming influence upon its actions. In particular, the matter of the Declaration of Principles had still not been resolved and the Nixon administration now pushed for its conclusion. Kissinger was determined to exploit US security guarantees towards Europe to accomplish this. As Kissinger explained in conversation with Schlesinger:

> The Europeans have no strategy. We have to create the impression that to cross us is at least as dangerous as to cross the French. We can't let the

> Europeans organise on an anti-American basis. We have a good opportunity now, with a new British government, and the Germans are weak ... If Europe gets the idea that unity prevents them from talking to us, they will withdraw more and more from NATO in the EC. We want to counter Europe by using NATO.[28]

The question arises as to what Kissinger meant by using NATO to counter Europe. The answer to this soon became clear. During internal discussions in Washington, Kissinger concluded that the US should threaten to withdraw troops from Europe, because this would critically undermine their security in relation to the Warsaw Pact. This, in turn, would produce a more cooperative political attitude from the EEC towards the US.[29] All of this was coupled with a wider effort on Kissinger's part to influence members of the EEC by utilising American economic power.[30] On 15 March 1974, Nixon deployed this tactic publicly during a speech at the Executives Club in Chicago. Here, the president explained that he would not tolerate 'a situation where the nine countries of Europe gang up against the United States ... the United States which is their guarantee of security'. The president was even more explicit in outlining that the EEC could not 'have ... US participation and cooperation on the security front and then proceed to have confrontation and even hostility on the economic and political front'.[31] Following the Washington Energy Conference, British officials feared that Nixon and Kissinger would start 'throwing their weight around' and, as shown earlier, this was the very 'lesson' that both Nixon and Kissinger had taken from the conference. Nixon's speech, therefore, was another example of the Nixon administration's determination to more robustly defend US interests in relation to the EEC.

What is of interest at this point is that Kissinger's private conversations in Washington reveal that Nixon was making rather empty threats. In reality, the president and Kissinger had little intention of reducing America's military commitment to Europe.[32] As US internal assessments suggested, there were very few long-term methods available for punishing Western Europe that would not simultaneously damage US interests. Nevertheless, the US had been successful in manipulating British foreign policy decisions when Kissinger and Schlesinger had temporarily suspended intelligence and nuclear cooperation in 1973. In a similar fashion, US threats to withdraw their forces had a profound impact upon European policy-makers. As Kissinger noted gleefully, his bluff had not been called and the Europeans were 'pissing in their pants'. As Kissinger reported, 'The Germans have promised to have consultation with us before they take decisions. The British have gone even further.'[33] In this light, it is perhaps not surprising that, on 19 March 1974, the president gave a conciliatory speech on the subject of US–EEC relations.[34]

What was meant by the British having 'gone even further' is unclear, but it probably referred to Callaghan's promise to Helmut Sonnenfeldt (15 March 1974) that Britain would engage bilaterally over the creation of the Declaration of Principles. This, Callaghan assured Sonnenfeldt, would be conducted without the knowledge of Britain's EEC partners.[35] By April 1974, this process was under way when the newly appointed British ambassador to Washington, Sir Peter Ramsbotham, met with Kissinger to discuss the declaration.[36] Perhaps this signalled a new level of exclusive interaction between US and UK officials. Certainly, the Wilson government could point to the fact that it had secured US–UK private discussions prior to a 'Big Five' discussion about the monetary and oil crises engulfing the Western powers.[37] US policy-makers would also make their British counterparts aware of their policy initiatives towards the ongoing SALT negotiations and the Middle East peace process.[38] All of this was undertaken, however, on the proviso that this information was to remain exclusively within the British government. Indeed, the US made it explicit that this information was not to be transmitted to Britain's EEC partners. Of course, the British were under no legal obligation to provide this information to their EEC allies. Nevertheless, as this illustrates, the US could have a profound impact upon Britain's interaction with the EEC.

Even though the Wilson government had managed to secure a level of interaction in US–UK relations which they believed had been missing under Heath, British officials still remained sceptical about the course of US policy. 'Despite the President and Dr. Kissinger's recent public criticism of Europe in general, Dr. Kissinger has gone out of his way to be friendly to HMG [Her Majesty's Government] since it took office,' Wilson was warned. This was occurring because Kissinger wanted to 'influence our policies at what he will judge to be a formative stage; and to ensure that we help steer Europe away from a course damaging to US interests'.[39] The US had singled out Britain 'for favourable mention' but the trouble existed that 'we may be unable to deliver what the US Administration expects of us'.[40] Several other senior British officials provided comparable advice and, given what was being stated privately in Washington, this advice does appear rather pertinent.[41]

Even in the face of such warnings, US–UK bilateral discussions continued as the 'Year of Europe' slowly petered out. The Declaration of Principles was eventually signed during the Ottawa conference (June 1974) but its eventual contents – as Kissinger lamented – were hardly the 'far reaching embodiment of shared purpose we had in mind'.[42] Or as one unknown author argued in *Foreign Affairs*:

> What the United States had envisioned as the 'Year of Europe', a period of imaginative updating and refurbishing of the NATO alliance, capped with a

new Atlantic Charter, has become instead the year in which Washington's relationship with its European partners has struck an all-time low.[43]

Moreover, as one CIA brief explained in August 1974, the new Declaration of Principles would not guarantee when and if the EEC would ever act as a collective. As the brief neatly summarised: 'Since EC members retain the option to act independently on many issues, there is the even greater problem of unpredictability. The US can never be certain when, or if, the Nine will act collectively.'[44] Given this, it is hardly surprising that scholars refer to Kissinger's initiative as 'the year that never was'.[45]

## Discord in Cyprus

On 9 August 1974, Richard M. Nixon became the first man to resign the office of the presidency and Gerald R. Ford was thus sworn in as the 38th president of the US.[46] Facing the new president were a multitude of problems including Nixon's potential pardon, rising inflation and unemployment, and the continuing problems in Vietnam. Ford's top priority was hardly, then, the conduct of US–UK relations.[47] In spite of this, the new president was soon confronted with something approaching a crisis in US–UK relations, because of differences over the evolving situation in Cyprus.

The Cyprus crisis is important for understanding US–UK relations in the 1970s for a number of important reasons. It serves as a clear example of how the US undermined the policy objectives of the UK in trying to resolve the conflict. It further demonstrated that the US would pursue its own regional interests at the expense of the concerns of its British ally. If further proof were needed that the US−UK special relationship did not apply to all facets of US−UK interaction, then events during the Cyprus crisis would act as a timely reminder. As two scholars noted about the Suez crisis, 'For Europeans, "Suez" stood for the moment when they had been shocked into awareness of how ... inferior in power they were to the United States, and how dependent on that power [they were]'.[48] The Cyprus crisis demonstrated this fact once again.

On 15 July 1974, the Greek government inspired a military coup in Cyprus, which removed Archbishop Makarios and installed Nico Sampson as the new Cypriot leader which sparked an ethnic conflict between the Greek and Turkish Cypriot populations.[49] Though US intelligence had noted that relations on the island were steadily worsening, for both the American and British intelligence community events in Cyprus came somewhat as a surprise.[50] For the British, events were worrisome on a number of levels, because as a guarantor power – established under the 1960 Zurich Accords – the British had a legal obligation to uphold the status quo in Cyprus.[51] More important still was the likely reaction of Turkey and Greece, because Cyprus was comprised of a mixed Turkish and Greek population. Nico Sampson was an ardent supporter of enosis, meaning he wanted Cyprus to accede to Greece, and his firebrand personality and history of political violence only increased the likelihood that the coup would lead to violence. In particular, the rights of Turkish Cypriots were likely to be targeted by Sampson, and Turkey threatened to intervene militarily if Turkish Cypriots came under attack. Greece responded by declaring that such Turkish action would be taken as a *casus belli*.[52]

From the British perspective this was all rather troublesome for a number of interconnected reasons. First, they feared that such a conflagration would have damaging repercussions for NATO. As the British ambassador in Athens, Sir Robin Hooper, warned, a war between Turkey and Greece would challenge the entire 'credibility' of NATO. According to Hooper, at the very least a war would leave NATO's southern and eastern flanks seriously weakened.[53] Slightly less melodramatically, the FCO brief on the conflict outlined that ethnic violence in Cyprus had to stop in order to restore stability to NATO's position.[54]

The other main anxiety for Wilson's government was the status of British sovereign bases on Cyprus, because they provided Britain with significant intelligence abilities. Most obviously, they provided an important listening post into the Middle East. Cyprus also acted as Britain's base into the Mediterranean, and had done so since the withdrawal from Egypt/Suez in 1956.[55] The maintenance of such facilities was, however, financially expensive, and contributed negatively to Britain's balance of payments. The Wilson government had therefore highlighted these bases for potential closure in its ongoing defence review. The possibility of conflict in Cyprus would only add further burden to sustaining such facilities.[56] Of course, less geopolitical matters were also in the forefront of British policy-makers' concerns. While more mundane, the most immediate problem facing Wilson was how to ensure the safe passage of British holidaymakers on the island.[57]

In order to prevent a Turkish–Greek war, British officials concluded that they would have to remove Sampson and re-install Makarios as president. This, it was felt, would prevent a Turkish invasion of Cyprus, which would in turn avoid a wider conflagration, thus maintaining NATO's integrity and protecting Britain's sovereign bases.

## Washington's thinking

On learning of the coup, Kissinger chaired a session of the WSAG.[58] Confusion reigned as to what had actually occurred in Cyprus, and it was still unclear as to what had triggered the hostilities. US policy-makers, however, were deeply concerned about the probable actions of the USSR.[59] 'I think our first objective should be to prevent any kind of Soviet action. We must keep this as an internal affair and keep it from becoming internationalized,' Kissinger concluded.[60] The foremost worry of the US, then, was preventing the USSR from gaining any sort of advantage from the conflict. In keeping with the geopolitical vision of the Nixon–Ford administrations, events in Cyprus were of importance, because of the likely wider ramifications they could have upon the Cold War. One intelligence briefing on Cyprus captures this thinking rather well:

> Cyprus is a foreign policy problem for the United States because strife between the Greek Cypriots and Turk Cypriots brings Greece and Turkey into military confrontation unhinging NATO's southern flank; because Cyprus's crises are invariably raised in the Security Council; and because such crises have the potential to complicate our evolving relations with the Soviets and affect the atmosphere in which the United States and the Soviet Union deal with the Arab/Israeli conflict.[61]

A second WSAG was convened on 16 July 1974 and again – despite the uncertainty regarding the details of the coup – the clear consensus was that the US had to prevent Soviet intervention.[62] The British idea of returning Makarios to power was met with both consternation and trepidation in US policy-making circles, because it was believed that this would only encourage Makarios loyalists to continue fighting, which would lead to a situation where they would then seek military aid from any source willing to provide it: i.e. the USSR.[63] Moreover, Makarios was considered by Washington to be a communist sympathiser. His return to power, then, was not viewed as something which the US should be actively seeking to achieve. Kissinger was explicit in articulating this thinking during the WSAG meeting:

> As I assess the situation, for us the best outcome would be a Clerides government. I just don't understand why the Turks would want to bring Makarios back. I don't think [the Turks] understand our analysis of the situation. Somebody has to go to London and explain our position.[64]

Kissinger then explained to the WSAG that the US would seek to utilise its influence with Turkey to make this point clear.[65]

From the outset of the crisis British and American objectives clearly differed. Claims from Callaghan that 'our two countries were agreed on broad objectives, we differed on procedures and tactics' thus appear less convincing.[66] US policy-makers viewed the coup predominantly as a potential opportunity for

Soviet aggrandisement. Returning Makarios to power was never an objective of US policy either. More importantly from the perspective of US–UK relations was that the US secretary of state was actively charting a policy in direct opposition to that of London and would over the course of the next weeks pursue a diplomatic course that undercut British efforts at implementing both a ceasefire and a lasting political solution.

As the violence continued in Cyprus, Turkish and Greek representatives convened in London and, under the auspices of British chairmanship, the terms of a possible ceasefire were negotiated. At the conference, Callaghan declared that the 'ideal solution' was to see Makarios return to power and, in order to achieve this, Callaghan suggested that military intervention may be required.[67] Such thinking was anathema to US objectives. First, the return of Makarios was not an ambition of the US, and the idea of utilising military force against a NATO member only soured US opinion further. Given recent American experiences in Vietnam, coupled with Nixon's domestic woes, one can appreciate why such a suggestion was met with incredulity. Kissinger therefore proposed that he would 'work for a compromise in which neither Makarios or the other guy take over', reasoning that this would prevent Soviet intervention in the conflict.[68]

Determined to ensure that the London conference did not reach any firm decisions without US representation, Kissinger had despatched Joseph Sisco, the under-secretary of state for political affairs, as his envoy. On 18 July, Sisco reported back to Washington that Callaghan was still supporting the restoration of Makarios, and that he had still not ruled out the possibility of utilising force to achieve this objective.[69] Kissinger remained sceptical as to whether such rhetoric was really indicative of likely British action.[70] Meanwhile, as Washington continued to analyse likely British motives, the ceasefire negotiations were stalling. By 19 July, it was apparent that Callaghan's intermediary efforts had failed to break the Turkish–Greek impasse.[71] Consequently, Turkey took a more direct approach in protecting their interests.

## Invasion and coup

In the early hours of 20 July 1974, Turkey launched an invasion of Cyprus. The Greeks responded by placing their military on high alert, and prepared for hostilities on their northern border with Turkey.[72] Only direct threats from Washington to permanently withdraw all military aid from Greece prevented further Greek action.[73] The evolving situation was deemed so serious by Washington that discussion took place as to whether the ruling Greek junta should be overthrown by some US-sponsored covert action. James Schlesinger, in particular, was keen to pursue such a path. In contrast, Kissinger was rather more circumspect, and was reluctant to follow such a course. 'I don't like overthrowing governments,' Kissinger retorted. As Kissinger then explained, 'I'm not sure the Greek government will last out the week, anyway. It seems to me there is no way it will survive.'[74]

Events in Greece would prove Kissinger's assessment correct, as the Greek military junta's Cypriot adventure led to a collapse of its authority. Subsequently, the ruling junta was replaced by the former leader, Constantine Karamanlis.[75] Such a turn of events was hardly welcomed in Washington. Kissinger's reluctance from the outset of the conflict to 'rake the Greeks' was dictated by a concern that a Greek government sympathetic to Moscow would attain power, and Karamanlis was deemed to hold such sympathies.[76] The British, on the other hand, were troubled by such events for different reasons. British efforts at finding a peaceful solution had been for naught, and Turkish action had endangered British sovereign bases in Cyprus. It also raised the spectre of a wider war between Turkey and Greece that would undermine NATO.

Following the Turkish invasion, Callaghan again offered the auspices of the British government to broker a peace settlement.[77] After a further round of diplomatic negotiations, which produced UN Security Council Resolution 353, Callaghan called for peace negotiations on neutral territory. After much wrangling over location and participation, it was finally settled that Geneva would act as the venue, and negotiations would commence on 24 July 1974. This conference was designed to broker the terms of a ceasefire and another conference, scheduled to begin on 8 August 1974, would attempt to produce a lasting political settlement.[78]

At the conference, Callaghan stuck to his original intention of restoring Makarios to power. He also outlined that Cyprus should be administered on a bi-federal basis.[79] Such a policy did not have the backing of the US and, following their briefing of the Turkish on this point, they too announced that they would not support this. The Turkish also insisted that in order for them to begin negotiations on a lasting political settlement the north-eastern third of Cyprus would have to be ceded to their authority.[80]

With such diametrically opposed positions, the Geneva peace conference turned into a somewhat rancorous affair. Nevertheless, Callaghan managed to establish terms for a ceasefire agreement which included the halting of all offensive activities and an agreement that phased withdrawal of all military forces from Cyprus would begin. Following the successful adherence to this, a second conference would convene to work out how a buffer zone between the two sides would be created.[81] In London, the prime minister was especially pleased with Callaghan's efforts, and believed that it afforded the opportunity for the British to create a lasting political settlement in Cyprus. As Wilson noted to Callaghan, 'We have the chance to create a more stable Cyprus, better relations between Greece and Turkey, and (for the first time ever) an alliance in NATO consisting of fully democratic states'.[82]

Callaghan was rather less confident than his boss and remained suspicious of Turkish ambitions. He suspected that the Turkish would use the period between the conferences to gain more territory in Cyprus that would be of strategic value.[83] He therefore informed Washington that if the Turkish undertook further military measures then Britain would respond in kind.[84] Wilson supported Callaghan by providing a demonstrable sign of Britain's seriousness – he reinforced Britain's sovereign bases on Cyprus.[85]

## Geneva: Part II

As the second Geneva talks convened, British officials in the FCO were deeply pessimistic about finding a lasting settlement. One noted that the exercise was a 'dead duck' and, in the assessments of senior FCO officials, Callaghan's stated objective that Cyprus should be administered on a bi-federal basis was simply unrealistic. The return of Makarios was also felt to be implausible.[86] Events would prove such pessimism accurate, because British interlocutors were confronted with deadlock at the talks. The Turkish demanded that Cyprus be administered on a bi-regional basis and that, to achieve this, a population transfer on the island – that separated Turkish and Greek Cypriots – would have to take place. Clerides, the acting president of Cyprus, requested that he be allowed 24 hours to consider this Turkish proposal. This, however, was rejected by the Turkish delegation. The conference therefore collapsed without any settlement being reached. Less than two hours after the conference had finished the Turkish made further military moves, seizing approximately 35 per cent of the island. This included the port city of Famagusta. However, Famagusta contained few Turkish Cypriots, thus undermining the Turkish argument that all of their military moves were designed solely to protect Turkish Cypriots.[87]

Callaghan was infuriated with such action, believing that the Turkish had been negotiating in bad faith and felt he had been vindicated in arguing that Turkey was seeking military-strategic aggrandisement.[88] President Ford was now faced with the first foreign policy crisis of his administration, because Callaghan had suggested that Britain would respond militarily to further Turkish actions. For the US, this situation was an incredible one. The possibility of a UK–Turkish war, which would likely descend into a wider Greek–Turkish conflict, appeared to now be a real possibility. Ford, barely 24 hours into his presidency, was confronted with the possibility of three NATO members being at war with one another! However, as with earlier British threats of military intervention, the US did not believe them to be credible. 'One of the stupidest thing[s] I have heard,' Kissinger told Ford. The president evidently concurred and ordered Kissinger to 'calm down our British friends a bit'.[89]

In London, Wilson convened a meeting to discuss the possible ways in which Britain should react to Turkish moves. As Callaghan noted, Britain's 'real' interests in Cyprus – the sovereign bases – had been left alone by the Turkish military. He explained further that British military intervention was unlikely to succeed without full US support. This, as Callaghan informed the prime minister, was unlikely to be forthcoming. Kissinger's efforts to calm the British had worked. As Wilson understood, without US backing the British were unlikely to be able to easily remove the Turkish military. More importantly, the Turkish had not infringed upon Britain's sovereign bases, and Wilson concluded that military action would not be undertaken.[90]

British indignation towards Turkey was met with little sympathy in Washington, and Callaghan's inability to find a peaceful solution to the crisis was met with scorn.[91] 'In this business you are paid by your results, and [Callaghan] didn't deliver a damn thing,' Kissinger complained.[92] Kissinger, while far from happy about Turkish actions, did not believe that a military response was required. Ultimately, Turkey's strategic importance to the US meant any military response was unpalatable. A reading of Kissinger's memoirs makes it quite apparent that he believed Turkey was of considerable strategic importance to the US.[93] At the time, Kissinger was rather less articulate in making this same point. 'Whether Turkey occupied a third of Cyprus or not did not affect US interests,' Kissinger informed the president.[94] In sum, Kissinger was not prepared to sacrifice Turkey as an important regional ally to ensure a bi-federal peace settlement in Cyprus. Rather, in Kissinger's assessment, a bi-regional solution, where Turkey controlled one portion of Cyprus and Greece the other, was acceptable.[95]

Washington's analysis of the Cyprus crisis was therefore driven largely by overarching Cold War considerations. Events in Vietnam, the rise of Eurocommunism, and the emergence of communist influence across Africa all contributed to Kissinger believing that another Soviet advancement could occur in Cyprus. Divorced from such geopolitical considerations, Kissinger was concerned about the impact of Watergate on America's international standing. He believed that Watergate was undermining US foreign policy, and he suspected that the USSR would exploit the president's domestic troubles for their own aggrandisement.[96] Kissinger also suspected that the advance of North Vietnamese forces once again could be explained by the domestic situation in Washington.[97] It is within this context, then, that events must be viewed. This, however, is not to suggest that Kissinger was supporting Turkish military action. Contrary to the claims of some authors, Kissinger was against Turkish military action from the outset of the crisis, and he had worked laboriously, if ultimately ineffectively, to prevent the escalation of hostilities.[98] Once the Turkish had gained a foothold on the island, Kissinger was opposed to further military action. As Kissinger made clear to the president on 10 August 1974, the US could not support any unilateral military action in the first 48 hours of Ford's new presidency. As such, Kissinger warned Ankara against taking further military action.[99]

For US–UK relations the episode had demonstrated a number of important points. It reiterated the fact that the special relationship between the two countries was largely limited to specific areas, such as intelligence or nuclear cooperation, and was becoming a lot narrower in its scope. When US interests were perceived to conflict with those of the United Kingdom, then the United States was prepared to fully pursue its aims with little concern for London's ambitions. Again then, the disparity in power within the US–UK relationship was evident. Wilson and Callaghan both sought a close relationship with Washington so as to influence its policies. On this occasion, the absence of influence was apparent.

## Détente and economic decline

This chapter now turns its attention to Britain's economic plight, and the ramifications it had for Britain's defence posture. By doing so, one can trace a systematic shift in US–UK relations, in that the UK came to be viewed as a less useful ally by the US. It also illustrates that Wilson's efforts at restoring closer US–UK interaction were largely ineffective, because of such defence cuts. From here, areas of international diplomacy which sought to push forward the process of détente, such as the CSCE and MBFR, are also reviewed in this section. This again allows for a broader assessment of the relationship to be provided and counterbalances the impression that US–UK relations were constantly beset by acrimony.

Wilson assumed power at the time when Britain had come to be regarded as the 'sick man of Europe'.[100] Heath's mismanagement of the economy, coupled with the inflationary pressures generated by the oil embargo, had led to an unsupportable budget deficit. To combat this, public expenditure cutbacks had been enacted in Anthony Barbour's budgets of 1973–74 in order to reduce Britain's borrowing requirements.[101] Britain's defence budget, however, remained largely unaffected by such cutbacks until December 1973, when it was announced that defence would incur a cut of £178 million.[102] Such was the seriousness of these economic problems that the likes of Lord Rothschild – who headed up Heath's economic think tank – were predicting that the

UK would be one of the poorest countries in Europe by 1985, unless serious defence cuts were enacted.[103]

Given this, Wilson inherited a situation where defence expenditure was to be reduced, but internal party politics within the Labour government also encouraged the new prime minister to look for defence spending reductions. At the Labour Party conference of October 1973, there had been vociferous demands for defence expenditure to be reduced, and £1,000 million had been suggested as the figure that a new Labour government should be looking to reduce Britain's defence expenditure by.[104] Wilson, while privately scornful of such thinking, did accede somewhat to these demands in the Labour Party manifesto of February 1974.[105] As it outlined, a new Labour government would seek to find savings of 'several hundred million pounds per annum' in the defence budget.[106] Consequently, on assuming office, the chancellor of the exchequer Denis Healey cut an additional £50 million from defence expenditure in his first budget. This, however, was only an interim solution, and Wilson ordered a full defence review to be undertaken. This, as Wilson warned, could result in reductions 'amounting to hundreds of millions of pounds'.[107]

Washington observed Wilson's defence policy closely, and was none too pleased by what it believed were the 'soft' policy choices being made in London.[108] From the military-strategic perspective, American officialdom did not wish to see Britain lessen its pre-existing commitments, and senior US policy-makers – including Nixon, Kissinger, Haig and Schlesinger – lamented Britain's global military decline. Yet during their time in office, they had been unable to prevent this decline, and had little success in convincing London to reverse its East of Suez policy or contribute more heavily to NATO. Nevertheless, this had been viewed as the limit of Britain's military downsizing. Now it appeared, from Washington's perspective, as if further large-scale military cutbacks were to be enacted by the new Labour government, which would have the likely effect of increasing the military burden upon the US.

Further to this, in Kissinger's assessment, such policies acted as another example of the European states trying to 'cop out' of the Cold War.[109] By this it was implied that with the onset of détente and improved superpower relations, NATO members would wrongly conclude that the Soviet threat no longer existed, and could reduce their defence commitments accordingly. Along with this, US officials were also concerned that British defence expenditure cuts would have more practical effects on US–UK cooperation. Most obviously, the worries of the US surrounded the issue of whether Wilson would endorse the decisions made by the Heath government to upgrade Polaris and retain intelligence posts in Cyprus.[110]

Washington, therefore, sought to convince their British allies that they should not embark on another round of deep defence cuts. Thus, during a meeting between Kissinger and John Hunt, the US secretary of state outlined his concerns. Hunt assured Kissinger that rumours referring to substantial defence cuts were unsubstantiated, and that Wilson was committed to the upgrading of Polaris and to retaining Britain's existing NATO commitments.[111] American elites remained sceptical of such assurances and this can be partly explained by the low opinion that prominent US policy-makers, including Ford and Kissinger, had of Wilson and his government. Kissinger regarded Wilson as a 'greasy sort of man' and 'Healey is a shit who can't be trusted' was his even more scathing verdict of the British chancellor of the exchequer.[112]

Significant concerns surrounded the suitability of Roy Mason as defence secretary, especially in regard to whether or not he would be able to function independently from his former boss, Denis Healey. The US ambassador in London, Walter Annenberg, warned Washington that Healey would be able to cajole Mason into making substantial reductions in the British defence budget.[113] It was also felt that Healey's first budget was indicative of things to follow in the future. Earl Sohm, the chargé d'affaires at the US Embassy in London, predicted that once Wilson had assured his position as prime minister, more significant cuts would follow.[114] The turn of events would prove this assessment correct. The general election of October 1974 solidified Wilson's authority somewhat, and both he and Healey could now begin to tackle Britain's budget deficit. It took no great leap of faith, then, to think that Britain's defence budget would once again be coming under severe scrutiny, and that cutbacks would follow in the near future.[115]

Throughout the winter of 1974, the US maintained a keen interest in British debates about possible defence cutbacks. Washington repeated its earlier position that it did not wish to see any substantial defence reductions undertaken by the British government. More specifically, the Ford administration articulated clearly that it believed the British government should maintain several key areas of its defence commitment, which included the Polaris upgrade, the retention of Britain's presence in Cyprus, and the continuation of the US–UK Diego Garcia commitments.[116] Such suggestions appeared not to have resonated in London, because reports soon arrived in Washington that suggested that Wilson was 'agonising' over whether to continue with the Polaris upgrade. Additionally, Kissinger was informed that the British sovereign bases in Cyprus were set to be disbanded.[117]

Evidently, US diplomacy had failed to achieve the desired outcome from the British government, so Kissinger set about taking a more rigorous approach with his British allies. He first despatched a cable to Callaghan where he warned a British withdrawal from Cyprus would 'undermine our overall position in the Mediterranean'.[118] Kissinger, along with Schlesinger and the CIA director, William Colby, took an even sterner tone with John Hunt during a meeting in

Washington. Apparently, Kissinger's explanation that the US did not want the British to close their bases in Cyprus was laced with a series of expletives. Given that America's relationship with Turkey was strained because of the Cyprus crisis, and the US Congress was threatening to halt all military assistance to Turkey (this was achieved in January 1975), the British presence in Cyprus took on a greater degree of importance. Indeed, Britain's intelligence facilities in Cyprus assumed extra significance when US posts in Turkey were shut down in retaliation to the Congress's termination of military aid.[119]

Following Washington's warnings, debate continued in Wilson's government regarding the scope of defence cuts, and after much wrangling Mason announced the preliminary results of the defence review to the House of Commons on 4 December 1974.[120] In retrospect, Mason claimed that the defence review 'preserved our core defensive interests in Europe and fully maintained the integrity of NATO' and at the time he was equally confident.[121] Wilson, in a number of his public speeches, was just as self-congratulatory, yet in private he was rather more reticent about the likely American reaction.[122] Thus, Wilson reported to his Cabinet that in the opinion of the Ford administration, defence cuts had reached 'the limit of what is tolerable'. In confidential correspondence with his chancellor of the exchequer, Wilson was even more forthright in expressing the same sentiment.[123]

Wilson was correct to be apprehensive about the reaction of the US given that even before the latest defence review had been completed, key US policy-makers were privately bemoaning the likely results. 'You have to operate on the assumption that Great Britain is through', was Kissinger's candid judgement.[124] The results of the defence review only soured Kissinger's opinion further.[125] Other influential US policy-makers were equally irritated with the British defence review. The US could 'no longer expect Britain to pull any weight,' Schlesinger allegedly stated.[126] Alexander Haig, now the supreme commander of allied forces in Europe, believed that the defence review was not 'reassuring'. As Haig articulated to Ford, the British had become 'spongy'.[127] Clearly this was not meant as a term of endearment. Indeed, under Haig's direction, NATO responded rather sourly, with a public spokesman complaining that British defence cuts were 'hard to swallow and there is no doubt that they will do some damage'.[128]

Not all US officials were as critical as the aforementioned. The US ambassador to the UK, Elliot Richardson, gave a rather more positive appraisal of the defence review: 'Britain and NATO have come away from the defence review rather better than initially might have been expected. Nothing vital has been lost, and the ingredients for a continued, meaningful British contribution to Western defense are still present'.[129] Such opinion was in the minority, however, and Ford's two most influential officials for foreign and security affairs,

Kissinger and Schlesinger, agreed that the defence review had done significant damage to Britain's standing with America. Additionally, US officials perceived the British defence review to have harmed US interests on several fronts. For example, the decision to reduce the scope of British bases in Cyprus and Malta was seen to have undermined America's ability to gather intelligence in the region. British actions were also seen to have undermined US efforts at promoting burden-sharing, and US attempts at negotiating an MBFR agreement with the USSR were deemed to have also been dealt a blow.[130]

Such evidence could lead one to conclude that US–UK relations were critically undermined by Wilson's defence review. Nevertheless, on closer inspection it is remarkable just how little impact the defence review of March 1975 actually had upon existing US–UK cooperation. As US policy-makers concluded, the types of cooperation undertaken with the UK – especially in the nuclear and intelligence realms – still benefitted the US. As the US Embassy in London noted, to cancel such mutually beneficial cooperation would only have a '"cut off your nose to spite your face" quality' about them.[131] Given the international environment, it becomes clearer as to why the Ford administration was unwilling to terminate mutually beneficial arrangements with a friendly country. The likes of Kissinger, Schlesinger and perhaps even Ford believed that the US was experiencing a period of power decline, and the events unfolding in Vietnam acted as a timely reminder of the limits of American power. US concerns abounded over the future stability of countries such as Greece, Italy and Portugal, and the spectre of 'Euro-communism' was – from the perspective of the Ford government – a very real danger to American interests in Europe. Moreover, in terms of proportion of GDP, Britain still remained the largest contributor to NATO. Wilson continued with the Polaris upgrade and gave in to US demands to retain intelligence posts in Cyprus. To put it simply, allies for the US in 1975 were in short supply. Terminating military cooperation with a country which, even given the latest round of defence cuts, still promoted US interests made little sense from the perspective of the Ford White House.[132]

Britain's economic difficulties in this period were the backdrop behind all of these other events. Economic recession, stagflation and an ever-growing deficit were the driving forces behind Wilson's need to reduce public expenditure. Moreover, the policies undertaken by the Wilson government to solve Britain's economic problems were to have an impact on US–UK relations. Most obvious were the defence cuts enacted to help reduce Britain's public expenditure. Besides, there was the broader concern in Washington about the economic policies pursued by Wilson's government. For instance, the president complained to the US ambassador designate for the UK, Elliot Richardson, about the Wilson government and ordered Richardson to 'get close' to the unions in the UK, so they would not follow 'disastrous' policies. In other words, Ford was asking his ambassador to involve himself in the domestic affairs of the UK.[133]

Throughout 1975, the president continued to take an interest in the British economy, and was vocal in chastising the policies pursued in London. Ford admonished Wilson's economic policies during one interview with the magazine *Fortune*:

> If that growth in transfer payments continues, we can't have the same economic system by the year 2000 that we have now. I don't think that we are over the cliff, but it is something we have to stop now. As more people get on those transfer payments they become a political force and the programs are sort of self-perpetuating. In my opinion, the best example of how the matter can get out of hand is the situation in Great Britain today. They just don't seem to be able to stop the momentum.[134]

This was followed by a speech in San Francisco on 4 April 1975, where again Ford labelled the UK as a prime example of a government that mismanaged its economy. These comments raised eyebrows in London, and Peter Ramsbotham lodged a complaint with the Ford administration and was granted an apology, along with a promise that the president would not publicly talk about Britain's economic problems in such a fashion again.[135] In spite of such promises, in October 1975 Ford once again spoke candidly about Britain's economic problems, with the *New York Times* reporting that Ford had said that a 'horrible example of a government that spends itself sick was Britain's with its Labour Government and its Welfare State'.[136] If the public statements were causing disquiet in British circles then one can only imagine what would have been made of the private comments being made in Washington. Kissinger, in one remark to President Ford, was particularly scathing, stating: 'Britain is a tragedy – it has sunk to begging, borrowing, stealing until North Sea oil comes in ... That Britain has become such a scrounger is a disgrace.'[137] Even if one allows that Kissinger may have been talking in a moment of exasperation, the fact remains that Ford's other advisers were just as critical; for example, US Treasury Secretary William Simon, Chairman of the Federal Reserve Arthur Burns, and Ford's special adviser on economics, Alan Greenspan, all lambasted the British government's economic policies.[138]

This low opinion of Britain became obvious during President Ford's tour of Europe in May 1975. Kissinger advised that Wilson was a 'marginal' figure and as such Ford was best spending 'a lot of time' with the West German chancellor, Helmut Schmidt.[139] In practical terms, how much time the president spent with foreign leaders had little effect upon US–UK bilateral cooperation. Nonetheless, if the defence cutbacks are viewed in conjunction with Britain's economic troubles, it becomes clear that the Ford administration viewed Wilson's government as an increasingly less reliable ally for promoting US interests.

Due to Britain's continuing economic problems, rumours soon began circulating that further defence cuts were forthcoming and Ford was kept informed of these developments.[140] This advice was well founded because Healey was arguing that further public expenditure cutbacks were required to control Britain's expanding borrowing requirements and this would likely involve bigger cutbacks in defence expenditure.[141] America's reaction to these proposed defence cuts was even more belligerent than that exhibited earlier in the year. At the Helsinki conference (July 1975), Ford articulated American displeasure about further British defence cutbacks.[142] Schlesinger was less diplomatic and employed rather bellicose tactics in an effort to convince the Wilson government to maintain its defence spending, when he threatened to permanently terminate US–UK nuclear and intelligence cooperation if substantial defence cuts were made. Mason reported Schlesinger as follows to the prime minister:

> If the British Government were to make further cuts in defence expenditure, the US government would have to re-consider its bilateral arrangements with us [Britain] on the exchange of communications and intelligence information and on assistance in respect of nuclear weapons, including specifically our POLARIS force and the improvement of its missiles.[143]

Following Schlesinger's warning, it was Kissinger's turn to convey the Ford administration's displeasure and he did so in conversation with James Callaghan. Whilst demonstrating a significantly more subtle approach than Schlesinger had with Mason, he articulated much the same point: US–UK security collaboration would be re-assessed if a further round of UK defence cuts was enacted.[144]

If this type of diplomacy was supposed to cause Wilson to rethink his defence policies then it appears to have failed. In fact the prime minister blithely dismissed these warnings and informed Mason that he should have told Schlesinger 'to get stuffed'.[145] Wilson also doubted whether the president or Kissinger 'would have supported this kind of pressure on us'.[146] Callaghan questioned this assessment, believing Ford would support Schlesinger if he suspended US–UK intelligence collaboration and, from his conversations with Kissinger, it was clear that the Ford administration was generally unhappy about further British defence cuts.[147] Healey, meanwhile, advised Wilson that Schlesinger's remarks should be considered, but the fundamental objective had to remain getting the economy 'right'. In Healey's assessment, this would require 'major reductions in public expenditure' and defence could not be exempt, given that 'desirable features of other public expenditure programmes were having to be foregone'.[148]

Of all the advice given to Wilson, it was Callaghan's that most accurately portrayed US opinion. To be sure, Wilson's thinking was not illogical given that Schlesinger's public differences with the president and Kissinger gave a clear impression of a divided administration.[149] However, while Wilson may have doubted that Ford and Kissinger would have supported Schlesinger, the fact was that they had actually sanctioned his actions.[150] This, though, was all a moot point from the perspective of the Wilson government and, in the final assessment, Schlesinger's threats and Kissinger's more subtle suggestions were ignored. On 24 June 1975, Mason announced that further defence cuts were to be expected in the near future.[151] Interestingly, US pressure had been unable to prevent a further round of defence cuts, and threats to cancel intelligence or nuclear cooperation had, on this occasion, been futile.

The US secretary of defense made a scheduled visit to London in September 1975, and it was here that Schlesinger again made his opposition to defence cuts known. He told Mason that the March 1975 defence review should be a 'one time' process and he made similar arguments to Wilson and Healey.[152] The chancellor responded by making it known that public expenditure related to the 'social services' was going to be cut, thus meaning it was rather self-evident that the defence budget would also be reduced.[153] Wilson was not as blunt with Schlesinger, informing him that, 'There was no need to expect any major changes in our defence expenditure'.[154] In spite of such assurances, Wilson had been careful not to make any specific promises about upholding Britain's defence expenditure and, given the economic and political realities which confronted the prime minister, this was a wise decision. Britain's deepening recession and increasing borrowing levels meant that public expenditure was going to be reduced further, and it was, therefore, a case of how substantial, rather than if, defence cuts would be implemented.[155]

How public expenditure would be cut was being rigorously debated in London. Healey sought to introduce an aggressive programme of tax increases and public expenditure cutbacks, which was dubbed the 'civil formula'. The civil formula was not accepted in its entirety; however, on 13 November 1975, the Cabinet gave its approval for public expenditure cutbacks of £3,750 million. One hundred million pounds of this total was designated to come from the defence budget up to Financial Year (FY) 1979–80. The Treasury, however, demanded a further reduction from the defence budget throughout the winter of 1975. Such demands were made because Healey had only managed to find some £2,600 million in savings, leaving a shortfall of £1,150 million from the agreed £3,750 million target. It was therefore evident that there would be increased pressure to reduce the size of the defence budget. As it turned out, it did not take long for these calls to materialise as Healey called for the defence budget to be slashed by an additional £550 million.[156]

Healey's demands encountered immediate opposition from Roy Mason, who argued that such cutbacks would terminally damage Britain's relationship with the US. John Hunt lent his support to Mason's appeals, advancing a similar argument which resonated with the prime minister. Wilson therefore rejected Healey's demands, and asked the various Cabinet ministers to re-submit their budget proposals with increased savings.[157]

Kissinger decided that he had to strengthen the resolve of Wilson against those arguing for substantial defence cutbacks, and thus despatched a scathing cable to London. 'I am sure that you are aware that America's long-term relations with the UK will inevitably have to take into account Britain's standing as a partner in our common security exercise,' Kissinger ominously warned.[158] While not specifically stating so, it is reasonable to suggest that Kissinger was referring to US–UK nuclear and intelligence cooperation. Kissinger, following Schlesinger's earlier path, invoked the possible re-assessment of the US–UK nuclear and intelligence relationship as a means of convincing Wilson that a substantial reduction in Britain's defence expenditure should not be undertaken.

Kissinger's actions, however, were largely irrelevant in deciding the final outcome of the defence reductions debate. Throughout the whole of the deliberations, it is evident just how little credibility Wilson gave to US threats.[159] As Wilson had learned in the 1960s, bellicose US diplomacy could not actually force his government into maintaining defence commitments which he was determined to scrap.[160] More importantly, Wilson was not prepared to accept Healey's suggestion that defence expenditure should be so radically reduced. As a trained economist himself, Wilson had always been sceptical of the Treasury's advice, and he remained unconvinced by the balance that Healey's civil formula approach was trying to strike between tax increases and public expenditure cutbacks. In Wilson's estimation, Healey was focusing too much on public expenditure cutbacks and not enough on ways to bolster the economy, in order to raise tax receipts, or enact new means of taxation. Added to this, Wilson still believed that Britain could not reduce its defence expenditure by the sums Healey was demanding because he desired to safeguard certain projects, such as the Polaris update, in order to, as he saw it, retain influence with Washington. One particularly ill-tempered retort to his Cabinet colleagues demanding defence expenditure be more significantly reduced that military spending 'was more important than school meals, or social security for Irishmen with 18 children' captures this thinking rather well.[161] Thus, in the series of Cabinet debates that followed, Wilson skilfully managed to ensure that defence's contribution to the overall public expenditure cutbacks fell from an initially 'scored' agreement of £225 million, to £193 million.[162] This was 5.5 per cent of the total public expenditure cutbacks of £3,750 million. Perhaps more importantly from Wilson's perspective was the fact that the figure the defence budget had been reduced by was less than half the figure Healey had been seeking.

The majority of the defence cutbacks involved manpower reductions, extending the duration of defence projects and delaying infrastructure programmes.[163] The major defence projects, such as the Polaris upgrade and the Harrier jet programme, continued and the intelligence posts in Cyprus were also retained. In Washington, the announced British defence cuts were being analysed closely and, in the final analysis, they were deemed not to have been as bad as was initially feared. Whilst private complaints in Washington ensued, rather less bellicosity was exhibited in bilateral contact with British officials. Perhaps given that the Ford administration had itself decided to cut its own defence expenditure in October 1975, lecturing the British on their own efforts was seen as less than wise.[164]

## Finding a CSCE agreement

As shown earlier, Heath's government had been sceptical as to how the CSCE and MBFR would benefit the UK. At their most melodramatic, the British regarded both sets of negotiations as having the potential to critically undermine European security. For US–UK relations, the negotiations had been a point of disagreement and Wilson's return to office did little to alter this. Shortly after returning to power, Wilson had read an article in the *Economist* about the CSCE which sparked his interest in the subject and he therefore ordered a full review of British policy towards the CSCE.[165] After receiving various opinions on the CSCE, Wilson decided that any summit designed to conclude the CSCE should not be agreed to without first obtaining major concessions from the USSR.[166]

This line of thinking was at variance with that of Washington. As shown earlier, the Nixon administration had initially wished to delay progress on the CSCE as a means of enacting leverage upon other areas of US–Soviet diplomacy. By the middle of 1972, agreements on subjects such as SALT and a Berlin Treaty had been reached and movement on CSCE was now sought. Now, US policy sought a swift resolution to the ongoing CSCE to ensure that nothing of real substance was reached in this multilateral negotiation. Accordingly, the visit of Nixon to Moscow in June 1974 was envisaged as a cut-off point. In sum, once the summit was over, the US wanted the CSCE to be promptly settled.[167]

What divided British and American policy were fundamentally different ideas about both what the CSCE could achieve and what could reasonably be expected to be extracted from the USSR in exchange for agreeing to the CSCE. For instance, the issue of Confidence Building Measures (CBMs), which included things such as the right of free movement throughout Europe, was one example of British and American policy being deeply divided.[168] Wilson's government sought tangible concessions from the USSR in these areas as the British believed these would be granted because the USSR was determined that the CSCE would act as a substitute treaty for ratifying Europe's post-World War II borders. This thinking was based on information garnered from Soviet and American sources that indicated that Brezhnev was personally determined to hold a CSCE summit. British policy-makers thus concluded that there existed a potential to extrapolate Soviet concessions for agreeing to such a summit.[169]

US thinking differed from this. It must be recalled that from the outset of the process the CSCE was never seen solely as something that would benefit US interests on its own. Rather, the CSCE was useful in so much as it allowed the US to apply leverage upon other areas of US–Soviet interaction. As a result of this, CBMs were viewed as peripheral factors, and what really mattered for the US was getting Soviet movement on issues deemed more important to US interests. In particular, Washington wanted progress on SALT II and MBFR. However, as US policy-makers were aware, events in the Middle East had damaged détente and made it less likely that the Soviets would offer the US an agreement which they could realistically be expected to agree to. Events were proving such conclusions correct given that SALT II was becoming mired in technical debates and MBFR discussions had progressed little. As Helmut Sonnenfeldt succinctly summarised for Kissinger, negotiations had moved at a 'snail's pace'.[170]

In order to garner a more responsive attitude from Moscow, Kissinger informed Nixon that he was 'holding up' progress on the CSCE until after the Moscow summit. This, as Kissinger explained, would give the US leverage over the USSR because they wanted to conclude the CSCE at a summit meeting. Refusing to move towards this would encourage the Soviets to be more forthcoming in both the SALT and MBFR discussions.[171] Indeed, this belief was not without foundation given Soviet interlocutors had intimated that progress in SALT and MBFR was directly linked to the condition that the US agreed to hold a CSCE summit.[172] Therefore, a CSCE summit was something that could be offered to the Soviets as a means of ensuring progress in areas deemed more important to the US.[173] Kissinger explained this policy approach candidly to Schlesinger: 'What can we do to keep the Soviet Union happy? We have MBFR, but that may be premature. CSCE is cheap. The Germans or French will probably give it away anyway and we should beat them.'[174] By August 1974, this had become official US policy, and consequently the CSCE and MBFR were explicitly linked and a conclusion to the CSCE at a summit would be agreed to only as a means of producing movement on MBFR.[175]

Earlier in the year, Kissinger had indicated to the Soviets that a CSCE would be concluded in the near future.[176] In the communiqué following the Moscow summit of June 1974, this private assurance was given a public endorsement.[177] For US–UK relations, this was to create further disagreement. Kissinger had provided Wilson with prior notice that the US would, at the conclusion of the Moscow summit, announce its intention to hold a CSCE summit.[178] The British informed Kissinger that they were not averse to settling the CSCE quickly, but they doubted whether Kissinger's timeframe was realistic.[179] Certainly, the negotiations at the CSCE were complicated and intricate. Less kindly, William Hyland noted that the CSCE had a 'Talmudic nature' which featured 'esoteric debates'.[180] It was certainly the case that the CSCE involved over 30 countries which were seeking to find agreement on a wide range of issues.[181] Completing the CSCE according to Kissinger's timetable was, if one wishes to be charitable, a rather ambitious objective.

Causing further frustration to Kissinger's ambition of settling the CSCE quickly was the actions of the British CSCE delegation which, according to one US observer, enjoyed debating complicated technical matters.[182] As the year progressed, the British delegation continued to debate the finer points of what the final CSCE agreement would include with their Soviet counterparts which left the clear impression that the talks were rapidly reaching a stalemate.[183] Such a situation angered Washington. In the opinion of Scowcroft, there was 'little to commend' in Britain's CSCE approach; Kissinger, therefore, attempted to break this impasse.[184] How this would be achieved presented an obvious problem. Trying to enforce US views on the Western negotiators was likely to create a rift amongst the Western alliance, and risk a repetition of US–European troubles witnessed throughout 1973. More dangerously, a fractured negotiating stance would provide the USSR with an opportunity to exploit this weakness. Nevertheless, from the standpoint of the US, the negotiations could not just be allowed to continue at their current rate for the above-mentioned reasons. This predicament was neatly summarised by Arthur Hartman, the assistant secretary of state for European affairs:

> The issue then is how to nudge the Allies along toward a more precise and realistic definition of objectives in Basket III and toward an agreed fallback position on CBMs without pressing them so hard we would risk a new US–European confrontation, but in a way that this autumn we would be in a position to show the Soviets that we have made a strong effort to bring CSCE to a conclusion.[185]

Kissinger consequently injected himself into this and encouraged the US delegation to hasten the rate of the negotiations. In his assessment, this would be achieved by the West largely accepting the terms of the agreements already reached, and by the British dropping their demands concerning CBMs. As a result, the US delegation insisted that 'we understand and support the Allied wish for progress in the Basket III area, although realistically we must not set our sights too high'.[186] Such an attitude, however, was met with consternation by the British delegation. In London, it was met with equal incredulity. Callaghan wanted something 'concrete' on Basket III before agreeing to the Soviet demand to settle the CSCE at a summit.[187]

British inflexibility was again met with little sympathy in Washington. Accordingly, Kissinger instructed his delegation to support the 'Finnish compromise', which meant that the Soviets would give some concessions over the issue of 'freer exchanges'. Crucially, however, this would be monitored by an internal regulatory apparatus, rather than by an outside body. Thus, Soviet sovereignty would not be violated by having to accept outside observers in their state, and would enhance the likelihood that the USSR would accept this condition.[188]

## A divided West

As negotiations continued, Callaghan and Kissinger – during a meeting in July 1974 – took the opportunity to explain their respective approaches to the CSCE. Kissinger pressed Callaghan to accept that the CSCE should be concluded at a summit, and further suggested that the USSR could not be expected to accept Britain's preferred level of CBMs. Callaghan remained unconvinced by Kissinger's line of reasoning. Instead he argued that the West should be pushing for greater concessions from the USSR, and would achieve them as long as the West remained resolute in its demands. At the end of the discussion it was evident that little agreement between the two sides existed. This said, it was agreed that it was essential for the Western bloc to unify its own negotiating position and only once these internal differences had been settled could a final CSCE be concluded.[189] Reaching this point, however, was going to be an obviously difficult task.

Given that Kissinger had failed to convince the British to alter their position, the contents of Basket III remained the principal sticking point in the negotiations. In December 1974, this impasse appeared to have been potentially broken. During Brezhnev's visit to Paris, the French, acting on behalf of the entire Western bloc, found agreement on the contents of Basket III. Following this, the Austrian delegation at the CSCE negotiation in Geneva was used to table the Soviet–French agreement. As a part of the agreement, the French had agreed to the Soviet demand that the CSCE should be concluded at an international summit.[190]

As seen above, a major summit to conclude the CSCE was something that both the US and British governments had not wanted to agree to without the Soviets offering something significant in return. French agreement to do this angered Ford and Kissinger with both reasoning that French actions had undermined the Western negotiating position, but, more importantly, it meant that the US could not extract concessions from the USSR in other areas of their diplomacy.[191] British officials were divided in their assessments of French behaviour. Crispin Tickell (the FCO's head of western organisations department and therefore responsible for the CSCE negotiations) informed Ronald Spiers, the US chargé d'affaires in London, that the French had not broken with the agreed Western position.[192] Tickell, however, was in the minority.

Michael Alexander, the chief negotiator for the British at the CSCE negotiations, agreed with the American opinion that French actions had undermined the entire Western negotiating position. Moreover, the chances for obtaining further CBMs now that the 'carrot' of a CSCE summit had been agreed to seemed remote. In London, Callaghan held a similar viewpoint.[193] French actions had a profound impact upon British policy towards the CSCE. Now that the summit had been agreed to, it was deemed unwise to deviate from this position because it would likely ostracise Britain and present an image of them being particularly belligerent. Moreover, British policy-makers figured that British opposition to a summit was not going to prevent it from occurring now it had been publicly agreed to. Thus, British policy-makers deemed that it was imperative to finalise the terms of Basket III and to quickly move to a summit so that the final CSCE agreement could be signed.

French actions should have brought US and UK policy closer together, as both countries understood that reaching an agreed Western position was required. British policy-makers believed that their complaints involving CBMs would have to be watered down (the very thing the US had been requesting throughout the past year), in order for an agreement to be reached in time for the summit.[194] As such, when Callaghan met with Kissinger in January 1975, he informed him that 'we won't get out of line with you' over the CSCE.[195] However, the reversal in British policy was unwelcome. Kissinger now argued that the summit should not be held unless the Soviets agreed to include further CBMs in Basket III. Ironically, the very thing the British had originally been arguing for now had Kissinger's support![196]

How then is this curious shift in US policy explained? Ultimately it comes down to Kissinger's overarching concern to obtain possible leverage over other areas of Soviet policy via the CSCE, and agreeing to a summit to settle the CSCE was seen as a trump card for influencing Soviet policy. Although the summit had been scheduled, little movement in Soviet foreign policy had been forthcoming. Kissinger, noting that the West had agreed to the summit, believed that the US may as well attempt to extract concessions on the contents of the CSCE. As Kissinger explained in conversation with President Ford, Brezhnev personally attached great significance to agreeing to a CSCE at a summit. Therefore, if the West could delay the summit by refusing to agree terms on CBMs, this would harm Brezhnev's position within the ruling elite of the USSR and could result in him accepting these demands in order for the summit to take place.[197] However, as Kissinger realised, the US could hardly make demands about CBMs, given they had to this point barely mentioned them in US–Soviet negotiations. Thus, other countries which had made an issue of CBMs should act as America's proxies; hence, the US secretary of state sought to convince the British that they should act as the American stalking horse.[198] Similarly, Kissinger ordered the US delegation at the CSCE to encourage their allied counterparts to stand firm against Soviet demands.[199]

This last-minute diplomacy by Kissinger was successful in extracting several concessions from the USSR. For instance, the USSR agreed that Europe's borders could only be altered via peaceful means, in accordance with international law. As Kissinger convincingly argued:

> American influence had helped to confine the recognition of borders to an obligation not to change them by force, which was a mere duplication of the UN Charter. Since no European country had the capacity to bring about a forcible change or a policy to that effect, the formal renunciation was hardly a Soviet gain. Even this limited recognition of legitimacy was vitiated by a statement of principles which preceded it ... It declared that the signatory states consider that their frontiers can be changed, in accordance with international law, by peaceful means and by agreement.[200]

Nevertheless, Kissinger failed to achieve the level of leverage in other areas of US–Soviet relations that he wanted. For instance, there was little movement over SALT II and MBFR. Consequently, as a tool of leverage over Soviet foreign policy, the CSCE failed to produce the type of result which Kissinger had envisaged was likely.

Helsinki was chosen as the location for the signing of the CSCE documents, and negotiations on the content of the CSCE continued until the actual date of the summit (30 July – 1 August 1975). Yet, following last-minute wrangling on the substance of the CSCE, the 'Helsinki Accords' were eventually signed on 1 August 1975.[201] For Kissinger, he doubted whether the CSCE would mollify Soviet behaviour and worried that it would only encourage 'communist inroads' throughout Europe.[202] Worse still for the president, the signing of the accords became a political liability, with the *New York Times* parodying Winston Churchill when it opined that 'Never have so many fought for so little'.[203] Other media outlets were equally scornful.[204] Former government officials, such as George Ball, and the Soviet dissident Alexander Solzhenitsyn attacked Ford's decision to attend the summit. Large and vocal elements within the Republican Party were equally critical, and this fuelled the challenge to Ford's presidency from the right of the party. As Ford would soon discover during his election campaign, the signing of the accords would prove to be a domestic burden that provided ammunition for his political opponents.[205]

Likewise, Harold Wilson faced vitriolic attacks from his political opponents, and Margaret Thatcher, the then leader of the opposition Conservative Party, vehemently attacked the CSCE and the entire process of détente.[206] Certainly, some elements of the popular British press agreed with her stance. The *Daily Express*, for instance, believed that if Wilson believed the 'guff' he had spoken at Helsinki then he should be prevented from 'going out alone' in the future.[207] But, as Thatcher accepted, her opinions placed her largely as the 'odd woman out'.[208] In the main, the British public appeared to be embracing improved East–West relations and the signing of the CSCE was somewhat of a political boost for Wilson's leadership.[209]

## MBFR

In both Washington and London, the MBFR had been seen as a rather more significant aspect of East–West relations. It is worth reflecting on how British and American policy had evolved. First, Wilson's return to power marked a subtle change in British policy towards MBFR. Most obvious was the fact that British enthusiasm for MBFR grew throughout this period which can be attributed largely to Britain's continuing economic problems. Simply, MBFR presented an opportunity for Britain to reduce its defence commitments in a multilateral format that would not undermine Western security. Nevertheless, British officials remained sceptical of US motives towards MBFR. In particular, the British were concerned that an MBFR agreement would be agreed regardless of NATO's concerns, and therefore severely damage British security interests.[210]

Perhaps the British were correct to be suspicious given that we now know that Nixon had suggested that the MBFR should be settled on a bilateral basis between the US and USSR. Kissinger persuaded Nixon against such a course of action, citing that it would create innumerable problems for the US within NATO.[211] But, following the US–Soviet summit (June 1974), it was

Kissinger that was now suggesting that MBFR should be settled bilaterally because he was growing impatient with its lack of progress.[212] Kissinger's entire détente strategy was also coming under increasing pressure, both domestically and from within the administration. MBFR, therefore, was becoming an issue of growing significance for US–Soviet relations, and as such Kissinger now suggested it should be conducted bilaterally with the USSR. 'If we get serious about MBFR, we should do it like SALT – give them proposals through your channel before surfacing them,' Kissinger advised Ford.[213]

Kissinger's suggested approach, however, was being challenged within Washington. Helmut Sonnenfeldt had consistently advised that US intentions vis-à-vis MBFR should be made abundantly clear to US allies and continued to argue this.[214] Sonnenfeldt could hardly act as a bureaucratic rival to Kissinger, but James Schlesinger certainly could and he was also not convinced that moving so quickly over MBFR suited US interests. He also remained sceptical about whether settling MBFR bilaterally with the Soviets was the preferable route to take. As Schlesinger reminded the president during one National Security Council meeting:

> Our objectives on MBFR have been two. First, to improve security in Western Europe. This has led us to concentrate on getting out the tank army. And we have agreed not to be stampeded into movement that does not serve our ultimate objective of improved security. Second, we want to get the Allies to do more. If we place limits on Western forces, we cannot get them to increase their manpower and budgetary support. It is important not to undermine these basic objectives by accepting some short term possible deal held out by the Soviets.[215]

Following this conflicting advice, the president ordered that US MBFR proposals should be given to the British and West Germans before other NATO members.[216] This was done largely because it was hoped that by engaging with the British at this early stage they would be able to mollify their likely resistance towards MBFR in forthcoming NATO meetings.[217] Regardless of this preferential treatment, US policy-makers were confident that they would obtain British support for their policies because Britain's economic woes would increase their desire to reduce military spending.[218]

The Ford administration continued to push for agreement within NATO about the contents of an MBFR settlement, and thus proposed that 1,000 nuclear warheads, 54 nuclear capable F-4 aircraft and 36 Pershing surface-to-surface missile launchers should be removed from Europe. This would be the fundamental basis from which NATO would negotiate an MBFR settlement with the Warsaw Pact.[219] The US was correct in its earlier thinking that the British would present the sternest challenge to its MBFR proposals. Within NATO, British officials pressed their American counterparts on both the substance of their proposals and the logic that supported them. According to one report, Callaghan had 'cornered' Kissinger at a NATO conference and had proceeded to list a whole series of complaints over the US's MBFR proposals.[220]

British officials had spent the opening months of 1975 opposing the US's MBFR proposals. However, by May this stance had completely altered, and London notified Washington that it would negotiate for an MBFR along the lines the US had proposed in January 1975.[221] Elliot Richardson gave further impetus to this, confirming that the British would genuinely seek an MBFR agreement.[222] This change in policy is best explained by Britain's economic difficulties. As predicted by US policy-makers in 1974, the MBFR afforded the British the opportunity to reduce their defence commitments within a multilateral framework, and would thus reduce the risk of damaging Britain's security interests within Europe.

In spite of Britain's new-found enthusiasm, the MBFR process remained painfully slow in achieving anything of substance and it also continued to be a source for US–UK disagreement.[223] British officials complained that the US no longer seemed interested in substantively negotiating the contents of MBFR, and this was hardly an unfair assessment given that the Ford administration came to view MBFR as an increasingly meaningless exercise which was unlikely to benefit US interests.[224] Ford, for instance, complained that the only accomplishment his MBFR approach had achieved was to give an impression that he was seeking to 'de-nuclearise' Europe which had only managed to raise the ire of the NATO alliance. Kissinger had reached a similar conclusion.[225] It was apparent that, by the latter part of 1975, the Ford administration had effectively lost interest in reaching a substantive MBFR agreement in the near future.

This loss of interest can be explained because of an intermixing of strategic and domestic political factors: US–Soviet diplomacy was stalling in a number of areas, internationally the entire détente project appeared to be collapsing, SALT II had become mired in technical debate with little likelihood of further progress, the Paris Peace Agreement collapsed in April 1975 when North Vietnam captured Saigon, and the USSR appeared to be advancing in Africa. The CSCE summit in July–August 1975 had also not resulted in any discernible shifts in Soviet foreign policy.[226] Domestically, the continuation of détente was coming under severe attack. Henry 'Scoop' Jackson, the likely Democratic nominee for president, vocally admonished Ford's foreign and defence policies. With Jackson's encouragement, domestic critics of détente became more vocal in the ensuing years. Jimmy Carter's campaign for the presidency also accused the Ford administration of pursuing a weak foreign policy towards the USSR.

For the president, then, the continuation of détente was becoming a prominent political issue that was hurting his chances of winning the 1976 presidential election. Such was the fear of appearing to be pursuing a 'weak' foreign policy, Ford had forbidden the word 'détente' being used to describe his foreign policy during his campaign for the presidency.[227]

Within the administration itself the challenge to détente was just as great, with Schlesinger leading the charge for a new foreign policy approach. Indeed, he would openly challenge official US policy aims in SALT II, and argued that the US should seek much tougher terms than those sought by Kissinger. Schlesinger would find himself fired as secretary of defense in November 1975, but his successor, Donald Rumsfeld, argued along similar lines.[228] Moreover, events in Asia, Africa and Southern Europe appeared to undermine the argument that détente was producing a more amenable foreign policy from the USSR. It appeared as if both superpowers were coming to the conclusion that détente would not provide them with what they wanted. In the case of the US, it could not prevent the Soviet arms build-up, nor obtain Soviet assistance in extracting itself from Indochina. For the Soviet Union, détente would not provide the anti-Chinese alliance it sought, or the economic assistance it required.[229]

Coupled with all of this was Henry Kissinger's dwindling influence on the course of US foreign policy. Kissinger's position within the administration as the chief architect and implementer of US foreign policy was being undermined by both changing international and domestic circumstances. While he had been largely unaffected by the scandal of Watergate, he was now becoming embroiled with similar controversies as the Church Committee (the Congressional inquiry into the CIA) began to reveal Kissinger's association with the more controversial activities of the agency. As the most visible member of the Ford administration associated with the détente project, such revelations were damaging to Kissinger's reputation and standing within the administration. Coupled with this, the challenge from the right of the Republican Party began to make Kissinger a political liability for the president. Ronald Reagan attacked the administration's détente policies and based this as his challenge against Ford as the Republican nominee for the presidency.[230]

Ford was not immune to these pressures, and he began to rely less upon Kissinger's policy advice.[231] Thus, when Kissinger lost his position as national security adviser in November 1975 (something Ford had never been comfortable with, and had been advised to change at the outset of his presidency),[232] it signalled that the president was now determined to chart a more independent and perhaps alternative course in foreign affairs.[233] The likes of Donald Rumsfeld and Dick Cheney offered this alternative, advising the president to take a much sterner approach in their diplomacy with the USSR.[234] As John

Lewis Gaddis – the eminent historian of the Cold War – has noted, 'whatever "thaw" had occurred in the Cold War now seemed to be ending'.[235] Given this, projects closely associated with détente, such as SALT II or MBFR, became less significant for the Ford administration.[236] It is of little surprise then that MBFR failed to substantively advance during the final year of the Ford administration.

## Conclusion

During Wilson's final premiership, he had sought to repair the relationship with Washington and from here ensure that relations remained as close as possible in order to influence Britain's superpower ally. In some ways, Wilson was highly successful in that he managed to improve personal relations with the key policy-makers in Washington and, at least in the public arena, the impression of a close and harmonious relationship was presented.[237] Along with this, the areas traditionally seen as the most 'special' in the US–UK relationship continued under his government. Finally, as witnessed during both the CSCE and MBFR negotiations, US–UK negotiations, if not always in agreement, showcased that a significant amount of interaction, discussion and cooperation continued between the two sides.

Yet, underneath the surface, US–UK disagreement was never far away and it even threatened to impact upon the intelligence and nuclear relationship. As such, a constant feature of the relationship was the coercive diplomacy employed by Washington against its British ally. Threats to curtail, limit, or even permanently cancel, nuclear and intelligence cooperation with London were made periodically by Washington in order to persuade London not to enact sweeping defence budget cuts which would harm perceived US interests. Wilson, having been well versed in experiencing the more belligerent policies of Washington during the presidency of Lyndon Johnson, was able to largely ignore the threats emanating from across the Atlantic. Indeed, Wilson, unlike his predecessor Edward Heath, had judged, quite correctly as it would turn out, that Washington would not act upon its threats because, in the final analysis, this cooperation benefitted the United States. As Wilson well understood, even an ally that was of declining utility remained, nonetheless, useful.

## Notes

1 Memorandum of Conversation, 18 October 1974, File: October 18, 1974, Ford–Kissinger, NSAMC, Box 6, GFL.

2 Peter Rose, 'The Long Agony in No. 10', *The Sun*, p. 1.

3 TNA: PREM 15/2069; TNA: PREM 16/231 Note for the Record: Events leading to the Resignation of Mr Heath's Administration, 4 March 1974. On Heath's last year in office see: Anthony Hornett, *The Fall of Mr Heath's Government, 1973–1974* (St Albans: A. Hornett, 1991).
4 Hathaway, *Great Britain and the United States*, pp. 105–10; Dickie, *'Special' No More*, pp. 154–7; Ovendale, *Anglo-American Relations in the Twentieth Century*, pp. 137–8.
5 Morgan, *Callaghan*, pp. 437–9; Renwick, *Fighting with Allies*, pp. 214–17; Ann Lane, 'Foreign and Defence Policy,' in Anthony Seldon and Kevin Hickson (eds.), *New Labour, Old Labour: The Wilson and Callaghan Governments, 1974–1979* (London: Routledge, 2004), p. 167; Graeme S. Mount, *895 Days that Changed the World: The Presidency of Gerald R. Ford* (London: Black Rose Books, 2006), pp. 3–18.
6 Baylis, *Defence Relations*, pp. 164–80; Dobson, *Anglo-American Relations in the Twentieth Century*, pp. 142–6; John Dumbrell, *A Special Relationship. Anglo–American Relations From Cold War to Iraq* (Basingstoke: PalgraveMacmillan, 2006), pp. 78–84; Burk, *Old World*, pp. 627–30.
7 Baylis, *Defence Relations*, pp. 99–115; Chichester and Wilkinson, *The Uncertain Ally*, pp. 43–56.
8 Baylis, *Defence Relations*, pp. 109–115.
9 Jonathan Aitken, *Nixon: A Life* (London: Weidenfeld & Nicolson, 1993), pp. 380–1.
10 Kissinger, *WHY*, pp. 222–5.
11 John Young, 'John Freeman' in Hopkins et al. (eds.), *The Washington Embassy*, pp. 177–80; Alexander J. Banks, 'Britain and the Cambodia Crisis of Spring 1970', *Cold War History*, 5:1 (2005), 87–105.
12 Telcon: The President–Secretary Kissinger, 13 March 1974, HAKTELCONS.
13 Black, *The Invincible Quest*, p. 763.
14 John Young, *Britain and European Unity, 1945–1999* (Basingstoke: Macmillan, 2000), pp. 111–20; Andrew Geddes, *The European Union and British Politics* (Basingstoke: Palgrave, 2003), pp. 74–8; Möckli, *European Foreign Policy*, pp. 302–9.
15 Bernard Donoughue, *Prime Minister: The Conduct of Policy Under Harold Wilson and James Callaghan* (London: Jonathan Cape, 1987), p. 86; Kavanagh and Seldon, *The Powers Behind the Prime Minister*, pp. 103–5; James Callaghan on the Common Market, MS Callaghan, Box 139, James Callaghan Papers, Bodleian Library, Oxford University, United Kingdom (hereafter: JCP). Also see the contents of MS Callaghan, Box 42, JCP. Further on this see: Michael Palliser, BDOHP, p. 31; Juliet Campbell, *ibid.*, p. 29; Rodric Braithwaite, *ibid.*, p. 15; Nicholas Henderson, *Mandarin: The Diaries of Nicholas Henderson* (London: Weidenfeld & Nicolson, 1994), pp. 59–60, 62–6, 72–3.
16 Emmanuel Mourlon-Druol, 'Filling the EEC Leadership Vacuum? The Creation of the EEC Council in 1974', *Cold War History*, 10:3 (2010), 321–3.
17 Patrick Bell, *The Labour Party in Opposition 1970–1974* (London: Routledge, 2004), pp. 75–88.
18 David McKie and Dennis Barker, 'We're In but Without the Fireworks', *Guardian*, 1 January 1973.
19 'Let Us Work Together: Labour's Way Out of the Crisis', February 1974, available at: www.labour-party.org.uk/manifestos/1974/Feb/1974-feb-labour-manifesto.shtml (Accessed 20 October 2012).

20 Quote in Michael Alexander, BDOHP p. 45. On the points made in the text see: Young, *Britain and European Unity*, pp. 111–20; David Reynolds, *Britannia Overruled: British Policy and World Power in the 20th Century* (London: Longman, 1991), p. 248; Bernard Donoughue, *Downing Street Diary: With Harold Wilson at No. 10* (London: Pimlico, 2006), pp. 251–2; TNA: PREM 16/72 Meeting of Ambassadors to EEC Countries, 20 March 1974; Roy Hattersley, *Fifty Years On: A Prejudiced History of Britain Since the War* (London: Little, Brown and Company, 1997), p. 226.

21 Young, *The Labour Governments 1964–70*, pp. 142–65; Lane, 'Foreign and Defence Policy,' in Seldon and Hickson (eds.), *New Labour*, p. 167; Morgan, *Callaghan*, pp. 437–9.

22 TNA: PREM 16/200 Harold Wilson to the President of the United States, 7 March 1974.

23 From AmEmbassy London to SecState Washington DC, 5 April 1974, Document Number: 1974LONDON04301, from: http://aad.archives.gov/aad/createpdf?rid=62352&dt=1572&dl=823 (Accessed 11 August 2009).

24 Notes of Cabinet Meeting, 20 June 1974, President's Office Files: Memoranda for the President, Box 94, NPMP.

25 Telcon: The President–Secretary Kissinger, 13 March 1974, HAKTELCONS; Telcon: Hal Sonnenfeldt–Secretary Kissinger, 5 March 1974, *ibid*; James Callaghan: Secretary of State for Foreign and Commonwealth Affairs, 20 January 1975, File: Great Britain Visit of Prime Minister Wilson 1–2–75 (2). Edward J. Savage Files, Box 3, GFL.

26 Telcon: The President–Secretary Kissinger, 13 March 1974, HAKTELCONS; Telcon: Hal Sonnenfeldt–Secretary Kissinger, 5 March 1974, *ibid*.

27 Memorandum of Conversation, 8 March 1974, File: March 8, 1974, Kissinger, Schlesinger, Colby, NSAMC Box 3, GFL; Telcon: The President–Secretary Kissinger, 14 February 1974, HAKTELCONS; Telcon: The President–Secretary Kissinger, 13 March 1974, *ibid*.; Telcon: Hal Sonnenfeldt–Secretary Kissinger, 5 March 1974, *ibid*.

28 Memorandum of Conversation, 8 March 1974, File: March 8, 1974, Kissinger, Schlesinger, Colby, NSAMC, Box 3, GFL.

29 Memorandum of Conversation, 11 March 1974, File: March 11, 1974, Kissinger, Schlesinger, Joint Chiefs, NSAMC Box 3, GFL.

30 Kissinger was working closely with George Schultz and Arthur Burns with regard to applying economic pressure upon the EEC. See: Ferrell (ed.), *The Secret Diary of Arthur Burns*, pp. 123–4; Telcon: Secretary Kissinger–Secretary Schultz, 16 March 1974, HAKTELCONS.

31 Question and Answer Session at the Executives Club of Chicago, 15 March 1974, in *Public Papers of the President, Richard Nixon, 1974*, p. 276.

32 Memorandum of Conversation, 11 March 1974, File: March 11, 1974, Kissinger, Schlesinger, Joint Chiefs, NSAMC, Box 3, GFL.

33 Both quotes within: Memorandum of Conversation, 19 March 1974, File: March 19, 1974, Kissinger, Schlesinger, NSAMC, Box 3, GFL.

34 Question and Answer Session at the Annual Convention of the National Association of Broadcasters, Houston, Texas, 19 March 1974, *Public Papers of the President, Richard Nixon, 1974*, pp. 282–98.

35 TNA: PREM 16/419 Draft Record of a Conversation between the Foreign and Commonwealth Secretary and Mr Helmut Sonnenfeldt, 15 March 1974.

36 TNA: FCO 82/471 Henry Kissinger to James Callaghan, 13 April 1974; TNA: FCO 82/471 Callaghan to Washington, 24 April 1974.

37 TNA: FCO 82/442 Record of Conversation between the Foreign and Commonwealth Secretary and Dr Henry Kissinger, 8 July 1974.

38 TNA: PREM 16/728 Ramsbotham to the FCO, 31 January 1975; TNA: PREM 16/728 Note of a Meeting held in the Oval Office, White House, 31 January 1975.

39 Both quotes within: TNA: FCO 82/441 Steering Brief, J. E. Killick to Private Secretary, 26 March 1974.

40 TNA: PREM 16/419 Richard Sykes to Thomas Brimelow, 2 April 1974.

41 TNA: PREM 16/419 Ramsbotham to the FCO, Tel. 1066, 25 March 1974; TNA: PREM 16/419 A. A. Acland to Lord Bridges, 25 March 1974; TNA: PREM 16/419 H. T. A. Overton to Private Secretary, 14 March 1974; Memorandum for the President from Henry Kissinger, 22 September 1974, File: United Kingdom (2), National Security Adviser Presidential Country Files for Europe and Canada, Box 15, GFL.

42 Hanhimäki, *Flawed*, p. 351. For other authors who agree the project was a failure see: Hynes, *The Year*, pp. 196–231; Garthoff, *A Journey Through the Cold War*, p. 288; Pietrantonio, 'The year that never was', 158–77; Weisbrode, *The Atlantic Century*, pp. 267–8.

43 Z, 'The Year of Europe?', *Foreign Affairs*, 52:2 (January 1974), 237.

44 William Farmenter memorandum, 5 August 1974, File: NSA: NSC Europe, Canada and Ocean Affairs, Staff Files Box 48 (2), Ford Library Project File of Documents Declassified Through the Remote Archive Capture Program, Box 6, GFL.

45 See the following: Hynes, *The Year*; Pietrantonio, 'The Year That Never Was'.

46 Barry Werth, *31 Days: Gerald Ford, The Nixon Pardon, and a Government in Crisis* (New York: Anchor Books, 2006); James Cannon, *Time and Chance: Gerald Ford's Appointment with History* (London: HarperCollins, 1994), pp. 321–78.

47 Clark Mollenhoff, *The Man who Pardoned Nixon: A Documented Account of Gerald Ford's Presidential Retreat from Credibility* (New York: St Martin's Press, 1976), pp. 80–8.

48 Ernest May and Philip Zelikow (eds.), *The Kennedy Tapes: Inside the White House During the Cuban Missile Crisis* (Cambridge, MA: Harvard University Press, 1997), p. 17.

49 Jan Asmussen, *Cyprus at War: Diplomacy and Conflict during the 1974 Crisis* (London: I.B. Tauris, 2008), pp. 21–5.

50 Intelligence Report Prepared in the Central Intelligence Agency, 24 September 1973, *Foreign Relations of the United States, 1969–1976: Greece; Cyprus; Turkey, 1973–1976* (Washington: United States Government Printing Office, 2007), Vol. XXX, Doc. 73, p. 253; Panagiotis Dimitrakis, *Military Intelligence in Cyprus: From the Great War to Middle East Crises* (London: Peter Lang, 2010), pp. 133–58.

51 Alistair Horne, *Macmillan 1957–1986* (London: Macmillan, 1989), pp. 99–104.

52 Asmussen, *Cyprus at War*, p. 26.

53 TNA: FCO 9/1921 Hooper to FCO, Tel. 430, 12 August 1974.

54 TNA: FCO 9/1916 British objectives in a Cyprus Conference, attached to J. E. Cable to Sir J. Killick, 22 July 1974.

55 Aldrich, *GCHQ*, pp. 320–30.

56 Ritchie Ovendale, *British Defence Policy since 1945* (Manchester: Manchester University Press, 1994), pp. 153–4.

57 Harold Wilson, *Final Term: The Labour Government 1974–1976* (London: Michael Joseph, 1979), pp. 62–3; Callaghan, *Time*, p. 342; Roy Mason, *Paying the Price* (London: Robert Hale, 1999), pp. 128–9.
58 Marc Susser, 'Preface,' in *FRUS, 1969–1976: Greece*, Vol. XXX, p. iv.
59 Memorandum from Rosemary Niehuss of the National Security Council Staff to Secretary of State Kissinger, 15 July 1974, *FRUS, 1969–1976: Greece*, Vol. XXX, Doc. 79, pp. 275–6.
60 Minutes of Meeting of the Washington Special Actions Group, 15 July 1974, *ibid.*, Doc. 80, p. 279.
61 Study Prepared by the Interdepartmental Group for Near East and South Asia, 6 May 1974, *ibid.*, Doc. 75, p. 263.
62 Minutes of Meeting of the Washington Special Actions Group, 16 July 1974, *ibid.*, Doc. 86, pp. 288–94.
63 Telegram from the Embassy in Greece to the Department of State, 16 July 1974, *ibid.*, Doc. 89, p. 300.
64 Minutes of Meeting of the Washington Special Actions Group, 17 July 1974, *ibid.*, Doc. 91, pp. 306–16; Telegram from the Embassy in Greece to the Department of State, 16 July 1974, *ibid.*, Doc. 89, p. 305.
65 Minutes of Meeting of the Washington Special Actions Group, 17 July 1974, *ibid.*, Doc. 91, pp. 304–8; Telegram from the Embassy in Greece to the Department of State, 16 July 1974, *ibid.*, Doc. 89, p. 305.
66 Callaghan, *Time*, p. 339.
67 *Ibid.*
68 Transcript of Telephone Conversation between President Nixon and Secretary of State Kissinger, 17 July 1974, *FRUS, 1969–1976: Greece*, Vol. XXX, Doc. 93, pp. 311–12.
69 Editorial Note, *ibid.*, Doc. 96, p. 320.
70 Telegram from the Department of State to Certain Posts, 18 July 1974, *ibid.*, Doc. 97, pp. 322–3.
71 The British record of these discussions can be followed throughout: TNA: FCO 9/1916; TNA: FCO 9/1917; TNA: FCO 9/1918.
72 Brendan O'Malley and Ian Craig, *The Cyprus Conspiracy: America, Espionage and the Turkish Invasion* (London: I.B Tauris, 2001), pp. 187–98.
73 Minutes of Meeting of the Washington Special Actions Group, 20 July 1974, *FRUS, 1969–1976: Greece*, Vol. XXX, Doc. 105, pp. 341–7; Transcript of Telephone Conversation between Secretary of State Kissinger and Deputy Secretary of State [Ingersoll], 20 July 1974, *ibid.*, Doc. 106, pp. 348–9.
74 Minutes of Meeting of the Washington Special Actions Group, 21 July 1974, *ibid.*, Doc. 110, pp. 361–2.
75 Callaghan had warned Kissinger that a possible coup was imminent and claimed that the information was from an 'excellent source'. Given that the coup took place the following day, it would appear this was indeed an 'excellent source'. See: *ibid.*, p. 363.
76 Briefing Memorandum from the Assistant Secretary of State for European Affairs [Hartman] to Secretary of State Kissinger, 23 July 1974, *ibid.*, Doc. 118, pp. 391–2; Transcript of Telephone Conversation between President Nixon and Secretary of State Kissinger, 17 July 1974, *ibid.*, Doc. 93, pp. 311–12; Memorandum of Conversation, 23 July 1974, *ibid.*, Doc. 119, p. 393.

77 TNA: FCO 9/1918 Record of a Telephone Conversation between the Secretary of State for Foreign and Commonwealth Affairs and Dr Kissinger, 21 July 1974.
78 TNA: FCO 9/1916 Callaghan to Athens, Tel. 168, 22 July 1974; TNA: FCO 9/1916 Callaghan to Athens, Tel. 173, 22 July 1974. The talks can be followed throughout: TNA: FCO 9/1918; TNA: FCO 9/1919, TNA: FCO 9/1920; TNA: FCO 9/1921; TNA: FCO 9/1922; TNA: FCO 9/1935.
79 Telcon: Kissinger–Callaghan, 22 July 1974, HAKTELCONS.
80 Telegram from the Embassy in Greece to the Department of State, 16 July 1974, *FRUS, 1969–1976: Greece*, Vol. XXX, Doc. 89, p. 305; Callaghan, *Time*, pp. 338–41.
81 Kissinger, *YOR*, p. 226.
82 The Prime Minister to the Foreign and Commonwealth Secretary, 31 July 1974, MS Wilson c. 1597, Prime Minister's Personal Minutes, 1974–75, File: 794 y(108), Harold Wilson Papers, Bodleian Library, Oxford University (hereafter: HWP).
83 Callaghan, *Time*, p. 350.
84 Telegram from the Mission in Geneva to the Department of State, 9 August 1974, *FRUS, 1969–1976: Greece*, Vol. XXX, Doc. 125, p. 416.
85 Dimitrakis, *Military Intelligence in Cyprus*, pp. 146–7.
86 TNA: FCO 9/1916 British Objectives in a Cyprus Conference, attached to J. E. Cable to Sir J. Killick, 22 July 1974; TNA: FCO 9/1921 J. R. Freeland to Mr Goodison, 10 August 1974; TNA: FCO 9/1921 Hooper to FCO, Tel. 430, 12 August 1974; TNA: FCO 9/1917 A. C. Goodison to Mr Brenchley, 13 August 1974.
87 TNA: FCO 9/1921 Phillips to UKMIS Geneva, Tel. 21, 14 August 1974; Dimitrakis, *Military Intelligence in Cyprus*, pp. 146–9.
88 Callaghan, *Time*, pp. 353–4.
89 Telcon: Ford–Kissinger, 10 August 1974, HAKTELCONS.
90 TNA: FCO 9/1927 Record of a Meeting at 10 Downing Street, 14 August 1974.
91 Telegram from the Mission in Geneva to the Department of State, 9 August 1974, *FRUS, 1969–1976: Greece*, Vol. XXX, Doc. 126, pp. 416–18; Memorandum of Conversation, 15 August 1974, *ibid.*, Doc. 133, p. 444; Memorandum of Conversation, 17 August 1974, *ibid.*, Doc. 137, p. 452.
92 Minutes of a Meeting of the Washington Special Actions Group, 14 August 1974, *ibid.*, Doc. 131, p. 435.
93 Kissinger, *YOR*, pp. 192, 225.
94 Memorandum of Conversation, 13 August 1974, *FRUS, 1969–1976: Greece*, Vol. XXX, Doc. 129, p. 424.
95 Telcon: The President–Secretary Kissinger, 10 August 1974, File: CyprUS–Kissinger Telcons 8/6/74, Henry Kissinger and Brent Scowcroft Temporary Parallel File, Box A1, GFL.
96 Craig and Logevall, *America's Cold War*, pp. 252–5; Paul Kennedy, *The Rise and Fall of the Great Powers: Economic Change and Military Conflict From 1500 to 2000* (London: Fontana, 1987), pp. 526–8.
97 Werth, *31 Days*, pp. 135–6.
98 Andreas Constandios, *America, Britain and the Cyprus Crisis: Calculated Conspiracy or Foreign Policy Failure?* (London: AuthorHouse, 2009); O'Malley and Craig, *The Cyprus Conspiracy*; Aldrich, *GCHQ*, p. 326.

99 Telcon: The President–Secretary Kissinger, 10 August 1974, File: CyprUS–Kissinger Telcons 8/6/74, Henry Kissinger and Brent Scowcroft Temporary Parallel File, Box A1, GFL. Not that this won the US much sympathy amongst Greek nationalists given the US Ambassador in Nicosia, Rodger P. Davies, was murdered by a sniper during a protest outside the US Embassy on 19 August 1974.

100 Mancur Olson, *The Rise and Decline of Nations: Economic Growth, Stagflation and Social Rigidities* (Cambridge, MA: Harvard University Press, 1982), p. 6.

101 Alec Cairncross, 'The Heath Government and the British Economy', in Ball and Seldon (eds.), *The Heath Government*, pp. 107–38.

102 See: *Hansard*, 17 December 1973, Vol. 866, column 967.

103 David Harris, 'Poor Man of Europe "by 1985"', *Daily Telegraph*, 25 September 1973.

104 Mason, *Paying the Price*, p. 123.

105 The Prime Minister to the Chief Whip, 24 October 1974, File: 794 y(108), Box MS Wilson, c.1597, Prime Minister's Personal Minutes, HWP; The Prime Minister to the Secretary of State for Industry, 4 July 1974, File: 794 y(108), Box MS Wilson, c.1597, Prime Minister's Personal Minutes, HWP.

106 'Let Us Work Together – Labour's Way Out of the Crisis', February 1974 (Labour Party Manifesto), www.labour-party.org.uk/manifestos/1974/Feb/1974-feb-labour-manifesto.shtml (Accessed 20 October 2012).

107 *Hansard*, 26 March 1974, Vol. 871, column: 302–3; Mason, *Paying the Price*, p. 123.

108 From AmEmbassy London to SecState Washington DC, 26 March 1974, Document Number: 1974LONDON03821, from: http://aad.archives.gov/aad/createpdf?rid=46515&dt=1572&dl=823 (Accessed 11 August 2009); Yanek Mieczkowski, *Gerald Ford and the Challenges of the 1970s* (Lexington: University of Kentucky Press, 2005), pp. 95–156.

109 Rodman, *Presidential Command*, pp. 106–7.

110 From AmEmbassy London to SecState Washington DC, 26 March 1974, Document Number: 1974LONDON03821, from: http://aad.archives.gov/aad/createpdf?rid=46515&dt=1572&dl=823 (Accessed 11 August 2009).

111 Memorandum of Conversation, 26 April 1974, RG 59 Records of Henry Kissinger, 1973–1977, NODISMEMCONS, Box 7, NAII.

112 For the Wilson quote see: Memorandum of Conversation, 14 August 1974, File: August 14, 1974–Ford, Kissinger, NSAMC, Box 4, GFL. The Healey quote is within: Memorandum of Conversation, 13 October 1975, *FRUS 1969–76: Foreign Economic Policy*, Vol. XXXI, Doc. 235, p. 810.

113 From AmEmbassy London to SecState Washington DC, 7 March 1974, Document Number: 1974LONDON02926, from: http://aad.archives.gov/aad/createpdf?rid=43444&dt=1572&dl=823 (Accessed 13 August 2009).

114 From AmEmbassy London to SecState Washington DC, 19 April 1974, Document Number: 1974LONDON04861, from: http://aad.archives.gov/aad/createpdf?rid=63550&dt=1572&dl=823 (Accessed 22 August 2009); From AmEmbassy London to SecState Washington DC, 2 August 1974, Document Number: 1974LONDON09893, from: http://aad.archives.gov/aad/createpdf?rid=131207&dt=1572&dl=823 (Accessed 28 August 2009).

115 Wilson, *Final Term*, pp. 9–11.

116 Ziegler, *Wilson*, p. 459.

117 Memorandum for Secretary Kissinger from Jan Lodal and Helmut Sonnenfeldt, 9 November 1974, File: United Kingdom (3), National Security Adviser Presidential Country Files for Europe and Canada, Box 15, GFL; From SecState WashDC (Ingersoll) to AmEmbassy London, November 1974, Tel. 251716, File: United Kingdom (3), National Security Adviser Presidential Country Files for Europe and Canada, Box 15, GFL.
118 TNA: PREM 16/21 Henry Kissinger to James Callaghan, 16 November 1974.
119 Aldrich, *GCHQ*, p. 329–31.
120 Mason, *Paying the Price*, pp. 130–4; David Greenwood, 'The 1974 Defence Review in Perspective', *Survival*, 17:5 (1975), 223–9.
121 Quote in Mason, *Paying the Price*, p. 132. Also: Roy Mason, 'Britain's Security Interests', *Survival*, 17:5 (1975), 219.
122 Speech for Glasgow Keir Hardie House, 1 March 1975, File: 16 December 1974–7 April 1975, MS Wilson c. 1263, Prime Minister's Speeches, HWP.
123 Quote in Barbara Castle, *The Castle Diaries 1974–76* (London: Weidenfeld & Nicolson, 1980), p. 227. Also: Prime Minister to the Chancellor of the Exchequer, 19 November 1974, File: 794 y(108), Box MS Wilson, c.1597, Prime Minister's Personal Minutes, HWP.
124 Memorandum of Conversation, 18 October 1974, File: October 18, 1974 Ford–Kissinger, NSAMC, Box 6, GFL.
125 Memorandum of Conversation, 8 January 1975, File: January 8, 1975 Ford–Kissinger, NSAMC, Box 8, GFL.
126 From AmEmbassy London to SecState Washington DC, 5 December 1974, Document Number: 1974LONDON15875, from: http://aad.archives.gov/aad/createpdf?rid=192618&dt=1572&dl=823 (Accessed 26 July 2009).
127 Memorandum of Conversation, 27 March 1975, File: March 27, 1975, Ford, SACEUR Alexander Haig, Donald Rumsfeld, NSAMC, Box 10, GFL.
128 'Fasten Your Gun Belts', *Daily Express*, 20 March 1975.
129 From AmEmbassy London to SecState Washington DC, 14 March 1975, Document Number: 1975LONDON04000, from: http://aad.archives.gov/aad/createpdf?rid=47399&dt=1822&dl=823 (Accessed 3 September 2009).
130 Ovendale, *British Defence Policy*, pp. 153–4; Baylis, *Defence Relations*, pp. 109–10; From SecState WashDC to AmEmbassy London, November 1974, Tel. 262034, File: United Kingdom State Department Telegrams From Secstate NODIS (1), National Security Adviser Presidential Country Files for Europe and Canada, Box 15, GFL; From SecState WashDC to AmEmbassy London, November 1974, Tel. 251716, File: United Kingdom State Department Telegrams From Secstate NODIS (1), National Security Adviser Presidential Country Files for Europe and Canada, Box 15, GFL.
131 From AmEmbassy London to SecState Washington DC, 9 July 1975, Document Number: 1975LONDON10476, from: http://aad.archives.gov/aad/createpdf?rid=122713&dt=1822&dl=823 (Accessed 9 November 2009).
132 On all of these points see: Greenwood, 'The 1974 Defence Review', 223–6; Frederic Heurtebize, 'The Union of the Left in France, 1971–1981: A Threat to NATO? The View from Washington', *Journal of Transatlantic Studies*, 9:3 (2011), 244–56; Mario Del Pero, '"Which Chile, Allende?" Henry Kissinger and the Portuguese Revolution', *Cold War History*, 11:4 (2011), 625–57; John Lewis Gaddis, *Strategies of Containment:*

*A Critical Appraisal of American National Security Policy during the Cold War* (Oxford: Oxford University Press, 2005), pp. 307–41; Westad, *The Global Cold War*, pp. 194–206; Melvyn P. Leffler, *For the Soul of Mankind: The United States, the Soviet Union and the Cold War* (New York: Hill & Wang, 2007), pp. 234–7.

133 Memorandum of Conversation, 27 February 1975, File: February 27, 1975 Ford–Kissinger–Ambassador Elliot Richardson (Great Britain), NSAMC, Box 9, GFL.

134 TNA: FCO 82/576 Extract from *Fortune*, April 1975.

135 TNA: FCO 82/576 V. Dixon to David Shore, 4 April 1975.

136 A. H. Raskin, 'Streamlining in Britain', *New York Times*, 28 October 1975, p. 33.

137 Memorandum of Conversation, 8 January 1975, File: January 8, 1975 Ford–Kissinger, NSAMC, Box 8, GFL.

138 Simon, *Reflection*, pp. 152–3; Memorandum for the President from Alan Greenspan, 23 April 1975, File: CO160-2/1/75-4/30/75, White House Central Files, Box 56, GFL; Memorandum of Conversation, 24 February 1976, File: European Community, National Security Adviser International Economic Affairs Staff Files, Box 5, GFL; From AmEmbassy London to SecState Washington DC, 21 January 1975, Document Number: 1975LONDON00950, from: http://aad.archives.gov/aad/createpdf?rid=14885&dt=1822&dl=823 (Accessed 22 July 2009); From AmEmbassy London to SecState Washington DC, 19 May 1975, Document Number: 1975LONDON07544, from: http://aad.archives.gov/aad/createpdf?rid=92491&dt=1822&dl=823 (Accessed 3 August 2009); From AmEmbassy London to SecState Washington DC, 17 June 1975, Document Number: 1975LONDON09263, from: http://aad.archives.gov/aad/createpdf?rid=104634&dt=1822&dl=823 (Accessed 4 August 2009).

139 Memorandum of Conversation, 9 May 1975, File: May 9, 1975, Ford–Kissinger, NSAMC, Box 11, GFL.

140 From AmEmbassy London to SecState Washington DC, 14 March 1975, Document Number: 1975LONDON04000, from: http://aad.archives.gov/aad/createpdf?rid=47399&dt=1822&dl=823 (Accessed 22 August 2009); Department of State Briefing Paper: Status of NATO, undated (July 1975), File: July 26–August 4, Europe Briefing Book CSCE Copy 1 (1), National Security Adviser Trip Briefing Books and Cable for President Ford, Box 10, GFL.

141 Edward Pearce, *Denis Healey: A Life in our Times* (Boston, MA: Little, Brown and Company, 2002), pp. 428–50.

142 Meeting with Prime Minister Wilson Briefing Papers, 30 July 1975, File: July 26–August 4, 1975–Europe, Briefing Book–CSCE Bilateral Book, Volume II (6), National Security Adviser Trip Briefing Books and Cables for President Ford 1974–76, Box 11, GFL.

143 TNA: PREM 16/733 R. M. [Roy Mason] to the Prime Minister, 19 June 1975.

144 TNA: PREM 16/733 Background Notes: The Monterey Warning, undated (circa 23 September 1975).

145 TNA: PREM 16/733 Handwritten note written by Wilson on RM [Mason] to the Prime Minister, 19 June 1975.

146 TNA: PREM 16/733 R. H. Wright to J. F. Mayne, 23 June 1975.

147 TNA: PREM 16/733 James Callaghan to the Prime Minister, 22 July 1975. It is within this document that reference is made to the 1973 suspension of US–UK intelligence

cooperation. Evidently both the prime minister and Callaghan were aware of the precedent set by Kissinger and Schlesinger.

148 TNA: PREM 16/733 DWH to the Prime Minister, 23 June 1975.

149 Ford believed that Schlesinger was insubordinate and had a habit of 'talking down' to him. As he told one journalist, 'He was the one that I was not comfortable with ... He was a talented guy, but we just didn't fit.' Thomas M. DeFrank, *Write it When I'm Gone: Remarkable Off-the-Record Conversations with Gerald R. Ford* (New York: G. P. Putnam's Sons, 2007), p. 97.

150 Telcon: Secretary Schlesinger–Secretary Kissinger, 14 June 1975, HAKTELCONS.

151 The US Embassy in London reported Mason's announcement. See: From AmEmbassy London to SecState Washington DC, 25 June 1975, Document Number: 1975LONDON09764, from: http://aad.archives.gov/aad/createpdf?rid=106620&dt=1822&dl=823 (Accessed 8 September 2009).

152 TNA: PREM 16/733 Meeting between the Defence Secretary and the Hon. James R. Schlesinger, United States Secretary of Defense, in the Ministry of Defence, 24 September 1975; TNA: PREM 16/733 Note of a Meeting over Lunch between the Prime Minister and the United States Secretary of Defense at Chequers, 27 September 1975; TNA: PREM 16/733 Note of a Meeting held in the Chancellor of the Exchequer's Room, 24 September 1975.

153 TNA: PREM 16/733 Note of a Meeting held in the Chancellor of the Exchequer's Room, 24 September 1975.

154 TNA: PREM 16/733 Note of a Meeting over Lunch between the Prime Minister and the United States Secretary of Defense at Chequers, 27 September 1975.

155 This was the very same point that the US Embassy in London warned Washington about. See: From AmEmbassy London to SecState Washington DC, 21 September 1975, Document Number: 1975LONDON14337, from: http://aad.archives.gov/aad/createpdf?rid=163320&dt=1822&dl=823 (Accessed 14 August 2009).

156 Denis Healey, *The Time Of My Life* (London: Michael Joseph, 1989), p. 400; Mason, *Paying the Price*, pp. 138–9; TNA: CAB 128/57/18 Conclusions of a Meeting of the Cabinet, 13 November 1975; TNA: PREM 16/330 John Hunt to the Prime Minister, 28 November 1975; TNA: PREM 16/330 T. F. Brenchley to the Prime Minister, 2 December 1975.

157 Donoughue, *With Harold Wilson*, p. 561; TNA: PREM 16/330 T. F. Brenchley to the Prime Minister, 2 December 1975; TNA: PREM 16/330 John Hunt to the Prime Minister, 28 November 1975; TNA: PREM 16/330 T. F. Brenchley to the Prime Minister, 2 December 1975.

158 From SecState WashDC [Kissinger] to AmEmbassy London, December 1975, Tel. 289664, File: United Kingdom State Department Telegrams From Secstate NODIS (4), National Security Adviser Presidential Country Files for Europe and Canada, Box 15, GFL.

159 The Cabinet discussions can be followed throughout: TNA: CAB 128/57/54; TNA: CAB 128/58/1; TNA: CAB 128/57/25.

160 John Dumbrell, 'The Johnson Administration and the British Labour Government: Vietnam, the Pound and East of Suez', *Journal of American Studies*, 30:2 (1996), 211–31.

161 The quote is referenced within Donoughue, *With Harold Wilson*, p. 594. On Wilson's dislike of the Treasury see: Peter Hennessy, *The Prime Minister: The Office and Its*

*Holders since 1945* (London: Penguin, 2000), p. 362. Wilson had studied at the University of Oxford where he had obtained a 1st class degree in Politics, Philosophy and Economics. At the age of only 21 Wilson was appointed as a Lecturer in Economic History at New College, Oxford University. It was here that Wilson would establish a reputation as a highly talented economist. On Wilson's education see Ben Pimlott, *Harold Wilson* (London: HarperCollins, 1992), p. 59; Ziegler, *Wilson*, p. 24.

162 TNA: CAB 128/57/54 Conclusions of a Meeting of the Cabinet, 9 December 1975; TNA: CAB 128/57/25 Conclusions of a Meeting of the Cabinet, 11 December 1975; TNA: CAB 128/58/1 Conclusions of a Meeting of the Cabinet, 15 January 1976.

163 TNA: PREM 16/330 John Hunt to the Prime Minister, 28 November 1975.

164 President Ford to Harold Wilson, October 1975, MS Wilson, c. 1592: Messages to and from Heads of State, HWP.

165 TNA: PREM 16/391 HW [Harold Wilson] to Lord Bridges, 1 June 1974.

166 TNA: PREM 16/391 Callaghan to Washington, 2 May 1974.

167 Memorandum of Conversation, 31 May 1974, File: May 31, 1974 Nixon, Kissinger, Alexander Haig, National Security Adviser: Memoranda of Conversations, 1973–1977, Box 4, GFL.

168 Davy, 'Helsinki Myths', 1–22. The CSCE was negotiating various and interrelated aspects of East–West interaction. Subsequently, the conference agenda was divided into what was termed 'baskets'. Basket I was to deal with questions related to the security of Europe. Basket II dealt with questions of economic and scientific cooperation. Basket III related to cooperation in the humanitarian field. Thus CBMs were contained within Basket III and were proving to be the biggest obstacle to East-West agreement.

169 Bennett and Hamilton (eds.), *DBPO: CSCE*, p. xxvi. Also see: TNA: PREM 16/391 Translation of a Message from Mr Brezhnev, delivered to the Prime Minister by the Soviet Ambassador in London, 10 June 1974; TNA: FCO 28/2451 Meeting with Mr William Hyland, Head of INR, State Department, 29 April 1974, filed by Malcolm Makinstosh, 30 April 1974.

170 For the quote see: Memorandum for the Secretary from Helmut Sonnenfeldt, 31 May 1974, National Security Council Files: Henry A. Kissinger Office Files, Europe, Box 69, NPMP. Also see: Memorandum for the President from Henry A. Kissinger, 26 March 1974, NSC Files: Henry A. Kissinger Office Files, Country Files, Europe–USSR, Box 76, NPMP; Hanhimäki, *Flawed*, pp. 359–81; Kissinger, *Diplomacy*, p. 759.

171 On Washington's thinking see: Memorandum of Conversation, 31 May 1974, File: May 31, 1974 Nixon, Kissinger, Alexander Haig, NSAMC, Box 4, GFL; Memorandum of Conversation, 18 March 1974, *FRUS 1969–1976, European Security*, Vol. XXXIX, Doc. 190, pp. 557–61; Backchannel Message from the President's Deputy Assistant for National Security Affairs [Scowcroft] to Secretary of State Kissinger in Jerusalem, 6 May 1974, *ibid.*, Doc. 202, p. 617.

172 Brezhnev Note to the President, 8 June 1974, National Security Council Files: Henry A. Kissinger Office Files, Country Files, Box 71, NPMP; Memorandum of a Conversation, 15 April 1974, National Security Council Files: Henry A. Kissinger Office Files, Country Files, Europe–USSR, Box 82, NPMP; Memorandum of Conversation, 24 October 1974, *FRUS 1969–1976*, *European Security*, Vol. XXXIX, Doc. 258, pp. 749–55.

173 US policy had previously sought to obtain Soviet agreement on MBFR prior to the conclusion of any CSCE. National Security Decision Memorandum 162, undated (circa April 1972), *FRUS 1969–1976, European Security*, Vol. XXXIX, Doc. 89, p. 271.

174 Memorandum of Conversation, 31 May 1974, *ibid.*, Doc. 190, p. 633.

175 Minutes of a Verification Panel Meeting, 1 August 1974, *ibid.*, Doc. 349, p. 1021.

176 Memorandum of Conversation, 25 March 1974, National Security Council Files, Henry A. Kissinger Office Files, Country Files–Europe–USSR, Box 76, NPMP.

177 Bennett and Hamilton (eds.), *DBPO: CSCE*, p. xxvi.

178 TNA: PREM 16/391 Extract from PM's Talks with Dr Kissinger, 8 June 1974.

179 TNA: FCO 21/1284 Ramsbotham to the FCO, 15 April 1974; TNA: FCO 82/446 A. A. Acland to Mr Tickell, 26 September 1974.

180 Hyland, *Mortal Rivals*, pp. 116–17. Hyland was appointed in 1969 as a member of the National Security Council. In 1973 he was appointed as the Director of the Bureau of Intelligence and Research, and in November 1975 he would serve as the Deputy National Security Adviser under Brent Scowcroft until the end of the Ford presidency.

181 Davy, 'Helsinki Myths', 1–22.

182 Memorandum for Secretary Kissinger from William Hyland, 8 January 1974, National Security Council Files: Henry A. Kissinger Office Files, Country Files, Box 68, NPMP.

183 A point made clear to Kissinger in May 1974. Sonnenfeldt and Hartman to Secretary Kissinger attached within Secretary of State to Ambassador in Jerusalem, Tel. State 107292, May 1974, National Security Council Files, Henry A. Kissinger Office Files, Europe, Box 69, NPMP.

184 Backchannel Message from the President's Deputy Assistant for National Security Affairs [Scowcroft] to Secretary of State Kissinger in Jerusalem, 6 May 1974, *FRUS 1969–1976, European Security*, Vol. XXXIX, Doc. 202, p. 617; Memorandum of Conversation, 11 April 1974, *ibid.*, Doc. 199, pp. 606–7; Sonnenfeldt and Hartman to Secretary Kissinger, attached within Secretary of State [Kissinger] to Ambassador in Jerusalem, Tel. State 107929, May 1974, National Security Council Files: Henry A. Kissinger Office Files, Europe, Box 69, NPMP; Memorandum for Secretary Kissinger from Jan M. Lodal and Helmut Sonnenfeldt, 31 May 1974, *ibid.*

185 Action Memorandum from the Assistant Secretary of State for European Affairs [Hartman] to the Counsellor of the Department of State [Sonnenfeldt], 19 July 1974, *FRUS 1969–1976, European Security*, Vol. XXXIX, Doc. 236, p. 700.

186 Telegram from the Department of State to the Mission in Geneva, 8 June 1974, *FRUS 1969–1976, European Security*, Vol. XXXIX, Doc. 210, pp. 638–9; Bennett and Hamilton (eds.), *DBPO: CSCE*, pp. xxvi.

187 Telegram from the Mission in Geneva to the Department of State, 23 July 1974, *FRUS 1969–1976, European Security*, Vol. XXXIX, Doc. 238, pp. 706–7; Sir E. Peck to Mr Callaghan, 4 July 1974, in Bennett and Hamilton (eds.), *DBPO: CSCE*, Doc. 89, p. 306; TNA: FCO 30/2481 Community Briefing on Visit by Herr Genscher to Dorneywood on Saturday 15 June, 19 June 1974.

188 Memorandum from the President's Assistant for National Security Affairs [Kissinger] to President Nixon, 27 June 1974, *FRUS 1969–1976, European Security*, Vol. XXXIX, Doc. 224, p. 666.

189 Memorandum of Conversation, 7 July 1974, *ibid.*, Doc. 234, pp. 695–8.
190 Romano, *Détente in Europe*, pp. 199–200.
191 Memorandum of Conversation, 9 December 1974, *FRUS 1969–1976, European Security*, Vol. XXXIX, Doc. 266, p. 782.
192 From AmEmbassy London to SecState Washington, December 1974, Tel. London 15934, File: United Kingdom State Department To SECSTATE EXDIS (1), National Security Adviser Presidential Country Files for Europe and Canada, Box 16, GFL.
193 Michael Alexander, BDOHP, pp. 14–16.
194 For reports of British demands on CBMs being less stringent see: Conference on Security and Cooperation in Europe, attached to Memorandum for Brent Scowcroft from George Springsteen, 14 January 1975, File: Conference on Security and Cooperation in Europe, 1974 WH (1), National Security Adviser NSC Europe, Canada and Ocean Affairs Staff Files 1974–1977, Box 44, GFL.
195 Memorandum of Conversation, 30 January 1975, *FRUS 1969–1976, European Security*, Vol. XXXIX, Doc. 269, p. 788.
196 Memorandum of Conversation, 26 May 1975, File: May 26, 1975 Ford–Kissinger, NSAMC, Box 12, GFL.
197 *Ibid.*
198 Memorandum of Conversation, 7 May 1975, File: May 7, 1975, Ford, Kissinger, UK Prime Minister Wilson, Foreign Secretary Callaghan, NSAMC, Box 11, GFL.
199 Memorandum for Secretary Kissinger from Mr Clift, 16 May 1975, File: Conference on Security and Cooperation in Europe, 1974 WH (3), National Security Adviser NSC Europe, Canada and Ocean Affairs Staff Files 1974–1977, Box 44, GFL.
200 Kissinger, *Diplomacy*, p. 759.
201 This was not settled until 19 July 1975, as the various delegates in Geneva continued to debate the various parameters of Basket III. The Soviets made a number of bilateral efforts to persuade the British to hold a summit in the summer of 1975. See: TNA: PREM 16/392 Soviet Ambassador's Call on the Prime Minister: CSCE, P. J. Weston to John [Killick] 16 June 1975; TNA: PREM 16/392 L. I. Brezhnev to the Prime Minister, 16 June 1975.
202 Stephen Kieninger, 'Transformation of Status Quo', in Bange and Niedhart (eds.), *Helsinki 1975*, p. 78.
203 Editorial, *The New York Times*, 21 July 1975.
204 News Report, NBC News, 2 August 1975, Tape F380, GFL.
205 George Ball, 'Capitulation at Helsinki', *The Atlantic Community Quarterly*, 3:3 (1975), 286–8; Alexander Solzhenitsyn, 'The Big Losers in World War III', *The Atlantic Community Quarterly*, 13:3 (1975), 293–5; Del Pero, *Eccentric Realist*, pp. 110–44.
206 Speech to Chelsea Conservative Club, 26 July 1975, available at: www.margaretthatcher.org/speeches/displaydocument.asp?docid=102750 (Accessed 21 September 2009).
207 'Stopping the Rot', *Daily Express*, 4 August 1975, p. 6.
208 Margaret Thatcher, *The Path to Power* (London: HarperCollins, 1995), p. 353.
209 Pimlott, *Wilson*, p. 703.
210 TNA: FCO 82/584 Note of a Meeting between the Prime Minister and the President of the United States, 30 July 1975; Editorial Note, *FRUS 1969–1976, European Security*, Vol. XXXIX, Doc. 231, p. 685.

211 This was discussed between Kissinger and Sonnenfeldt on 21 June 1974. See: Editorial Note, *ibid.*, Doc. 215, p. 653.
212 Minutes of a Verification Panel Meeting, 1 August 1974, *ibid.*, Doc. 349, p. 1021.
213 Memorandum of Conversation, 23 January 1975, File: January 23, 1975 Ford–Kissinger, NSAMC, Box 8, GFL.
214 Memorandum for Mr Kissinger from Helmut Sonnenfeldt, 1 August 1973, National Security Council Files, Henry A. Kissinger Office Files, Country Files, Box 68, NPMP; Memorandum of Conversation, undated (circa October 1975), *FRUS 1969–1976, European Security*, Vol. XXXIX, Doc. 364, p. 1071.
215 Minutes of a National Security Council Meeting, 23 January 1975, *FRUS 1969–1976, European Security*, Vol. XXXIX, Doc. 355, p. 1047.
216 National Security Decision Memorandum 284, 4 February 1975, *ibid.*, Doc. 357, p. 1054.
217 Editorial Note, *ibid.*, Doc. 358, pp. 1055–6.
218 Minutes of National Security Council Meeting, 23 January 1975, File: NSC Meeting January 23, 1975, National Security Adviser NSC Meeting File, Box 1, GFL.
219 US National Security Decision Memorandum, Henry Kissinger to the Secretary of Defense et al., undated (circa January 1975), File: Outside the System Chronological File 1/22/75–1/25/75, National Security Adviser Outside the System Chronological File 1974–1977, Box 2, GFL.
220 US National Security Decision Memorandum, Henry Kissinger to the Secretary of Defense et al., undated (circa January 1975), File: Outside the System Chronological File 1/22/75–1/25/75, National Security Adviser Outside the System Chronological File 1974–1977, Box 2, GFL; Memorandum for Brent Scowcroft from Richard Boverie, 18 November 1975, File: Meeting Materials–NSC Meeting Dates (4), US National Security Institutional Files 1974–1977, Box 23, GFL.
221 From AmEmbassy London to SecState Washington, May 1975, Tel. London 5081, File: United Kingdom State Department To SECSTATE EXDIS (2), National Security Adviser Presidential Country Files for Europe and Canada, Box 16, GFL.
222 From AmEmbassy London to SecState Washington, June 1975, Tel. London 8715, *ibid.*
223 Memorandum from William Shinn of the Office of the Counsellor of the Department of State to the Counsellor [Sonnenfeldt], 21 October 1975, *FRUS 1969–1976, European Security*, Vol. XXXIX, Doc. 363, p. 1065.
224 Briefing Memorandum from the Assistant Secretary of State for European Affairs [Hartman] and the Director of the Bureau of Political-Military Affairs [Vest] to Secretary of State Kissinger, 28 November 1975, *ibid.*, Doc. 365, p. 1073.
225 Editorial Note, *ibid.*, Doc. 366, p. 1078; Editorial Note, *ibid.*, Doc. 356, pp. 1052–3.
226 Garthoff, *Détente and Confrontation* pp. 489–520, 596–600.
227 Douglas Brinkley, *Gerald R. Ford* (New York: Henry Holt, 2007), pp. 105–12; Gordon Barrass, *The Great Cold War: A Journey Through the Hall of Mirrors* (Stanford: Stanford University Press, 2009), pp. 184–92; Nicholas Thompson, *The Hawk and the Dove: Paul Nitze, George Kennan, and the History of the Cold War* (New York: Henry Holt, 2009), pp. 250–75; Jussi Hanhimäki, *The Rise and Fall of Détente: American Foreign Policy and the Transformation of the Cold War* (Washington: Potomac, 2012), pp. 77–100.

228 Rodman, *Presidential Command*, pp. 109–11; Rumsfeld, *Known and Unknown*, pp. 222–32.

229 Westad, *The Global Cold War*, pp. 207–87; Burr (ed.), *The Kissinger Transcripts*, pp. 322–66; Robert Gates, *From the Shadows: The Ultimate Insider's Story of Five Presidents and how they won the Cold War* (New York: Simon & Schuster, 1996), p. 49.

230 John Prados, *Presidents' Secret Wars: CIA and Pentagon Covert Operations From World War II Through The Persian Gulf* (Chicago: Ivan R. Dee, 1996, revised edition), pp. 326–56; Zelizer, *Arsenal of Democracy*, pp. 259–72; Cannon, *Time and Chance*, pp. 405–8; Randall B. Woods, *Shadow Warrior: William Egan Colby and the CIA* (New York: Basic Books, 2013), pp. 437–63.

231 Van Atta, *Melvin Laird*, pp. 483–92.

232 George H. Bush, as the Republican Party National Chairman, had given such advice to Ford on 8 August 1974, the day prior to Nixon's resignation as president. See: George Bush, *All the Best: My Life in Letters and Other Writings* (New York: Simon & Schuster, 1999), pp. 193–4. On Ford's scepticism of Kissinger holding the position of National Security Adviser and Secretary of State, see: DeFrank, *Write It When I'm Gone*, p. 91.

233 Kissinger, *YOR*, pp. 834–45. It should be remembered that Kissinger's replacement, Brent Scowcroft, was a close associate of his. However, Anatoly Dobrynin noted that once Scowcroft had been appointed, he was 'more open' and less reserved now that he had been released from 'Kissinger's constant control'. Dobrynin, *In Confidence*, p. 351. On Scowcroft's role in the Ford administration, see: David F. Schmitz, *Brent Scowcroft: Internationalism and Post-Vietnam War American Foreign Policy* (New York: Rowman & Littlefield, 2011), pp. 42–60.

234 Rumsfeld, *Known and Unknown*, pp. 222–32; Dick Cheney, *In My Time: A Personal and Political Memoir* (New York: Simon & Schuster, 2011), pp. 72–94. Rumsfeld took over as Ford's chief of staff from Alexander Haig soon into Ford's term. Cheney served initially as Ford's deputy chief of staff and, following Rumsfeld's promotion to defense secretary, he assumed the role of chief of staff.

235 John Lewis Gaddis, *The Cold War* (London: Allen Lane, 2005), p. 184.

236 Westad, *The Global Cold War*, pp. 207–87.

237 See for example Ford's speech welcoming Wilson to the White House in January 1975: The American Presidency Project, 'Remarks of Welcome to Prime Minister Harold Wilson of the United Kingdom', 30 January 1975 available at: www.presidency.ucsb.edu/ws/?pid=5260 (Accessed 11 January 2013).

# 5

# All out of money
## 1976–77

*There is a difference between being a charitable benefactor and host to a parasite.*

William Simon's explanation of US policy towards Britain during the IMF crisis[1]

## Introduction

Allegedly suffering from the first stages of Alzheimer's disease, Harold Wilson announced he would resign as prime minister in March 1976. As one close associate of the prime minister recalled, Wilson had simply 'had enough'.[2] A battle for the party leadership (and thus to become prime minster) ensued which the 'champion of the moderates' James Callaghan eventually won.[3] Callaghan took office on 5 April 1976, and Anthony Crosland took over from the new prime minister as foreign and commonwealth secretary. In his previous position, Callaghan had been influential in the formulation of British foreign policy and he was determined to retain a dominant role in foreign policy-making. Callaghan's promotion to number 10 Downing Street thus ensured a degree of continuity in the conduct of British foreign policy.[4]

On the other side of the Atlantic, events were tumultuous for the Ford administration, both domestically and in the realm of international relations. The SALT II negotiations with the USSR effectively ground to a halt, and US diplomacy with the PRC was failing to produce any discernible results for the US. This was most obvious in respect to America's long war in South East Asia and, in May 1975, US forces were ejected from Vietnam. In Africa, a Soviet-inspired revolution appeared to be taking hold throughout Angola. The situation in Europe did not appear much better, given that the rise of Euro-communism was perceived as a growing challenge to American interests. In the economic realm there was little cheer for the president, given that international recessions were deepening and the solutions reached amongst the major Western economies appeared to be making little positive difference. Domestically, the president had to survive Ronald Reagan's challenge to become the actual Republican nominee for president. Barely surviving this, Ford found himself involved in an arduous and closely fought presidential campaign with the Democrat nominee, Jimmy Carter. After months of lengthy campaigning, Ford would eventually lose the general election in November 1976. The year 1976–77 was, on all fronts, a difficult one for the Ford White House.[5]

US–UK relations were not to be an exception to this. Following a summer of economic turmoil, which included speculative pressure on the UK currency (sterling), and the refusal of international markets to lend further credit to Britain to finance its spending, James Callaghan was forced to seek a loan from the International Monetary Fund (IMF). The IMF insisted that a loan would only be provided if Britain cut its projected Public Sector Borrowing Requirement (PSBR) for the financial years 1976–77, 1977–78 and 1978–79. The IMF wanted to see a reduction in the UK's PSBR from a projected £12 billion to a figure in the region of £9 billion by FY 1978–79. This policy was designed to deflate the British economy and restore borrowing to levels that would be deemed 'credible' by international markets.[6] Callaghan, however, believed the IMF's proposed PSBR reduction was too high because it would lead to increased unemployment and, moreover, fail to resolve the problem of sterling being utilised as an international reserve currency. Instead, Callaghan wanted a loan from the IMF that did not require such large cuts in the PSBR, and also a 'safety net' loan that could be drawn upon to defend against currency speculation.[7]

The UK–IMF loan application dominated US–UK relations at this juncture because Callaghan wanted the Ford administration to intercede on Britain's behalf to reduce the IMF's PSBR demands. The US – given its economic influence, coupled with its preferential position within the world's economic institutions – did have the ability to do this.[8] The real test for Callaghan, though, was to convince the Ford administration to use its influence to assist the UK. Callaghan therefore sought to convince Washington that the IMF's economic reasoning behind such a large PSBR reduction was flawed. The prime minister, however, had a contingency plan which involved Britain's security commitments to the Western alliance acting as a sort of 'bargaining chip'. In essence, Britain's nuclear deterrent, its contribution to NATO's conventional forces and its intelligence facilities would all be threatened to be reduced, or even disbanded, if the US did not provide the level of economic assistance that London desired. It was believed that by threatening such action, the US would provide economic assistance for fear that the British would undermine US security interests.

Events would prove that Callaghan's thinking was misplaced. The Ford administration refused to directly interfere in the UK–IMF loan negotiations, and the final safety net loan it assisted with did not meet Callaghan's expectations. In the final assessment, the Ford administration was unwilling to acquiesce to Callaghan's request for a number of interlinked reasons. The most obvious was that they simply did not agree with his argument that Britain's public expenditure only required a small reduction. Secondly, the drawn out negotiating process between the British government and the IMF showcased how a number of longer-term trends in British economic and defence policy had undermined the US–UK relationship to a point that the US did not believe Britain any longer warranted preferential treatment in its dealings with the IMF so it could maintain its defence commitments. In essence, when the Labour government of James Callaghan needed the US–UK's special relationship to deliver material benefits, it came up rather short.

## The context of the IMF crisis

Whilst this chapter is focused predominantly upon the political–diplomatic US–UK relationship, the economic context to the IMF crisis needs to be explained in order to contextualise the wider political issue. Throughout 1974–76, the Wilson government had implemented a series of public expenditure cutbacks and tax rises in order to control inflation, reduce the budget deficit and restore international confidence in would-be creditors that Britain remained a sound investment destination. Such measures, however, failed to achieve Wilson's ambitions, and by the spring of 1976 the issue of Britain's budget deficit had become a major concern for the Callaghan government.[9] The forefront of British concerns surrounded both the size of Britain's PSBR and the level to which it had grown throughout the past two years. For example, in March 1974, the PSBR stood at £2.7 billion but, by 1975, Denis Healey had outlined that a PSBR of £9 billion was needed. By 1976, the figure had grown even further to approximately £12 billion. Lack of economic growth, rising unemployment, industrial unrest and more aggressive inflation all contributed to the new prime minister's woes. Given Callaghan's inheritance, it is understandable that some have seen Wilson as having exited 'in the nick of time'.[10]

Given these economic difficulties, sterling – in a repeat of what had occurred only ten years previously – came under speculative pressures from international money markets. In its simplest terms, this meant that holders of sterling began to offload the currency, and the price of sterling began to plummet.

Thus, those holding sterling deposits were seeing the value of their investment fall and this increased the likelihood that they too would look to offload their deposits. The Bank of England responded to this by purchasing sterling; it was believed that this would provide a demonstrable sign of confidence in the currency's stability, and thus convince investors to hold on to their sterling deposits. This, it was hoped, would stabilise the currency and prevent its further depreciation. By June 1976, it was apparent that this had failed and, on 3 June 1976, Callaghan was informed that the Bank of England – having spent some £3 billion in trying to defend the rate of sterling – had exhausted its capacity to continue purchasing sterling. Consequently, Callaghan was advised that Denis Healey should hold a meeting with both US and European officials to begin preliminary discussions about obtaining further funds to support sterling.[11] Healey himself urged Callaghan to agree to a swap facility with the US Federal Reserve and European central banks, which would allow Britain to draw on further credit to defend sterling. It should be noted at this point that US assistance in defending sterling from speculation was not unique to this period, given that in 1974 Wilson had attempted to get a 'cooperative attitude' from the US if sterling came under speculative attack.[12] Given also the US's economic power, looking for US assistance was an entirely natural option for British policy-makers to take.

Other options were suggested, which included a 'sweating it out' approach, or to seek an IMF tranche support loan. Both, however, were quickly dismissed by Healey who believed the 'sweating it out' option would only lead to sterling's price collapsing even more quickly. The IMF route appealed less given that it would seek to link any loan with a number of political conditions. For Healey, these would be politically unpalatable because they would likely involve the British government having to make large public expenditure cutbacks which would harm the social welfare programmes that the Labour government was both committed to and electorally reliant upon. Healey's thinking was based on good foundations given that Dr Johannes Witteveen, the Managing Director of the IMF, had told Healey in November 1975 that any loans provided to the UK would be conditioned on the British government enacting large public expenditure cutbacks.[13] Reinforcing this position was the fact that only a week after Healey had proffered his advice to Callaghan, Witteveen reiterated a similar warning to him.[14]

Callaghan accepted Healey's advice and a meeting with William Simon, the secretary of the Treasury, and Arthur Burns, the chairman of the Federal Reserve, was arranged. Once the meeting commenced, Simon and Burns explained that they wanted to help Britain in 'every way they could'.[15] Yet, as they informed Healey, it was believed in 'some quarters' that Britain was not doing everything it could to rectify its increasing budget deficit. 'Some quarters' clearly referred to people such as Robert Hormats, the senior staff member for International Economic Affairs on the National Security Council.[16] Hormats had made it known earlier in the year that the British government's incompetence was leading the country towards economic ruin, and Healey's budget of February 1976 would not control inflation or stabilise the price of sterling.[17] When Healey had announced in February 1976 that Britain would be cutting its PSBR by £1 billion, senior Ford administration officials had to be instructed to welcome the news. Though the announcement was viewed as a positive signal, the cut of £1 billion in Britain's PSBR was still deemed insufficient to rectify Britain's economic problems.[18] As Simon and Burns reminded Healey, if this type of thinking won through, there would be little chance of market confidence in sterling returning until radically different economic policies were pursued by the British government.[19]

Given all of this, Sir Kenneth Berrill, the head of the Central Policy Review Staff, was surely correct when he warned Callaghan that Britain would likely meet a frosty response from Simon and Burns at the upcoming international economic conference in Puerto Rico. As Berrill suggested, US officials were likely to respond with a 'putting your house in order first' attitude.[20] In practice, this meant the extension of further credit would not be forthcoming until deeper cuts in Britain's public expenditure occurred. Events soon demonstrated the accuracy of such advice.

Stories throughout the newspaper media suggested that Arthur Burns would be particularly unwilling to offer Britain an extension of credit unless it involved the British government enacting serious economic reforms.[21] At the Puerto Rico conference, these stories were proven to be well founded, given that Burns informed Callaghan:

> We in the United States wish to support you in every way that we can but we could not consider the provision of further credit. Without a change in underlying economic and financial policy, financial assistance would merely increase your external debt and delay the inevitable.[22]

Burns had demonstrated his hostility to providing further credit unless some type of fundamental adjustment to British economic policy was forthcoming and therefore, when the British agreed to a loan from the Federal Reserve in June 1976, it was attached with a series of conditions. The most important one was that the loan had to be repaid in full by December 1976, and if Britain was unable to do this then a loan from the IMF would have to be sought in order to repay this American credit.[23]

At this stage though, British policy-makers were not overly concerned about these conditions attached to the Federal Reserve's loan. In fact, Healey was confident that Britain would be able to repay the American loan on time, as he reasoned that economic growth would reduce Britain's deficit by bringing in extra taxation for the Treasury. Accordingly, the PSBR could be reduced and a surplus would be left to repay the loan.[24] US officials were of the opposite opinion. 'At the present rate the British, who have yet to make the substantive policy changes necessary, will have to borrow from the IMF,' Edwin Yeo – the under-secretary for monetary affairs at the US Treasury – informed the president.[25] Yeo's assessment would prove to be rather more accurate than Healey's and by September his prediction was coming true. Britain had been unable to reduce its deficit because Healey's projected economic growth had simply not happened. Market confidence in sterling, and Britain's economic policies more generally, also remained low. Despite earlier predictions that Britain would not require an IMF loan, Healey was now seriously contemplating undertaking this course.[26] As Simon informed Kissinger and Scowcroft, 'Healey appears to be readying himself for negotiations with the IMF. He indicated quite clearly that he plans to begin negotiations with the Fund – probably in late October'.[27]

Whether Healey would have attempted to gain an IMF loan to repay the standby credit is a moot point, because events surrounding sterling forced his hand. Throughout the summer of 1976, sterling's rate steadily depreciated, which, in large part, had been promoted by the UK Treasury as a means of making British export goods more competitive internationally. However, by September 1976, sterling had begun to slide uncontrollably, and holders of sterling began to offload it en masse.[28] Further reducing confidence in the British economy were the events of the Labour Party conference – held in Blackpool at the end of the month – that gave the impression to the financial markets that Callaghan was losing his grip over the party. As the *Daily Express* noted in its lead article, James Callaghan would be 'cracking the whip amid mounting squabbling behind the scenes'.[29] Events at the conference hardly gave an impression that Callaghan was fully in control of his party, given that when Healey took to the stage to explain that some level of public expenditure cutbacks was required to stabilise the economy, he was roundly booed by the audience.[30]

Events soon took an even worse turn for the British economy when on 28 September the situation surrounding sterling 'exploded'.[31] In practical terms, this meant that the value of sterling had begun to tumble uncontrollably as holders of the currency sought to offload their deposits. This resulted in the infamous episode where Healey did not travel to an IMF conference in Manila. Instead, he returned from Heathrow airport to provide a public sign that he was in control of the situation. The markets took the opposite impression and the price of sterling plummeted further.[32] To combat this, the Bank of England attempted to stabilise sterling by purchasing a further $100 million of the currency. This bought the government some temporary respite with sterling stabilising somewhat, yet – in spite of such efforts – Callaghan was informed that sterling was going to fall to at least $1.50 (to place this in perspective, on 27 September sterling stood at $1.70, and had lost over 12 per cent of its value). More worryingly, this could not be guaranteed as the floor rate, i.e. sterling would keep falling in value.[33] Thus, it is with only a touch of hyperbole that one national newspaper would exclaim the need to 'Save our Sterling'.[34] Callaghan's government, without the necessary funds to indefinitely defend the rate of sterling, restore market confidence or repay the standby credit loans due in December 1976 to the US Federal Reserve, decided an application for an IMF loan was the only recourse available.[35]

An important point to be added at this juncture is that the IMF does not always have enough money in convertible currency to lend to foreign governments. Accordingly, it must go to central banks to request these funds, and from here the IMF negotiates with a government and then presents the loan conditions to the Group of Ten (G10). The G10 (comprised of the world's leading industrial nations, plus Switzerland) then decides whether to provide the necessary currency for the loan. The US, given its powerful economic position, had an influential role within the G10, and the US Federal Reserve was probably the single most powerful member of the central banks represented.[36]

Callaghan expected the IMF to demand a major reduction in Britain's PSBR which would only be accomplished by reducing Britain's public expenditure programmes. For Callaghan this was unpalatable politically, but he also believed that Britain's economic problems were magnified by sterling acting as an international reserve currency. In his assessment, this meant that the British economy was exposed to international speculative pressures on sterling, which could force significant price fluctuations and damage Britain's economic performance.[37]

Internal Labour Party politics was the other key factor influencing the prime minister's decision-making. For the Labour government, the form of any IMF loan was a matter of vociferous debate. Healey had suggested that Britain should seek a loan of £2.3 billion from the IMF, and that this would finance the projected budget deficit of £3 billion and would involve public expenditure cuts of £700 million.[38] Anthony Crosland was opposed to Healey's plans, and argued that such a reduction in Britain's public expenditure would only deepen Britain's recession and make economic recovery more difficult.[39] For the left-wing members of the government (which included Deputy Leader of the Party Michael Foot, Business and Energy Secretary Tony Benn and Secretary of State for the Environment Peter Shore), the concept of public expenditure cuts while unemployment remained at over 5 per cent of the workforce was anathema.[40] Moreover, the idea of having to sacrifice aspects of welfare spending in order to repay loans to central banks was deeply unappealing for the Labour government. The trade unions, which provided strong support to the Labour Party, were also making their opposition known to accepting deep PSBR cuts as a condition of the IMF loan.[41] The trade unions were hardly being encouraged to shift from this position given that the likes of Michael Foot were giving rousing speeches proclaiming that public expenditure on social services should not be reduced.[42] The prime minister therefore had a divided Cabinet, and more worrying was the fact that his two most senior Cabinet officials, Denis Healey and Antony Crosland, held diametrically opposed positions.[43]

To work his way from this impasse, Callaghan believed that he could convince President Ford to utilise US influence with the IMF to ensure that the loan conditions set by the IMF would not demand such a substantial reduction in Britain's PSBR. The prime minister therefore began the process of acquiring US support. He arranged for a telephone call with Ford and began drafting a letter to the president outlining Britain's position. Callaghan's initial draft letter was in keeping with the 'pugnacious' mood he held towards the entire IMF application.[44] In the 1960s, when he had been chancellor of the exchequer, Callaghan had suggested that a reduction in the British Army of the Rhine (BAOR) should be threatened to ensure US financial assistance. The thinking behind this idea was that the US would not want to see one of its key alliance partners withdrawing from the defence of Europe so would supply the necessary financial support.[45] Callaghan, now as prime minster, once again suggested a similar course.[46] However, Callaghan was persuaded against pursuing a path that so explicitly linked US financial assistance to Britain upholding its security commitments for fear this would appear as a type of blackmail and needlessly irritate opinion in Washington. Thus, direct references to BAOR commitments were omitted from his letter to Ford.[47] The letter did note, however, that without financial assistance Britain – 'as an ally and a partner in the western alliance' – could no longer be expected to continue with its current commitments.[48] While not as bellicose as originally intended, Callaghan had signalled his intent to utilise Britain's position within the Western security alliance as a means of obtaining financial assistance.

The Ford administration evaluated Callaghan's letter, and particular attention was given to his suggestion that the US should pressure the IMF into giving Britain less stringent loan terms. Ford's economic advisers were deeply sceptical about pursuing such a course of action. Throughout the 1970s, large reports received from the US ambassador in London had been sent to the State Department expressing concern about Britain's economic plight.[49] Recent events only confirmed the suspicions of prominent US economic policy-makers, such as Simon, Yeo and Burns, that Britain had to enact serious economic reforms. Such measures would include a reduction in the PSBR, a cut in public expenditure and a tightening of monetary policy (which an IMF loan would all be conditioned upon). Accordingly, they advised Ford that the US should refuse the British request to intervene in the UK–IMF negotiations.[50] Ford's political advisers agreed with this. As Scowcroft noted, 'It is clearly undesirable for us to become involved in negotiations with the IMF'. He reasoned that if the IMF was pressed into being 'more lenient on the UK,' it would likely see the Callaghan government refuse to make the necessary cuts in the PSBR. This would only 'postpone the inevitable crisis', because Britain's substantial levels of borrowing would remain.[51]

To support his case, Callaghan also arranged for a telephone conversation with Ford. Scowcroft prepared the president with a 'talking points' memorandum for this conversation, which again illustrated the US's disinclination to accept Callaghan's proposal for intervening in the UK–IMF negotiations.[52] As Scowcroft's talking points outlined, 'We will give our full support to whatever agreement is reached between the UK and the IMF'. He further made clear that the British government alone would have to reach an agreement with the IMF, and that the US should refrain from applying bilateral pressure on the IMF to advance Britain's cause.[53]

Though receiving this briefing, the president failed to precisely follow Scowcroft's advice during his telephone conversation with Callaghan. Rather than clearly articulating that the US would wait for the UK and IMF to reach an accommodation by strictly bilateral methods, Ford told Callaghan that his government would 'do whatever we can to be helpful'.[54] From the British perspective, the offer to 'do whatever we can to be helpful' was taken to mean that the US would use its influence with the IMF into providing lenient loan terms. Indeed, this is exactly the fashion in which Healey interpreted Ford's statement.[55] In Washington, however, the president's advisers made it clear they did not want to pursue such a course of action. One can infer that this was the belief of Ford also given that, if he did not agree with Scowcroft's advice, he would have asked for a different memorandum for his discussion with Callaghan.

## Safety net

Having been chancellor of the exchequer during the 1960s, Callaghan was well acquainted with the fluctuations in the rate of sterling. He therefore saw the current difficulties as an opportunity to not only overcome the short-term fluctuations in sterling, but also as a means for ensuring its longer-term stability. For the immediate problem of sterling's significant depreciation, Callaghan envisaged Britain obtaining a safety net loan, which would be acquired from the G10 (though it would predominantly be financed by the US Federal Reserve and the West German Deutsche Bundesbank). The safety net would be designed as a means of easing any speculative pressures on sterling in the event that if sterling was being offloaded en masse, thus driving its value downwards, the British government could draw on this safety net to buy sterling and defend its value. The safety net would therefore provide a visible sign to investors that the currency could be defended from speculators, and offer investors the much-needed assurance that sterling was a stable currency in which to invest. In the longer term, Callaghan actually wanted to see the liquidation of sterling balances.[56]

On 1 November 1976, the IMF negotiating team, headed by Johannes Witteveen and Alan Whittome, landed in the UK to begin negotiations. Callaghan was determined to achieve parallel objectives. Negotiations with the IMF would establish the terms of a future loan to cover Britain's budget deficit and repay its international loans, and a safety net loan designed to protect sterling against future currency speculation would also be sought. Callaghan saw these two negotiations as intertwined, noting that 'it was important to get international agreement on the safety net/bond scheme in parallel with the IMF negotiations'. He also wanted the safety net loan to be announced simultaneously with the terms of the IMF loan.[57]

Callaghan's wishes were well understood in Washington, and his position was deemed an opportunity for the Ford administration to ensure that the UK agreed to the IMF's loan conditions.[58] As Scowcroft informed the president, Callaghan 'implied in this message the possibility that Britain might accede to the tough terms likely to be required by the IMF if agreement on sterling balances could be announced at the same time'.[59] With Kissinger also supporting Scowcroft's analysis, the Ford administration appeared quite confident that the British government would agree terms with the IMF.[60]

Callaghan, however, still wanted support from the Ford administration in obtaining preferential loan conditions from the IMF and information obtained from Helmut Schmidt, the chancellor of West Germany, suggested that this was a possibility.[61] Schmidt convinced Callaghan (and a number of his advisers) that the US would sanction the safety net loan prior to the finalisation of the IMF loan, and he was further advised by his private secretaries that appealing to the US on grounds of international security would yield results. For instance, during the Cabinet meetings which discussed the IMF negotiations, one of Callaghan's private secretaries noted to him that he was 'certain' that the tactic of reaching out to Ford and Kissinger would get Britain a 'safety net' prior to the conclusion of the IMF negotiations. Michael Palliser wrote in a similar fashion to Callaghan's principal private secretary, Kenneth Stowe.[62]

Following such confident advice, Callaghan attempted to use his relationship with Henry Kissinger as a means of ensuring the US would pressure the IMF into providing preferential loan conditions. The prime minister wanted Kissinger to ensure that the IMF negotiating team would not receive encouragement from US economic officials to demand stringent British spending cuts as a condition of any loan. It soon became apparent that such tactics were not producing the results that those in London had predicted. The British ambassador to Washington, Peter Ramsbotham, reported on his efforts with Kissinger, informing London that Kissinger wished to take a 'compassionate approach' towards Britain, but within the administration there existed a strong clamour for the IMF to demand stringent terms because the 'needed' economic changes would fail to be implemented otherwise.[63]

Certainly it was clear that Callaghan's appeals were unlikely to convince the president's economic team. Simon, Yeo and Burns wanted to keep the two loan negotiations separate, because they feared Britain would use the safety net as a substitute for the IMF loan. As a result, they demanded the IMF negotiations be concluded prior to any safety net being agreed.[64] The president largely agreed with such advice, and Ford had little inclination to apply the necessary leverage upon the IMF so they would provide preferential lending terms to the British government. As Ford wrote in a handwritten comment on 11 November 1976, 'British Cab must accept IMF'.[65]

In contrast to Callaghan's misjudgement of the Ford administration, Healey was much more in tune with American thinking. In Healey's opinion, the US held a 'totally uncooperative attitude' and it appeared unlikely that the US government would support the safety net loan until the IMF negotiations were concluded. As for the IMF negotiations, Healey noted that the US was not placing any pressure on the negotiators to offer Britain less stringent terms.[66] Nevertheless, many of the outward signs emanating from the Ford administration appeared to contradict this. Kissinger was claiming to be 'sympathetic' yet Simon, Yeo and Burns were clearly less so. Yet, at the outset of the IMF negotiations Ford had personally informed Callaghan that he 'would do whatever he can' to assist the British. Not surprising then that policy-makers in London were confused about the likely course of US policy.

The apparent contradictions stemming from Washington led Callaghan to send Harold Lever, the chancellor of the duchy of Lancaster, as a personal envoy to the US. Lever, a self-made millionaire and former businessmen, was seen by Callaghan as something of an economics expert.[67] Callaghan again sought to utilise his relationship with Ford and Kissinger as a vehicle for mitigating the demands of the IMF, and wanted Lever to emphasise the repercussions for 'the alliance' if Britain had to accept the IMF terms.[68] Callaghan also backed up such attempts by directly contacting Ford by telephone, and again reiterated the negative consequences for the Western alliance if Britain was forced into enacting substantial public expenditure cutbacks.[69]

Douglas Wass, the permanent under-secretary at the Treasury, has questioned the logic of the Lever mission. According to him, Callaghan had been informed on several occasions that Britain would have to reach agreement on terms with the IMF prior to any safety net loan being granted. As shown above, this was undoubtedly the case, and Wass was certainly more attuned to the reality that the US was not going to pressure the IMF into providing less demanding loan conditions.[70] Scowcroft had advised the president against following such a course and Kissinger also reinforced such advice prior to Lever's visit.[71] Kissinger's advice was given even though he suspected it would lead to the collapse of the Callaghan government![72] Callaghan's judgement, that appealing to the political masters in Washington would be met with more sympathy, was clearly misguided. US policy-makers both in the political and the economic realm were in complete agreement that the US would not involve itself in the UK–IMF negotiations.

## The Lever mission

Harold Lever flew to Washington and met with Henry Kissinger and, following the instructions of the prime minister, he attempted to link the nature of the IMF loan to Britain's existing security commitments. Lever argued that the IMF's demands would result in a critical reduction in Britain's defence expenditure, which, in turn, would severely damage NATO, and undermine broader US security interests.[73] Kissinger's response indicated that he was less than convinced by such an argument, and he informed Lever that both he and the president supported the idea that Britain had to reduce its PSBR and would have to achieve this by reducing its public expenditure. Clearly this was unwelcome news for the British government. Kissinger did, however, offer a caveat of hope when he suggested that the level of public expenditure cuts would be mitigated by 'political considerations'. Added to this he also gave his support for the safety net loan. As Kissinger told Lever, he was going to push the 'political aspects' of the situation, and try to convince Simon, Yeo and Burns to provide the safety net once the IMF loan had been agreed.[74]

As with most international events, Kissinger's thinking was dictated predominantly by political, rather than economic, considerations. Ultimately, on this occasion, Kissinger did not feel Britain was important enough to warrant US interference in the UK–IMF negotiations. He did, however, conclude that the safety net was needed in order to restore confidence in Britain's currency. Furthermore, this approach demonstrated the consistency behind Kissinger's thinking. For instance, during the Italian IMF negotiations in the summer of 1976, Kissinger had been keen to ensure that it was 'not simply economic conditions' that mattered in an overall settlement.[75] From the British viewpoint, it was perhaps rather worrisome that they were to receive little more assistance than Italy had from the US, in spite of efforts by the Wilson and Callaghan governments to nurture close US–UK relations.

By utilising Kissinger, Callaghan had attained some minor achievements. As Kathleen Burk and Alec Cairncross have noted, Lever was able to secure US agreement to help provide the safety net.[76] Critically, however, Arthur Burns remained unconvinced. Moreover, Yeo was making it known to the West Germans that he wanted to see the IMF demand substantial PSBR cuts from Britain.[77] Given this then, the Lever mission must be deemed a failure, because Callaghan wanted the 'political considerations' placed at the forefront of the IMF debate so as to temper 'the orthodoxy of the monetarists'.[78] Callaghan was still hoping that the Lever mission would convince the US to use its influence with the IMF negotiating team in London. As seen above, Lever's mission did not accomplish this. Even Kissinger, believed by Callaghan to have most clearly understood the wider political implications of the IMF loan, refused Callaghan's wishes. Therefore, on 24 November 1976, Callaghan was informed that Kissinger would not intervene in the UK–IMF negotiations.[79]

To compound Callaghan's predicament was the clear indication he received from Washington that the US was unlikely to support the simultaneous conclusion of the IMF and safety net loans. While Kissinger had informed Lever that he would support this, those authorised in Washington to implement such a deal (Simon, Yeo and Burns) were unwilling to undertake the necessary procedures to create this.[80] The hope that Kissinger could overrule this opposition was dealt a blow by Ford's election defeat to Jimmy Carter. Kissinger was soon to be out of office and his ability to influence other actors, especially the likes of Arthur Burns who did not rely on the president for his position as chairman of the Federal Reserve, was reduced.[81]

Callaghan could also be in no doubt that American approval for the safety net was conditioned upon Britain concluding terms with the IMF. The IMF negotiators had made it clear that, if Britain was to receive an IMF loan, it would have to enact public expenditure cutbacks. Callaghan thus convened his Cabinet, where he attempted to convince them of the necessity to accept a loan with such stipulations. As he explained to his colleagues, whilst 'good will' existed in the US, a 'general view' existed that Britain had to make significant cuts in its PSBR if a loan was to be granted. However, the level of the PSBR reduction was still something to be debated within the Cabinet.[82]

At the end of these Cabinet meetings, Callaghan authorised Healey to negotiate a loan agreement with the IMF that would involve a cut in the PSBR from

£12 billion to £9.5 billion for FY 1978–79. This would involve public expenditure cutbacks of roughly £1.25 billion for FY 1977–78 and 1978–79. Healey, however, disagreed with Callaghan's proposals. As he had been negotiating with the IMF, it was evident that a reduction in the PSBR to £9.5 billion fell short of the IMF's expectations. Witteveen for instance had informed Healey he wanted Britain to reduce its PSBR to £8.8 billion by FY 1978–79.[83] Added to this, the IMF had made it known publicly that a reduction of £3 billion was what it were aiming for. Healey believed he would be able to negotiate the figure slightly downwards, and suggested he would target a PSBR of approximately £9 billion. Such advice was ignored and Callaghan assured his Cabinet that he would utilise his relationship with President Ford to ensure an agreement was reached at £9.5 billion.[84]

Callaghan's bravado in front of his Cabinet colleagues did not accurately reflect his real level of influence in Washington. As US policy-makers were aware, Callaghan would likely again seek to convince the president to interfere in the IMF negotiations and were thus preparing contingency plans for this. Accordingly, Brent Scowcroft and Alan Greenspan once again warned Ford against agreeing to support any British request to pressure the IMF into providing less stringent loan conditions.[85] This course of action was pertinent given that Callaghan would again telephone the president and ask for assistance. In spite of Callaghan being 'tough with Ford', he again came away with nothing of substance.[86] As Ford had decided prior to Callaghan's call, Britain's PSBR had to be cut below £9.5 billion.[87] Other last ditch efforts from British officials to get the president to change his mind were equally fruitless.[88]

Callaghan had to return to the Cabinet and inform them that he could not deliver on his £9.5 billion target. The Cabinet now debated the best course of action. Healey reported that his discussions with the IMF indicated that reducing the PSBR to a figure of £9 billion was deemed insufficient. He therefore proposed that he should seek agreement with the IMF to reduce the PSBR to £8.7 billion for FY 1977–78, and £8.6 billion for FY 1978–79. These cuts would be supplemented by the sale of British petroleum (BP) shares that were worth in the region of £500 million.[89] Healey, however, encountered stern opposition from his colleagues and the Cabinet was split into three main factions. One group supported Healey's proposal to reduce the PSBR and sell the BP shares. One opposing faction was headed by Crosland, who argued that such a reduction in the PSBR could not be accepted and proposed that Britain enact a 'leverage' strategy. By this, he meant that Britain could threaten to withdraw from NATO or enact trade tariffs, unless US pressure was placed on the IMF to lessen its demands.[90] The final faction within the Cabinet was led by Michael Foot. This group, which included Benn, Shore and Minister of State for Social Security Stan Orme, argued that Britain should refuse an IMF loan with such conditions and should instead implement trade tariffs in order to raise additional funds for the Treasury and thus protect public expenditure. Benn, in a moment of flamboyance, noted that if Callaghan accepted the IMF terms it would be the 'political tomb for the Government'.[91]

The extent to which the Cabinet was divided was openly speculated about throughout the media, and one newspaper even suggested that Healey was on the verge of submitting his resignation.[92] Regardless of the Cabinet's apparent division, the prime minister was confident that if he decided upon a course of action he would have the numbers to push it forward. While reluctant to do so, Callaghan decided that he would have to support his chancellor's proposals.[93] Efforts to convince the US had failed and pursuing the alternative strategies appealed little to Callaghan. Crosland's proposal to threaten NATO withdrawal was deemed too dangerous a course to pursue and, moreover, when similar suggestions had been made subtly, they had failed to make any discernible impact upon US policy. More significantly for Callaghan, he believed that agreeing to the IMF loan would guarantee a quick settlement on the safety net loan, which in his opinion was more important than the actual IMF loan. Therefore, the idea of erecting trade tariffs which would antagonise the international community and likely prevent a G10-sponsored safety net loan would simply contradict his wider objectives.[94] Following heated Cabinet discussions Callaghan won support for Healey's proposals and, following tense negotiation with the IMF, the terms of the loan were settled. Callaghan agreed to reduce Britain's PSBR to £8.7 billion for FY 1977–78 and £8.6 billion for 1978–79, and BP shares worth approximately £500 million were also sold to help reduce Britain's PSBR.[95]

Even if one is exceedingly charitable towards Callaghan, it cannot be ignored that his tactic of appealing to the US for assistance had failed. Compounding this was the fact that it was public knowledge that both President Ford and Chancellor Schmidt had rebuffed his efforts to obtain financial assistance.[96] Throughout the negotiations, Callaghan had been told on numerous occasions that no US interference in the UK–IMF negotiations would be forthcoming, yet this was seemingly ignored.[97] Why the prime minister ignored this advice is curious. Perhaps Callaghan believed Britain's political significance in relation to the US would have resulted in preferential economic treatment. Certainly, Britain – despite its defence reductions in 1974–76 – retained its nuclear and intelligence relationship with the US. However, Callaghan had witnessed American displeasure at Britain's defence cuts, and he must have realised how much the US believed that the UK had declined in importance given that Kissinger had told him as much on several occasions.

Perhaps, therefore, Callaghan's situation within the Labour Party better explains his determination to stubbornly cling to the idea that he could influence US policy. Callaghan was a firm believer in the social contract with the trade unions, and he knew that breaking with the trade unions would severely damage Labour's electoral and financial situation. The terms of the IMF loan would enforce deflationary measures on the British economy, which meant that public expenditure cutbacks would be invoked and would inevitably lead to job losses. For the trade unions, this was a deeply unpopular policy, and Callaghan therefore had to reduce the IMF demands in order to mitigate trade union disgruntlement. Accepting the IMF terms without even attempting to make them less stringent would have seriously undermined Callaghan's political position.[98]

Of course, this line of argument should not be taken too far. Edmund Dell, the secretary of state for trade, has made a convincing counter-argument which suggests that Callaghan could always convince his Cabinet to follow his lead, simply because the collapse of the Labour government would have led to Margaret Thatcher's Conservative party – which would have implemented the PSBR reductions on a larger scale – obtaining office. Indeed, during the crisis itself Thatcher was publicly talking of the need for much larger scale reductions in the PSBR in order to ward off the bailiffs.[99] Given this, for the left wing of the Labour Party to have brought down the Callaghan government would have been a futile effort to prevent the PSBR cuts. For Dell, therefore, arguments that Callaghan's room to manoeuvre was prohibited by his domestic position are unconvincing.[100] Interestingly, this is exactly what one of Callaghan's private secretaries advised him at the time.[101] However, by presenting himself in opposition to Healey's more demanding PSBR cuts, Callaghan managed to escape the full vitriol of the Labour Party. Instead, it was Healey who was largely blamed for having forced through the IMF terms.[102] This, as the archival record now suggests, is an unfair categorisation.

## Obtaining the safety net

Although the issue of obtaining the safety net remained unresolved, Callaghan envisaged that it would be announced simultaneously, or very soon after Britain publicly announced its application for an IMF loan. He also wanted the safety net to be in the region of \$3.5 billion.[103] Callaghan agreed to the terms of the IMF loan on the proviso that the safety net would be swiftly granted, and this was certainly the impression Ford had given to Callaghan.[104] Ford remained unconvinced as to whether the US should agree to such a loan but, by 3 December 1976, Ford had been persuaded by Kissinger that Britain should be granted the safety net loan, as long as Britain agreed terms with the IMF. Ford therefore instructed William Simon to undertake the necessary preparations for providing the safety net loan.[105] This was reported to London, but the British ambassador in Washington warned against placing too much confidence in Ford.[106] As he explained, the president could not guarantee the safety net because it was not his constitutional authority to do so; rather, this decision would come about at the behest of the US Federal Reserve. It was Chairman Arthur Burns, and not President Ford, who was the man who would have final authority over providing the safety net. This was a point that would become of supreme importance in the following weeks.[107]

The prime minister expected stern opposition from the US Treasury and Federal Reserve against providing the safety net, and his mood consequently deteriorated. In a handwritten note Callaghan scrawled, 'Do [the] US ... want us to do this with consequences?'[108] What these consequences were soon became apparent as British officials in discussion with their NATO counterparts suggested that substantial defence cutbacks would likely be enacted if significant financial support was not forthcoming. Subtle suggestions within this context, however, failed to significantly alter American policy.[109] Callaghan therefore decided to analyse whether invoking Britain's Western security commitments more explicitly with the Ford administration would persuade the US to offer the necessary financial support. He ordered John Hunt and Michael Palliser to provide him with a survey of British defence commitments, and from this he wanted to know whether threatening the cancellation of such commitments would engender a more cooperative attitude from the US.

Hunt and Palliser produced this for the prime minister and outlined several possibilities, which included the abandonment of the British nuclear deterrent and the cancellation of the Chevaline improvement to Polaris.[110] Further ideas ranged from a total withdrawal from Cyprus or a reduction in Britain's BAOR commitments to a complete abandonment of Britain's extra-European military capabilities. Hunt and Palliser concluded that a complete withdrawal from Cyprus or the disbandment of Polaris were the only measures likely to influence US policy.[111]

John Hunt was in a very good position to make such judgements given that he had witnessed first-hand the American aversion to seeing Britain withdraw from Cyprus, or perhaps scrapping its update to Polaris.[112] Hunt, however, warned about the wisdom of using such tactics and the biggest problem he noted was the fact that the British were still, at this juncture, negotiating the final terms of the PSBR reduction with the IMF. An argument employed by the British government against reducing the PSBR much below £9 billion was that they were committed to retaining costly defence projects. If Britain threatened to cancel these, then the IMF could potentially demand Britain make an even greater reduction in its PSBR.[113]

While the British government debated its own course of actions, events in Basle, where representatives from the G10 were discussing the structure of the proposed safety net, were coming to a conclusion. Healey reported that the US delegation was taking a line far from the 'sympathetic' one that Ford had promised and noted that the US was reluctant to agree to any safety net loan.[114] The US now reasoned that, since Britain had concluded its IMF loan, market confidence in sterling had been restored and it was now unnecessary to provide a loan to defend the rate of the sterling.[115]

Although Callaghan had been provided with a number of alternative areas in which to exert political leverage upon the US, he decided not to use them. Perhaps the late advice received from John Hunt convinced the prime minister against pursuing such a course.[116] Instead, Callaghan wrote directly to Ford, arguing that the safety net was imperative to restore market confidence in sterling.[117] Callaghan also sought to use his relationship with the West German chancellor, Helmut Schmidt; he wanted Schmidt to convince Ford that the safety net should be given to Britain. Schmidt obliged, and wrote to Ford on 12 December arguing Callaghan's point.[118]

Very little appears to have come from Schmidt's efforts to convince Ford to provide a safety net to Britain, and reports from Washington suggested that the US would refuse to sign up to a G10 safety net loan. Derek Mitchell, the deputy permanent under-secretary at the Treasury, reported that both Burns and Yeo remained reluctant to support the safety net.[119] Callaghan attempted to circumvent such opposition by appealing to Washington's political elites, and Ramsbotham was tasked with persuading Kissinger and Scowcroft that they should convince Ford to overrule Burns and Yeo. The British ambassador had some success as Scowcroft agreed to speak with Yeo and make him more 'reasonable' and he promised to get Kissinger to 'weigh in' his support for providing the safety net.[120] Ramsbotham remained pessimistic as to whether this would achieve much and repeated his earlier warnings that it was Burns' constitutional right, and not Ford's, to agree to the safety net.[121]

Ramsbotham's assessment was astute given the turn of events that would transpire in the following days. While Ford had ordered the US to sign up to the safety net, the US delegation in Basle simply ignored this and continued to present counter proposals to that of the safety net. Thus, progress in finalising the safety net was being prevented by the US.[122] The British once again looked to Kissinger and Scowcroft for assistance and Ramsbotham liaised with both. However, both appeared rather uninterested in the safety net negotiations and Kissinger went on to claim that he did know what the US delegation was up to, and merely reiterated that Ford had given his backing to the safety net.[123] Kissinger was not being disingenuous as Ford had ordered the safety net to be granted, but the US Federal Reserve and Treasury continued to block approval for it at the Basle negotiations.

Following heated debate in Washington, Burns and Simon succumbed to the wishes of the president and American agreement for the safety net was transmitted to the British.[124] Though US approval for the safety net had finally been given, the actual details of the safety net would still have to be worked out and this would obviously take some time.[125] In the interim, Ford offered public support for the British IMF agreement which came about at Kissinger's suggestion. Indeed, Kissinger noted that Ford had never intended to 'weasel' out of the safety net commitment, but that he had been constrained by his constitutional role vis-à-vis the Federal Reserve.[126] The president, Kissinger and Scowcroft all realised that Callaghan would be 'disappointed' with this, and this was clearly the case as Callaghan again floated the idea of sending a recriminatory letter to Ford.[127] Douglas Wass claims that Healey had 'to beg [Callaghan] not to send such a message to President Ford'.[128] Healey's efforts paid off, and Callaghan's letter to Ford illustrated none of the frustration that the prime minister felt.[129]

The final safety net was secured in the second week of January 1977.[130] The US would initially allow Britain to draw up to $250 million from a safety net of $3 billion. This agreement, however, came with a number of caveats. The British could only draw on this fund on condition that the PSBR reductions agreed with the IMF were implemented.[131] At the very least, Callaghan had obtained the safety net which he felt was imperative for Britain's long-term economic well-being. Nevertheless, the safety net was loaded with a number of conditions that Callaghan had sought to avoid. It had also failed to be delivered at the time he believed was economically necessary, and politically convenient to stave off domestic criticism. For Callaghan, then, this had been a politically calamitous affair.

Moreover, the IMF crisis demonstrated the lack of influence which the prime minister had with the Ford administration. Callaghan had spent considerable effort in trying to garner a warm relationship with both the president and Henry Kissinger, in order to *influence* US policy. As Callaghan claims within his memoirs, this was something which he believed he had achieved, and this is something that both Ford and Kissinger corroborate in their own retrospective accounts of their relationship with Callaghan.[132] Regardless, throughout the IMF crisis, Callaghan's personal relationship did little, if anything, to alter the course of US policy along lines more amenable to his wishes. Even when Kissinger suspected that the Callaghan government could fall as a result of the IMF terms, it did not alter US policy. In fact, the biggest concern for Kissinger was to avoid the impression that the Ford administration had caused the Callaghan government to collapse. As he noted to the president, it was imperative that the image of 'sinking the British' was not attributed to the Ford administration.[133]

Personal relations, therefore, were secondary to broader considerations. When Kissinger would talk about not being a 'sentimental' person, it clearly applied to the conduct of US–UK relations in spite of public statements to the contrary.[134]

## US–UK relations within the economic context

There has been considerable debate over the reasons for US policy taking the course it did throughout the IMF crisis. Some writers have suggested that Ford's electoral defeat to Jimmy Carter in November 1976 undermined his authority. As such, an unelected president who was sympathetic to Britain's predicament was unable to exercise his authority vis-à-vis the Federal Reserve and Treasury.[135] Callaghan, in his memoirs, provided a similar analysis.[136] Certainly, throughout the crisis, Kissinger used the impending election as a reason why the US could not be seen to be placing pressure upon the IMF.[137] Others, however, have dismissed this explanation.[138] This latter interpretation is much more convincing because, as the documentation in the Ford Library shows, Carter's election did not constrain Ford in his foreign policy-making. Even if Kissinger saw the election of 1976 as a potential problem in aiding the British, he admitted that once it was over he would be a lot freer to tackle the issue.[139]

Instead, other factors better explain US policy. The first point to remember was that the fashion in which the Ford administration dealt with Britain's IMF application would have ramifications in other areas in the world, most notably in regard to the IMF applications being made by Mexico and Italy.[140] The Ford administration was consistent in the advice it offered to Mexico, Italy and Britain: public spending had to be curbed in order to bring down the level of borrowing each power undertook in order to generate economic productivity; only by doing this would speculative pressures on their respective currencies come to an end. Along with this, the Ford administration was concerned that pressuring the IMF into providing beneficial loan terms for Britain would establish a worrying precedent for future IMF bailouts.[141]

Callaghan's policy of linking Britain's defence commitments to the IMF loan also failed to have a discernible impact upon the course of US policy, and was largely ineffective for several important reasons. First, Britain's global importance to the US as a military ally had steadily declined throughout the past 20 years. The most dramatic demonstration of this was the East of Suez withdrawal, but, as shown in earlier chapters, the 1970s had witnessed further defence retractions that had severely dented Britain's standing in Washington. Added to this was the important fact that key policy-makers in Washington believed that the UK would likely reduce its military commitments still further.

By the summer of 1976, such fears were proved correct as the British issued a defence white paper which outlined further reductions. Such action hardly enamoured the British to the Ford administration.[142]

In response to this latest defence cutback, Roy Mason promised Donald Rumsfeld, the US defense secretary, that this would be the final cutback for the foreseeable future.[143] Throughout 1974–76, other British policy-makers had made similar promises, but had then gone on to break them. Clearly then, Mason was stretching credibility when he made such assurances. This is an important point to remember when understanding the Ford administration's policy. In 1965–67, sterling came under speculative pressures, but the Johnson administration provided the demanded economic support. This was done partly to ensure that Britain retained its presence East of Suez.[144] In 1976, Britain was no longer East of Suez, and Wilson's last two governments had further reduced Britain's military commitments. By 1976, Britain's importance for the US had waned significantly, and its status as the key military ally in Europe had arguably been eclipsed by that of West Germany. In April 1976, General George Brown, the chairman of the joint chiefs of staff, symbolised just how far the UK's significance had fallen in American military opinion, when he expressed that the military of the UK was 'pathetic' and consisted of nothing more than 'generals and admirals and brass bands'.[145] This perhaps overstates the degree to which the UK had fallen in official US thinking, but the fact remains that the UK no longer assumed the level of importance that it once had.[146]

British threats of curtailing its military commitments were also less credible than in previous years. Making further military reductions was thus seen to have the potential to undermine vital British security interests. In particular, a reduction in the BAOR would have negatively impinged upon NATO, and would also have undermined the ongoing MBFR negotiations.[147] As Hunt reminded Callaghan throughout the IMF negotiations, reducing the BAOR would set in motion the 'dismantling of NATO'.[148] Perhaps Hunt was being slightly melodramatic, but if Callaghan had threatened such a course – and perhaps even enacted such measures – it would have had significant ramifications for British policy. In the final assessment, Callaghan was not prepared to risk this.

Another point of significance is that within the US documentary record it is remarkable just how little time was spent discussing possible British military reductions as a consequence of an unfavourable IMF loan. Perhaps, then, this can be interpreted as a sign of just how un-credible such threats were viewed in Washington or, worse still for the British, just how unimportant they were deemed in American eyes. While it would be too harsh to suggest that 'Britain no longer mattered ... as a world power or as a political example', it was evident during the IMF crisis that Britain no longer mattered enough to constitute preferential economic consideration from the US.[149]

One crucial factor does remain however, that being that Callaghan never tried to extract US cooperation by issuing threats pertaining to Britain's most important defence contributions. The most obvious examples were Britain's Polaris force, its intelligence stations in Cyprus and the Indian Ocean, the American bases located in Britain and its BAOR commitment. These were seen by British policy-makers as areas which promoted US interests and the American reaction to the Wilson government when it suggested that it would cancel or reduce such things indicated this was so. An interesting counterfactual therefore presents itself. Whilst it would be foolhardy to suggest that, had such a tactic been utilised, the Ford administration would have immediately pressured the IMF into proffering less demanding loan conditions, it is worth considering whether Crosland's 'leverage' strategy would have been more successful. Given that key US policy-makers believed that American primacy in international affairs was being severely challenged and that Southern Europe was succumbing to communist influence, then perhaps Callaghan would have obtained the type of assistance he desired had he followed Crosland's more bellicose strategy. However, as noted earlier, there was very little discussion in Washington about the British actually implementing such drastic cutbacks. This could either indicate that such matters were deemed so unlikely as to warrant discussion, or perhaps these interests were not deemed that important by the Americans.

## Economic thinking

The economic philosophy of key US officials in the Treasury, Federal Reserve and in Ford's government was of course highly important in determining US policy throughout the IMF crisis. The likes of Arthur Burns, Edwin Yeo, Alan Greenspan and William Simon were ardent fiscal conservatives.[150] Simon was described by Denis Healey as somewhere 'to the right of Genghis Khan'.[151] Michael Palliser described the American administration less dramatically for the prime minister when he noted that they were in a 'fundamentally conservative mood'.[152] Such British assessments were largely accurate if the private papers of American officials are anything to go by. In one example from Simon's private correspondence, he bemoaned American fiscal policy for resembling a 'socialist' agenda. If such a course was not reversed, then Simon predicted that 'socialism' would take hold in the US.[153] Socialism was clearly used by Simon as a pejorative term in this context.

Ford's other economic advisers were just as disdainful about Britain's economic position. Greenspan and his staff for instance provided damning verdicts on Callaghan's economic policies. Further to this, information received by Greenspan from his staff about the British government's economic policies was usually laced in negative or sarcastic commentary. Robert Hormats was equally critical of Britain's economic performance. Some outside of government – such as Milton Friedman, the influential economist at Chicago University – publicly predicted Britain would become the European equivalent of Chile. Given the predicament of Chile in the mid-1970s, this was clearly not meant as a favourable comparison.[154] In sum, the medicine that the IMF was prescribing was fully endorsed by the economic masters in Washington.

On the safety net issue, the role of the US Federal Reserve was even more important. Constitutionally, it was the purview of Arthur Burns to commit the US to the safety net. Therefore, appealing to the president, whilst not inconsequential, was no guarantee for securing the safety net loan. The president, Kissinger and Scowcroft were fully aware of their lack of control over the Federal Reserve.[155] As William Simon told Kissinger, 'I will have to get with Arthur Burns because in the final analysis that is where the buck or pound goes'.[156] If Callaghan was to get US assistance then convincing the likes of Simon and Burns was just as important as securing the support of Ford or Kissinger. Ultimately, Burns and Simon were unconvinced that Britain should receive preferential treatment from the IMF, and British diplomacy failed to convince them to alter their position.

There has been a tendency by former British officials to paint the likes of Simon, Yeo and Burns as the bogeymen who scuppered British hopes of negotiating more lenient IMF terms, and subsequent writers have followed suit.[157] While not inaccurate, it does omit several important points, and the biggest of these is that Ford himself was fiscally conservative. Therefore, the idea of providing bailout money to a country or institution deemed to be 'living beyond their means' did not sit well with the president. Balanced budgets, reduction of deficits and free markets were the key to economic success in Ford's assessment. The president articulated this vision when he stated: 'I propose that we make a substantial and permanent reduction in our Federal taxes, and second that we make a substantial reduction in the growth of federal spending.'[158] During the New York City financial crisis of 1975, Ford would demonstrate his adherence to such principles. The city had, in a similar fashion to the British government, extended all of its available credit lines and requested assistance from the Federal government in order to meet its spending commitments. Ford refused this appeal and the city had to make sweeping public expenditure cuts in order to balance its budget.[159] Accordingly, British appeals to Ford for economic assistance were always likely to be met with reluctance.

Perhaps even more important was the fact that Ford's government never accepted the economic arguments put forward by Callaghan and Healey: that was, Britain's economic problems originated from short-term speculative pressures on sterling and 'malignant interaction between the exchange rate, the money supply and interest rates'.[160] This line of argument was deemed unconvincing in Washington because US policy-makers believed that Britain's problems stemmed from long-term structural imbalances within its economic system. The intellectual tide of monetarism, and all that entailed, challenged the largely Keynesian remedies which the British government was proposing.[161] Britain was judged to have too high a rate of taxation which stifled economic productivity. Its trade unions were considered to be too powerful, which resulted in too many working days being lost due to strikes. Britain's social security system was regarded as having been inflated beyond the country's capacity to finance it.[162] As William Simon noted in correspondence with Lord Hartwell (the owner of the *Daily Telegraph* newspaper which attacked his conduct throughout the IMF crisis), it was the economic mismanagement by successive British governments which had led to Britain's current predicament.[163]

More damning was that Ford's economic team did not trust the Callaghan government to implement the economic reforms it promised it would enact if it was provided with additional credit to help finance its sterling balances. As Yeo noted:

> From a technical standpoint we have examined the various ways this could be done [providing a 'safety net' loan for sterling]. But from a policy standpoint a substitution account means additional credit, probably of an unconditional nature, for the UK. A proposal or feeler on a substitution account would support the view that the UK still does not appreciate the gravity of its situation and/or lacks the will to deal with it in terms of substantive policies.[164]

Such opinions were not exclusive to Ford's economic advisers. The IMF itself was so sceptical about Callaghan's government implementing the promised expenditure cuts that it would only provide the loan in instalments, with each additional one conditioned on the necessary cutbacks being enacted.[165] Those who were believed to be sympathetic to Britain's predicament were also critical of its economic policies. David Bruce, the former US ambassador to the UK, who was viewed as somewhat of an Anglophile, told President Ford that Britain suffered from 'fundamental problems'.[166] The people that Callaghan used throughout the IMF crisis to mitigate the demands of the IMF – for example, Kissinger and Scowcroft – were of the same opinion.[167]

In sum, the key actors within the Ford administration believed that the economic measures demanded by the IMF were necessary to prevent future British economic problems. Furthermore, there was an entrenched belief that, if the British were not given the strictest of terms by the IMF, then it was unlikely that Callaghan would ever implement the economic changes which Washington deemed necessary.[168] Given such conditions, it was always likely that Callaghan's calls for US financial support would fall on deaf ears.

## Conclusion

Callaghan's first ten months in office were dominated by Britain's economic crisis. The re-establishment of the Atlantic relationship at the centre of Britain's foreign policy, which began when Callaghan was foreign secretary and continued throughout his premiership, was unable to produce the type of results he desired during the IMF crisis. Such criticism needs to be issued with a caveat, which is that given President Ford's fiscally conservative nature it was always going to be difficult to obtain an IMF loan without making what Ford believed were necessary cuts in Britain's PSBR.

Even though he had won the safety net, Callaghan had clearly been outmanoeuvred by Washington's economic masters. Britain had to accept the terms demanded by the IMF in spite of a great unwillingness to cut the PSBR. Callaghan, however, had envisaged that once the IMF agreement had been settled the British would be granted the safety net. Callaghan regarded the safety net as the most important matter; he had, for instance, even refused to implement import tariffs as a means of ensuring the good will of the international economic community. Yet, despite obtaining the safety net, this was only achieved following arduous negotiations; it was nowhere near the size Callaghan wanted, and was delivered a month later than he had envisaged.[169] Whilst a little unfair, the sentiments expressed by one British national newspaper that 'Jim and Denis play IMF Tune Dance of the Puppets', does capture the British situation nicely.[170] In the final assessment, Callaghan had to yield to the demands of the IMF and implement austerity measures upon the British economy.

It is certainly apparent from Callaghan's papers that he believed Britain's importance as an ally to the US to be sufficient enough to force the US to restrain the demands of the IMF. Callaghan's appeals to the likes of Ford, Kissinger and Scowcroft demonstrated this line of argument, yet this ultimately failed to deliver the kind of results he wanted. His investment in close US–UK relations failed to materially manifest into political capital when it was most needed during the IMF crisis. It is difficult to disagree with Kathleen Burk's opinion that: 'Britain had ... been humiliated, not only because this was the first case of a modern industrial country turning to the IMF for this type of loan, but also because she was treated the same way as any other indigent country.'[171]

Though British elites clearly had little influence over their American counterparts, the fact remained that the institutionalised aspects of US–UK cooperation – notably in the security/defence realms – continued and, in other areas, US–UK interaction functioned smoothly. For instance, the US and UK worked efficiently in evacuating their citizens from Lebanon in June 1976, and ongoing diplomatic cooperation continued over the future of Rhodesia.[172] This even saw Kissinger trying to alleviate domestic troubles for Callaghan vis-à-vis criticisms emanating from Margaret Thatcher. Kissinger went as far as to provide a brief for Thatcher so she would understand the situation more fully and would, accordingly, lessen her criticism of the Labour government. As Kissinger put it, 'I thought it would be a good idea if Rogers briefed Mrs Thatcher – to get her off Crosland's back'.[173] Likewise, the visit of Queen Elizabeth II to celebrate the bicentennial of the founding of the United States was an occasion which was marked with great fanfare and gave the public impression of close US–UK relations.[174]

This presents an interesting paradigm for historians in assessing the US–UK relationship during the Ford–Callaghan era. If one looks at the IMF crisis, it becomes apparent that Callaghan never received the type of support from Ford that he believed Britain warranted because of its position in the Western alliance. Alternatively, if one focuses upon the ongoing security–military relationship then one can see a rather different impression. Ultimately, however, one must view this period for US–UK relations as one where the disparities in their respective international positions were more apparent, and when a number of longer-term trends in British foreign and defence policy began to have profound effects on US–UK interaction. British defence commitments since World War II had gradually been reduced and the East of Suez withdrawal had markedly altered Britain's position as a global actor. Britain's economic policies were also viewed unfavourably and, by 1976, there was a clear sense throughout US policy-making circles that Britain had to undertake a series of austerity measures, because it had an overinflated public sector, coupled with an unproductive private sector. Callaghan thus inherited a set of circumstances that made any appeal for US assistance throughout the IMF crisis likely to be met with a less than enthusiastic response. As events unfolded throughout the year, he found this to be the case.

## Notes

1 Simon, *Reflection*, pp. 152–3.

2 Joe Haines, *Glimmers of Twilight: Harold Wilson in Decline* (London: Politico's, 2003), p. 116. On Wilson's health see: David Owen, *In Sickness and in Power: Illness in Heads of Government during the Last 100 Years* (London: Methuen, 2008), pp. 84–5.

3 This was what one newspaper dubbed Callaghan. See: *Evening News*, 5 April 1976, p. 1. On Callaghan's rise to power, see: Paul Deveney, *Callaghan's Journey to Downing Street* (Basingstoke: Palgrave Macmillan, 2011).

4 Morgan, *Callaghan*, pp. 588–60.

5 Gaddis, *The Cold War*, pp. 171–94; Gerald Ford, *A Time to Heal: The Autobiography of Gerald R. Ford* (New York: Harper and Row, 1979), pp. 209–407.

6 On the centrality of 'credibility' to the British government's entire economic strategy see: Ben Cliff and Jim Tomlinson, 'Negotiating Credibility: Britain and the International Monetary Fund, 1956–1976', *Contemporary European History*, 17:4 (2008), 545–66.

7 Kathleen Burk and Alec Cairncross, *Goodbye Great Britain: The 1976 IMF Crisis* (New Haven: Yale University Press, 1992), pp. 1–10. For an explanation on the safety net loan, see: Catherine Schenk, *The Decline of Sterling: Managing the Retreat of an International Currency, 1945–1992* (Cambridge: Cambridge University Press, 2010), pp. 368–77.

8 Burk and Cairncross, *Goodbye Great Britain*, pp. 1–10.

9 Donoughue, *The Conduct of Policy Under Harold Wilson*, pp. 83–4; Wilson, *Final Term*, pp. 234–6; Healey, *My Life*, pp. 372–427.

10 Quote in Pimlott, *Wilson*, p. 724. Statistics from Burk and Cairncross, *Goodbye*, pp. 14–15.

11 TNA: PREM 16/796 Sir Kenneth Berrill to the Prime Minister, 3 June 1976.

12 From the President to the Prime Minister via the Cabinet Line, 24 September 1974, File: Outside the System Chronological File 9/20/74–9/24/74, National Security Adviser Outside the System Chronological File 1974–1977, Box 1, GFL; Memorandum for the President from Henry Kissinger, 21 September 1974, *ibid.*; Message from the Prime Minister to President Ford, 18 September 1974, *ibid.*

13 For this being mentioned see: TNA: PREM 16/796 Note of a meeting between the Prime Minister and the Chancellor of the Exchequer, 4 June 1976; TNA: T 386/15 Note for the Record, 10 June 1976.

14 TNA: T 386/69 Note of a Working Dinner at No. 11 Downing Street, 2 November 1975.

15 TNA: PREM 16/796 Note for the Record, undated (circa June 1976).

16 Hormats has written widely on the problems of global finance and financial institutions. See: Robert D. Hormats, *American Albatross: The Foreign Debt Dilemma* (New York: The Century Foundation, 1988); Robert D. Hormats, *Reforming the International Monetary System: From Roosevelt to Reagan* (Washington DC: Foreign Policy Analysis, 1987).

17 Memorandum for Brent Scowcroft from Robert Hormats, 17 March 1976, File: Outside the System Chronological File 3/5/76–3/30/76, National Security Adviser Outside the System Chronological File, Box 4, GFL.

18 Memorandum for Alan Greenspan from Brent [Scowcroft], 24 February 1976, File: CO160-1/1/76–2/29/76, White House Central Files Box 57, GFL; Memorandum for Brent Scowcroft from Mr Clift, 20 February 1976, File: CO160-1/1/76–2/29/76, White House Central Files Box 57, GFL.

19 TNA: PREM 16/796 Note for the Record, undated (circa June 1976).

20 TNA: PREM 16/796 Sir Kenneth Berrill to the Prime Minister, 3 June 1976.

21 Media opinion summarised for Arthur Burns: Additional Press Coverage of $5.3 billion stand-by Credit, within AmEmbassy London to Treasury Department Washington

DC, Tel. EO 11562, File: Bank of England 1976–77, Arthur Burns Papers (hereafter: ABP), Box B9, GFL.

22 Talking Point: Conversation with Callaghan, attached to F. Widman to Chairman Burns, 25 June 1976, File: International Economic Summit Puerto Rico June 1976: Treasury Briefing Papers, ABP, Box B62, GFL.
23 Notes from Scott Pardee on the cable from Bank of England, 6 June 1976, File: United Kingdom: Loan from Group of Ten 1976, ABP, Box B113, GFL.
24 TNA: CAB 134/4025 EY(76) 5th Meeting, Ministerial Committee on Economic Strategy, Minutes of a Meeting held at 10 Downing Street, 7 June 1976.
25 Memorandum for the President from Edwin Yeo III, 24 June 1976, File: International Economic Summit Puerto Rico June 1976: Treasury Briefing Papers, ABP, Box B62, GFL.
26 Summary of Discussion by William Simon, 15 September 1976, File: Treasury Department 5/24/76–10/27/76, Henry Kissinger and Brent Scowcroft Files Temporary Parallel File, Box A1, GFL.
27 TNA: T 381/16 Nick [Jordan-Moss] to W. S. Ryrie, 20 September 1976.
28 Chris Rogers, 'Economic Policy and the Problem of Sterling under Harold Wilson and James Callaghan', *Contemporary British History*, 25:3 (2011), 353–4.
29 'Blackpool Follies', *Daily Express*, 27 September 1976.
30 Healey, *My Life*, p. 427.
31 Burk, *Old World*, p. 628.
32 Healey, *My Life*, pp. 428–9.
33 Callaghan, *Time*, pp. 427–8.
34 'Save our Sterling', *The Sun*, 29 September 1976.
35 Edmund Dell, *Hard Pounding* (Oxford: Oxford University Press, 1991), p. 236; TNA: T 381/16 Note of a Meeting held in the Chancellor of the Exchequer's Room, 28 September 1976.
36 Burk and Cairncross, *Goodbye*, pp. 8–9.
37 *Ibid.*, pp. 1–9.
38 Callaghan, *Time*, p. 428.
39 On Crosland, see: Kevin Jeffreys, *Anthony Crosland* (London: Pimlico, 2008).
40 Hennessy, *The Prime Minister*, pp. 384–9.
41 Mark Harmon, *The British Labour Government and the 1976 IMF Crisis* (London: Macmillan, 1997), pp. 55–8.
42 Speech given by Michael Foot at the Barrow in Furness CLP Annual Dinner, 25 September 1976, File: MP7/3, Michael Foot Papers, Labour Party Archive, Manchester, UK.
43 On the Crosland–Healey rivalry during the IMF Crisis, see: Giles Radice, *Friends & Rivals: Crosland, Jenkins and Healey* (London: Abacus, 2003), pp. 243–69.
44 TNA: T 381/16 Nick [Jordan-Moss] to W. S. Ryrie, 20 September 1976.
45 TNA: DEFE 25/99, Note from MOD: NATO Special Committee of Defence Ministers, Nuclear Planning Working Group, Brief for Defence Secretary, 15 September 1966; Francis M. Bator to President Johnson, 30 September 1966, Head of State Correspondence File, Box 10, LBJ Library; Message from Prime Minister to President, 7 October 1966, *ibid.*; Text of Message from the President to the Prime Minister, *ibid.*

46 TNA: T 381/16 Nigel Wicks to N. J. Monck, 30 September 1976; TNA: T 381/16 F. R. Barratt to Principal Private Secretary [Wicks], 30 September 1976.

47 TNA: T 381/16 F. R. Barratt to Principal Private Secretary [Wicks], 30 September 1976.

48 Jim Callaghan to the President of the United States, 30 September 1976, File: United Kingdom–Prime Minister James Callaghan, National Security Adviser Presidential Correspondence with Foreign Leaders, Box 4, GFL.

49 From Ambassador in London (Annenberg) to Department of State, Ref: State 8317, 11 February 1971, RG 59 General Records of the Department of State, Subject Numeric Files, 1970–73, Political and Defense, Box 2658, NAII, From Ambassador in London (Annenberg) to Department of State: Annual Assessment for the United Kingdom, 14 February 1972, *ibid.*; Intelligence Note, by Bureau of Intelligence and Research, 30 June 1972, RG 59 General Records of the Department of State, Box 962, NAII.

50 Burk and Cairncross, *Goodbye*, p. 64.

51 Underlined in the original. See: Memorandum for the President from Brent Scowcroft, undated (circa 1 October 1976), File: United Kingdom-Prime Minister James Callaghan, National Security Adviser Presidential Correspondence with Foreign Leaders, Box 4, GFL.

52 Memorandum for the President from Brent Scowcroft, undated (circa 28–29 September 1976), File: Country File-United Kingdom (1), National Security Adviser International Economic Affairs Staff Files, Box 3, GFL.

53 Memorandum for the President from Brent Scowcroft, undated (circa 30 September 1976), *ibid.*

54 TNA: PREM 16/798 Transcript of a Telephone Conversation between the Prime Minister and President Ford, 29 September 1976.

55 TNA: T 381/16 N. Jordan-Moss to Principal Private Secretary [Wicks], 1 October 1976.

56 Schenk, *The Decline*, pp. 372–4. Sterling balances were large amounts of sterling held in London by foreign countries which would use these as a currency for international trade transactions. By 1979 Callaghan had got his wish as sterling balances had disappeared.

57 Quote in TNA: PREM 16/800 Note for the Record: The IMF Loan and Safety Net for Sterling Balances, 5 November 1976. Also TNA: CAB 134/4025 EY(76) 19th Meeting, Ministerial Committee on Economic Strategy, 17 November 1976.

58 Meeting on the UK Economic Situation from Brent Scowcroft, 19 November 1976, File: United Kingdom (10), National Security Adviser Presidential Country Files for Europe and Canada, Box 15, GFL.

59 Underlined in the original. *Ibid.*

60 Memorandum of Conversation, November or December 1976, File: November 18 (?), 1976 Ford, Kissinger, NSAMC, Box 21, GFL.

61 TNA: T 381/17 Ken Stowe to N. J. Monck, 3 November 1976; TNA: PREM 16/799 Note of a Telephone Conversation between the Prime Minister and the Federal German Chancellor, 2 November 1976; TNA: PREM 16/800 Prime Minister's Conversation with Chancellor Schmidt, 5 November 1976.

62 Callaghan had all of the handwritten papers from the Cabinet sessions discussing the IMF loan placed into a brown envelope marked with: 'Not to be Destroyed.' See: TNA:

PREM 16/808 This Envelope contains notes made by the Prime Minister and Private Secretaries during the Cabinet Meetings discussing the IMF Negotiations: Not to Be Destroyed, undated (circa September–December 1976); TNA: PREM 16/799 Michael Palliser to K. R. Stowe, 4 November 1976.

63 TNA: PREM 16/800 Ramsbotham to FCO, Tel. 3794, 11 November 1976.

64 TNA: PREM 16/798 KRS [Kenneth Stowe] to the Prime Minister, undated (circa 5 November 1976); TNA: PREM 16/798 Note of a Meeting held in 10 Downing Street, 6 October 1976.

65 President: IMF loan to Great Britain, 12 November 1976, Box President Handwriting File, File: Countries-United Kingdom, GFL. Special thanks to the archival staff at the Gerald R. Ford Library for locating and providing me with a copy of this document.

66 TNA: T 381/17 Note of a Meeting held in the Chancellor's Room, 9 November 1976.

67 Hennessy, *The Prime Minister*, pp. 361–2.

68 TNA: PREM 16/800 JC [James Callaghan] to the President of the United States, 12 November 1976; TNA: PREM 16/801 Ramsbotham to FCO, Tel. 3828, 14 November 1976.

69 TNA: PREM 16/801 Telephone Conversation between President Ford and the Prime Minister, 16 November 1976.

70 Douglas Wass, *Decline to Fall: The Making of British Macro-economic Policy and the 1976 IMF Crisis* (Oxford: Oxford University Press, 2008), pp. 251–2.

71 Memorandum of Conversation, 16 November 1976, File: November 16, 1976 Ford, Kissinger, NSAMC, Box 21, GFL; Telcon: Secretary Kissinger-Secretary Simon, 17 November 1976, HAKTELCONS.

72 *Ibid.* Kissinger would make similar remarks later in the year. Memorandum of Conversation, 13 December 1976, File: December 13, 1976, Ford, Kissinger, NSAMC, Box 21, GFL.

73 TNA: PREM 16/801 Ramsbotham to FCO, Tel. 3845, 16 November 1976.

74 TNA: T 381/17 Ramsbotham to John Hunt, Tel. 3874, 17 November 1976.

75 Telcon: Mr William Rogers–Secretary Kissinger, 31 July 1976, HAKTELCONS.

76 Burk and Cairncross, *Goodbye*, p. 82.

77 TNA: PREM 16/801 Ramsbotham to FCO, Tel. 3845, 16 November 1976; Memorandum for Brent Scowcroft from Robert Hormats, 2 November 1976, File: Country File-United Kingdom (3), National Security Adviser International Economic Affairs Staff Files, Box 3, GFL.

78 TNA: PREM 16/800 JC [James Callaghan] to the President of the United States, 12 November 1976.

79 TNA: PREM 16/802 Ramsbotham to FCO, Tel. 3969, 24 November 1976.

80 TNA: PREM 16/801 Ramsbotham to FCO, Tel. 3874, 17 November 1976; TNA: PREM 16/801 Transcript of a Telephone Conversation between the Prime Minister in his room at the House of Commons and the Chancellor of the Duchy of Lancaster at the British Embassy in Washington, 17 November 1976; TNA: PREM 16/801 Crosland to FCO, Tel. 2507, 18 November 1976; TNA: PREM 16/801 Ramsbotham to FCO, Tel. 3907, 18 November 1976.

81 Kissinger, *YOR*, pp. 1059–64.

82 TNA: CAB 128/60 CM(76) 32nd Conclusion, Minute 3, 18 November 1976.

83 TNA: CAB 128/60 CM(76) 33rd Conclusion, Minute 2, 23 November 1976.

84 As reported in: 'Welcome to the Club, Denis', *The Sun*, 6 December 1976.
85 Memorandum for the President from Brent Scowcroft and Alan Greenspan, 1 December 1976, Box Presidential Handwriting File, File: Countries-United Kingdom, GFL.
86 Bernard Donoughue, *Downing Street Diary: With James Callaghan in No. 10* (London: Jonathan Cape, 2008), p. 110.
87 Memorandum of Conversation, 23 November 1976, File: November 23 (?), 1976, Ford, FRG Chancellor Helmut Schmidt (phone call), NSAMC, Box 21, GFL.
88 TNA: PREM 16/802 Ramsbotham to FCO, Tel. 3969, 24 November 1976; TNA: PREM 16/803 Ramsbotham to FCO, Tel. 3986, 25 November 1976.
89 TNA: PREM 16/804 Note for the Record: IMF Negotiations, 1 December 1976.
90 TNA: CAB 128/60 CM(76) 34th Conclusions, Minute 4, 2 December 1976. Crosland was supported by Harold Lever, Roy Hattersley, Secretary of State for Prices and Consumer Protection, and Shirley Williams, the Paymaster General. See: Dumbrell, *Anglo–American Relations From the Cold War to Iraq*, p. 84.
91 TNA: CAB 128/60 CM(76) 34th Conclusions, Minute 4, 2 December 1976. For other accounts from those present, see: Donoughue, *With James Callaghan*, pp. 90–126; Tony Benn, *Against the Tide: Diaries 1973–76* (London: Arrow, 1990), pp. 610–94.
92 David Harris, 'Healey at Bay over Package', *Daily Telegraph*, 2 December 1976.
93 Pearce, *Healey*, pp. 480–2.
94 Burk and Cairncross, *Goodbye*, pp. 111–12.
95 TNA: PREM 16/804 Note for the Record: IMF Negotiations, 1 December 1976; TNA: CAB 128/60 CM(76) 34th Conclusions, Minute 4, 2 December 1976; Hennessy, *The Prime Minister*, pp. 386–7.
96 Ian Ball, 'Callaghan Agrees to £3,494m Cut', *Daily Telegraph*, 6 December 1976, p. 1.
97 TNA: PREM 16/802 Ramsbotham to FCO, Tel. 3969, 24 November 1976; TNA: PREM 16/803 Ramsbotham to FCO, Tel. 3986, 25 November 1976; TNA: T 381/18 Note of a Meeting held at 11 Downing Street, 28 November 1976.
98 For a similar thesis, see: Hennessy, *The Prime Minister*, pp. 386–8.
99 'The Purse Busters', *Daily Express*, 9 October 1976.
100 Edmund Dell, *The Chancellors: A History of the Chancellors of the Exchequer, 1945–90* (London: HarperCollins, 1997), pp. 435–7.
101 TNA: PREM 16/808 This Envelope contains notes made by the Prime Minister and Private Secretaries during the Cabinet Meetings discussing the IMF negotiations: Not to Be Destroyed, undated (circa September–December 1976).
102 Pearce, *Healey*, pp. 500–1.
103 Burk and Cairncross, *Goodbye*, pp. 118–20.
104 TNA: PREM 16/802 President Ford to Prime Minister Callaghan, 20 November 1976.
105 Memorandum of Conversation, 3 December 1976, File: December 23, 1976, Ford, Kissinger NSAMC, Box 21, GFL.
106 TNA: PREM 16/805 Ramsbotham to FCO, Tel. 4120, 3 December 1976.
107 *Ibid.*; TNA: PREM 16/807 DHW [Douglas Wass] to the Prime Minister, 10 December 1976.
108 TNA: PREM 16/808 This Envelope contains notes made by the Prime Minister and Private Secretaries during the Cabinet Meetings discussing the IMF Negotiations: Not to Be Destroyed, undated (circa September–December 1976).

109 From AmEmbassy Bonn to the Secretary of State, 15 November 1976, Tel. 6311, File: Germany-State Department Telegrams to SecState NODIS (1), National Security Adviser, Presidential Country Files for Europe and Canada, Box 7, GFL.

110 'Chevaline' was the code name given to the project for updating Polaris.

111 TNA: T 364/51 Annex B, attached to John Hunt to the Prime Minister, 4 December 1976.

112 See Chapter 4.

113 TNA: PREM 16/805 John Hunt to Mr Stowe, 3 December 1976.

114 For Ford's offer to be 'sympathetic' see TNA: PREM 16/802 President Ford to Prime Minister Callaghan, 20 November 1976. On Healey's complaints, see: Wass, *Decline to Fall*, p. 255.

115 Harmon, *The British Labour Government*, p. 222. This position was consistent with internal thinking within the US Federal Reserve. See: Sterling Balances, David Howard to Mr Reynolds, 23 November 1976, File: United Kingdom General November 1976–1977, ABP, Box B113, GFL.

116 TNA: PREM 16/805 John Hunt to Mr Stowe, 3 December 1976.

117 TNA: PREM 16/807 Prime Minister to the President, 10 December 1976.

118 TNA: PREM 16/807 Telephone Conversation between the Prime Minister and Chancellor Schmidt, 11 December 1976; Memorandum for the President from Brent Scowcroft, 12 December 1976, File: Germany (FRG)-Chancellor Schmidt (3), National Security Adviser Presidential Correspondence with Foreign Leaders, Box 2, GFL.

119 TNA: PREM 16/807 Ramsbotham to FCO, Tel. 4284, 12 December 1976.

120 TNA: PREM 16/807 Ramsbotham to FCO, Tel. 4285, 12 December 1976; TNA: T 381/19 Front End Loading and Safety Net: Points for Telephone Conversation, Mrs Hedley-Miller, Mr Ryrie, 13 December 1976.

121 TNA: PREM 16/807 Ramsbotham to FCO, Tel. 4285, 12 December 1976.

122 For the advice being sent to the US delegation at the conference see: To Governor Wallich from Paul A. Volker, 9 December 1976, File: United Kingdom Sterling Balance Problem (1), ABP, Box B113, GFL.

123 TNA: PREM 16/808 Ramsbotham to FCO, Tel. 4189, 13 December 1976.

124 Simon, *Reflection*, p. 153; Raj Roy, 'Peter Ramsbotham, 1974–77', in Hopkins et al., *Washington Embassy*, p. 223.

125 Wass, *Decline to Fall*, pp. 256–7.

126 Memorandum of Conversation, 13 December 1976, File: December 13, 1976, Ford, Kissinger, NSAMC, Box 21, GFL.

127 TNA: PREM 16/808 Ramsbotham to FCO, Tel. 4213, 13 December 1976; TNA: PREM 16/808 Draft Message to President Ford, attached to K. R. Stowe to N. J. Monck, 14 December 1976.

128 Wass, *Decline to Fall*, p. 256. For the letter sent to Callaghan, see: TNA: PREM 16/808 N. Monck to Ken Stowe, 15 December 1976.

129 Prime Minister Callaghan to President Ford, December 1976, File: Backchannel-Hotline Cabinet Office London Incoming, 12/76, Henry Kissinger and Brent Scowcroft Files Temporary Parallel File, Box A1, GFL.

130 Wass, *Decline to Fall*, p. 256.

131 Arthur Burns to Gordon Richardson, 7 January 1977, File: United Kingdom Sterling Balance Problem (2), ABP, Box B113, GFL.

132 Callaghan, *Time*, p. 430; Kissinger, *YOR*, pp. 608–10; Simon, *Reflection*, p. 154.
133 Memorandum of Conversation, 23 November 1976, File: November 23, 1976, Ford, Kissinger, Scowcroft, National Security Adviser Memoranda of Conversations, Box 21, GFL.
134 Henry A. *Kissinger, 'Reflections on a Partnership:* British and American Attitudes to Post-war Foreign Policy', *International Affairs*, 58:4 (1982), 577.
135 Morgan, *Callaghan*, pp. 538–42; Renwick, *Fighting With Allies*, p. 216.
136 Callaghan, *Time*, p. 430.
137 Telcon: Kissinger–Scotty Retson, 28 October 1976, HAKTELCONS; TNA: PREM 16/799 Ramsbotham to FCO, Tel. 3594, 27 October 1976.
138 Burk and Cairncross, *Goodbye*, pp. 63–4.
139 Telcon: Kissinger-Scotty Retson, 28 October 1976, HAKTELCONS.
140 On Mexico, see: Memorandum for Brent Scowcroft from Robert Hormats, 20 August 1976, File: 8/3/76–8/23/76, National Security Adviser Outside the System Chronological File 1974–1977, Box 5, GFL. On Italy see: From AmEmbassy Rome to the Secretary of State, September 1976, Tel. 2110, File: Italy-State Department Telegrams To SecState-NODIS (5), National Security Adviser, Presidential Country Files for Europe and Canada, Box 9, GFL; From AmEmbassy Rome to the Secretary of State, September 1976, Tel. 685, *ibid.*
141 On Italy follow the material in: Talking Point: Conversation with Moro, undated, File: Country File-Italy, National Security Adviser, International Economic Affairs Staff Files, Box 2, GFL; Memorandum for the President from William Simon, undated, *ibid.*; Memorandum for the President from Edwin Yeo, 24 June 1976, *ibid.*; Stabilization Program for Italy, undated, *ibid.*; Memorandum for General Scowcroft from Edwin Yeo, 9 September 1976, *ibid.*
142 Memorandum for the President from Brent Scowcroft, 21 July 1976, File: United Kingdom-Prime Minister James Callaghan, National Security Adviser Presidential Correspondence with Foreign Leaders, Box 4, GFL.
143 TNA: FCO 46/1374 Note of a Bilateral Discussion between the Defence Secretary and the Hon. Donald Rumsfeld, the US Secretary of Defence, 15 June 1976.
144 Dumbrell, 'The Johnson Administration, and the British Labour Government', 211–31.
145 Rumsfeld, *Known and Unknown*, p. 236.
146 Memorandum for the President from Brent Scowcroft, 21 July 1976, File: United Kingdom-Prime Minister James Callaghan, National Security Adviser Presidential Correspondence with Foreign Leaders, Box 4, GFL; Reynolds, *Britannia Overruled*, pp. 249–52.
147 Robert Boyce, 'In Search of the Anglo-American Special Relationship in the Economic and Financial Spheres' in A. Capet and A. Sy-Wonyu (eds.), *The 'Special Relationship': La 'Relation Speciale'* (Rouen: University of Rouen, 2003) pp. 84–5; Dobson, *Anglo-American Relations*, pp. 143–5.
148 TNA: PREM 16/805 John Hunt to Mr Stowe, 3 December 1976.
149 Dimbleby and Reynolds, *An Ocean Apart*, p. 319.
150 W. C. Wells, *Economist in an Uncertain World: Arthur F. Burns and the Federal Reserve, 1970–1978* (New York: Columbia University Press, 1994); William Simon, *A Time for Truth* (New York: Readers Digest Association, 1978); William Simon, *A Time for*

*Action* (New York: Readers Digest Association, 1980); Simon, *Reflection*, pp. 152–5; Alan Greenspan, *The Age of Turbulence: Adventures in a New World* (London: Penguin, 2008).

151 Healey, *My Life*, pp. 419–20.

152 TNA: PREM 16/798 Note of a Meeting held in 10 Downing Street, 6 October 1976.

153 William Simon to William Peterson, 1 December 1976, William Simon Papers, Box 8 Series 1, Drawer 8, Folder 8, GFL.

154 For the points made in the text see: Memorandum for the President from Alan Greenspan, 23 April 1975, File: CO160-2/1/75–4/30/75, White House Central Files. Box 56, GFL; For the Desk of Alan Greenspan, 15 May 1975, File: CO 160-5/1/75–6/3/75, *ibid.*, GFL; Memorandum for Brent Scowcroft from Robert Hormats, 12 November 1976, File: Country File-United Kingdom (3), National Security Adviser International Economic Affairs Staff Files, Box 3, GFL; John E. Reynolds to Chairman Burns, 5 May 1976, File: International Finance May 1976, ABP, B63, GFL; Reynolds, *Britannia Overruled*, p. 253.

155 Memorandum of Conversation, 16 November 1976, File: November 16, 1976 Ford, Kissinger, NSAMC, Box 21, GFL; Memorandum of Conversation, November or December 1976, File: November 18 (?), 1976 Ford, Kissinger, NSAMC, Box 21, GFL; Memorandum of Conversation, 23 November 1976, File: November 23, 1976, Ford, Kissinger, Scowcroft, NSAMC, Box 21, GFL.

156 Telcon: Secretary Kissinger-Secretary Simon, 17 November 1976, HAKTELCONS.

157 Callaghan, *Time*, pp. 430–40; Healey, *My Life*, pp. 419–20; Dell, *A Hard Pounding*; Burk and Cairncross, *Goodbye*; Harmon, *The British Labour Government*; Kevin Hickson, *The IMF Crisis of 1976 and British Politics* (London: I.B. Tauris, 2005).

158 Ford, *A Time to Heal*, pp. 313–14.

159 Brinkley, *Ford*, pp. 123–5.

160 Denis Healey, 'Foundation for Growth', *Financial Times*, 31 December 1976.

161 Donoughue, *The Conduct of Policy*, pp. 79–85.

162 International Labour Comparisons, 22 November 1976, File: International Economic Reports 1, L. William Seidman Files, Box 137, GFL; Memorandum for Brent Scowcroft from Robert Hormats, 8 July 1976, File: Country File-United Kingdom (2), National Security Adviser International Economic Affairs Staff Files, Box 3, GFL; United Kingdom Economic Situation and Policy Problems, undated (circa June 1976), File: International Economic Summit Puerto Rico June 1976: Treasury Briefing Papers, ABP, Box B62, GFL.

163 William Simon to Lord Hartwell, 12 September 1976, William Simon Papers, Box 6, Series I, Drawer 6, Folder 2, GFL.

164 Memorandum for the President from Edwin Yeo III, 24 June 1976, File: International Economic Summit Puerto Rico June 1976: Treasury Briefing Papers, ABP, Box B62, GFL.

165 Peter Riddell, 'IMF Plans Close Watch on U.K.', *Financial Times*, 30 November 1976.

166 Memorandum of Conversation, 12 November 1974, File: November 12, 1974 Ford-Ambassador David Bruce, NSAMC, Box 7, GFL. Bruce was serving as the US ambassador to NATO at the time.

167 Meeting with Anne L. Armstrong from Brent Scowcroft, 14 January 1976, File: FO2/CO151–164A, White House Central Files Subject File, Box 8, GFL; Memorandum

for the President from Brent Scowcroft, undated (circa 1 October 1976), File: United Kingdom-Prime Minister James Callaghan, National Security Adviser Presidential Correspondence with Foreign Leaders, Box 4, GFL; Memorandum for the President from Brent Scowcroft, undated, File: Europe-General (2), National Security Adviser Presidential Country Files for Europe and Canada, Box 1, GFL; Memorandum of Conversation, 18 October 1974, File: October 18, 1974-Ford–Kissinger, NSAMEMCON, Box 6, GFL; Memorandum of Conversation, 8 January 1975, File: January 8, 1975 Ford–Kissinger, NSAMEMCON, Box 8, GFL; United Kingdom, undated, File: Economic Summits-Rambouillet (1), National Security Adviser International Economic Affairs Staff Files, Box 4, GFL; Memorandum of Conversation, 24 February 1976, File: European Community, National Security Adviser International Economic Affairs Staff Files, Box 5, GFL.

168 Memorandum for Brent Scowcroft from Robert Hormats, 12 November 1976, File: Country File-United Kingdom (3), National Security Adviser International Economic Affairs Staff Files, Box 3, GFL; Memorandum for the President from Edwin Yeo III, 24 June 1976, File: International Economic Summit Puerto Rico June 1976: Treasury Briefing Papers, ABP, Box B62, GFL.

169 Hattersley, *Fifty Years On*, p. 252.

170 'Dance of the Puppets', *Daily Express*, 1 October 1976.

171 Burk, *Old World*, p. 629.

172 Kissinger, *YOR*, pp. 1006–10.

173 Telcon: Ambassador Armstrong–Secretary Kissinger, 13 October 1976, HAKTELCONS.

174 The Gerald R. Ford presidential library maintains a detailed exhibit of Queen Elizabeth II's visit. See: www.fordlibrarymuseum.gov/library/exhibits/queen/queen.asp (Accessed 22 February 2013).

# 6

# Conclusion

As Henry Kissinger noted in 2001, the contemporary strains in the transatlantic relationship mirrored those experienced throughout the Cold War.[1] As shown in the previous chapters, such an interpretation holds considerable merit. Given the political, economic and social changes witnessed in this era, perhaps scholars should not be surprised that the US–UK relationship was fraught with difficulties. Nevertheless, the traditional interpretation that the Nixon–Heath years were a period of constant acrimony for US–UK relations requires clarification. Nixon's policies in Vietnam were publicly supported by Heath and, even in the face of stern criticism from other European leaders, Heath remained resolute in his support. Nixon's détente policies were also publicly supported and US–UK interaction in a number of other areas continued. Intelligence cooperation was a continual feature of the relationship and Heath revitalised US–UK nuclear cooperation. The upgrading of Polaris was a subject that saw continual discussion amongst US–UK policy-makers, and the final decision to upgrade Polaris (in November 1973) confirmed that the US–UK nuclear relationship would continue in spite of the prime minister's flirtation with the idea of an Anglo-French nuclear deterrent.[2]

Such information should not lead to a total reversal of our understanding of the Nixon–Heath years. Whatever was stated publicly to the contrary, Heath's government remained suspicious of Nixon's détente policies. In particular, there was a constant concern that superpower cooperation could morph into superpower condominium, and the secretive fashion in which the US–PRC rapprochement was conducted only increased London's suspicions. US–Soviet negotiations concerning SALT were viewed with particular trepidation because Heath's government believed it could result in the curtailment of US–UK nuclear cooperation. Such concerns had a direct impact on British nuclear policy and Heath's nuclear overtures to France, and the final decision to opt for the Chevaline upgrade to Polaris, were driven, in part, by a concern that SALT would limit US–UK nuclear cooperation.[3]

Other elements of détente, especially the CSCE and MBFR negotiations, were another source of disagreement for US and UK policy-makers. To be sure, the Nixon and Heath governments were in agreement about the undesirability of both projects. Nixon and Kissinger viewed the CSCE with derision, and this was something that British officials largely shared. Nonetheless, there existed a point of clear difference between US and UK policy. Nixon saw the CSCE as a potential avenue for pressuring Soviet foreign policy in other areas deemed more important to US interests. Thus, the CSCE was initially directly linked to reaching a Berlin settlement and, when this was concluded in 1971, the CSCE was linked to progress on SALT and MBFR. Heath's government viewed the CSCE differently. As détente improved East–West relations, it was believed that the CSCE would inevitably be concluded. It was, as Douglas-Home noted, 'unavoidable'.[4] Accordingly, Heath sought to settle the CSCE as quickly as possible as a way of ensuring that the CSCE would not actually deal with anything deemed to be of extreme importance. This was clearly at variance with US policy and, as such, between 1970 and 1972 this was a continued source of divergence in US and UK policy.

MBFR was an area of deeper concern for both US and UK policy-makers. If not handled correctly, the British government believed MBFR could critically undermine NATO, and Heath wanted the issues surrounding MBFR to be vigorously analysed within NATO. Only once this had been accomplished would NATO undertake serious discussions with the Warsaw Pact. Nixon initially gave little attention to the concept, but by 1971 – due to a mixture of domestic, international and economic motives – the president gave the idea more interest. US policy was designed to press forward with the idea whilst the British continued to debate the merits of the negotiation.

In existing accounts, SALT, MBFR and the CSCE are often depicted as being major sources of antagonism for US–UK relations.[5] Certainly they were subjects where differences were apparent, but the point that should be remembered is that they were matters to be negotiated. Difference of opinion, in and of itself, does not indicate that US–UK relations were in a crisis. Rather, it merely demonstrates that states have differing interpretations on matters. Indeed, throughout 1969–72 US–UK officials engaged in detailed bilateral discussions on these topics. It was only in 1973–74 when wider US–UK political differences intensified that these differences assumed greater importance. Where US–UK differences on MBFR were once viewed as natural policy divergences that could be negotiated, they were now seen as further proof of a more uncooperative US–UK relationship. Kissinger and Schlesinger viewed British differences as indicative of wider British attempts to undermine US foreign policy. Initially, however, they were viewed as natural points to be debated amongst allies. It is within this context that US–UK differences on international diplomacy can be properly understood.

## Britain's future role

In the opinion of the Nixon White House, several aspects of Heath's foreign policy were regrettable. Nixon had enthusiastically welcomed Heath's election in June 1970, believing that he would reverse Britain's global decline – a point which he felt had only undermined US interests because 'the United States would by necessity be forced to "go it alone" in the foreign policy leadership of the free world'.[6] Nixon's hopes for Heath were misplaced as Heath fundamentally endorsed Wilson's East of Suez withdrawal in his much-anticipated defence review of 1970. From Washington's perspective this was an annoyance given that the Nixon Doctrine aspired to reduce America's global commitments, and their attempts to promote burden-sharing and improve NATO's conventional forces were also dealt a further blow. Nonetheless, at this stage, the president accepted the British decision philosophically because he accepted that Britain still contributed, as a proportion of GDP, the most of any European state to NATO. Polaris had been kept, intelligence facilities in Cyprus remained and the UK's other global bases, notably in Diego Garcia, were also retained. As Kissinger concluded, Heath's government was 'doing as much as they can'.[7]

Heath's overriding foreign policy priority was to obtain British membership of the EEC but he did not view it as a zero sum game. He had no intention of ending aspects of US–UK bilateralism which remained relevant for promoting British interests. The objective was, as Douglas-Home articulated, to have the 'best of both worlds'.[8] By the end of 1972, Heath had managed to achieve his main foreign policy objective. Britain, at the third time of trying, had attained membership of the EEC. For the Nixon administration this was perceived as potentially troublesome. The US had traditionally supported British membership of the EEC yet Nixon would come to question this. His economic advisers persistently warned about the economic challenges that EEC expansion would pose for US interests and the international economic policies pursued by the president would only further enflame US–EEC economic competition. In 1971, the implementation of a 10 per cent surcharge on imports and the refusal to convert dollar-gold transactions demonstrated Nixon's determination to safeguard US economic interests. Therefore, the expansion of the EEC was largely seen by the president as an economic competitor, rather than as a potential partner.[9]

For Nixon, however, the political, rather than economic, consequences of British EEC membership were more important. Here, Kissinger provided Nixon with several areas where future problems could arise. An 'independent

Europe could prove to be a competitive power center with the US,' Kissinger warned. Nixon feared that the US was potentially losing a close British ally in which confidential and close matters could be discussed. In its place was an enlarged EEC, built on cooler ties and with no foreign policy machinery to work through.[10] Ultimately, despite these concerns, Nixon endorsed British membership of the EEC and even offered clandestine assistance for aiding the UK–EEC negotiations. As Nixon concluded, the US could do very little to prevent British membership of the EEC and, more importantly, he believed British membership could potentially benefit US interests in the longer term as it could turn the EEC into an 'entity'.[11] More simply put, the EEC could become a more equitable partner within the Western alliance which would advance the cause of burden-sharing and promote the Nixon Doctrine's wider aspiration of lessening direct US involvement globally.

The year 1973–74 illustrated how misdirected such thinking was. Predictions from the likes of Kissinger that EEC expansion would mark the onset of a more competitive relationship were proving to be accurate. Kissinger's warnings that the EEC's lack of foreign policy apparatus would prohibit easy bilateral relations were clearly highlighted during his 'Year of Europe'. So too was Kissinger's fear that US–UK bilateral contact would be less easy now that Britain was a member of the EEC. Kissinger's wider concern that the EEC would actually challenge US primacy within the Western alliance was also apparent, as the EEC refused to cede to American demands that a higher degree of linkage between economic and political matters should be implemented. When the EEC sought a separate policy initiative towards the Arab–Israeli conflict which directly contradicted US policy at the end of 1973, it was with some justification that US policy-makers lamented the expansion of the EEC.

It was Kissinger's 'Year of Europe', however, that sparked considerable US–UK disagreement. The 'Year of Europe' initially illustrated procedural problems for US–UK interaction now that Britain was a member of the EEC, especially in regard to how the US would negotiate the Declaration of Principles. Kissinger desired to operate bilaterally with European governments and Heath's government, whilst indicating a willingness to follow this course, soon backtracked. The prime minister wanted the EEC to unify a common position, and, once this was achieved, negotiate with the US as a collective.

Procedural issues aside, fundamental differences divided US and UK policy throughout the 'Year of Europe'. Most alarming yet, for US–UK relations, was that Heath and his senior advisers suspected Kissinger's 'Year of Europe' had rather more sinister objectives than those claimed, believing it was the intention of the US to divide and rule the nascent common foreign policy of the EEC. While several scholars have accepted this was Kissinger's objective, there is very little evidence to support such an interpretation. Kissinger certainly wanted more from the 'Year of Europe' than his stated intentions to improve NATO's forces and provide a symbolic gesture of Atlantic solidarity. Indeed, US policy was designed so that direct linkage was made between US–EEC economic and political interaction. More simply, the Nixon–Kissinger theory of linkage, primarily driving US foreign policy vis-à-vis the USSR, was to be applied to US–EEC relations.

It is this crucial point which really created discord amongst US and UK policy-makers. Heath did not want this conceptualised approach applied to US–EEC relations, because he feared that the US would exploit its security guarantees to Europe as a means of extracting more amenable trade and economic agreements with the EEC. Moreover, Heath did not want the US to influence EEC policies which were at a formative stage. Subsequently, Heath's government sought to resist US policy and did this initially when he let it be known that any US–UK discussions pertaining to the Declaration of Principles would be transmitted to Britain's EEC partners. Following French pressure, and further evidence that Kissinger's real motivations were less altruistic than he presented, Heath suspended all US–UK discussion about the declaration. As Heath informed the US, they would simply have to wait until the EEC had formulated a common position before negotiations could proceed further.

Heath's actions were viewed with incredulity in Washington, because his policy was effectively scuppering any hope of a quick foreign policy success – which Nixon personally wanted to distract attention from his Watergate troubles. More substantively, Heath's decision was seen to mark the end of close US–UK diplomacy, and both Nixon and Kissinger talked about the end of the 'special relationship'.[12] However, Kissinger was determined that his declaration be created along the lines he sought, and therefore exerted bilateral pressure upon Britain to achieve this. This took the form of US–UK intelligence and nuclear cooperation being suspended temporarily. Such tactics soon yielded results for Kissinger, and Heath reversed his policy that US–UK discussions on the declaration could not occur. Indeed, such was the pressure put on the British government that Heath not only allowed US–UK discussion on the declaration, but he also provided the US with reports about UK–EEC discussions about the declaration.

By the beginning of October, the EEC had produced a draft declaration, and British officials were also discussing the declaration with their US counterparts. US–UK relations were, at some level then, recovering from their summer of hostility. The outbreak of the fourth Arab–Israeli war was soon to ruin any hopes of relations being quickly repaired. During the war, Heath was foremost concerned with protecting Britain's oil supplies, but he also envisaged an Arab–Israeli settlement that would follow the general outlines of UN Resolution 242. The conflict for Heath presented both difficulties and opportunities but, by adopting a neutralist stance towards the war, Heath believed he could bolster his chances of producing an Arab–Israeli settlement as well as protect Britain's oil supplies.

Oil, whilst of course not unimportant in the American opinion, was of secondary concern to larger geopolitical factors. The greatest concern for Washington, then, was the likely reaction of the USSR, and the peace settlement that the US sought was designed to largely omit them from the region. US policy was predicated upon the assumption that Israel would be militarily dominant at the end of the war, because this would ensure that the Arab states would negotiate. In turn, because of the severe losses induced by the surprise Egyptian–Syrian assault, Kissinger believed this would make Israel more susceptible to American pressure to negotiate a lasting political settlement with its Arab neighbours. Accordingly, presenting America as the only power able to broker a peace deal would prise Soviet influence away from its Arab allies.[13]

Given these radically different agendas it was always likely that US and UK policy would come into conflict. This quickly manifested when the British refused to table in the UNSC Kissinger's ceasefire proposals that were predicated upon the idea that all belligerents returned to the status quo ante bellum. In effect, the land occupied by Israel in 1967, and now re-captured by Egyptian and Syrian forces, would have to be given back to Israel. Heath believed that supporting this would be perceived as a pro-Israeli act by the Arab states, and his attempts to pursue a neutral course would be undermined. Heath would again infuriate Washington when he refused to allow US reconnaissance aircraft to fly from British bases in Cyprus to survey the warzone. The US airlift to Israel similarly was not allowed to utilise British air bases.

This level of disagreement was to be dwarfed by the ramifications that emanated from the aftermath of the DEFCON III decision. While Kissinger had informed Cromer of this decision, it was never communicated to the prime minister. Further, Heath believed the US was endangering all of the Western alliance without even consulting those states which would be affected by such a decision. Moving to DEFCON III was also viewed by Heath as a gross overreaction to the situation, and he believed it was largely driven by Nixon's Watergate induced troubles.

Heath's distancing from US policy had serious consequences for British interests when the US once again temporarily suspended its intelligence cooperation with London. This was done as a form of punishment, but Kissinger's ideas for longer-term punishments were never implemented. A series of possible 'pressure points' drawn up for Kissinger all concluded that the cancellation of bilateral security cooperation would only undermine US interests. This Kissinger accepted and, when a British request for additional assistance in upgrading Polaris was made at the beginning of January 1974, this was duly approved.

The Washington Energy Conference was a watershed for US foreign policy towards the enlarged EEC and Britain. It was seen as a lesson in the Nixon White House in how to conduct future diplomacy with its allies. In particular, the US had learned that by utilising a number of tactics, including the temporary cancellation of nuclear and intelligence cooperation, they had managed to ensure that the British would, if forced, operate bilaterally with the US in opposition to Heath's desire to formulate common EEC political and foreign policies. As shown in Chapter 3, US bilateral pressure on British interests could have profound effects upon the direction of British foreign policy. It is the coercive elements in US diplomacy towards its British ally that are currently omitted from existing accounts of the Nixon–Heath years. Yet, as shown above, this was a feature of the relationship, and, more importantly, was an element of US policy that had considerable success at influencing the course of London's policy decisions.

The year 1973–74 was a difficult one for US–UK relations as disagreement, suspicion and recrimination dominated the relationship. Nonetheless, other areas of US–UK interaction indicate that such an analysis must be tempered somewhat. Kissinger tasked Thomas Brimelow with drafting a US–USSR treaty which eventually manifested as the 'Agreement on the Prevention of Nuclear War (signed in Washington DC on 22 June 1973). Even though senior British officials enjoyed an often fraught relationship with Kissinger, this did not prevent the continuation of close cooperation. The choice in upgrading Polaris, of course informed by a concern about the future reliability of US nuclear cooperation, did cement US–UK ties.[14] Heath had also illustrated during the Washington Energy Conference his propensity for close US–UK cooperation when he believed that it would better suit UK interests. Indeed, the EEC's disunity at the Washington Energy Conference dealt a blow to Heath's wider aspiration of producing common EEC policies.

Accordingly, a rather more mixed assessment of the Nixon–Heath years than currently exists is required. US–UK relations undoubtedly witnessed severe problems and adapting to British membership of the EEC created numerous difficulties. Détente and the subsequent diplomacy it created – be it the CSCE, MBFR or SALT – continued to be points of US–UK disagreement. Yet in other realms US–UK cooperation remained remarkably close and consistent. Thus, the portrayal of the US–UK relationship in the Nixon–Heath period must be one that emphasises discord, cooperation and diplomatic coercion.

## Wilson's return

Wilson's return to office saw renewed efforts to re-establish closer US–UK relations. Both Wilson and Callaghan were much cooler towards the EEC and, whilst the renegotiation of the terms of EEC entry were mainly a facade generated by Wilson to appease his domestic critics, it did signal Wilson's intention to refocus upon US–UK relations. This, Wilson believed, would allow Britain to influence US policy more directly, whilst accepting that EEC membership would allow Britain to derive a number of economic benefits. Indeed, what Wilson had sought in the 1960s was the basis of his foreign policy throughout the 1970s.

Wilson's defence cutbacks, coupled with Britain's economic troubles, were to undermine his foreign policy ambitions. US–UK relations were blighted by Britain's chronic economic problems and the unwillingness of Wilson to maintain Britain's defence efforts. However, as previous studies have illustrated, Wilson's defence cuts had little effect on the more practical aspects of US–UK defence cooperation.[15] Such arguments are correct but, given what new material from the archives highlights, this analysis requires further qualification. Firstly, US–UK nuclear and intelligence cooperation was utilised by the Ford administration to influence the scope of British defence cuts, and the nature of US–UK cooperation exposed the British to this type of US pressure. This was evident during Wilson's decision to retain Britain's intelligence facilities in Cyprus when he had initially wanted to close them yet, following US opposition, the British prime minister reversed his decision. On other occasions US efforts were rather less successful. Wilson enacted defence cuts even when Kissinger and Schlesinger threatened to permanently suspend nuclear and intelligence assistance. Wilson calculated, correctly, that the US would not terminate this cooperation because it enhanced US interests. In sum, the coercive diplomacy practised by the US at this juncture was rather less successful than its practitioners hoped for. Nevertheless, the fact that this coercive diplomacy existed is telling about the fashion in which the 'special relationship' was viewed by both the Nixon and Ford administrations.

## Callaghan and Ford

Callaghan's first ten months in office were dominated by Britain's economic crisis. Due to Britain's worsening recession, the speculative attacks on sterling and the growing rate of the PSBR, Callaghan had to seek an IMF loan. The greatest concern for the prime minister was to avoid having to accept a loan that insisted on a significant reduction in Britain's PSBR. Callaghan also wanted a safety net loan from the G10 to defend sterling from currency speculation. In order to obtain all of this, Callaghan wanted the Ford administration to pressure the IMF into providing Britain with preferential loan conditions. This, he believed, would be forthcoming because of Britain's military and strategic importance to the US.

This was a fatal misjudgement by Callaghan. His appeals to Ford, Kissinger and Scowcroft ultimately failed to deliver the type of results he wanted. Ford's political advisers did not believe Britain warranted preferential economic treatment. Meanwhile, Ford's economic advisers believed the IMF's demand that Britain significantly reduce its PSBR was a necessity and, moreover, in Britain's long-term interests. Consequently, the Ford administration refused to intercede in the UK–IMF negotiations.

The IMF crisis illustrated a lack of US–UK cooperation in the form that Callaghan wanted. Nevertheless, as other commentators have noted, the more institutionalised aspects of US–UK cooperation continued to function smoothly in this period.[16] Even in spite of this, it is apparent that the courting of the US–UK special relationship – at first by Wilson, and then pursued by Callaghan – had failed to provide the political influence within Washington when London needed it most. The *Daily Telegraph*, in its review of 1976, captured Britain's declined position rather well when it noted: 'Thus 1976 ends in total disarray, and perhaps the only consolation to the bewildered onlooker is that the farce is now rapidly drawing to its close, and a dénouement at hand.'[17] Of course, the British foreign policy-making establishment did not articulate British decline in such a manner. But one FCO briefing memorandum for David Owen, appointed foreign and commonwealth secretary in February 1977, articulated a very similar point about the continuing significance of the US–UK relationship:

> During the last administration our relations with the US were generally good, due both to mutual interest and to the close relationship which Mr Callaghan and later Mr Crosland developed with Dr Kissinger ... But even at the height of the good relationship with Dr Kissinger, the relationship was no longer an exclusive one: the FRG now matters as much to the US as does the UK, and even US–French relations are on a firmer setting.[18]

## Conclusion

This then serves as an interesting episode in which to draw some broader conclusions about the nature of the US–UK relationship. Certainly the idea that the most 'special' aspects of the relationship were immune to the 'transitory' effects of politics is a highly questionable one, given that intelligence and nuclear cooperation were to be affected because of political disputes in this period.[19] However, longer-term consequences were avoided. Despite the level of political dissatisfaction in Washington towards their British ally, the US–UK relationship was still deemed to promote US interests. It is quite clear from this period that the 'functional' aspects of the US–UK relationship triumphed over any short-term political differences.

The other striking feature of this period was the level of coercion that US policy-makers practised in their diplomacy towards their British ally. The vast number of studies on the diplomacy of the Nixon–Kissinger–Ford years usually associates this practice with US foes. However, this study has shown that coercion was part and parcel of US alliance diplomacy also. Studies on US–UK relations during the years under study here omit this element of the relationship altogether.[20] Of course, it should be remembered that coercion in US diplomacy was not the dominant theme in US–UK relations. Indeed, quite the opposite was the case, as diplomatic cooperation on a number of issues – along with security cooperation – was far more common than coercive diplomacy was.

Further to this, when coercion was utilised by the US it had quite mixed results. It was most successful during the 'Year of Europe' period when US pressure was able to reverse Heath's policy course. Likewise, US pressure later on in the year was to have a profound influence upon Heath's wider European ambitions, when he chose to side with the US at the Washington Energy Conference. Given such success, then, it was only ever likely that US policy-makers would seek to utilise coercive diplomacy in future political disputes with the UK. Yet the government of Harold Wilson proved itself far more resilient to US pressure. In fact, Wilson had a far more accurate understanding of the dimensions of power in the US–UK relationship. Whilst aware that the US could retract its intelligence and nuclear cooperation, he correctly concluded that the US would never do this because it actually promoted US interests. Wilson, far more so than Heath, understood the functional aspects of the US–UK relationship.

Whilst the US–UK relationship declined in importance during this period, in both the international arena and as an aspect of bilateral relations between the two states, it did not mark a terminal decline for the US–UK relationship either. With the Soviet invasion of Afghanistan (1979), the onset of more bellicose US–Soviet relations, the coup in Iran by Islamic fundamentalists (1979) and the steadily worsening US economy, US–UK interaction and cooperation increased.[21] As John Dumbrell points out, the US–UK relationship was forged in war, and is at its most 'special' during such moments.[22] As readers will note, the US–UK 'special relationship', for better or worse, continues to function within the contemporary world of international relations.

Détente, therefore, was a curious phenomenon in which the US–UK relationship was to operate. Throughout, there was – as a former British ambassador to the US noted of the entire US–UK relationship – a level of 'mutual assured schizophrenia' which permeated the relationship in this period.[23] Even so, US–UK cooperation remained remarkably consistent despite numerous policy clashes and differences throughout 1969–77. Perhaps Kissinger sums up the relationship best: 'Nobody ever said that the special relationship precluded disagreements' but 'we had a degree of confidence in British leaders that we did not have in leaders of any other country'.[24]

## Notes

1 Henry Kissinger, *Does America Need a Foreign Policy? Toward a Diplomacy for the 21st Century* (New York: Simon & Schuster, 2001), p. 33.
2 On the possibility of Anglo–French nuclear weapons co-operation see: Kristan Stoddart, 'Nuclear Weapons in Britain's Policy towards France, 1960–1974', *Diplomacy and Statecraft*, 18:4 (2007), 719–44.
3 This theme is pressed keenly within Baylis, 'Moscow Criterion'.
4 TNA: FCO 82/197 Record of Conversation, 14 September 1972.
5 Hynes, *The Year*; Rossbach, *Rebirth*.
6 Nixon, *Memoirs*, p. 179.
7 Memorandum for the President from Henry A. Kissinger, 3 November 1970, NSCIHF, National Security Decision Memorandums, Box H-219, NPMP.
8 TNA: PREM 15/2089 Douglas-Home to Prime Minister, 17 October 1973.
9 Matusow, *Nixon's Economy*, pp. 130–3.
10 Discussion of United States Policy Toward Europe: NSC Meeting, 28 January 1970, NSCIHF, Meeting Files, National Security Council Meetings, Box H-026, NPMP.
11 Memorandum of Conversation, 17 December 1970, NSCIHF, Presidential-HAK Memcons, Box 1024, NPMP.
12 Telcon: The President–Kissinger, 13 August 1973, HAKTELCONS; Telcon: The President–Kissinger, 14 August 1973, HAKTELCONS.
13 Suri, *Kissinger*, pp. 257–65.
14 Twigge, 'Operation Hullabaloo', 689–701.
15 Baylis, *Defence Relations*, pp. 109–15.
16 *Ibid.*
17 Paul Johnson, 'Democracy – at Pistol Point!', *Daily Telegraph*, 31 December 1976.
18 TNA: FCO 82/687 G. N. Smith to Mr Edmonds, 16 February 1977.
19 Keith Jeffery, *MI6: The History of the Secret Intelligence Service, 1909–1949* (London: Bloomsbury, 2010), p. 721; Richard J. Aldrich, 'British Intelligence and the Anglo-American "Special Relationship"', *Review of International Studies*, 24:1 (1998), 337.
20 Hynes, *The Year*; Rossbach, *Rebirth*; Scott, *Allies Apart*.
21 David Owen, *Time to Declare* (London: Michael Joseph, 1991), pp. 283–5, 307–18; Cyrus Vance, *Hard Choices: Critical Years in America's Foreign Policy* (New York: Simon & Schuster, 1983), pp. 256–83.
22 Dumbrell, *Anglo–American Relations From the Cold War to Iraq*, pp. 1–10.
23 Christopher Meyer, *DC Confidential: The Controversial Memoirs of Britain's Ambassador to the US at the Time of 9/11 and the Iraq War* (London: Weidenfeld & Nicolson, 2005), p. 173.
24 Ziegler, *Heath*, p. 378.

# Select bibliography

Listed below are the primary sources utilised in the writing of this book. All of the other sources utilised in the writing of this work are listed within the endnotes.

*Primary sources*


**The National Archives, Kew, Surrey, UK (TNA)**

Cabinet Files
CAB 128; CAB 130; CAB 133; CAB 134; CAB 164; CAB 185

Defence Files
DEFE 13; DEFE 25; DEFE 48

Foreign and Commonwealth Office Files
FCO 7; FCO 9; FCO 21; FCO 28; FCO 30; FCO 41; FCO 44; FCO 45; FCO 46; FCO 59; FCO 73; FCO 82; FCO 93; FCO 96; FCO 146

Prime Minister Office Files
PREM 15; PREM 16

Treasury Files
T 355; T 364; T 381; T 386

**John F. Kennedy Presidential Library, Boston, Massachusetts, USA**
Henry A. Kissinger Files

**Lyndon Johnson Presidential Library, Austin, Texas, USA**
National Security Files

### Nixon Presidential Materials Project, National Archives II, College Park, Maryland, USA (NPMP)

Henry A. Kissinger Office Files
Henry Kissinger Telephone Conversation Transcripts
H. R. Haldeman Files
National Security Council Files
National Security Council Institutional (H) Files (NSCIHF)
President Office Files
President's Office Files, Memoranda for the President

### Gerald Ford Presidential Library, Ann Arbor, Michigan, USA (GFL)

Edward J. Savage Files
Henry Kissinger and Brent Scowcroft Files Temporary Parallel File
L. William Seidman Files
National Security Adviser International Economic Affairs Staff Files
National Security Adviser NSC Europe, Canada and Ocean Affairs Staff Files 1974–1977
National Security Adviser Outside the System Chronological File 1974–1977
National Security Adviser Memoranda of Conversations, 1973–1977 (NSAMC)
National Security Adviser Presidential Correspondence with Foreign Leaders
National Security Adviser Presidential Country Files for Europe and Canada
National Security Council Files
National Security Institutional Files 1974–1977
Presidential Handwriting Files
Richard Cheney Files
White House Central Files

### National Archives II, College Park, Maryland, USA (NAII)

RG 59 General Records of the Department of State

### Private Papers

Arthur Burns Papers, Gerald Ford Library, Ann Arbor, Michigan, USA (ABP)
Harold Macmillan Papers, Bodleian Library, Oxford University, UK
Harold Wilson Papers, Bodleian Library, Oxford University, UK (HWP)
James Callaghan Papers, Bodleian Library, Oxford University, UK (JCP)
Michael Foot Papers, Labour Party Archive, Manchester, UK
William Simon Papers, Gerald Ford Library, Ann Arbor, Michigan, USA

### Published collections of primary sources

Bennett, Gillian and Hamilton, Keith A. (eds.) *Documents on British Policy Overseas: Britain and the Soviet Union 1968–1972*. London: The Stationery Office, 1997, Volume I.

Bennett, Gillian and Hamilton, Keith A. (eds.) *Documents on British Policy Overseas: The Conference on Security and Cooperation in Europe, 1972–1975*. London: The Stationery Office, 1997, Series III, Volume II.

Bennett, Gillian and Hamilton, Keith A. (eds.) *Documents on British Policy Overseas: Détente in Europe, 1972–1976*. London: The Stationery Office, 2001, Volume III.

Burr, William (ed.) *The Kissinger Transcripts: The Top Secret Talks with Beijing and Moscow*. New York: The New Press, 1998.

Engel, A. Jeffrey (ed.) *The China Diary of George H. W. Bush: The Making of a Global President*. Princeton: Princeton University Press, 2008.

*Foreign Relations of the United States 1969–1976: Foundations of Foreign Policy, 1969–1972*. Washington: United States Government Printing Office, 2003, Volume I.

*Foreign Relations of the United States 1969–1976: Organization and Management of U.S. Foreign Policy, 1969–1972*. Washington: United States Government Printing Office, 2006, Volume II.

*Foreign Relations of the United States 1969–1976: Foreign Economic Policy; International Monetary Policy, 1969–1976*. Washington: United States Government Printing Office, 2002, Volume III.

*Foreign Relations of the United States 1969–1976: Soviet Union January 1969–October 1970*. Washington: United States Government Printing Office, 2006, Volume XII.

*Foreign Relations of the United States 1969–1976: Soviet Union October 1971–May 1972*. Washington: United States Government Printing Office, 2006, Volume XIV.

*Foreign Relations of the United States 1969–1976: Greece; Cyprus; Turkey, 1973–1976*. Washington: United States Government Printing Office, 2007, Volume XXX.

*Foreign Relations of the United States 1969–1976: Foreign Economic Policy, 1973–1976*. Washington: United States Government Printing Office, 2009, Volume XXXI.

*Foreign Relations of the United States 1969–1976: European Security*. Washington: United States Government Printing Office, 2007, Volume XXXIX.

Hamilton, Keith and Salmon, Patrick (eds.) *Documents on British Policy Overseas, Series III, Volume IV, The Year of Europe: America, Europe and the Energy Crisis, 1972–1974*. London: Routledge, 2006.

*Hansard: 1973*. London: Her Majesty's Stationery Office, 1974, Volume 866.

*Hansard: 1975*. London: Her Majesty's Stationery Office, 1976, Volume 871.

Mayall, James and Navari, Cornelia (eds.) *The End of the Post-War Era: Documents on Great-Power Relations, 1968–1975*. Cambridge: Cambridge University Press, 1980.

*Public Papers of the Presidents of the United States: Richard Nixon 1969*. Washington: United States Government Printing Office, 1971.

*Public Papers of the Presidents of the United States: Richard Nixon 1970*. Washington: United States Government Printing Office, 1971.

*Public Papers of the Presidents of the United States: Richard Nixon, 1972*. Washington: United States Government Printing Office, 1974.

*Public Papers of the Presidents of the United States: Richard Nixon, 1974*. Washington: United States Government Printing Office, 1975.

## Oral history interviews

Author's interviews conducted on behalf of Chatham House:

Lord Owen

Lord Robertson

Sir Kevin Tebbit

Sir Richard Mottram

### British Diplomatic Oral History Project (BDOHP), Churchill Archive, Churchill College, Cambridge University, UK

Charles Powell
Denis Greenhill
Donald Maitland
John Killick
Juliet Campbell
Michael Alexander
Michael Palliser

### Center for Strategic and International Studies Nuclear History Oral History Project

David Gill, 'Lord Carrington', in Jenifer Mackby and Paul Cornish, *US–UK Nuclear Cooperation after 50 Years*. Washington: CSIS Press, 2009.

David Gill, 'Sir Michael Quinlan', in Jenifer Mackby and Paul Cornish, *US–UK Nuclear Cooperation after 50 Years*. Washington: CSIS Press, 2009.

### Memoirs and diaries

Agnew, Spiro. *Go Quietly or Else*. London: William Morrow, 1980.

Barber, Anthony. *Taking the Tide: A Memoir*. London: Michael Russell, 1996.

Benn, Tony. *Against the Tide: Diaries 1973–76*. London: Arrow, 1990.

Blair, Tony. *A Journey*. London: Hutchinson, 2010.

Brandt, Willy. *People and Politics: The Years 1960–1975*. Boston, MA: Little, Brown and Company, 1978.

Callaghan, James. *Time & Chance*. London: Collins, 1987.

Carrington, Peter. *Reflect on Things Past*. London: Collins, 1988.

Castle, Barbara. *The Castle Diaries 1974–76*. London: Weidenfeld & Nicolson, 1980.

Connally, John. *In History's Shadow: An American Odyssey*. New York: Hyperion Books, 1993.

Dean, John. *Blind Ambition*. New York: Simon & Schuster, 1976.

Donoughue, Bernard. *Downing Street Diary: With Harold Wilson in No. 10*. London: Jonathan Cape, 2005.

Donoughue, Bernard. *Downing Street Diary: With James Callaghan in No. 10*. London: Jonathan Cape, 2008.

Douglas-Home, Alec. *The Way the Wind Blows*. London: Collins, 1978.

Eban, Abba. *An Autobiography*. London: Weidenfeld & Nicolson, 1977.

Ehrlichman, John. *Witness to Power: The Nixon Years*. New York: Simon & Schuster, 1982.

Ferrell, H. Robert. *Inside the Nixon Administration: The Secret Diary of Arthur Burns, 1969–1974*. Lawrence: University of Kansas Press, 2010.

Garthoff, Raymond. *A Journey through the Cold War: A Memoir of Containment and Coexistence*. Washington: The Brookings Institute, 2001.

Greenhill, Denis. *More by Accident*. York: Wilton, 1992.

Greenspan, Alan. *The Age of Turbulence: Adventures in a New World*. London: Penguin, 2008.

Haig, Alexander. *Inner Circles: How America Changed the World*. New York: Warner Books, 1992.

Haldeman, Harry Robbins. *The Ends of Power*. New York: Times Books, 1978.

Haldeman, Harry Robbins. *The Haldeman Diaries*. New York: Putnam, 1994.

Hattersley, Roy. *Fifty Years On: A Prejudiced History of Britain Since the War*. London: Little, Brown and Company, 1997.

Heath, Edward. *The Course of My Life*. London: Hodder & Stoughton, 1997.

Hurd, Douglas. *An End to Promises: Sketch of a Government, 1970–74*. London: Collins, 1979.

Hyland, G. William. *Mortal Rivals: Superpower Relations from Nixon to Reagan*. New York: Random House, 1987.

Jenkins, Roy. *A Life at the Centre*. London: Macmillan, 1991.

Johnson, Lyndon Baines. *The Vantage Point: Perspectives of the Presidency 1963–1969*. London: Weidenfeld & Nicolson, 1972.

Kissinger, Henry. *White House Years*. Boston, MA: Little, Brown and Company, 1979.

Kissinger, Henry. *Years of Upheaval*. Boston, MA: Little, Brown and Company, 1982.

Kissinger, Henry. *Years of Renewal*. New York: Simon & Schuster, 1999.

Kissinger, Henry. *A History of America's Involvement in and Extrication from the Vietnam War*. New York: Simon & Schuster, 2003.

Kissinger, Henry. *Crisis: The Anatomy of Two Major Foreign Policy Crises*. New York: Simon & Schuster, 2003.

Maitland, Donald. *Diverse Times, Sundry Places*. London: The Alpha Press, 1996.

Meir, Golda. *My Life*. London: Putnam, 1975.

Nixon, Richard. *RN: The Memoirs of Richard Nixon*. London: Grosset & Dunlap, 1978.

Nixon, Richard. *The Real War*. London: Sidgwick & Jackson, 1980.

Nott, John. *Here Today Gone Tomorrow: Memoirs of an Errant Politician*. London: Politico's, 2002.

Owen, David. *Time to Declare*. London: Michael Joseph, 1991.

Price, Raymond. *With Nixon*. New York: The Viking Press, 1977.

Sadat, Anwar. *In Search of Identity*. London: Collins, 1978.

Schultz, George. *Turmoil and Triumph: My Years as Secretary of State*. Oxford: Maxwell Macmillan International, 1993.

Seitz, Raymond. *Over Here*. London: Weidenfeld & Nicolson, 1998.

Simon, William. *A Time for Truth*. New York: Readers Digest Association, 1978.

Simon, William. *A Time for Action*. New York: Readers Digest Association, 1980.

Simon, William. *A Time for Reflection*. New York: Regnery Publishing, 2003.

Smith, Gerard. *DoubleTalk: The Story of SALT I*. New York: Doubleday, 1980.

Sulzberger, L. C. *An Age of Mediocrity, Memoirs and Diaries: 1963–1972*. New York: Macmillan, 1973.

Vance, Cyrus. *Hard Choices: Critical Years in America's Foreign Policy*. New York: Simon & Schuster, 1983.

Wass, Douglas. *Decline to Fall: The Making of British Macro-economic Policy and the 1976 IMF Crisis*. Oxford: Oxford University Press, 2008.

Zumwalt, Elmo. *On Watch: A Memoir*. Arlington: Zumwalt & Associates, 1976.

# Index